Texas Politics
Economics, Power
and Policy
THIRD EDITION

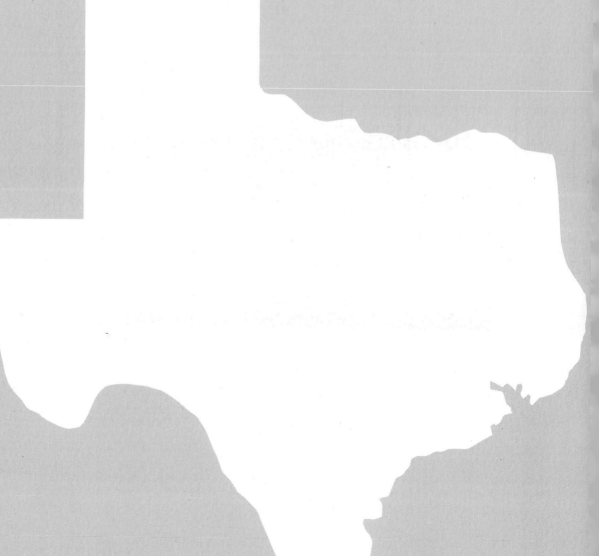

Texas Politics
Economics, Power
and Policy

THIRD EDITION

JAMES W. LAMARE

WEST PUBLISHING COMPANY
St. Paul • New York • Los Angeles • San Francisco

COPYEDITING: David Dexter

DESIGN: Lucy Lesiak Design

COVER ART: Stephen T. Rascoe
Blue Summer Rain Storm/Oil

Printed in the United States of America

Library of Congress Cataloging in Publication Data
Lamare, James
Texas Politics

Includes Index.

1. Texas—Politics and government—1951–
2. Texas—Economic conditions. 3. Elite (Social sciences)—Texas. I. Title.
JK4816.L36 1988   320.9764   87–31467
ISBN 0–314–64226–9

CONTENTS

— 12 — Highways and Welfare: Contrasting Policy Priorities   199

— 13 — Fiscal Policy in Texas   215

PREFACE

The third edition of this book coincides with a dynamic period of economic and political turmoil in the state of Texas. Economic dislocation, principally the result of falling oil prices, has sent shock waves through the state. Once well established economic institutions have disintegrated, some vanishing from the economic scene altogether. Bankruptcies are rampant. Jobs have been lost. People are leaving the state in search of a better economic climate. Confidence in the state's economy—once the envy of the nation—has eroded. The economic elite of Texas have been rocked by economic events, many of which are beyond their control.

The economic crunch has created a fiscal crisis for state government in Texas. Simply put, there isn't enough tax revenue being generated to cover the costs of state services and programs at their current level of funding. The time has been ripe for a new approach with fresh ideas to state policy, especially in the areas of education, welfare, and highways.

During this time of great difficulty a statewide election transpired. The Texas Legislature convened more times than it has in the prior decade. Major changes in the electoral and party system of the state have occurred. New public policy, some of which is aimed at improving the lot of the poor, has been enacted. The scent of change is in the air.

This edition comprehensively treats the economic crisis and the new political developments that have been registered recently in Texas. A new chapter has been added on the fiscal crisis facing state government. The chapter on elections has been broadened to more fully cover the emerging two-party system in the state. More attention has been paid to the office of the governor. The political changes evident in local politics are discussed. Public policy changes are incorporated into the text. The transformation of the economic sector is a major theme of the chapters on economic relations in the state.

In making these alterations I have benefited immensely from the comments of various readers. I would particularly like to thank the following for their suggestions: Tom Bass, John R. Bauer (University of Texas at San Antonio), Patricia J. Caperton (Southwest Texas State University), Carolyn J. Davis (North Harris Community College), Bryan D. Jones (Texas A&M University), Bob Little (Brookhaven College), and Roland E. Smith (Texas Tech University). Coping with the mechanics of revision has been greatly facilitated through word processing. For their help in this area I am most appreciative of the skills of Liz Dobson, Jill Dolby, and Janis Storer, as well as of the various corporations making personal computers and word processing software programs.

To Nappy and Alice,
who have touched many lives

The Texas Economy

Exploring the impact of economic forces on the politics of Texas requires an analysis of the state's economy. In particular, the key economic actors must be identified. The first part of this book pursues this goal. Chapter 1 is an introduction to the concepts of power and economic rule as they relate to the political situation in Texas. Chapter 2 outlines the major economic arenas in the state. The core of the economy is composed of the petroleum industry, agriculture, and financial transactions conducted through banks, insurance companies, and savings and loan firms. Large-scale corporations dominate each of these important economic arenas. Chapter 3 shows that these distinct sectors of the state's economy are interconnected. Mergers, shared ownership, and interlocking directorates link seemingly disparate members of the economic elite operating throughout Texas.

1

Power, Pluralism, and Economic Rule: An Introduction

This is a book about the distribution of political power in the state of Texas. Its aim is to determine who has this power, and why.

Power simply refers to the ability to achieve one's goals. The struggle for power is most obvious in situations in which individuals, groups, or institutions compete for scarce resources. The actor that accomplishes his, her, or its purpose is generally recognized as the more powerful. After numerous victories, a party might reach a position of such superiority that it no longer faces any serious challenges. In this case power has become highly structured. The powerful actor, sometimes without exerting much effort, can control the agenda of pending social action to minimize the materialization of any threats to its position. Realizing the awesomeness of this power, potential opponents may forgo any challenge. There are times, in other words, when goals are secured without much, if any, meaningful conflict.

Political power is a distinct type of power. It refers to actions that affect a substantial segment of the population. One has political power if, in trying to obtain his, her, or its goals, the general society is affected.

Any social organization that makes decisions that have an impact on the general public is politically powerful. It is possible for institutions to have such power independent of the government, but, in modern industrial societies such as the United States, government is inextricably involved in the relationships of political power. Political groups often align themselves with and rely on the government because people are more likely to obey the group's decisions if the government has sanctioned them. There are two reasons for this widespread obedience.

First, most modern governments are considered to be the highest level of protectorate by their constituent populations. So overwhelming is this supportive feeling that a governmental request for adherence is frequently acceded to by most citizens simply out of respect for the government.

Second, government can compel obedience through the threat or actual use of coercion. The most distinguishable characteristic of a government, according to the eminent sociologist Max Weber, is that it "successfully upholds a claim to the monopoly of the legitimate use of physical force in the enforcement of its order." [1]

The government in the United States traditionally has been accepted by its citizens as the legitimate source of rules and regulations. Quite understandably, private interests have sought the sanction of government in their quest for political power. Requests for government assistance have taken two general forms. At times, the government is asked to adopt and implement the programs and ideas on the behalf of groups and individuals. On other occasions, private interests seek government assurance that the former can engage in certain activities without the intervention of the latter. In either case, the government becomes deeply involved in the distribution of political power in this country.

The governments of the fifty states play a major role in the allocation of resources for the overall society. The expansion of the federal government throughout the first eight decades of this century has encouraged, not discouraged, a greater involvement of state government in public policy. All states are heavily engaged in formulating policies in the areas of education, welfare, transportation, taxation, and the regulation of business, labor, and social behavior. Indeed, it has been concluded that "the states are growing in importance more than any other level of government in the United States." [2]

City and county governments have a very immediate effect on citizens. Local governments are primarily responsible for providing basic public services such as education, water delivery, sanitation facilities, streets, and police protection.

This book analyzes political power at the state and local levels in Texas. There are two prevailing theoretical approaches to studying the distribution of political power in the United States. One is *pluralism;* the other is the *economic rule* perspective. [3]

As theories, pluralism and economic rule are at odds in their interpretations of almost every aspect of the political power question. They do, however, have one belief in common: each school of thought agrees that government at all levels in the United States is actually run by a relatively small group of people—an elite. As to the nature of the elite, its composition and its accountability to the mass public, disagreement is the norm. An analysis of the pluralist and economic rule theories follows.   ★

PLURALISM

Pluralism contends that political power is widely dispersed in the United States. [4] No one group or person has a monopoly on it. Political decisions are made for the most part openly in government institutions by officials representative of, and accountable to, the general public. The ties between the rulers and the ruled are quite intricate, and both parties benefit from the relationship.

With regard to political leaders, many things keep them close to the public:

1. *Political leaders are plentiful.* Thousands of Americans hold offices in local, state, and federal government. Leadership positions tend to cluster around specific policy issues. For example, those who make decisions in the area of education—

members of school boards, superintendents, and the like—do not enter into other areas, such as agriculture. Tax collectors do not plan city traffic light patterns. Consequently, numerous leadership groups have emerged in the government. Each is quite autonomous from the others, and each specializes in a given policy area. As the public increasingly demands resolution of crucial issues, many new leadership groups (boards, commissions, agencies, legislative committees, etc.) are born. The public thus is not without government institutions to hear complaints and redress grievances. The more formidable problem often becomes finding the right group of officials to address. Pluralism holds that in those rare instances in which one leader or a small group of leaders dominates the decision-making process, the leader or group is usually very visible, and therefore accountable to a large constituency.

2. *Diversity, both in the social background and in the issue orientation of the political elite, is quite pronounced.* Within each specialized leadership group, and across the broad spectrum of political leaders, officials are drawn from all walks of life. No one social group, such as based on race, region, economic class, sex, or religion, dominates all leadership posts; each social group is represented in the elite. Moreover, pluralism contends that elite members vary in their perspectives on the issues; their outlooks are as distinct as the social backgrounds from which they come.

3. *Political leaders firmly believe in democratic values.* Although diversity marks the issue orientations of officials, they are alike in their adherence to the democratic creed. They share a common commitment to procedural fair play, tolerance for all points of view, and respect for individual liberties. They encourage nonviolent solutions to social problems and emphasize the importance of mass participation in the political process; hence, disagreements over policy matters are conducted within a democratic atmosphere.

The masses also play a crucial role in pluralist thinking. The elite are cognizant of the many in several ways:

1. *It is not difficult for the average person to join the ranks of political decision makers.* The line between the two is thin. Becoming a leader is mostly a matter of desire, for if one wants to seek office, opportunities are ample. A general disinterest in politics found among the public is the major barrier preventing most people from seeking a position of leadership. Accordingly, a citizen outraged at the behavior of decision makers can quickly exorcise his or her feelings by seeking a political post.

2. *Citizens control leadership behavior through the electoral process.* The ultimate route to becoming a leader includes winning votes; failure at the polling booth effectively bars attainment of a leadership post. Even appointed officials are influenced by mass preference since they are selected by popularly elected leaders. The threat of electoral defeat is often enough to shape the behavior of officeholders. Candidates hence pay close attention to the opinions held by the public.

3. *Citizens affect the political process through membership in interest groups.* Group membership is effectuated either by physically joining an organization or by simply being in an identifiable categorical group such as Texans, or Southerners, or blacks. Either type of membership is bound to have leaders who present demands to the political elite. Indeed, many political officials begin their careers as group leaders. Through the active participation of groups in political decision making, ranging from candidate selection to lobbying for specific policy proposals, members have their viewpoints presented—whether they are fully aware of it or not.

The results of the mingling between leaders and followers are these:

1. *Political leaders make decisions based on input from various groups and individuals.* The government listens to the proposals of all concerned parties and formulates its policy after a neutral weighing of each side.

2. *Final decisions reflect the interests of a large and diverse section of the population.* Because of the many voices aimed at the government's ear, public policy usually is a compromise of many viewpoints. It is through the art of negotiation that the bargain among competing interests is struck.

3. *A change in policy is often initiated by the masses or in anticipation of demands from the public.* Since many perspectives enter into policy discussions, change is usually moderate and arrived at slowly.

In short, pluralism depicts the political system in the United States as one that is close to the interests of the masses. The beneficiaries of public policy are many, many people—usually more than a majority. Hence, large segments of the population reach their goals through the political system: each group has political power.

ECONOMIC RULE

The economic rule model asserts that political power in the United States is concentrated in the hands of the top economic elite.[5] Put simply, those people and institutions that dominate the production and distribution of goods and services also collect most of the rewards to be gained from governmental decision making. The average citizen takes a backseat to the economic elite in affecting and benefiting from public policy.

The following points about the economic elite stand out:

1. *Members of the economic elite are people who command the operations of the major businesses in America.* They are principal stockholders, managers, and members of the boards of directors of the country's largest corporations. These institutions set the tone of the economy. Since there are relatively few big businesses with such economic clout, the elite comprise an extremely small minority of Americans. By the very nature of their lofty status and their unique experiences, members of the economic elite are mostly atypical of the general population.

2. *Basically, members of the elite see eye-to-eye on pecuniary matters.* The prevailing goal in the economic world is to maximize profits. Given this orientation, there is little internal dissension. There may be conflict over which firms should acquire the most profit and over the best means to obtain profit, but it is rare for the giant corporations to publicize these disagreements. Usually, conflicts are short in duration and are resolved within the brotherhood of the business community.

3. *The economic elite are united through many bonds.* Purely economic connections prevail among distinct corporate entities; companies are drawn together through interlocking directorates, shared stock ownership, and joint business agreements. Interest groups, such as the Business Council, the Business Roundtable, the Council on Foreign Relations, the Committee for Economic Development, the Texas Research League, and the Trilateral Commission, consolidate corporate viewpoints. And there are social ties among partisans of the business community; membership in private clubs, marriage, and common school experiences are vital points of linkage.

The interests of the economic elite are communicated to the government in the following manner:

1. *Initial selection of candidates for electoral office is influenced by the economic sector.* Care is taken to screen potential candidates to insure that the field of choices available to the electorate is composed of people not at odds with the priorities of the economic leadership. The campaigns of favored candidates are assisted through generous financial contributions by members of the economic elite.

2. *The appointment of persons to government posts is also influenced by the economic elite.* Many times appointees are members of the elite. In this way economic leaders become political leaders with official positions that frequently directly benefit their interests.

3. *Extensive lobbying of the government by big business is common.* In an attempt to influence the policy-making process, the economic elite provide research, experts, entertainment, financial inducements, and basic support to government officials.

4. *The structure of government institutions in the United States simplifies the corporate lobbying and campaign contribution process.* Government decisions are primarily made in decentralized quarters. The major work on policy proposals occurs in legislative committees, in specialized administrative agencies, and in obscure courtrooms. Consequently, efforts to influence decisions need only be directed at the appropriate targets. It is not necessary for dominant economic interests to be concerned with contacting and influencing all personnel in the government.

The relationship between the dominant economic sector and the political leadership yields a number of results:

1. *Public policy mostly reflects the interests of the economic notables.* Government decisions further the priorities of the economic sector. Others might benefit from policy making, but only if their interests coincide with the goals of the economic elite or if the economic elite have no particular interest in the policy.

2. *The masses exercise little control over the political process.* The citizenry is relegated to voting for the candidates who have been handpicked by members of the higher economic circles. Moreover, public interest groups are secondary in importance to the lobbying efforts undertaken by dominant economic forces.

3. *Changes in policy initiated by average citizens only stand a chance of success if the members of the elite adopt the cause.* It is necessary to show the elite that it is in their interest to alter the status quo.

Neither the economic rule nor the pluralistic perspective concludes that the American political process is fully democratic. In a democracy, all people would be knowledgeable and concerned about political matters and directly involved in political decision making. No political system has ever reached this democratic ideal. Consequently, democratic theory is not an accurate description of the real world of politics, although it may be a good guide to what the political process should be like.

The major point of contention between the two theories centers on whether the economic elite has political influence. Pluralists hold that business is no more powerful than many other groups. To be sure, leading economic actors might have some valuable political resources (such as wealth). However, noneconomic groups and individuals also have political inducements (such as social standing, strength in numbers, and the vote) that offset advantages possessed by business. Furthermore, many pluralists discount the likelihood that an economic elite even exists in the United States. Competition—not cohesion—characterizes business relations.

Conversely, the economic rule perspective not only argues that an economic elite is present in America it also contends that this elite prevails in the political system. In short, it purports that politics is run by and for people and institutions that dominate the economy.

ABOUT TEXAS

A portrait of the social characteristics of Texans makes an interesting pluralistic mosaic. The people of Texas, some 16 million strong, are a diverse lot. This is particularly true in terms of race, national origin, religion, residence, and economic status. Each of these characteristics will be discussed in more detail.

Racial and Ethnic Origins

Texans can trace their roots to many points of origin. Twelve percent of the state is black. With 1.7 million blacks Texas ranks third in the nation in total black population. Blacks were first imported into Texas in the nineteenth century as slaves. Although during the 1980s the percentage of black Texans has been on the decline, the absolute number of blacks living in Texas has increased slightly owing to in-migration from other states. Today, blacks are heavily concentrated in the rural areas of East Texas and in two urban centers, Houston and Dallas.

Around 21 percent of the state population is Mexican American. Indeed, fully one-fifth of the nation's Hispanics reside in Texas. Most of these people have migrated from Mexico in this century and now live in hamlets, towns, and cities in the south and west of the state, especially on or near the Mexican border.

Other nationalities are well represented in Texas. Some 22 percent of the population has at least some English in their origin; another 17 percent has ancestral ties with Ireland; around 15 percent can trace its lineage to Germany. Smaller numbers (less than 10 percent of the statewide population) of Texans have ancestral roots in France, Italy, and Poland.[6] Sprinkled throughout the state are enclaves where cultural patterns of the country of origin are still quite pronounced.

Religion

About six of every ten Texans profess a preference for a Protestant religion.[7] Far and away, the most common Protestant affiliation is Baptist, in particular Southern Baptist. Twenty-two percent of the population identifies with the Roman Catholic church, a figure that mostly reflects the religious preference of the state's large Hispanic population. Only about 1 percent of Texans are Jewish. Fully 70 percent attend religious services at least once a month and also claim that religion is "very important" in their lives.

A zealous religious spirit is alive and well in Texas. Fundamentalist Protestants and doctrinaire Catholics are pervasive. When asked if they had "ever tried to encourage someone to believe in Jesus Christ or accept Him as ... Savior," almost two-thirds of the population answered yes, a response registered by only 45 percent of a national sample of Americans. In dramatic distinction, Austin is the home of one of the country's most vocal atheists: Madalyn Murray O'Hair. Ms. O'Hair once won an important Supreme Court case that limited the use of public schools for religious purposes. Incidentally, less than 1 percent of Texans share her atheist beliefs and only 8 percent concur that the public school is no place for "reading the Lord's Prayer or Bible verses."

Geography and Residency

Texas contains some 260,000 square miles of land and water—second only to Alaska among all states. At its extremes Texas runs 801 miles in length and its width covers 773 miles. Such vastness presents distinct problems in transportation and communication for the state's residents. For example, it is farther from El Paso to Houston than it is from El Paso to Los Angeles, Salt Lake City, or Denver. It would be a shorter trip to travel from New York City to Atlanta, New York to Chicago, or Washington, D.C. to St. Louis than from El Paso to Houston!

Most of the state's population resides in a few urban centers. Houston, the fifth largest city in the United States and the most populous in Texas, is inhabited by 1.6 million people. Dallas contains just under a million. San Antonio with nearly 800,000 people is the third largest Texas city. Rounding out the top six are El Paso (425,000 residents), Fort Worth (385,000 strong), and Austin (population 346,000).

A century ago more people lived in the rural sectors of Texas. Now, as of 1987, less than one-fifth do, although rural Texas has experienced a small increment in population growth in recent years. Nonetheless, much of the state's land mass is virtually unpopulated. Loving County in West Texas, for instance, covers some 671 square miles but contains only 100 people, a substantial drop from the 164 who lived there in 1970. Less than 2 percent of the people of Texas now live on farms; in 1940 some 23 percent of the population were farmers or ranchers. Rural areas still maintain unique and distinct traditions, but the importance of these traditions has waned considerably with the large shifts in population to urban and suburban areas.

Until 1986 the population in Texas grew at a rapid pace. Between 1980 and 1984, for instance, the state experienced a 12.4 percent rise in population. This rate of growth was some three times the national average. Much of this increase came from net-migration into the state; it is estimated that around 300,000 more people entered than left Texas annually during the first four years of the 1980s. All told, in-migration accounted for fully 58 percent of the state's recent population growth.[8] Most Texans (some 60 percent) are lifelong residents of the state. But the relative proportion of newcomers has been increasing; about 20 percent of the population moved to Texas within the last decade.[9]

During 1986 more people moved out of Texas than entered the state. This was the first time in the 150–year history of the Lone Star State that out-migration surpassed in-migration. The principal reason for this exodus was the decline of the state's economy.

Economic Status

Throughout the 1970s the Texas economy was the envy of the nation. During that period it ranked at or near the top in total personal income, employment opportunities, retail and agricultural sales, bank deposits, construction contracts, manufacturing output, and petroleum and mineral production. The recession that bedeviled most of the rest of the nation hardly slowed the economic boom in Texas.

The tide began to turn in 1982, at which time a noticeable surplus of oil became available on the world market. Inevitably the oil glut resulted in a lowering of the price of oil and petroleum-based products. The effect was almost immediately felt in the opulent oil industry of Texas. Oil recovery, refining, drilling, and marketing were cut back. Jobs, especially in the oil service industry, were lost. By January 1983 unemployment in the state reached a high of 8.3 percent of the work force, which was almost double the rate of joblessness recorded in Texas in the late–1970s.[10] Nevertheless, there still was a cautious optimism that recovery was in the air. Leading economic indicators geared to the state economy signaled in mid–1983 an end to the recession.[11] Indeed, one expert concluded from this information that "the worst of the Texas economic recession [was] probably over." [12]

Instead, however, the downward economic slide became an avalanche. Oil prices continued to fall. A barrel of crude oil that went for $27 as of December 1985 could be purchased some three months later for only $10. Every dollar drop in the price of a barrel of oil brought with it a loss of 25,000 jobs. By June 1986 unemployment reached a post-Depression high of 10.5 percent; fully 846,000 Texans were out of work.[13]

Agriculture also experienced hard times. Drought and contracting markets converged on the state's already struggling farm and ranching community. One source estimated that during 1986 a weekly average of 173 farms and ranches faced economic disaster.[14]

The economic downturn in petroleum and agriculture had a major effect on Texas society overall. People moved away from the state in droves. Real estate markets in major cities, especially Houston, strained to the point of collapse. During 1986 an all time high of 33,869 petitions for bankruptcy were filed in Texas's courts by businesses.[15]

The state's banks felt the economic crunch directly. Many financial institutions, including the state's foremost commercial banks, had invested heavily in

Courtesy of Ben Sargent, *The Austin American—Statesman*. Reprinted by permission.

energy, real estate, and farming and ranching. The lack of profitability in these economic sectors seriously impaired repayment of the principal and interest on these loans. Houston's First City Bancorporation reported that by the fall of 1986 loans valued at $857.4 million were nonperforming. James A. Elkins, Jr., chairman of First City, lamented: "We are dealing with an economic decline that has grown even more pervasive and more contracted." [16]

State government also was impacted by the economic slip. A large portion of revenue going into the state treasury comes from petroleum sales. Approximately $100 million in taxes is lost to the state with every dollar decline in the price of a barrel of oil.[17] Consequently, by the middle of 1986 the government was directly confronting a revenue shortfall of nearly $3 billion. Indeed, the revenue squeeze had become so acute that in late October 1986 the state was preparing to borrow between $300 million and $1 billion in order to pay its bills.[18] Governor Clements announced in early 1987 that the state government's deficit might reach $5 billion.

The people of Texas also experienced some doubt about the virtue, vitality, and viability of the state's economy. In 1983, two-thirds of the public rated Texas an "excellent" place to live; by 1986, this feeling had dropped 16 percent (to 51 percent).[19] Throughout 1986 a substantial amount of pessimism about economic conditions was reported. For instance, Texans were widely split over the question of whether people were getting along better financially these days. Thirty-nine percent agreed with this proposition; 26 percent thought things were worse than the previous year; the rest believed that matters remained the same as the previous year. Most (43 percent) concluded that their financial situation would stay the same in the near future. When asked about the future prospects of business conditions in the state, Texans were not so positive. Fully 47 percent felt that business would experience bad times financially during the next twelve months; only 28 percent anticipated good times a year on. Forty-five percent envisioned a five-year future of widespread unemployment or depression, compared with 30 percent who held that the economic conditions would turn around over this longer period.[20]

In the early part of 1987 signs of improvement in the state's economy were evident. Most important, the price of a barrel of oil was on the way up—by February a barrel of West Texas intermediate crude, the benchmark for oil prices worldwide, had risen to $18.50. Unemployment fell slightly, to around 9 percent of the work force. Moreover, the recent economic plunge generated a flurry of activity to lessen the state's dependency on the petroleum industry. Economic diversification was in the offing. The most promising new direction for the state's economy pointed toward the business of high technology.

Throughout the economic oscillations of the 1980s the gap between the state's rich and poor remained. To be sure, the recent economic dislocation spared hardly anyone in Texas. Ordinary workers, the poor, as well as major corporations felt the blows. However, during the boom times of the late 1970s a great mass of riches had accumulated in the state; Texas ranked among the top three states in total wealth. Moreover, this wealth was not evenly distributed. While, for instance, 434 Texans had incomes in excess of $1 million during 1979, at the same time over 15 percent of the population was officially classified as living below the poverty line.[21] As indicated in table 1–1, the upper and upper-middle classes prospered disproportionately from the good economic times in the state. As noted by one observer: "Income growth in Texas during the 1970s was not an equalizing force among income classes. If anything, more of the gains went to higher income groups, and income distribution became slightly less equal than it had been." [22] It is hence likely that richer Texans, all things being equal, weathered the recent economic crisis better than others.

Nonetheless, the great volatility of the Texas economy does suggest that the state's business elite cannot fully control its economic fate. Forces emerge from the structural operations of the economy to disrupt the best laid plans of the elite,

TABLE 1–1   Income Distribution in Texas, 1979

Annual Income (1979)	Percent of Total Federal Income Tax Returns Filed by Texans	Percent of Total Income (After Taxes) Held by Texans
Low ($10,000 or less)	44.8%	14.0%
Modest ($10,000 to $19,999)	26.7	26.0
Middle ($20,000 to $49,999)	25.8	45.2
Upper-Middle ($50,000 to $1,000,000)	2.7	14.0
Very Rich ($1,000,000 or more)	.008	.8

SOURCE: Adapted from Cadwell Ray, "Income Distribution and Economic Growth in Texas," *Texas Business Review* 57 (May-June 1983): 108–112.

forces coming from factors such as oversupply of a product (for instance, oil). Once in full swing it becomes extremely difficult for an elite to contain these structural forces. To be sure, the unleashing of such forces is a strong incentive for an elite to coalesce and try to anticipate, if not curb, unwanted economic disequilibrium. Hence Texas's economic crisis probably has fortified its business elite, while, at the same time, it has demonstrated the vulnerability of such an elite to inexpedient structural forces of the economy.

In conclusion, Texans can be categorized in terms of their race, national origin, religious preference, place of residence, and economic standing. Such classification reveals a pluralistic society within the state. But does a pluralistic society mean that *political power* is distributed pluralistically? Does each of these social groups exercise political power in the state? This book answers these questions largely in the negative.

ABOUT THIS BOOK

The major thesis of this book is that an economic elite dominates the political system of Texas. The principal political questions brought before state and local governments involve the allocation of economic resources. The resolution of these economic matters is usually to the benefit of those who control those resources. As such, this investigation endorses the economic rule perspective of political power.

Many diverse observers of modern Texas have attested to the inordinate importance of economic interests in the politics of the state. Writing in the late 1940s, political scientist V.O. Key, Jr., a native Texan, commented that "the Lone Star State is concerned about money and how to make it, about oil and sulfur and gas, about cattle and dust storms and irrigation, about cotton and banking and Mexicans." [23] Speaking at the state Democratic party convention in 1947, the party chairman proclaimed that "it may not be a wholesome thing to say, but the oil industry today is in complete control of state politics and state government." [24] In the mid–1970s, a survey administered by Dun and Bradstreet to businessmen found that they regarded the state "as having the most favorable climate for business in the nation." [25] One of Texas's large banks concluded from this study "that Texas government, by its actions and inactions, has created a climate which is very appealing to employers." [26] By the mid–1980s, the state's economy was ranked sixteenth by business leaders. Currently, politicians, academics, journalists, and business and social leaders, among others, are replete with advice to the government as to how to administer a quick-fix to the state's economic ills.

The reasons behind the political success of the economic elite in Texas are numerous. Some involve the attitudes and attributes of the citizenry of the state. Others concern the social, economic, political, and geographic structure of Texas. Usually both these sets of reasons combine in an intricate pattern to explain fully the lack of political power of the masses and the overwhelming influence of economic notables. Among the specific factors accounting for this inequitable distribution of political power, two stand out.

First, the pluralistic nature of Texas society inhibits mass political movements. Generally speaking, a person's social and political life is restricted to his or her immediate group setting. Social pressure and psychological needs compel, for most people, a close attachment to things and persons familiar. In addition, the overall structure of the society in which one lives also contributes to this phenomenon. Until the 1960s, for instance, it was against the law for racial groups to share a good many social experiences in Texas. Moreover, members of racial minorities were legally barred from the political process through statutes that prohibited their political participation (more about this in chapter 4). Even today, residentially segregated neighborhoods—often the result of past political and current economic practices—inhibit the crossing of group lines for the purpose of organizing mass political activities. The geographic vastness of Texas is also a major structural barrier to widespread statewide political organization.

Second, the prevailing political culture in Texas deemphasizes group political participation as well as direct challenges to existing authority. Individualism and deference to authority are the core elements of the traditionalistic belief system that permeates Texas.[27] It is a system in which each individual is thought responsible for his or her successes or failures in life. People who reach the top, especially of the economic heap, are perceived to be praiseworthy and respected for their accomplishments. Accordingly, those at the bottom have only their own slackness to blame for their lack of achievement.

In essence, Texans are mostly conservative in their political and social beliefs. Most (54 percent) are God-fearing Christians who "say that [they] have been born again or have had a born-again experience."[28] Fully 60 percent "consider the words of some rock music to be harmful to those under eighteen." A majority would like to see a rating system imposed on music so that so-called adult lyrics could be properly identified. Indeed, 34 percent would not allow persons under eighteen the right to purchase music with adult lyrics; 37 percent would ban rock videos with such words from television; and 22 percent would simply stop altogether the sale of "X-rated" music.[29] The right to purchase guns is another matter. Some 54 percent of the Texas public acknowledge possession of a gun in their homes.[30] Not unexpectedly, 38 percent of Texans consider themselves conservatives. Only 17 percent label themselves liberal. The rest prefer to be called moderate.[31]

Not all authorities are given the same amount of deference in Texas. It appears that Texans accord a great deal of legitimacy to business institutions. Banks that were targets of popular suspicion in the past are no longer suspect institutions. Three-fourths of Texans look favorably upon banks; only 20 percent have negative views.[32] Respect for government institutions varies. When Texans were asked to declare the most important problem facing the state, they were more likely in 1981 to say "elected officials than inflation, unemployment, energy, water supply, overpopulation, illegal aliens, education, or alcohol or drug abuse."[33] Some 64 percent rate the performance of Texas's court system as at best "fair." The legislature receives an "excellent" ranking from only 4 percent of the population; 36 percent rate it "good," 41 percent "fair," and 9 percent "poor." Conversely, nearly two-thirds applaud the work of the police.[34] Almost 75 percent feel that the regulatory powers of the state government are effective.[35] Deference to administrative authority seems well in place in Texas.

Commitment to a traditional, conservative culture is not evident among all Texans at all times. During the 1970s, for instance, Chicanos in Crystal City coalesced to challenge the dominant political and economic system in their city.[36] For a while this challenge proved successful; once-powerless people took the reins of the city's government. However, the Crystal City example is the exception that exemplifies the rule, for most Chicanos in Texas are well immersed in the state's traditional political culture. Individualism and deference to authority are main features of the belief system of most of the state's Mexican Americans.[37]

A great deal of what Texans think does not necessarily accord with reality. For instance, the pillars of the economic community of Texas (as will be detailed in chapters 2 and 3) have not been climbed by individuals who have reached their lofty status through lifelong struggle. Rather, impersonal, very stable giant corporations dominate the economy. Texans, like most Americans, suffer from a remarkable ignorance about the politico-economic system.[38] What people are led to hold true and dear are frequently perceptions, norms, things to be valued, or orientations important to others—usually those doing the socializing. As is often the case, these thoughts are not based on facts; rather they are grounded in feelings.

The economic elite enters into the socialization process in both overt and covert ways. Its presence is most manifest in the education system and in the mass media.

Schools are governed by local and state boards on which, traditionally, economic notables are heavily represented (see chapter 11). As such, these people are in a position to design curricula, hire and fire teachers, and keep the socialization process on a track favorable to the political and economic status quo.

A study of the schooling process in one city in the Southwest (probably Dallas) details the change of economic beliefs that transpires as children advance in school years. Children begin school with a rather naive view of economic matters. At an early age they tend toward equity and state-sponsored welfare as means by which goods and services should be distributed throughout society. As they progress through school, however, they come to believe in private property, private enterprise, and the value of private possessions. Government as well as labor unions become suspect economic forces in the minds of older children. People who are not successful economically are thought the ultimate cause of their own problems. By the ninth grade, the authors of this study conclude:

> Children appear to have developed a fairly explicit conception of free enterprise and a normative orientation favorably disposed toward private ownership of the means of production. ... Perhaps, most importantly, [they] begin to articulate the idea that private ownership and productivity are necessary and inescapable components of any smooth functioning economic system.[39]

Schools hence assist in a form of economic socialization that "functions primarily as a mechanism not only to legitimate the corporate order, but also the general structure of social inequality in American life." [40] Even some of the major universities in the state appear reluctant to introduce their students to divergent economic and political perspectives.[41]

Control over the mass media in Texas, especially in the populated markets, is concentrated in the hands of a relatively few corporations. Ten broadcasting companies are responsible for what appears on Texas television.[42] Many of these firms also possess newspapers and radio stations. The Belo Corporation of Dallas, for instance, owns that city's *Morning News,* WFAA–TV, and two radio stations (KROX–AM and KZEW–FM), as well as KHOU–TV, which serves the Houston metropolitan area. Belo has direct links with Dallas's influential corporate leaders. Sitting on its board of directors are representatives from key financial institutions, especially the city's foremost banks.

The Texas media rate low in providing their audiences with political news.[43] The media also rarely delve into much criticism of the economic or political "powers that be" in the state. However, there have been times (one of which will be discussed in chapter 6) when members of the economic elite have used the media to transmit messages directly to the public.

Economic elites also influence the socialization process tacitly. Basically, they set the tone for the core content of what is socialized. Corporations have managed to attach themselves to some of the more fundamental beliefs—patriotism, private property, and freedom—esteemed throughout America. An attack on the corporation often is interpreted as an assault on some of the most valued norms in the country. Consequently the fundamental importance of the corporation in the American belief system is no longer open to serious question, let alone doubt. It has become somewhat of a "given," a sacred cow, in the socialization process.[44]

In short, social diversity and a traditional political culture combine to impede sustained mass political action that runs contrary to the position of the economic elite. The door to control of state government is left mostly open to highly organized groups that are aware of the political process and willing to influence it. These groups invariably turn out to be the dominant economic interests of the state.

The remainder of part I details the makeup of the Texas economic elite. How it gains access to the state government is a story that unfolds in parts II and III. What benefits accrue from its penetration of the state's political institutions constitutes part IV. The fifth part of the book focuses on the impact of economic elites on local governments in Texas. A final note addresses the prospects of political and economic change in the state.

NOTES

1. Max Weber, *The Theory of Social and Economic Organization,* ed. Talcott Parsons (New York: The Free Press, 1964), p. 154. Emphasis in the original.

2. Ira Sharkansky, *The Maligned States: Policy Accomplishments, Problems and Opportunities,* 2d ed. (New York: McGraw-Hill, 1978), p. 1.

3. In discussing these two theories, I have only addressed the core elements in each. Variations in each school, subtle or more obvious, have been ignored.

4. The pluralistic literature is overwhelming. A comprehensive statement of the theory and its application to the understanding of the American political scene is found in Robert A. Dahl, *Pluralist Democracy in the United States: Conflict and Consensus* (Chicago: Rand McNally, 1967).

5. This view of the economic rule model is drawn from many sources. A fairly recent formulation of the perspective may be found in Edward S. Greenberg, *Understanding Modern Government: The Rise and Decline of the American Political Economy* (New York: John Wiley and Sons, 1979).

6. U.S. Department of Commerce, Bureau of Census, *1980 Census of Population and Housing: Congressional District of the 98th Congress, Texas* (Washington, D.C.: U.S. Government Printing Office, 1983), pp. 45–16. Nationality has been calculated on the basis of any ancestor coming from the country in question.

7. The information presented in this section on religion is from the *Texas Poll* of April 1985. Also see William C. Martin, "Texas and God," *Atlantic* 235 (March 1975): 89.

8. This information comes from the *Texas Almanac and State Industrial Guide: 1986–1987* (Dallas: A.H. Belo, 1985), p. 440.

9. *Texas Poll,* February 1984.

10. Thomas R. Plaut, "Energy and the Texas Economy," *Texas Business Review* 57 (March–April 1983): 71.

11. Paul J. Kozlowski, "An Index of Leading Economic Indicators for the State of Texas," *Texas Business Review* 57 (March–April 1983): 53–56.

12. Thomas R. Plaut, "The Texas Economy: Current Status and Short Term Outlook," *Texas Business Review* 57 (January–February 1983): 20.

13. *Texas Observer,* July 31, 1986.

14. Greg Moses, "Farm Aid for the Betrayed," *Texas Observer,* July 31, 1986, pp. 8–9.

15. *New York Times,* January 21, 1987, part IV, p. 1.

16. Quoted in Gregory Seay, "First City Reports $47.9 Million Loss," *Houston Post,* October 27, 1986, E–1.

17. House Study Group, *From Surplus to Shortfall* (Austin: House Study Group, April 22, 1985), p. 3.

18. Bruce Hight, "Treasury to Tell State of Need to Borrow Cash," *Austin American-Statesman,* October 25, 1986, p. 1.

19. *Texas Poll,* Winter 1986.

20. Information from the *Texas Poll,* May 1986.

21. Information on millionaires is from Cadwell Ray, "Income Distribution and Economic Growth in Texas," *Texas Business Review* 57 (May-June, 1983): 112. The poverty figure is from U.S. Department of Commerce, Bureau of Census, *1980 Census of Population and Housing, Texas* (Washington, D.C.: U.S. Government Printing Office, 1983), pp. 45–105.

22. Cadwell Ray, "Income Distribution," p. 108.

23. V.O. Key, Jr., *Southern Politics in State and Nation* (New York: Vintage, 1949), p. 254.

24. Quoted in Robert Engler, *The Politics of Oil: A Study of Private Power and Democratic Directions* (Chicago: University of Chicago Press, 1961), p. 354.

25. Robert Lockwood, "The Business Situation in Texas," *Texas Business Review* 50 (January 1976): 1.

26. Texas American Bancshares, *Annual Report, 1977,* p. 16.

27. Daniel J. Elazar, *American Federalism: A View from the States,* 2d. ed. (New York: Crowell, 1972), pp. 93–114.

28. *Texas Poll,* April 1985.

29. *Texas Poll,* June 1986.

30. *Texas Poll,* July 1985.

31. *Texas Poll,* October 1985.

32. *Texas Poll,* February 1984.

33. Institute for Constructive Capitalism, *Concerns, Issues and Attitudes: A Texas Survey* (Austin: U.T. Austin, Graduate School of Business Administration, 1981), pp. 4–7.

34. The ratings of courts, the legislature, and the police are in the *Texas Poll,* October 1985.

35. Institute for Constructive Capitalism, *Concerns, Issues, and Attitudes,* p. 6–6.

36. John Shockley, *Chicano Revolt in a Texas Town* (Notre Dame, Ind.: University of Notre Dame Press, 1974); Armando Gutierrez and Herbert Hirsch, "The Militant Challenge to the American Ethos: 'Chicanos' and 'Mexican Americans,' " *Social Science Quarterly* 53 (February 1973): 830–845.

37. James W. Lamare, "Language Environment and Political Socialization of Mexican American Children," in *The Politics of Future Citizens,* ed. Richard G. Niemi (San Francisco: Jossey-Bass, 1974), ch. 4; "The Political World of the Rural Chicano Child," *American Politics Quarterly* 5 (January 1977): 83–108; and "The Political Integration of Mexican American Children: A Generational Analysis," *International Migration Review* 16 (Spring 1982): 169–88.

38. The dearth of political information is a mainstay chapter in just about every book on American public opinion. For example, see Harry Holloway and John George, *Public Opinion: Coalitions, Elites, and Masses* (New York: St. Martin's Press, 1979), ch. 4. Economic socialization of children has been overlooked by most researchers, but for an initial summary of the existing literature see Barrie G. Stacey, "Economic Socialization in the Pre-Adult Years," *British Journal of Social Psychology* 21 (1982): 159–73.

39. Scott Cummings and Del Taebel, "The Economic Socialization of Children: A Neo-Marxist Analysis," *Social Problems* 26 (December 1978): p. 205.

40. Ibid.

41. William K. Stevens, "Politics an Issue in Texas Dispute," *New York Times,* June 9, 1981, part C, p. 1.

42. Margo Beutler, "Texas Broadcasting: Who Shall Govern?" *Texas Observer,* October 20, 1979, pp. 4–5.

43. Discussed in the June 1974 issue of the *Texas Monthly.*

44. More along this line can be found in Charles Lindblom, *Politics and Markets* (New York: Basic Books, 1978), ch. 15; and in Michael Parenti, *Power and the Powerless* (New York: St. Martin's Press, 1978), part 2.

2

The Texas Economy: What Dominates

Dominance over the Texas economy lies in the hands of a relatively few large corporations. Gone are the days when farmers, ranchers, innovative entrepreneurs, and local merchants, businessmen, and bankers controlled economic relations in the state. Their place of preeminence has been taken by impersonal institutions—corporations immense in assets, revenues, production and distribution of goods, manpower, and in the effect they have upon our daily lives. The transformation of the state's economy into a corporate one parallels nationwide trends. Today, fewer than 250 giant corporations exercise widespread control over industry, banking, life insurance, communications, utilities, and transportation in the United States.[1]

The search for the corporate elite of Texas begins in the important economic arenas of the state: energy, agriculture, and finance. A detailed sketch of corporate dominance in each of these three economic spheres follows. ★

ENERGY: THE ECONOMIC FOUNDATION

Texas and energy are almost synonymous words. Much of the twentieth century economic history of the state is written in the oil first discovered in large quantity at Spindletop in 1901. While oil still remains important, natural gas, coal, uranium, solar power, electricity, and chemicals have become component parts of the state's energy complex—an industrial matrix unmatched in economic significance anywhere in the country. By 1981, fully one-fourth of Texas's economic output was directly related to energy production and distribution.[2] Full appreciation of this energy empire requires a close scrutiny of six structural elements: crude oil operations, natural gas activities, alternate energy sources, electric companies, chemical plants, and manufacturers of the equipment that serves these enterprises.

Crude Oil

For the greater part of this century, Texas has supplied the bulk of the petroleum needs of the United States. About 27 percent of U.S. refining is done in Texas. One-third of the country's reserves lie in Texas.[3] In recent years, however, Texas's contribution to the production of oil has been declining. In 1975, for instance, 1.2 billion barrels of oil came from the state's fields; ten years later the output was 831 million barrels. Throughout the 1970s around one-third of the nation's petroleum came from Texas. In 1985 Texas provided 25 percent to the total, the lowest percentage recorded during this century. Yet with $20 billion of revenue generated in sales, recovery of crude oil still is the state's largest money producer.[4] In 1983, some 350,000 petroleum workers were paid a total of $10.5 billion in wages. In 1984, the state's public schools and universities received $532.2 million from petroleum sales, a reduction of some $200 million from 1981 receipts. Since the discovery of oil, Texas's schools have gained almost $6 billion from the state's lucrative oil industry.[5] Hence, although the overall value of the petroleum business has been on the wane in recent years, oil remains the foremost economic activity in Texas.

Who controls the petroleum industry in Texas? Objective, reliable data about the operations of oil companies are not easily obtained. One disgruntled investigator groused: "Even the CIA, with its presumably fathomless resources, has claimed difficulty in penetrating the petroleum curtain."[6] Available information generally comes from the oil industry itself and it is not widely circulated.

Table 2–1 presents details about the major oil producers in Texas. Although slightly more than 6,000 businesses produce oil in Texas, most of the discovery and recovery is accomplished by a relatively few companies. Just under 900 million barrels of oil came out of the ground in 1981. The statistics for that year reveal that the top ten producers were responsible for 60 percent of the oil

TABLE 2–1   Top Oil Producers in Texas

Company	Barrels per Year (1981)	Percent of Total	Cumulative Percent
1. Amoco	88.8 million	9.9	9.9
2. Exxon	79.2 million	8.8	18.7
3. Chevron (including Gulf's total)	74.2 million	8.3	27.0
4. Texaco (including Getty's total)	59.2 million	6.6	33.6
5. USX (Marathon and TXO)	52.6 million	5.9	39.5
6. Shell	49.2 million	5.5	45.0
7. Mobil (including Superior Oil)	48.2 million	5.4	50.4
8. Atlantic Richfield (ARCO)	31.4 million	3.5	53.9
9. Sun Oil	29.0 million	3.2	57.1
10. Amerada Hess	26.8 million	3.0	60.1
Remaining 6,000 Producers	359.4 million	40.0	100.1 *
Totals	898 million	100.1 *	100.1 *

* Does not add to 100 percent owing to rounding error.
SOURCE: Adapted from *Oil Directory of Texas* (Austin: R.W. Bryan Co., 1982).

produced. That left the large bulk of the remaining 6,000 companies to recover 40 percent (359 million barrels) of Texas crude.

A close inspection of table 2–1 shows that the top producers are major national companies. Amoco (Standard Oil of Indiana) leads the pack with 88.8 million barrels, or 10 percent of the total. Exxon, the world's foremost industrial firm, accounts for almost 9 percent. The next eight of the top ten producers include Chevron (which now owns Gulf Oil), Texaco (which now possesses Getty Oil), USX (formerly called U.S. Steel, which entered the oil market through its purchase of Marathon Oil and Texas Oil and Gas), Shell, Mobil (which now includes Superior Oil), Atlantic Richfield, Sun, and Amerada Hess.

Conspicuously absent from the list of producers are companies associated with wildcatters—those irrepressible oil barons portrayed in the media as the rugged individualists who form the backbone of the Texas oil business. To be sure, such individuals have drilled the land in Texas and through perseverance, guile, cunning, and sheer luck some struck it rich in the process. H.L. Hunt, Dad Joiner, Sid Richardson, Perry Bass, Edwin Cox, and Paul Haas come close to this stereotype. However, companies founded by such men are not among the top producers in Texas, regardless of their popular image. Hunt Enterprises, for instance, recovered only around 5.4 million barrels in 1981, a small fraction (.06 percent) of Amoco's production total.

Texas leads the nation in the refining of crude oil. In 1985, 1.64 million barrels were processed in the state, a slight decline in refinery runs done in the earlier 1980s. Forty-four companies own the 52 refineries operating in the state. Since 1982, eleven refining plants have been shut down, a further sign of the economic woes besetting the petroleum industry. As indicated in table 2–2, the major oil companies refine most of the oil, with ten companies performing over two-thirds of this task. The top seven—Exxon, Chevron (which now owns Gulf's facilities), Amoco, Texaco, Phillips, Mobil, and Shell, in that order—process 55 percent of the crude. A quick recheck of table 2–1 reveals a strong correspondence between the top producers and the leading refiners.

TABLE 2–2 Top Refineries in Texas

Company	Barrels Refined (1985)	Percent of Total	Cumulative Percent
1. Exxon	180.3 million	11.0	11.0
2. Chevron (including Gulf)	176.3 million	10.8	21.8
3. Amoco	146.0 million	8.9	30.7
4. Texaco	104.8 million	6.4	37.1
5. Phillips	100.4 million	6.1	43.2
6. Mobil	100.4 million	6.1	49.3
7. Shell	93.8 million	5.7	55.0
Remaining 37 Refiners	734 million	44.9	44.9
Totals	1636 million	99.9*	99.9*

* Does not add to 100 percent owing to rounding error.

SOURCE: Adapted from Oil and Gas Division of the Railroad Commission of Texas, *Annual Report, 1985*, pp. 99–101.

Hence two important phases of the petroleum business in Texas—production and refining—are dominated by the major oil companies. In addition, majors have extensive operations in the transportation (through pipelines and by rail and truck) and the distribution (through service stations, for instance) of oil. Although precise figures detailing the depth of these commitments in Texas are not readily at hand, there is strong impressionistic evidence pointing to the importance of these companies. For instance, gas stations owned by major oil companies have come to permeate this form of distribution. Until the energy crisis of 1973, gas was usually dispensed to the public at stations owned by individual dealers under contract with a major oil company for supplies. Since then, tens of thousands of smaller dealers have gone out of business, owing to shortages in supply and high prices for gas. These dealers usually have been replaced with self-service stations owned by majors. Gulf (now owned by Chevron), for example, between 1973 and 1976 severed ties with around 4,000 dealers while at the same time increasing its number of self-service stations to 900, a fourfold accretion.[7]

Hence the giants of the Texas crude oil business are major companies. Majors dominate production, refining, transportation, and distribution. These companies, in the jargon of economists, are vertically integrated. That is, all the essential functions of the petroleum process are performed by the same corporation. An independent company might specialize in one or two of these functions. As such, it is usually dependent on one of the majors to complete any given oil transaction and therefore it assumes a secondary position to the majors in the Texas oil industry.

Natural Gas

Natural gas is a tasteless, odorless, invisible substance sealed under great pressure within the earth. It is usually found in close proximity to crude oil. Gas was once considered so useless and difficult to harness for commercial purposes that it was burned as it escaped from the subsoil. (Flaring, as the practice was called, was stopped in Texas in 1949). Over the last thirty years, however, natural gas has become the major fuel responsible for producing electricity, heating homes, and supplying power for factory boilers in the United States.

Throughout this century, Texas has been the key source of the country's natural gas. In 1985, 5.81 trillion cubic feet of natural gas were produced in Texas. This figure represents 35 percent of the gas produced in the nation. Although unsteady prices led to the plugging of 14,479 natural gas wells in 1985, some 43,600 wells were still in operation that year. Around 25 percent of U.S. gas reserves are located in the state [8] and natural gas sales are still worth in excess of $13 billion a year.[9]

The natural gas business encompasses three distinct operations: discovery and production, transportation to market, and distribution to customers. As in the crude oil industry, giant corporations dominate each of these three phases in Texas.

Table 2–3 presents figures on natural gas production in 1981. Texas produced 6.73 trillion cubic feet of natural gas that year. Ten corporations accounted for 52 percent of this total. A minority of the gas recovered (48 percent) is in the domain of the remaining 6,000 or so producers.

TABLE 2-3 Top Natural Gas Producers in Texas

Company	Cubic Feet in Millions (1981)	Percent of Total	Cumulative Percent
1. Exxon	983	14.6	14.6
2. Mobil (including Superior Oil)	456	6.8	21.4
3. Chevron (including Gulf)	399	5.9	27.3
4. USX (including Marathon and TXO)	342	5.1	32.4
5. Texaco (including Getty Oil)	298	4.4	36.8
6. Amoco	264	3.9	40.7
7. Atlantic Richfield (ARCO)	220	3.3	44.0
8. Shell	215	3.2	47.2
9. Phillips	161	2.4	49.6
10. Sun Oil	152	2.3	51.9
Remaining 6,000 Producers	3240	48.1	51.9
Totals	6730 MCF	100.0	100.0

SOURCE: Adapted from *Oil Directory of Texas* (Austin: R.W. Bryan, 1982).

Some familiar names appear on the list. Exxon, with almost 15 percent of the total, heads the group. Mobil (Superior Oil), Chevron (Gulf), USX (Texas Gas and Oil and Marathon), Texaco (Getty), Amoco, Atlantic Richfield, Shell, Phillips, and Sun Oil round out the leading ten producers. Although the next dozen or so producers contain several independent firms, the preeminent position of the majors should not be underestimated. For instance, only when all the gas output of the top twelve independents is combined can the production figure of Exxon be surpassed.

Natural gas only became a valuable commodity when it could be safely and economically transported from the field to the commercial marketplace. The transmission problem was solved with the creation of pipeline systems in the 1930s and 1940s. The owners of the pipeline operations soon came to have a dominant role in the natural gas business. In 1985, 2.1 trillion cubic feet of gas, some 36 percent of the total produced, was exported from Texas.[10]

Texas has spawned several interstate pipeline carriers. The El Paso Company (now controlled by the Burlington Northern Corporation) delivered, in 1985, 351 billion cubic feet of gas, mostly to the Southwest (including about 50 percent of California's gas). Tenneco's pipeline carried 222 billion cubic feet to New York City and to the greater New England area. Texas Eastern supplied Ohio, West Virginia, and parts of Pennsylvania and New York. Transco serviced much of the Southeast and the eastern seaboard up to New York and Philadelphia, with 245 billion cubic feet of Texas gas. The combined totals of these firms account for about 45 percent of the gas transmitted onto the interstate market. The Natural Gas Pipeline Company (354 billion cubic feet) and the ENRON Company (169 billion cubic feet) added another 16.4 percent and 5.5 percent to the total transported. All told, five companies delivered over two-thirds of the state's gas to external customers.[11] Each of these pipeline companies has a virtual monopoly in their market areas; that is, competition among them is extremely rare.

More natural gas is consumed in Texas than in any other state. Most of it (some 52 percent) goes to industry. A third is delivered to utilities for the generation of electricity. Home consumption, usually for the heating of houses, takes only about 6 percent of the gas distributed within Texas.[12] ENSERCH (Lone Star Gas) distributes gas across the northern part of the state, including the Dallas Fort Worth metroplex. ENRON, which was formed when Houston Natural Gas and InterNorth of Omaha merged, covers the southeastern part of the state. Entex serves parts of Houston, East Texas, and areas along the Mexican border. Valero provides gas to much of Central Texas, including San Antonio. Southern Union supplies Austin and El Paso. These are Texas's largest domestic distributors of natural gas. Each has a near monopoly control over its respective market.

In short, the natural gas business is dominated by large-scale corporations. Major oil companies have a striking presence in the production of gas. They are joined in the gas elite by many Texas-born corporations that concentrate in the transportation and distribution phases of the natural gas business.

Alternate Energy Sources

Crude oil and natural gas have been the prime sources of energy in the U.S. throughout the twentieth century. But these are nonrenewable minerals and their stocks are being depleted. In Texas, for instance, reserves of oil and natural gas will probably decline at an annual rate of 1.4 percent through the year 2000: "Whereas conventional petroleum resources have constituted 98 percent of the historical production of Texas energy, they represent only 23 percent of the remaining endowment." [13]

What will become the future sources of energy? In the immediate time frame, coal, uranium, and geothermal resources are the prime candidates. Solar energy has yet to emerge as a meaningful source of power but may be a bright option in the future. Texas is blessed with an abundance of each.

Lignite, a brown, soft, porous type of coal, is plentiful in Texas. With a total of about 58.2 billion tons of lignite, Texas ranks third among all states in availability of this resource.[14] In 1985 Texas was sixth among states in coal production, 99 percent of which was lignite.[15] It is estimated that half of the lignite has commercial potential, usually made available through strip mining operations. Since 1972, about 158 million tons of lignite have been ripped from the earth of Texas, mostly for the generation of electricity.[16]

Some 620 million pounds of uranium—the third largest quantity among states—are blanketed beneath South and West Texas. The annual production rate has been 5.4 million pounds with an accumulation of some 33 million pounds mined by 1980.[17] Most of the uranium is destined to fuel nuclear power reactors, although a dramatic decline in price and demand in the early 1980s has put the uranium business somewhat on hold.

Hydrothermal and geopressure water formations, many containing methane, are located in the Gulf Coast, the TransPecos Arch, and South and Central Texas. The potential of geothermal sources is being researched closely. Finally, the sun shines brightly most of the year over much of the state. El Paso records more sunlight hours each year than any other metropolitan area in the country. Solar energy is a natural for Texas.

The corporate hand is clearly visible in the development of alternate energy sources. Currently, there are seven lignite strip mines in full production in Texas. Texas Utilities, the giant electric company, operates four of them—one in partnership with Alcoa. Fully 75 percent of coal produced in Texas is done by Texas Utilities, mostly to feed the utility company's electric power generators. Indeed, Texas leads the nation in the amount of coal consumed in any one state. The bulk of that total goes to one company, however—Texas Utilities.[18] Exxon, Dow Chemical, Shell, and Phillips Petroleum have smaller lignite mines in the state.[19] By the early 1980s, even uranium mining in Texas was mostly done by Dupont, Chevron, Anaconda Copper (ARCO), USX (Marathon Oil), Mobil, Exxon, Texaco, and Kerr-McGee.[20]

Furthermore, major oil companies have been quite active in solar energy through the absorption of smaller solar energy companies. For instance, photovoltaic cells are capable of converting the sun's rays into electricity and much of the original nongovernmental photovoltaic research and marketing was done by small- to medium-sized firms (such as Solarex). Over the years, however, large oil companies have moved into the photovoltaic market. In the 1980s Amoco, for example, purchased Solarex. By 1983, "almost 80 percent of the photovoltaic market was controlled by only three firms, each owned by an oil company: Arco Solar (Atlantic-Richfield), Solarex (Amoco), and Solar Power (Exxon)."[21] When the sun becomes an economically viable energy source (probably sometime toward the end of this century), the major oil companies will deliver its power.

Electric Companies

Electricity is generated when steam-driven turbines rotate rapidly. Since the superheated steam is produced mostly by burning natural gas and petroleum, electric utilities are thus directly dependent on the availability of these fossil fuels. At the beginning of 1985 there were 138 electric power plants in Texas. Some 30 percent of the state's electricity is generated by municipally owned utilities (such as those in Austin and San Antonio) and rural electric cooperatives (such as the Lower Colorado River Authority). Only six investor-owned companies, which are listed in table 2–4, supply the remaining 70 percent.[22]

Utility companies in Texas recently have begun switching to new energy sources to produce electricity. After the increase in price and decrease in abundance of crude oil and natural gas experienced in the 1970s, the power companies turned more and more to coal and uranium as alternate sources of generating electricity. Texas Utilities, the largest power company in the state, is in the process of constructing two nuclear reactors and eight coal-generating plants. Four of its coal-generating plants are now on-line; two more are to come into operation before 1989. At this writing, unit one of Texas Utilities' nuclear reactors located near Glen Rose is awaiting a federal license to begin production. Unit two is behind schedule and is not expected to be finished until 1988. Each unit is substantially above its originally estimated cost. Virtually every major electric company is financially committed to plants that will soon generate electricity from uranium or coal, or both.

The role of major oil companies in electrifying Texas should not be overlooked. As pointed out in previous sections of this chapter, major oil companies

TABLE 2-4   The Largest Privately Owned Electric Companies in Texas

Company	Assets (1985)	Revenues (1985)
Texas Utilities	$10.9 billion	$4.2 billion
Houston Industries (Houston Lighting and Power)	$ 8.8 billion	$4.0 billion
Central and South West (Central Power and Light, West Texas Utilities, Southwestern Electric Service, and Public Service of Oklahoma)	$ 6.8 billion	$2.7 billion
Gulf States Utilities	$ 5.6 billion	$1.9 billion
Southwestern Public Service	$ 1.6 billion	$832 million
El Paso Electric Company	$ 1.9 billion	$340 million

SOURCE: *1986 Annual Report* of each company.

produce most of the materials utilized in generating electricity. Hence power companies—through their dependence on natural gas, petroleum, uranium, and coal as sources of electricity—are, by and large, directly tied to the oil majors.

Chemicals

Raw crude oil and natural gas contain a plethora of chemicals that, in turn, are the core of a variety of commercial products. Xylene, toluene, ethylene, ammonia, and benzene are among the many valuable chemicals extracted from crude and gas. By-products of these compounds include insecticides, fertilizers, dyes, drugs, plastics, nylon, solvents, glue, rubber, and clothing.

About 41 percent of U.S. petrochemicals comes from factories situated in Texas. In total, 196 companies are engaged in the state's chemical industry, and the largest chemical companies are major oil companies.[23] In addition, the names of Dow Chemical, Dupont, Union Carbide, Monsanto, and Celanese are to be found among the chemical elite of the state.

Equipment and Machinery

Petroleum companies, natural gas firms, electric utilities, and chemical corporations all use highly specialized machinery to carry out their operations. Not surprisingly, Texas is the home of many corporations that concentrate on equipping these enterprises. These businesses build refineries, chemical plants, nuclear reactors, and coal-fired facilities that generate electricity. They also supply gas and oil drilling rigs, pipelines, and supertankers. Two-thirds of all domestic oil-drilling equipment is manufactured by Texas-based companies.[24]

The following are among Texas's leading construction firms: Halliburton (Brown and Root), Dresser, Zapata, and SEDCO. Vice-President George Bush, a Texan, founded Zapata. SEDCO was started and once headed by Texas Governor

Bill Clements. As a result of a merger in 1986, it is now a part of the giant Dutch multinational Schlumberger (1985 assets equaled $10.9 billion). When Mr. Clements was serving his first term as governor, one of SEDCO's drilling wells exploded off the Mexican coast, resulting in the worst oil slick in the history of the world. The mammoth blowout caused considerable damage to the economy along Texas's Gulf Coast.

Through its Brown and Root subsidiary, Halliburton has become a major builder of pipelines, chemical factories, coal-burning generating plants, and nuclear reactors, as well as other heavy construction projects. In 1985 Halliburton had an asset worth valued at $4.7 billion and revenues of $4.9 billion. Brown and Root is the prime contractor for Texas Utilities' Comanche Peak nuclear power plants located near Glen Rose. Until 1981, it also was constructing the South Texas Nuclear Power facility on Matagorda Island for Houston Lighting and Power, Central and South West, and the municipal electric companies of Austin and San Antonio.

In each case, Brown and Root became embroiled in investigations and controversy about the safety and cost-effectiveness of the nuclear power plants. Specific charges leveled at Brown and Root included the falsification of accounts and inspection documents and the harassment and intimidation of employees trying to report these illegalities.[25] The Nuclear Regulatory Commission of the federal government perceived that "the basic problem at [the] South Texas [project] can be summarized as inadequate licensee control of the construction process, leading to serious deficiencies in the quality assurance program."[26] Houston Lighting and Power, the principal partner in the South Texas project, was subsequently fined $100,000 for its part of the problem. In the midst of allegations, counterclaims, and lawsuits Brown and Root was relieved of its contractual obligation to build the plant. It was replaced by Bechtel. Brown and Root continues, however, to construct Texas Utilities' Comanche Peak reactors.

Energy and the Texas Economy

The discovery of oil has stimulated much economic activity and great wealth in Texas. The core of the energy complex revolves around the country's largest oil companies. The top twelve American oil companies, including U.S. Steel, account for 61.4 percent of Texas's oil production, 55.0 percent of its refining total, and 53.8 percent of its natural gas recovery.[27] Several of these firms hold most of the rights to alternate energy sources in the state. Consumers of these energy sources, whether they be the paying public, electric companies, or natural gas carriers, are thus structurally bound to the oil giants. The tentacles of the oil majors extend to the petrochemical industry. Finally, the manufacturers of energy equipment and machinery count on the majors to buy their wares or hire their services.

Although the majors have extensive holdings in, and influence over, Texas, only one company—Texaco—can trace its corporate origins to the state's oil fields. None now has its official worldwide corporate headquarters in Texas, although most have established secondary homes here. The oil bounty of Texas has generated a few important local energy firms distinct from the majors, but they generally are a notch below the national giants in economic importance.

Table 2–5 shows the lofty economic status achieved by the top twelve U.S. oil firms. Their numbers—assets, revenues, and domestic and international standing—are truly impressive. In a decade, their combined asset worth has grown from $144.9 billion (1976) to $359.6 billion (1986). To be sure, they have recently suffered some loss of revenue owing to falling petroleum prices. Between 1982 and 1986, collectively the major petroleum firms experienced a 27 percent decline in sales income.

Foremost among these giants is Exxon, whose nominal forerunner, Standard Oil of New Jersey, was founded by John D. Rockefeller, Sr. Interestingly, Standard was an uninvited participant in the early oil discoveries of Texas.[28] It circumvented resistance, some of which was quite violent, by forming a partnership with Humble Oil of Texas. Any distinction between the two was obliterated in 1972 when Standard of New Jersey and Humble officially merged into the Exxon Corporation. Presently, Exxon is Texas's leading energy merchant. Part of this dominance shows up in Exxon's current yearly profit margin of over $5.4 billion, the most earned by any of the world's businesses.

AGRICULTURE

The wealth generated from the land in Texas does not end with the rich natural resources beneath its surface. The state's land mass also has been generous to farmers, ranchers, and woodcutters, since the fertile soil is quite suitable for grazing and for cultivating fibers, foodstuffs, and timber. Cash receipts from the sale of agricultural products grown in Texas were around $10.2 billion in 1984. Texas consistently ranks among the top three states (along with Iowa and California) in gross earnings derived from the sale of its livestock, crops, and timber

TABLE 2–5   Revenues, Assets, and Industrial Standing of the Top Twelve Oil Companies

Company	Revenues (1985)	Assets (1985)	Industrial Domestic	Standing * International
Exxon	$86.7 billion	$69.2 billion	2	2
Mobil	$56.0 billion	$41.7 billion	3	4
Texaco	$43.2 billion	$37.7 billion	6	8
Chevron	$41.7 billion	$38.9 billion	7	9
Dupont	$29.5 billion	$25.1 billion	9	12
Amoco	$27.2 billion	$25.2 billion	11	14
Atlantic-Richfield	$22.4 billion	$21.6 billion	12	18
Shell	$20.3 billion	$26.5 billion	14	19
USX	$18.4 billion	$21.8 billion	15	26
Phillips	$15.7 billion	$14.0 billion	17	36
Occidental	$14.5 billion	$11.6 billion	19	40
Sun Oil	$13.8 billion	$12.9 billion	20	48

* Domestic and international standing is based on revenues.

SOURCES: 1986 Annual Report of each corporation; *Fortune*, April 28, 1986, p. 182; and *Fortune*, August 21, 1986, pp. 170–171.

products. All told, some $33 billion a year in state income is derived from agricul-
tural activities in Texas. The total asset value of land, machinery, livestock,
buildings, crops, and farming households and investments now exceeds $100
billion.[29]

There are three phases to the business of agriculture. One involves the actual
growth of products and commodities. The second covers the conversion of raw
agricultural items into consumable products. The third includes the retail sale of
agricultural goods to customers. The discussion now turns to land ownership,
agricultural processing, and distribution.

Land Ownership in Texas

The abundance of relatively inexpensive land in Texas has, over the years, given
many people more than just a means to make a living. It has also afforded the
opportunity to own private property and provided a strong rationale to believe in
the virtues of rugged individualism, self-reliance, and personal freedom and liberty. Recently, however, the number of people who own agricultural land in Texas
has been declining.

In 1940 there were 418,000 farms and ranches in Texas.[30] By 1950 that figure
had dropped to 331,567.[31] Over the course of the next three decades a steady
erosion in the number of agricultural units occurred until by 1982 only 185,026
farms and ranches were left.[32] With adverse economic conditions currently besieg-
ing many of the state's farmers, more owners will surely be forced to sell. One
source predicted that by the end of 1986 the number of farms and ranches would
be down to 160,000.[33] During this flurry of ownership change the average size of
agricultural units has almost doubled, from 439 acres in 1950 to 732 acres in
1984.[34]

There are great disparities in agricultural sales among Texas farmers and
ranchers. On average (in 1982), each agricultural unit earned $48,299 in sales. But
this figure disguises acute unevenness in the spread of sales. A majority of Texas's
farms and ranches received $5,000 or *less* in *gross receipts* in 1982. Almost two-thirds
could not surpass an annual *gross* sales figure of $10,000. Fully 90 percent of these
low-earning farms and ranches are run by families, indicating that agriculture is a
real struggle for Texas's typical family farmer and rancher.

Most of the income earned from agriculture goes to a small minority of
farms and ranches. In 1982, for example, 1,749 agricultural units grossed at least
$4.4 billion in sales. In other words, these top farms and ranches accounted for
almost 50 percent of all agricultural receipts. In 1974, the top farms and ranches
were responsible for 41 percent of sales. Hence the overall trend is toward
greater concentration of earning power in the hands of a very small number
(less than 1 percent) of the total agricultural units in Texas. Ironically, it is the
largest farms that receive financial aid from the federal government; the smaller,
more financially strapped units, do not benefit much from government assistance programs.[35]

Only 46 percent of these top earners are owned by individuals or families.
The majority are under the control of corporations or partnerships. To be sure,
most corporate farming and ranching in Texas is *not* done by public corporations.

Rather, farming and ranching corporations in the state are mostly formed by family members.[36]

Texas has some noteworthy large spreads run by family corporations. The King family corporation, for instance, owns 825,000 acres between Brownsville and Corpus Christi. The King Ranch is almost 200,000 acres larger than the state of Rhode Island. Other large family farming units are the Waggoner estate in Central Texas (525,000 acres), the O'Connor Ranches (500,000 acres), the Blakemore Ranch of West Texas (455,000 acres), the Burnett Ranches of Central Texas (451,000 acres), the Kenedy Ranch of South Texas (450,000 acres), former Governor Dolph Briscoe's holdings in Central Texas (450,000 acres), and the acreage (140,000 plus) owned by South Texas rancher Clinton Manges.[37]

Public corporations are only marginally involved in farm ownership. Less than 1 percent of the agricultural units in the United States falls under their ownership.[38] This low figure is probably representative of the fact that the greatest financial risk in agriculture is in producing farm or ranch products. Nonetheless, corporate farmers and ranchers generally make a good profit.[39]

There are some clear cases of corporately owned agricultural units in Texas. Much of the state's beef is raised on corporate feedlots located in the Panhandle area. The Iowa Beef Processors (now owned by the Occidental Petroleum Company), for example, has extensive interests in the cattle industry of the state. The hand of corporate farming is quite visible in the rich and fertile South Texas valley area. With over $320 million in farming sales annually, Hidalgo County is the wealthiest agricultural county in the state and third in the nation. Interestingly, Hidalgo ranks near the bottom nationally in per-capita income earned annually by its residents, many of whom are migrant farm workers. Corporate growers, such as Griffin and Brand, dominate agriculture there.

The most obvious case of corporate ownership of Texas's agricultural land occurs in the timber business. Some 10 million acres of commercially valuable forest land lie within the state, mostly in the East Texas region. Whereas two-thirds of this land is divided into small holdings, large corporations with interests in wood, paper, and pulp own the most productive units.[40]

The Temple Inland Company, with 1,090,000 acres of forest land, heads the list. Formerly this company was a subsidiary of Time, Inc., publisher of *Time* magazine, *Fortune, People, Money, Sports Illustrated,* and Little-Brown books. Time sold Temple Inland in 1984, although the chief stockholder in the timber company—Texan Arthur Temple—also is the principal investor in Time. The merger of the St. Regis Paper Company with Champion–U.S. Plywood has resulted in the new company now holding almost as many acres (some 1,022,000) as Temple Inland. The Southern Pacific Sante Fe Company possesses 550,000 timber acres; International Paper Company has 442,807 acres; Owens Illinois owns 171,776 acres.[41]

The title of the largest single owner of Texas's agricultural land goes to the Texas Pacific Land Trust. Altogether the Trust administers 1.2 million acres of land, primarily located in far West Texas. Most of this acreage was accumulated by the Texas and Pacific Railroad during the nineteenth century. At that time the state legislature encouraged railroads to construct track in exchange for land (to be discussed more fully in chapter 7). The trust is what remained after the Texas and Pacific Railroad went bankrupt. Most of its land is being leased to ranchers, who paid the Trust some $340,000 in grazing fees in 1982. Along with cattle, the land is host to many oil wells. Oil companies contributed $4.3 million in 1982 to the Trust for drilling rights.[42]

A few Texas-based corporations have extensive agricultural holdings in other states. Anderson-Clayton, a Houston agribusiness that converts raw materials into consumable items, has 33,000 acres in California.[43] Tenneco possesses nearly 700,000 acres of timberland in Alabama, Mississippi, Florida, Michigan, and Tennessee. It also owns or leases slightly over 1.1 million acres of fertile farmland in Arizona and California.[44] With so much land under its corporate belt, Tenneco is considered to be "the country's biggest farmer." [45]

Finally, 20 percent of the country's farmers and ranchers work under contracts with corporations. In certain food lines the figure is much higher. For instance, virtually every chicken farmer in America is under contract with a corporation for his or her produce.[46] These contracts are usually with corporations that link farmers and ranchers with consumers; it is here that the impact of big business in agriculture is the greatest.

Food Processors

The foremost food processors are primarily national and international corporations, such as Nestle, Philip Morris (owners of General Foods), R. J. Reynolds (owners of Nabisco Standard), and Dart Kraft. "While," in the words of Texas Commissioner of Agriculture Jim Hightower, "there are 32,000 food processing firms in America, . . . 50 of them now make more than 90 percent of the profits in the industry." [47] In any one line of food only a relatively few of these giants are responsible for what is processed. Specialization in food items is the norm. Consequently, at best only a few companies account for most of the sales of any one food product in the United States. For instance, three corporations produce 90 percent of the frozen dinners sold; four companies sell 85 percent of the cereal; nine of every ten desserts come from the kitchens of three corporations. All the way down the shopping list, one finds oligopoly (control by the few) rampant in the food processing industry.[48] Indeed, it is estimated (by the Federal Trade Commission) that consumers pay millions more each year for their food bill because of "monopoly overcharges." [49]

Because of its agricultural riches, many of the food giants flock to Texas. Del Monte (now a division of R. J. Reynolds), for example, processes many of the fruits and vegetables grown in South Texas. In the same area, Texsun, a subsidiary of Royal Crown Cola, turns fresh fruits into canned drinks. The Pet Company is firmly planted in the chili fields near El Paso. Pet, itself a part of the Illinois Central Railroad Company, uses the chilies to spice up its Old El Paso Mexican food line. Ralston Purina, one of the larger cereal and animal feed companies, has multiple plants across the Lone Star State. Finally, many of the country's biggest meat packers, including Occidental Petroleum's Iowa Beef Processors, slaughter and cure livestock in Texas. Indeed, Edwin Cox, Jr., an oilman from Dallas, recently purchased Swift and Company, one of the nation's premier packers of pork and meat.

Some corporations with headquarters in Texas are among the leading processors of food. Houston's Tenneco, for example, packages, crates, and distributes fruits, vegetables, and nuts in its California plants. Anderson-Clayton converts cotton and soybeans (among other raw food items) into finished products such as Seven Seas salad dressing, Log Cabin syrup, and Chiffon margarine. Wilson Meats, a subsidiary of Dallas's LTV corporation, produces and distributes hot dogs, hams, and other pork items. The Associated Milk Producers of San Antonio collects, refines, and distributes milk and other diary products throughout the nation. In some markets, such as San Antonio and El Paso, it has a virtual monopoly.

Retailers of Food

Consumers buy food either in grocery stores or in restaurants. In either place they mostly make purchases from corporations. Seven grocery chains—Safeway, Kroger, Southland (7–Eleven), American (Alpha Beta), Lucky, Winn-Dixie, and A & P, in that order—account for one-third of all food items sold in the United States.[50] Texas's contribution to the list is the Dallas-based Southland Corporation. With around 8,000 7–Eleven outlets across America, Southland is the country's foremost convenience store operator. Its annual sales now exceed $12 billion, some three times its sales of 1977.

Patterns of concentration somewhat higher than the national figure are found in the market control of grocery store chains in Texas cities. Safeway and Kroger control about 36 percent of the greater Houston market area (which stretches from Beaumont to Victoria and from College Station to Galveston). Safeway, Kroger, and Winn-Dixie divide 39 percent of the Dallas/Fort Worth area. H.E.B., a locally based chain, Kroger, and Safeway account for 52 percent of the sales in the San Antonio market, which ranges from Austin to Brownsville.[51]

Large-scale corporations have made impressive inroads into the nation's restaurant business. Almost half of *all* nationwide dining establishments are now owned by fewer than 100 corporations. Corporate restaurants and fast food chains amass a majority of all dollars spent dining out.[52] It has been accurately observed that "today, the fastest growing and most profitable segment of the food industry is the chain restaurant business."[53] Table 2–6 presents a selected list of corporate dining places operating in the state of Texas.

The Plight of the Small Family Farm in Texas

Economic disaster has stalked family farms ever since the advent of sophisticated farm machinery. Small growers who have survived mechanized farming now must confront the twin pressures exerted by suppliers and by the middlemen of agriculture.

Suppliers are plentiful. Machinery, fertilizer, seed, and fuel compose only a partial list of the commodities basic for successful modern farming. Each has its price, and currently that price is soaring. Over the last quarter century the expense of a new tractor has increased to around $50,000—more than a tenfold increase (in constant dollars).[54] Fertilizer, a petroleum by-product, doubled in cost over a short two-year span in the 1970s.[55] In the midst of the energy crisis Reeves County farmers saw their natural gas bills quintuple in one year.[56] Without fuel, farmers

TABLE 2–6   Corporate Owners of Some Chain Restaurants

Restaurant Chain	Corporate Owner
El Chico	Anheuser-Busch
Lum's and Ranch House	Colgate-Palmolive
Burger Chef	Philip Morris
Red Lobster	General Mills
Stuckey's	Illinois Central Railroad
Stouffer	Nestle
Pizza Hut, Taco Bell, Kentucky Fried Chicken	PepsiCo
Burger King and Steak and Ale	Pillsbury
Jack in the Box	Ralston Purina
Arby's	Royal Crown Cola
Dobb's House	Squibb
A & W Root Beer	United Brands
El Torito and Del Taco	W.R. Grace

SOURCE: Annual Report of each company.

could not operate the irrigation pumps needed to water their fields. Bank loans in the area began "to dry up just as fast as unirrigated land." [57] The dry spell continues well into the 1980s. Rising cost in fuel means that "farmers are facing serious management decisions in the use of irrigation for crop production." [58] Land irrigated in Reeves County decreased from 50,000 acres in 1980 to 29,000 acres by 1985.[59]

The need to contract with middlemen—food processors and retailers—adds to the economic woes of the family farmer or rancher. The costs of shipping, processing, storing, packing, and selling agricultural goods are very high. Frequently, agreements signed between middlemen and farmers work mostly to the economic benefit of the former. For instance, one family living in Presidio contracted with Griffin and Brand, the large agribusiness firm out of Hildago County, to deliver their onions and melons to market. The company earned four times more than the family from the sale of the produce. In the words of one family member, Griffin and Brand "came here and said 'We're a big outfit, and we've got a lot of money. We want to make some money and make the farmers a little.' Of course, they didn't say how little." The following year the family deliberately tried to avoid Griffin and Brand. Only after the family had lost $40,000 did it discover that their new middleman was in reality an agent of Griffin and Brand. In assessing the situation, one member of the family concluded that the company was "trying to break the farmers . . . and take their land." [60]

With a decline in market prices for their produce and a prolonged period of drought, it is no wonder that Texas's already beleaguered family farmer and rancher are under considerable stress in the 1980s. Many, as earlier figures suggested, have simply sold their holdings, usually at depressed value. Some have been forced off the land by their creditors. To help cope with this situation a farm crisis hotline was established in Texas with funds collected by Farm Aid. During the first six months of 1986, 2,500 phone calls were logged by the crisis center. The typical caller was 47 years old, with more than two decades of farming or ranching experience. Most (90 percent) were phoning to request the name of an attorney; half wanted information about indigent legal aid; around one-third inquired about job-training schemes; and an equal number were referred to authorities at the state's mental health units.[61]

Corporate growers generally are immune from the full force of the pressures that plague small family farms. Some of the large agribusinesses are integrated. That is, all aspects of farming (e.g., supplies, land, processing, and retailing) are done within the same company. Tenneco, for instance, grows food, processes it, sells it, and supplies itself with fertilizer (through its petrochemical division), farm equipment (through its J. I. Case and International Harvester subsidiaries), and fuel (though its oil and natural gas facilities). A harsh growing season or a stubborn market may mean the demise of the small farmer, but even those agribusinesses not as self-sufficient as Tenneco can withstand many agricultural uncertainties. Most can draw on other resources within the company—the profits gained from other economic activities, for instance—during these times of economic difficulty.

FINANCIAL INSTITUTIONS

Since the late 1960s, Texas has experienced tremendous economic development. New industries have relocated into the state and established firms have embarked on ambitious expansion plans. Consequently, construction permits and housing starts reached all-time highs during the early 1980s. It was a time when the need for capital was at a premium. The recession of the mid-1980s resulted in a period of economic slack, however. The state's financial institutions—principally the commercial banks, the savings and loan firms, and the insurance companies—have been fully caught up in this pendulum. This section explores each of these financial establishments.

Banks

In the past, Texans were very distrustful of banks. The framers of the Texas Constitution, ratified in 1876, in fact prohibited the granting of state charters for commercial banks. In 1904, after great wealth began to accumulate as a result of major oil discoveries, the ban against bank charters was removed through constitutional amendment. However, any newly authorized bank was confined to one location; that is, branch banking was forbidden. The aim of this restriction on multibanks was to inhibit the concentration of bank deposits and assets in the hands of a relatively few financial institutions.

In 1986, the state legislature and Texas voters approved a constitutional amendment that now legally authorizes branch banking. In effect, this change legitimates a practice that has been already in existence in the state for over a decade. While under the old law banning branch banking the state spawned over 1,853 separate commercial banks, a relatively few of these institutions were far more economically important than the rest. Table 2–7 displays the distribution of bank assets in Texas at the end of 1984.

TABLE 2–7 Assets and Number of Affiliates of the Top Bank Holding Companies in Texas

Bank Holding Company	Number of Affiliates (1985)	Assets (1984)	Percent of Total Assets	Cumulative Percent
InterFirst	67	$ 21.61 billion	11.5	11.5
Republic of Texas	39	$ 21.59 billion	11.5	23.0
M Corp	65	$ 20.74 billion	11.0	34.0
Texas Commerce	70	$ 20.73 billion	11.0	45.0
First City	64	$ 17.32 billion	9.2	54.2
Remaining Banks	1548	$ 6.4 billion	45.8	45.8
Totals	1853	$188.27 billion	100.0	100.0

SOURCES: *1985 Annual Report* of each bank holding company and the *Texas Almanac and State Industrial Guide: 1986–1987* (Dallas: A. H. Belo Co., 1985), p. 589.

By the end of 1984, 5 bank holding companies controlled 54.2 percent of all bank assets in the state of Texas. Fully 305 affiliates were members of these 5 bancorporations. The remaining 1,548 banks accounted for only 45.8 percent of all the state's bank assets. Public officials in Texas, as will be detailed in chapter 14, mostly saw a legal distinction between branch banking and a bank holding company. Consequently, bank holding companies continued to grow in economic strength by increasing their number of affiliates throughout the state. Table 2–8 documents the phenomenal expansion experienced by the large bank holding companies between 1978 and 1985.

On the average, the five largest banks increased their assets over this seven-year period by 62 percent. Correspondingly, the number of affiliates grew by 61 percent. Enlargement usually came through mergers. M Corp (formerly Mercantile Bank) led all rivals in expansion by making some shrewd acquisitions. During the 1980s, M Corp purchased El Paso's second largest bank group (Pan National) and effectuated a merger with Houston's Southwest Bancshares, then the sixth largest bank holding company in Texas. As a

TABLE 2–8 Seven-Year (1978–1985) Growth of Top Texas Bank Holding Companies

Bank Holding Company	Assets (1985)	Percent Gain since 1978	Affiliates (1985)	Percent Gain since 1978
InterFirst	$22.1 billion	54.8	67	56.7
Republic of Texas	$23.2 billion	60.3	39	56.4
M Corp	$22.6 billion	81.9	65	87.7
Texas Commerce	$20.1 billion	60.2	70	47.1
First City	$16.9 billion	52.0	64	56.3

SOURCES: *1978* and *1985 Annual Report* of each bank holding company.

result, M Corp's assets and affiliates increased by 82 percent and 88 percent, respectively. Between 1978 and 1985, it went from the state's fifth leading bancorporation to the number three position.

Not all of the large banks have fared as well. In fact the economic recession has had a strong negative impact on some of these banks, especially those that had extensive investments in the energy business and in the real estate market. Particularly hard hit have been Dallas's InterFirst and Houston's First City and Texas Commerce. Crisis has precipitated yet another wave of mergers among large-scale banks.

In December 1986, InterFirst and Republic of Texas—the state's two largest banks—announced their intention to unite. Assuming no legal obstacle has been put in the path of the merger after this writing, the new combined bancorporation (called First Republic) will become the twelfth largest bank in the United States.

Perhaps even more interesting is the proposed takeover of Texas Commerce by Chemical Bank of New York. Recent federal legislation now permits interstate banking. The 1986 special session of the Texas legislature passed a law that allows out-of-state banks access to the Texas market. In December 1986, Chemical Bank of New York, the nation's fifth largest commercial bank, absorbed Texas Commerce in what *Fortune* termed the "biggest bank deal ever." [62] If no legal barrier stops this merger, a new chapter in the history of Texas banking is about to be written.

In short, banking in Texas has experienced a tremendous transformation over time. The state has gone from no banks to heavy concentration in the banking industry over the course of eight decades. In between, a period of robust financial diversity characterized the state. Now all major regional areas are basically served by a relatively few banks, most with headquarters distant from their areas. The number of principal banks grows ever smaller, while the distance between customers and banking decision making centers grows ever greater.

Savings and Loan Firms

Uncertainty in Texas's financial world is not solely confined to banks. Savings and loan associations have also experienced the effects of boom and bust. Savings and loan institutions are the major source of money for buying homes. When Texas was leading the nation in housing starts in the late 1970s, these firms were steep in profit.[63] The collapse of the housing market in some areas (e.g., Houston) took its toll on some of these associations. Overall, the savings and loan business is today in great flux.

The number of savings and loan associations serving Texas has increased from 228 in 1982 to 275 in 1985. Also the overall assets of these firms during this three-year period have increased by two and a half times (from $38.1 billion to $95.5 billion). However, concentration in the industry has decreased significantly. Whereas the top six associations accounted for 39 percent of all savings and loan assets in 1982, the first six in 1985 were responsible for only 26 percent of the total.[64] The leading half-dozen companies in the latter year were: Gibraltar Savings Association ($4.93 billion in assets), United Savings ($4.84 billion in assets), Bright Banc Savings ($4.74 billion in assets), University Savings ($3.96 billion in assets), First Texas Savings ($3.76 billion in assets), and Sunbelt Savings ($3.14 billion in assets).

Gibraltar Savings has been Texas's premier savings and loan firm for the last decade. Until 1984 it was part of the California-based Imperial Corporation of America, but is now owned by private investors. United Savings has been a subsidiary of Kaneb Services, an oil and natural gas company. These days the relationship between United Savings and Kaneb is less clear. Bright Banc Savings entered the top six firms as a result of its 1985 take over of Dallas Federal Savings. Bright Banc is headed by Harry R. Bright, chairman of the East Texas Motor Freight trucking company and the principal owner of the Dallas Cowboys. University Savings has slipped from its number-two position among lenders in 1982 to fourth place; it still is owned by Houston's large natural gas distributor, Entex. First Texas Savings was formerly the property of the large Beneficial Corporation. Beneficial, however, divested itself of First Texas in 1982 by selling it to private investors. Sunbelt Savings is new to the top echelons of savings and loan firms in Texas. It has replaced Farm and Home Savings, a Missouri-based firm whose assets have not shown much recent growth.

Reflective of the uncertain times in Texas's savings and loan industry is the fact that 20 percent of these firms are on the watch list of state officials who regulate these associations. Indeed, six firms collapsed in 1985. With assets of $1 billion the failure of Mainland Savings of Houston "was billed as the biggest S & L insolvency in history." [65]

Conversely, Lomas and Nettleton of Dallas continues its ranking as the number-one mortgage banker in the United States. Lomas and Nettleton was the most profitable corporation with headquarters in Texas for 1985.[66] It principally serves as a broker in arranging loans for buyers of homes, offices, and buildings. All told, through its 678,456 loans to customers throughout the country, Lomas and Nettleton has accumulated over $1 billion in assets.[67]

Insurance Companies

Nearly 2,200 firms are licensed to issue insurance in Texas. About 1,400 national companies have operations in the state. These include the top six national life insurance companies (Prudential, Metropolitan, Equitable, Aetna, New York Life, and John Hancock), which in combination account for over 40 percent of the $655 billion in assets comprising the U.S. life insurance industry.[68] Also doing business in Texas are the top four property and liability insurance companies—Aetna, CIGNA, Travelers, and Texas's American General—which collectively possess 56 percent of the $232 billion in casualty insurance assets.[69]

Some 750 insurance companies have their headquarters in Texas. The largest is American General. With $13 billion in assets (1985), American General is not only the state's leading insurance outfit, it is also tops in the South. Three other major insurance firms have emerged from Texas: American National Financial Corporation (1985 assets of $3.74 billion), Southwestern Life (1985 assets of $4.89 billion and formerly a wholly owned subsidiary of Tenneco), and Southland Financial (1985 assets of $1.07 billion). Dallas is one of the major insurance centers in America.

HIGH TECH

Energy, agriculture, and financial matters have formed the core of the Texas economy for most of this century. Indeed, it would not be wrong to argue that Texas's financial well-being has been predicated largely on the value of its petroleum products. The fragility of such an unidimensional economic base was fully unveiled by the recession that struck the state in the 1980s. Falling prices for petroleum have played havoc with the economic health of Texas.

The rallying cry for many forward-thinking Texans is economic diversification. Stirring arguments for broadening the state's economic base are heard frequently these days from business, political, academic, and media leaders. The most mentioned candidate for economic development is high technology. Electronics should increasingly shape the economy of the state, so some futurists contend.

Not to be overlooked is the fact that Texas already had an electronics industry in place well before the current emphasis on developing high tech began. Fort Worth's Tandy, Dallas's Texas Instruments and Electronic Data Systems (recently purchased by General Motors), and San Antonio's Datapoint are four examples of indigenous electronics firms with some tradition in the state. In addition, a Texas-based defense industry, which is deeply involved in the manufacturing and testing of advanced electronic technology, has been in full swing since World War II. General Dynamics, which is among the leading national defense contractors, has been building fighter planes (and providing employment for around 17,000 people) for some time now. Texas Instruments has been employed by the Pentagon to supply electronic equipment, especially for missile systems, for a long time. So too, LTV of Dallas has been a major defense contractor for over two decades. By 1982, high tech firms employed some 190,000 Texans, less than 3 percent of the total work force.[70]

To be sure, sounding the clarion for more high tech in Texas has brought additional factories and business to the state. IBM, Westinghouse, Tracor, Rockwell International, and Textron have all either opened new facilities or expanded old ones in Texas. Between 1978 and 1984 the number of electronics firms doing business in Texas increased from 1,638 to 7,541.[71] The chief catch was Microelectronics and Computer Technology Corporation (MCC).

MCC is actually a consortium of several companies organized around the goal of innovation in, and advancement of, electronic technology. Originally, it consisted of ten electronics firms, including Control Data Corporation, Honeywell, Motorola, Mostek (a division of United Technologies), NCR, National Semiconductor, RCA (now owned by General Electric), and Sperry. By 1986, membership in MCC had improved to twenty-one, although some charter firms had departed the consortium. Austin became the home of MCC after it outbid several other cities for that distinction.

MCC has become the symbol of Texas's pursuit of high technology. Lately, however, some doubts about the possibility of a high tech transformation of business in Texas have been raised. Economists now estimate that high tech will not over the long haul have a major impact on the state's economy. At best maybe 200,000 jobs in this industry will be available to the state's labor force.[72] Although nearly 8 percent of the work force in Austin is currently employed by electronics firms, the president of the local Chamber of Commerce still doesn't "think that high tech will be our savior." [73] The major force behind MCC, Bobby Inman, left the consortium in 1986, leading one observer to note: "The magic about MCC has faded and reality has set in, revealing the research facility as it has always been, a fragile, high-risk venture whose value will not be known until the nineties ... Inman's departure certifies the end of the Austin high-tech boom, a phenomenon that was always more illusion than reality anyway." [74]

CONCLUSION

The principal economic arenas in Texas have been threefold: petroleum, agriculture, and finance. Most assuredly, other important business activities are to be found in the state. Electronics has a foothold in the economy. Some heavy manufacturing (of steel, for instance) occurs. But, oil, agriculture, and capital still form the core of the economy.

Both core and periphery have, however, been experiencing some difficulties in the 1980s. Still, the strength of the Texas economy cannot be underestimated. If viewed as an independent nation, Texas's economic system would rank thirteenth among all countries. Although Texas is the home for only 6 percent of the U.S. population, 12 percent of America's total corporate income is made in the state.[75] Most of this bounty goes to a relatively few companies, many of which are not headquartered in the state. In the words of a member of the Texas legislature: "Less than one-half of one percent of all corporations operating in Texas control nearly half of all state corporate wealth. Of this tiny ultrarich elite, over 70 percent are non-Texas firms." [76]

In short, a few firms dominate the economy of Texas. Moreover, there are signs that these leaders act in an economically cohesive manner. The following chapter explores these economic links.

NOTES

1. Thomas R. Dye, *Who's Running America? The Reagan Years,* 3d ed. (Englewood Cliffs, N.J.: Prentice-Hall, 1983), ch. 2

2. Thomas R. Plaut, "Energy and the Texas Economy," *Texas Business Review* 57 (March-April 1983): 83.

3. *Texas Almanac and State Industrial Guide: 1986–1987* (Dallas: A. H. Belo Co., 1985), pp. 598–600.

4. Oil and Gas Division of the Railroad Commission of Texas, *Annual Report, 1985,* (Austin: Texas Railroad Commission, 1985), p. 1.

5. *Texas Almanac: 1986–1987,* p. 601 and p. 603.

6. Robert Engler, *The Brotherhood of Oil: Energy Policy and the Public Interest* (Chicago: University of Chicago Press, 1977), p. 191.

7. Mitch Green, "Independent Service Stations: Fighting for Survival (and Losing)," *Texas Observer,* December 2, 1977, p. 191.

8. Figures from Oil and Gas Division, *Annual Report, 1985,* p. 1.

9. *Texas Almanac: 1986–1987,* p. 601.

10. Oil and Gas Division, p. 1.

11. Ibid., p. 51.

12. Governor's Energy Advisory Council, *A Teacher's Handbook on Energy, 1977* (Austin: Office of the Governor, 1977), p. F–5.

13. W. L. Fisher, "Texas Energy: Trends and Outlook to Year 2000," in the *Texas Almanac and State Industrial Guide, 1982–1983* (Dallas: A.H. Belo Co., 1981), p. 371.

14. Ibid.

15. W. R. Kaiser, *Texas Lignite—Status and Outlook* (Austin: U. T. Austin, Bureau of Economic Geology, 1985).

16. W. L. Fisher, "Texas Energy."

17. Ibid.

18. W. R. Kaiser, *Texas Lignite.*

19. House Study Group, *Strip Mining in Texas* (Austin: House Study Group, # 28, June 1, 1978), pp. 9–10.

20. Ibid.

21. Richard Munson, "Big Oil's Solar Power Eclipse," *The Nation,* December 17, 1983, p. 627.

22. *Texas Almanac: 1986–1987,* p. 578.

23. Parviz Manoucheri Adib, "The Petrochemical Industry in Texas and Louisiana," *Texas Business Review* 57 (July–August 1983): 165–170.

24. *1978 Annual Report* of Southwest Bancshares, p. 12.

25. Betty Brink, "Saving Utilities from Themselves," *Texas Observer,* November 9, 1984, pp. 11–13.

26. John F. Ahearne, Chairman of the Nuclear Regulatory Commission, *Regulation and Construction of Nuclear Power Plants—South Texas Nuclear Project,* hearing before the Subcommittee on Oversight and Investigations of the Committee on Interstate and Foreign Commerce, House of Representatives, 96th Congress, 2nd session, 1981, p. 3.

27. These figures are based on the data sources listed in tables 2–1, 2–2, and 2–3. After U.S. Steel acquired Texas Oil and Gas (TXO) in 1985, it changed its name to USX. USX now derives most of its annual revenue from its oil operations, hence its inclusion as a major oil firm.

28. Some of the obstacles placed in the pathway of Standard Oil's move into Texas are recounted in Carl Solberg, *Oil Power: The Rise and Imminent Fall of an American Empire* (New York: Mentor, 1976), ch. 3.

29. These figures are found in the *Texas Almanac: 1986–1987,* p. 612.

30. Ibid.

31. Bureau of the Census, Department of Commerce, *1982 Census of Agriculture: Texas* (Washington, D.C.: U.S. Department of Commerce, 1984), p. viii and p. 1.

32. Ibid.

33. *Texas Observer,* September 26, 1986, pp. 16–17.

34. The 1950 average acreage figure comes from the Bureau of the Census, *1982 Census of Agriculture;* the 1984 figure comes from the *Texas Almanac: 1986–1987,* p. 612.

35. Jim Hightower, "The Administration Gets Wind of a Farm Crisis," *Texas Observer,* October 12, 1984, pp. 9–11.

36. Unless otherwise indicated the statistics on farm and ranch earnings come from the Bureau of the Census, *1982 Census of Agriculture,* p. 8 and p. 34.

37. Catherine Chadwick, "The Big Country," *Texas Monthly,* February 1985, pp. 103–05.

38. Congressional Budget Office, *Corporations in Farming* (Washington, D.C.: Government Printing Office, 1980).

39. Ibid.

40. *Texas Almanac: 1986–1987,* p. 619; and Bruce Cory, "Taxing Timberland in East Texas," *Texas Observer,* July 21, 1978, p. 8.

41. Ibid.

42. *1982 Annual Report* of the Texas Pacific Land Trust.

43. Reported in Mary Ellen Leary, "The New Winning of the West," *Nation* 225 (December 1977): 649.

44. *Moody's Industrials,* 1983.

45. Jim Hightower, *Eat Your Heart Out* (New York: Crown Publishers, 1975), p. 126.

46. Congressional Budget Office, *Corporations in Farming.*

47. Interview with Jim Hightower in the *Texas Observer,* March 26, 1983, p. 11.

48. Jim Hightower, "Who's Who in the Thanksgiving Business," *Texas Observer,* November 17, 1978, p. 3.

49. Interview with Jim Hightower, *Texas Observer.*

50. *Progressive Grocer's Marketing Guidebook* (New York: Progressive Grocer Co., 1986).

51. Ibid.

52. "Top 100 Gain Further Sales Dominance," *Nation's Restaurant News,* August 8, 1978.

53. Jim Hightower, "Who's Who," p. 7.

54. Geoffrey Rips, "Planting a Few Seeds," *Texas Observer,* April 8, 1983, p. 3.

55. Testimony of Robert J. Mullins of the Texas Farmers Union given to the Subcommittee on Oversight and Investigation of the House Committee on Interstate and Foreign Commerce, *The Impact and Effect of Unregulated Natural Gas Prices on Labor, Consumers and Agriculture* (Washington, D.C.: Government Printing Office, 1977), p. 55.

56. Statement of Coy Nichols in ibid., pp. 46–47.

57. Testimony of Robert J. Mullins.

58. Carl G. Anderson, "Agriculture in Texas," in the *Texas Almanac: 1986–1987,* p. 614.

59. Compare figures about Reeves County irrigation in 1980 in the *Texas Almanac: 1982–1983,* p. 327 with those in the *Texas Almanac: 1986–1987,* p. 344.

60. The story, with quotes, is told by Paul Sweeney in "Small Growers Just Holding On," *El Paso Times,* July 1, 1978, p. 1–B.

61. Greg Moses, "Farm Aid for the Betrayed," *Texas Observer,* July 31, 1986, pp. 8–9.

62. *Fortune,* January 19, 1987, p. 10.

63. Jim Hightower, "Up, Up and Away: Mortgage Lenders Demand Higher Interest Rates," *Texas Observer,* February 16, 1979, p. 5.

64. Comparison based on the figures presented in the *Fifty-Fourth Annual Report* (1982) and the *Fifty-Eighth Annual Report* (1986) of the Texas Savings and Loan Department.

65. Sam Weiner, "Aliens," *Texas Business,* October 1986, pp. 58–59.

66. Michele Kay, "The Texas 400," *Texas Business,* June 1986, p. 65.

67. *Moody's Bank and Financial Manual,* 1986, p. 3138.

68. Calculations based on figures presented in the annual reports of each insurance company and in Department of Commerce, Bureau of the Census, *Statistical Abstract of the United States: 1985* (Washington, D.C.: Government Printing Office, 1985), p. 509.

69. Ibid.

70. Jeff Franks, "High Tech Highly Touchy," *Texas Business,* April 1986, p. 57.

71. *Texas Almanac: 1986–1987,* p. 572.

72. Jeff Franks, "High Tech," p. 57.

73. Quoted in Peter Elkind, "Why Inman Left," *Texas Monthly,* November 1986, p. 133.

74. Ibid., p. 249.

75. Senfronia Thompson, "Taxing Corporate Profits: A Proposal," *Texas Observer,* December 10, 1982, p. 20.

76. Ibid.

3

Cohesion in the Texas Economy

One way to unite the fortunes of large, distinct corporations is through the social ties of the people who lead these companies. Marriage, sharing a similar background, or mingling together at the same schools, country clubs, civic organizations, or cultural functions are major social means of achieving cohesion—a class perspective—among corporate executives. There is some evidence showing that America's corporate wealthy do indeed occupy the same social space.[1] The leaders of Texas-based companies have parallel social background characteristics as well. Most are white, Anglo-Saxon, Protestant, middle-aged men—born, reared, and educated in the Lone Star State.[2] Many are found on the membership rolls of the state's most prestigious country clubs, such as Houston's River Oaks, Bayou, University, Country, Ramada, and Petroleum Club, of which it has been said "belonging . . . is not nearly as important as failure to belong."[3]

There are, however, two problems with placing a great deal of confidence in the notion that social ties create cohesion among economic leaders. First, a large number of the corporate wealthy do not share the same social experiences. Most corporate executives, for instance, are not members of the same country clubs. Intermarriage among corporate executives is not the norm. There are, in other words, far too many deviations from any modal social pattern among corporate leaders to suggest, at least with much conviction, that class unity is effectuated through social contacts or background. Second, it is logically possible for people who mix together socially to be keen competitors once back in their separate corporate boardrooms. Rivals in business, as in sports, can have extensive personal interaction both before and after tense contests.

A more convincing case for cohesion would need to show that strong economic ties exist among leading corporations. Are there economic bonds that pull together the business activities of the dominant corporations in Texas? This chapter explores three means by which Texas business relations might be linked: mergers, interlocking directorates, and shared ownership. ★

MERGERS

A merger occurs when one company purchases another. A flood of major mergers has recently engulfed America's corporate world. Throughout the ten-year span of the 1970s, mergers of manufacturing and mining companies entailed $61 billion in expenses.[4] In 1981 alone, merger activity tallied almost $83 billion.[5] In 1984, acquisitions rose to $125 billion.[6] In 1985, the figure was even higher, leading investment adviser Felix Rohatyn to comment: "In my 35 years of business I have never seen anything remotely approaching this year's [1985] tidal wave of take-overs, mergers and buyouts of every size and shape, including both very good and sound ones and extremely ill-conceived ones."[7] By 1986, fully 14,000 mergers had transpired during the decade.[9]

There are three distinct types of mergers: horizontal mergers, vertical mergers, and conglomerate mergers. *Horizontal* mergers refer to rival companies uniting. In effect, competition is usually reduced in the aftermath of a horizontal merger and the major segments of the Texas economy have been caught up in the swirl of recent horizontal merger activity. The 1980s have witnessed several consolidations of oil firms with extensive operations in the state. In 1981 Dupont, a major petrochemical firm, outbid several other companies to take over Conoco, then the country's seventh largest oil firm. The following year saw Occidental Petroleum take over Cities Service.

The year 1984, however, stands out in the annals of oil company mergers. Texaco began the year by capturing Getty Oil—much to the chagrin of Houston's Pennzoil, which was in the hunt for Getty. Indeed, Pennzoil subsequently accused Texaco in a Texas court of unlawfully infringing on its deal with Getty. The court agreed and ordered Texaco to pay Pennzoil some $10.3 billion in damages. Texaco appealed the verdict and, to stave off actual payment of the fine, declared bankruptcy. Things went a bit smoother for Chevron when it snatched Gulf Oil from the hands of other pursuers, in particular Atlantic Richfield. Chevron bought out Gulf for around $13.5 billion in the largest and most expensive acquisition ever recorded. Rounding out the major oil mergers of 1984, Royal Dutch Shell fully took over all the operations of Houston's Shell Oil and Mobil purchased Texas's leading independent, Superior Oil.

Although oil company mergers have quieted some since the 1984 frenzy, U.S. Steel (now USX), which earlier in the decade had acquired Marathon Oil, became more a petroleum firm than a steel company when in 1985 it purchased Texas Oil and Gas (TXO), the fifth largest natural gas producer in the state. In 1986, Houston Natural Gas merged with InterNorth of Omaha to form the ENRON company. Coastal States became a major interstate gas distributor through its acquisition of American Natural Resources, a gas pipeline company. Finally, Houston's United Energy Resources became a part of MidCon, a Connecticut-based energy firm.

Agriculture has also been enveloped in the horizontal merger movement. Many agribusiness firms have recently consolidated. Among food processors, in 1985 R. J. Reynolds, the tobacco giant, absorbed Nabisco, which had just the year before acquired Standard Brands. Philip Morris, R. J. Reynolds's chief rival in the tobacco industry, followed a similar path of diversification and expanded its agribusiness holdings to include Heublein, Miller Brewery, Seven-Up, Del Monte, and General

Courtesy of Ben Sargent, *The Austin American-Statesman.* Reprinted by permission.

Foods. Philip Morris subsequently unloaded the international division of Seven-Up to PepsiCo. PepsiCo's acquisition is an attempt to keep abreast of the expansion of Coca-Cola, which now owns Texas's Dr. Pepper. Anheuser Busch (brewers of Budweiser beer) acquired Dallas's Campbell-Taggart, which is among the country's leading bakers (makers of Rainbo Bread and Meads Fine Bread).

Banking circles in Texas will become closer if the 1987–proposed merger of the state's two largest bank holding companies (InterFirst and Republic) is approved. Chemical of New York's takeover of Houston's Texas Commerce relocates control over a large segment of banking operations in the state into the hands of decision makers centered in New York City. With financial difficulties still besetting a few of the state's other major bank holding companies (most particularly, Houston's First City and Allied Bancshares), the prospects for further large-scale banking mergers seem quite good.

Vertical mergers occur when a company takes over a business that is essential to the production or distribution activities of the buyer. Texas Utilities, the state's giant electric company, for instance, over the last decade has been buying leases to coal and lignite fields. Ownership of these leases means that Texas Utilities has within its possession a major resource from which to generate and distribute electricity.

Conglomerates are formed when one company merges with another that is neither in direct competition with, nor functional to, the purchaser. In the mid–1970s, for example, Mobil acquired the giant retail outlet, Montgomery Ward. The Burlington Northern transport company recently acquired the El Paso Natural Gas Company. Dallas's LTV, in addition to buying three steel firms (Republic Steel, Jones and Laughlin, and Youngstown Sheet and Tube), has also purchased an aerospace concern (Vought), a meat processing firm (Wilson Meats), and a shipbuilding outfit (Lykes).

One of the most arresting examples of the many faces of mergers can be seen in the empire-building of the Tenneco company of Houston. This corporate giant—the world's thirty-sixth largest industrial company—began modestly in the mid-1940s by transporting natural gas through its pipelines. In 1966, Tennessee Gas Transmission Company changed its name to Tenneco. Since then, Tenneco has come to stand for much more than just the conveyance of natural gas. Through its various divisions, additions made mostly through mergers, Tenneco now means:

1. Producing, transporting, and marketing crude oil.
2. Owning farmland (Tenneco West), manufacturing farm implements (J. I. Case and, since 1985, International Harvester), processing foods, especially fruits and vegetables (Sun Giant), and distributing agricultural products through minimarkets in its gas stations.
3. Making cartons and packages to contain various items (Packaging Corporation of America).
4. Refining petrochemicals.
5. Building ships for other corporations (for instance, supertankers for Shell) and the federal government (for example, the Navy attack submarines Carl Vinson and Theodore Roosevelt) through its subsidiary, Newport News Shipbuilding.
6. Operating once-rival insurance companies (Philadelphia Life and Southwestern Life).
7. Developing land, including office-building sites and residential communities in and around Houston.
8. Felling trees from its timberlands for the manufacture of a variety of wood products.
9. Manufacturing parts for automobiles (Walker mufflers and Monroe shock absorbers).

Acquisitions have thus made Tenneco a conglomerate. But some of the company's foremost mergers have been horizontal. Two previously rival farm implement companies (J. I. Case and International Harvester) have been absorbed into Tenneco, for instance. Furthermore, vertical integration, especially in its farming and timber operations, has been accomplished through Tenneco's acquisitions. James L. Ketelsen, the chief executive officer of Tenneco, has said recently in reference to the conglomerate growth of his company: "We have only just begun." [9] Interestingly, the fall in petroleum prices appears to be taking its toll on Tenneco, for in 1987 it sold off its insurance holdings for $1.4 billion in order to raise some needed cash.

Mergers have the effect of shrinking the number of producers and distributors in the economy. When previously autonomous, perhaps rival, companies come within the orbit of a giant firm, economic competition—a major component of a free-enterprise, capitalistic economy—is lessened. Reduced competition between businesses means a loss of consumer control over important economic practices, such as the setting of prices for items. Even when competition is not at risk, mergers, through depleting the ranks of once-autonomous producers and distributors, have the effect of increasing concentration in the economy. Giant corporations defend mergers, however, in the name of efficiency and practicality.

INTERLOCKING DIRECTORATES

Interlocking directorates occur when a member of the board of directors of one company also sits on the board of another firm. Board membership is usually the result of several factors, including being a senior manager of a company, owning large shares of stock in the company, and having expertise that a company finds vital to its well-being. Most board members are drawn directly from within the ranks of the business community.[10] Since the board is ordinarily the final point of decision making in a company, interlocks open the possibility of linking together perspectives from distinct corporations and forging common corporate policy. As reported by a U.S. Senate committee:

> Interlocking directorates provide a special opportunity for intercompany communication and consensus. The linkages at the boardroom table are personal connections by which key information can be passed, arrangements can be made and policies formed. Board meetings are corporate proceedings where management policies are specifically reviewed and approved or corrected. Thus, to the extent that a board contains members who are also directors of actual or potential competitors, suppliers, customers or financial organizations, there is a potential for anti-competitive abuse.[11]

Federal law (the Clayton Act of 1914) forbids interlocks between directly rival firms. A member of the board of directors of Exxon is legally prohibited from serving on Shell's board. It is not illegal, however, for directors of competitive companies to sit on a third, nonrival board. A representative from Exxon and one from Shell could sit on a board, say, of a bank.

How widespread are board interlocks in the United States economy? According to one study, 90 percent of the boards of the country's 250 largest corporations are interlocked.[12] As summarized by sociologist William G. Roy, "virtually all studies of contemporary American interlocking directorates have found a single, unified network."[13] The center of this interwoven tapestry of business lies primarily in the banking world. One study found that in 1975 almost half of the 200 largest industrial corporations had an official from a major bank sitting on their boards.[14] A fairly recent report released by the U.S. Senate noted that Citibank of New York—the country's largest financial institution—had interlocks with 49 corporations, including rival oil companies, steel producers, retail stores, insurance companies, and communications firms, as well as other industrial giants. Through the interlocks with these companies, Citibank had 871 board ties, directly or indirectly, with other corporations.[15]

Interlocks don't necessarily result in bank control over connected firms. However, through a wide network of interlocks, banks are in a position to know a great deal about the operations of many firms. That knowledge can be communicated through these interlocks. Although knowledge might not directly lead to power, it perhaps does allow central banks the ability to at least constrain, if not overtly influence, decision making over a broad band of diverse firms.

Interlocking directorates abound in Texas. Again the banks are at the core of the interlock grid. Not only do they bring together many of the state's leading businesses, especially ones in the energy field, there is also evidence of board ties that bind the largest Texas banks.

Key to the state bank network is the board membership of Dallas's Lomas and Nettleton, the country's most prosperous mortgage banker. Lomas and Nettleton's board contains members also on the boards of InterFirst (Frank Crossen), Texas Commerce (Jon Newton), First City (Nat Rogers), and M Corp (Jess Hay, Dolph Briscoe, Gene Bishop, and Bill O. Mead). Republic is the only bank out of the top five bank holding companies in the state not represented on Lomas and Nettleton's board.[16] However, Lomas and Nettleton is interlocked with ENSERCH (Lone Star Gas), which, in turn, has a board tie with Republic.

Spanning from the bank boardrooms are interlocks with other significant financial institutions in Texas. First City, for instance, shares directors with American General—Texas's top insurance company—and Entex, the owner of University Savings—second largest savings and loan firm serving the state. Texas Commerce has a board member with each of the state's two foremost insurance firms, American General and Southwestern Life (formally a Tenneco subsidiary). M Corp and Republic each shares a director with Southland Financial, another important Texas-based insurance company. Republic also has common board membership with Bright Banc Savings, a leading home mortgage outfit.

The financial interlock network thus appears intact in Texas. No one major financial institution is very far away from information about the policy matters being considered by any of its counterparts. Board interlocks thus suggest an efficient and relatively direct communications transmission system in the financial world of Texas.

The bank boards are also a focal point for nonfinancial corporations with extensive holdings in Texas. M Corp's board is comprised of members who are associated with two major oil companies (Exxon and Occidental), two important independent oil producers (Mitchell Energy and Clayton Williams), and three of the state's principal suppliers of electricity (Houston Industries, Central and South West, and Southwestern Public Service). Texas Commerce shares directors with several major energy firms, including MidCon (formerly United Energy Resources), USX (formerly U.S. Steel), ENRON (formerly Houston Natural Gas), Burlington Northern (formerly the El Paso Company), Texas Eastern, Tenneco, Panhandle Eastern, Exxon, and Houston Industries. Republic Bank's board links ENSERCH, Tenneco, Atlantic Richfield, and Southwestern Public Service. InterFirst shares directorships with two major electric utilities (Texas Utilities and Gulf States) and ENSERCH. Finally, First City's board couples with Texas Eastern, Panhandle Eastern, Halliburton (Brown and Root), Gulf States Utilities, and ENRON.

The banks sit at the center of a widespread interlock network system. The most important corporations in Texas are relatively near to each other through interlocks that primarily flow from the boards of the leading banks in the state. Cohesion is further advanced by the fact that banks themselves are also within close proximity to each other through interlocking directorates.

SHARED OWNERSHIP

Shared ownership exists when companies have in common the same investors. If the shared investment is substantial, the common owner might be able to bring together the economic outlooks of otherwise separate corporations. Hence stock ownership patterns may have the effect of creating cohesion among dominant economic institutions.

Systematic study of this possibility has been difficult, however. Reliable and valid information about the principal owners of the major companies of America has not been readily forthcoming. When a U.S. Senate committee in the early 1970s asked the country's leading firms to reveal their top thirty investors, only one-third fully complied.[17] Others forwarded either incomplete or irrelevant data, or they simply refused to cooperate with the committee. Exxon, for example, reported a partial list of shareholders. It denied the committee additional names on the grounds that such information would be a violation of the investors' privacy and, moreover, that "the real owners are not disclosed to the company." [18]

More recent efforts to identify the owners of large companies have met with greater success.[19] Unraveling the evidence now available uncovers several interesting aspects about ownership of major U.S. corporations. Four points stand out:

1. *Major stockholders are relatively few in number.* Only about 10 percent of the U.S. population owns any stock in the country's public corporations. However, most of these investors possess a very small number of shares. To be influential in company matters a shareholder must have at least 1 percent of the total stock outstanding. Relatively few individuals or institutions hold this portion of shares in any one company.

On the average, for instance, only six investors held at least 1 percent of the stock in Texas's (and the country's) nine leading oil companies in the early 1980s.[20] Furthermore, concentration of stock in the hands of only a few major investors is the norm. For example, the twenty top stockholders of Texas's most important oil firms had an average possession of nearly one-quarter of the total shares of these corporations.[21]

2. *Most of the major stockholders are institutional investors.* Research into investors consistently corroborates that the preponderance of top owners—those with more than 1 percent of the stock—of U.S. companies are institutions. One study of the leading 166 American corporations, for instance, finds that 89 percent of the principal investors in these firms are institutionally based.[22] The ranks of top shareholders are replete with banks, insurance companies, investment houses, diversified financial houses, government agencies (usually through administering public employee pension funds), corporations, foundations, institutional endowments, and universities. It is rare to find individuals or families among the major stockholders; only 11 percent of the top investors in the leading U.S. firms are persons or families.[23]

To be sure, most corporations can trace their origins to the skills and actions of a single individual or to personal partnerships. Moreover, some of these entrepreneurs, along with their immediate relatives and direct descendants, still have large shares in their creations. For instance, the Rockefeller family has major holdings in the offshoots of the Standard Oil Company founded by John D. Rockefeller, Sr. The original Standard Oil was broken up by the U.S. Supreme Court in 1911 because it had a virtual monopoly over the country's oil business. Standard was restructured into separate companies: Standard of New Jersey (now Exxon), Standard of New York (now Mobil), Standard of California (Chevron), and Standard of Indiana (Amoco). Whereas these companies were to be run by autonomous management, the court permitted Rockefeller and his family to retain stock in each newly created firm. Currently, the Rockefeller family interests are among the top twenty investors of Exxon, Mobil, Chevron, and Amoco. The Pew family, creators of Sun Oil, has 32 percent of the stock of the company. The Mellons, founders of Gulf Oil, had (before Chevron took over Gulf in 1984) 18 percent of the corporation's shares. The family of the late George Brown, who had a hand in the establishment of several energy equipment and natural gas pipeline companies in Texas, is among the leading investors in Halliburton and Texas Eastern.

Most of the major stockholders, however, are institutions. On the average, for instance, eighteen of the twenty top stockholders of Texas's foremost oil companies are entities, not people. The Rockefeller family is the only important noninstitutional investor in Exxon, for example.

3. *The principal institutional stockholders in major companies are financial enterprises, especially banks.* Some 70 percent of the leading investors in America's foremost companies are financial institutions, namely, banks, investment companies, and insurance firms. Half of the key financial shareholders are commercial banks. Standing above this crowd of top investors is New York's J. P. Morgan bank, which possessed in the early 1980s 1 percent or more of the shares in sixty-seven (nearly a majority) of America's dominant corporations.[24] As concluded by a U.S. Senate study, J. P. Morgan is "far and away the most dominant investor. At the end of 1979, Morgan held $18.5 billion worth of equities in its portfolio." [25]

The presence of J. P. Morgan is evident in the ownership of corporations having a major impact on the Texas economy. Morgan possessed in 1980 at least some stock in fifteen of the twenty-two top corporations active in the energy sector of the state's economy.[26] The bank held more than 1 percent of the shares in eight of these firms—Exxon, Mobil, Chevron, Tenneco, El Paso (before it was merged into Burlington Northern), Panhandle Eastern, Transco, and Halliburton. Morgan's reach penetrates the Texas financial world as well. In the early 1980s the New York bank controlled 1.92 percent of the stock of the First International Bank (later called InterFirst), 2.50 percent of Mercantile (now M Corp), and 1.03 percent of First City.

4. *Separate corporations have common institutional owners.* When several companies have a major investor in common, the opportunity for economic cohesion is present.

Most certainly, a 1 percent share in numerous companies does not by itself afford an investor control over the policies of those corporations. However, it may compel ostensibly distinct companies at least to pay some attention to the interests of the common principal owner.

As noted above, financial institutions—especially banks—are top investors in numerous dominant firms. Research also indicates that within this financial community there is cohesion among a few of the most important banks. In particular, the four principal New York banks—Citibank, Chase Manhattan, J. P. Morgan, and Manufacturers Hanover—are tied together through several knots, including mutual respect, convergent lending policies, and shared ownership.[27] Each of these banks has substantial investments, for instance, in each other.[28] Indeed, there is so much unity among these four that it has been argued that they should be treated as a joint association, and not as four distinct banks.[29]

All told, the four leading New York banks possess, on the average, 2.8 percent of the stock of America's dominant firms. Their combined holdings are inclusive of 91 percent of these companies.[30] As such, these banks may be in a position to exercise some influence over decisions made by a large number of diverse corporations.

The combined holdings of this banking quartet extend to companies important to Texas. With the exception of Shell (now fully in the possession of Royal Dutch Shell) and Gulf (now a part of Chevron), these banks held significant shares in companies that dominated petroleum activities in the state during the early 1980s.[31] Specifically, they were top investors in Atlantic Richfield (6.33 percent share), Exxon (5.77 percent share), Phillips (5.16 percent share), Mobil (4.62 percent share), Chevron (3.71 percent share), Amoco (3.55 percent share), and Texaco (1.89 percent share). They also controlled substantial stock in important electric companies, especially Texas Utilities (2.51 percent) and Houston Industries (3.05 percent).[32] Furthermore, they were key investors in four of the principal natural gas pipeline companies: Transco (1.95 percent), Tenneco (1.99 percent), El Paso (Burlington Northern) (2.09 percent), and Panhandle Eastern (3.2 percent).[33] Finally, with a collective share of 8.17 percent, they had virtually a controlling position at Halliburton.

Hence many rival or functionally interdependent firms shared a core of common owners. It is thus possible that a modicum of cohesion might exist within the community of dominant energy firms in Texas.

The four New York–based banks also had important investments in some of Texas's leading banks. In particular, in 1980 they had a 3.66 percent share of First International (InterFirst), 3.54 percent of Mercantile (M Corp), and 1.03 percent of First City.[34] Therefore, some link between the center of the national economy—the New York banks—and the focal point of the Texas economy—the leading state banks—is forged through ownership patterns.

Moreover, within the financial community in Texas, there are signs of common ownership. Foremost is the fact that in the early 1980s First International (InterFirst)—the largest bank holding company in the state—held stock in each of its leading "rivals." First International (InterFirst) had .25 percent of Texas Commerce, 1.24 percent of Republic, 1.77 percent of Mercantile (M Corp), and a rather large 3.91 percent share of First City.[35] In other words, First International/InterFirst, a bank that has been well within the ownership orbit of the four principal

New York banks, has also been a key investor in most of Texas's other leading bank holding corporations. The potential for cohesion among the leading bank holding companies is facilitated through this ownership pattern.

In short, this chapter suggests that cohesion characterizes the economy of Texas. The dominant firms outlined in the previous chapter do not function in total isolation. Mergers have forced the collapse of some competition. Interlocking directorates, which emanate mostly from the board rooms of the state's major banks, cut across a wide spectrum of companies doing extensive business in the state. Ownership information points to a core of investors in the state's leading companies, a core that is structured around the key banks of New York. These banks have investment links to principal banks in Texas. The Texas premier financial institution, in turn, has an important financial stake in the workings of the state's other leading banks.

This web of connections does not necessarily mean that the core institutions control the decision making of other companies in the network. There is no doubt that most day-to-day corporate policy making is made by each company's management team. Nonetheless, these linkages do provide a comprehensive communications system through which information and messages can be readily and rapidly transmitted to most of the state's leading businesses. Furthermore, the institutions that form the nuclei of the communications network are also well-placed to constrain, if not directly influence, the decision making procedures and outcomes of firms dominant in Texas's economy.[36]

PRELUDE TO POLITICS

This chapter, along with the previous one, have outlined the composition of Texas's economic elite. The principal sectors of the state's economic system—primarily energy, agriculture, and finance—are dominated by a relatively few giant corporations. Like all businesses in a free enterprise economy, the principal goal of the corporation is, in the words of Dallas's Dresser company, "to provide a maximum return on invested capital over the long term and steady profit growth that results in growing stock market values per share of company stock."[37]

Because of the extensiveness of the operations of the large-scale corporation, however, it follows methods of obtaining a maximum rate of return that are somewhat different from those utilized by smaller businesses. A small enterprise is ordinarily subject to the marketplace (e.g., the vicissitudes of supply, demand, and competition) to determine its profitability. The modern large-scale company, however, cannot afford such uncertainty. It prefers predictability and planning to the vagaries of market forces. The giant company seeks not to be buffeted by its environment but to gain mastery over it—stability and harmony are the watchwords of the big firm.[38] Unforeseen events, such as a precipitous plummet in prices, a surprise revolution, a prolonged workers' strike, or an effective consumer boycott, disrupt corporate planning, and, ipso facto, profit making. Corporations utilize several means to minimize the unexpected and to insure a predictable future.

A company's first preference is to achieve a stable environment through its own endeavors. Several strategies may be employed by a company in its autonomous quest for a secure and profitable existence. For instance, it may negotiate long-term agreements with suppliers of raw materials and with labor organizations in order to guarantee steady prices and a predictable work force, respectively. A constant stream of customers may be courted through the use of sophisticated advertising techniques. Adventurous and risky production and distribution practices may be pursued as an extreme measure in order to corner a market.

When, however, a company cannot achieve a stable, profitable future solely on its own, it may then unify with other firms—even rivals—to obtain its goals. At times, control over the environment is more readily secured if companies work together and not against each other. In other words, self-interest sometimes dictates the promotion of the mutual interest of business. In this situation, institutions that can facilitate cohesion among diverse firms are quite useful. As we have seen, leading commercial banks fill this role admirably.

Cohesion, however, is difficult to sustain over the long haul. Any one firm is frequently tempted to bolt from the group in order to maximize its economic standing. Moreover, forces beyond the control of even the most tightly knit economic elite often create dramatic disequilibrium in the economy. For instance, oversupply of some items, undersupply of others, problems in productivity, and inflationary spirals—among other factors—have in recent years precipitated deep economic instability in the business world of Texas. It was almost impossible for even the most adept and adroit members of the state's economic elite to harness, yet alone counter, the unsettling impact of these forces.

The usual consequence of such dislocation is a major shakedown of the economic system. Under pressure some companies simply collapse. Others restructure. Mergers are common. Yet, barring a total renovation of the economic system, the survivors usually emerge from the chaos with their market position strengthened. Furthermore, such instability ordinarily reenforces the perceived advantages of unity among business leaders in order to gain control over environmental forces of disequilibrium. This impulse toward cohesion is also evident when outsiders (for example, workers, environmentalists, consumers, and small business people) pose a real threat to the hegemony of a corporation.

However, it frequently is the case that a business, either on its own or as a member of an elite group, cannot fully combat instability. In such times, business has sought governmental assistance to gain mastery over its environment. Government has a host of resources that can be instrumental for corporate dominance and growth. Through overt actions, such as legislation, administrative rule making, and court decisions, government can improve the market conditions and profitability of business. Inaction can be equally important when a corporation requires government neutrality in the pursuit of its goals. Since government has a great deal of legitimacy in the eyes of most Americans, its decisions are usually met without much hostility. Governmental acquiescence can thus be quite useful to business.

Conversely, government opposition could harm business. An antagonistic group of public officials could combine its legitimate status with its control over coercive force to stalemate, or even decimate, corporation hegemony. Hence it is at times within the rational self-interest of business to cultivate a positive, benevolent relationship with government—federal, state, or local.

True enough, the economic standing of the corporate structure *by itself* is often sufficient enough to insure for business the unfettered support of government. Political authorities are reluctant to work against the interest of a business that can fire thousands of employees (say an auto manufacturer), or cut back production of valuable items (such as oil and natural gas), or simply leave the country and relocate in areas where the political climate is more favorable. Often just the threat of such a drastic action guarantees quiescence on the part of government.

As such, the foundation of any corporate-government relationship usually is embedded with business in the privileged position.[39] Yet this special status does not relieve business of the necessity of being directly involved in the everyday activities of government. Quite the contrary. Political privilege, once obtained, is something that must be maintained and expanded. To do so, it is necessary for the business community to develop and utilize lines of communication with the political system. The next part of this book explores such connections as they exist in Texas.

NOTES

1. See G. William Domhoff, *The Higher Circles* (New York: Vintage, 1970), ch. 1; and Thomas R. Dye, *Who's Running America? The Reagan Years* (Englewood Cliffs, N.J.: Prentice-Hall, 1983), ch. 7.

2. This description is based on social background information contained in *Who's Who in America* (1977). About 45 percent of the members of the boards of directors of the top fifty corporations with headquarters in Texas were listed in *Who's Who.*

3. James Conway, "Oil: The Source," *Atlantic* 235 (March 1975):65.

4. Bureau of the Census, Department of Commerce, *Statistical Abstract of the United States: 1982–1983* (Washington, D.C.: Government Printing Office, 1983), p. 531.

5. *New York Times,* May 31, 1982.

6. *Time,* December 25, 1985, p. 31.

7. Quoted in ibid.

8. Ibid., p. 30.

9. Quoted in *Texas Business,* July 1986, p. 29.

10. See Michael Ussem, *The Inner Circle* (New York: Oxford University Press, 1984), p. 38.

11. Committee on Governmental Affairs, United States Senate, *Structure of Corporate Concentration: Institutional Shareholders and Interlocking Directorates Among Major U.S. Corporations* (Washington, D.C.: Government Printing Office, 1980), vol. 1, pp. 5–6.

12. Harold Salzman and G. William Domhoff, "The Corporate Community and Government: Do They Interlock?" in *Power Structure Research,* ed. G. William Domhoff (Beverly Hills: Sage Publications, 1980), p. 233.

13. William G. Roy, "The Unfolding of the Interlocking Directorate Structure of the United States," *American Sociological Review* 48 (1983): 257.

14. Edward S. Herman, *Corporate Control, Corporate Power* (Cambridge: Cambridge University Press, 1981), p. 129.

15. Committee on Governmental Affairs, *Structure of Corporate Concentration,* p. 12.

16. Since at this writing the merger proposals between InterFirst and Republic and between Chemical Bank of New York and Texas Commerce have not been completely finalized, I will treat the Texas banks as separate companies.

17. Subcommittees on Intergovernmental Relations and Budgeting, Management, and Expenditures, *Disclosure of Corporate Ownership,* U.S. Senate, 93rd Congress, 1st Session (Washington, D.C.: Government Printing Office, 1973), pp. 29–33.

18. Ibid., p. 243.

19. In 1979, Congress enacted a law compelling institutional investors with more than $100 million investment portfolios to register their holdings with the Securities and Exchange Commission; failure to comply could bring a substantial penalty. Consequently, information about stock holdings is now more complete. The following two sources have been used in my analysis of ownership patterns: Committee on Governmental Affairs, *Structure of Corporate Concentration;* and a series of reports issued by Corporate Data Exchange, i.e., *CDE Stock Ownership Directory: Energy* (New York: Corporate Data Exchange, 1980), *CDE Stock Ownership Directory: Banking and Finance* (New York: Corporate Data Exchange, 1980), *CDE Stock Ownership Directory: Fortune 500* (New York: Corporate Data Exchange, 1980), and *CDE Stock Ownership Directory: Agriculture* (New York: Corporate Data Exchange, 1978).

20. In 1981, the nine companies were Exxon, Amoco, Chevron, Mobil, Gulf, Phillips, Atlantic Richfield, Shell, and Texaco. Combined, these firms accounted for half the natural gas and oil produced and refined in Texas in 1981. Since that time Gulf has been absorbed into Chevron, Royal Dutch Shell is the sole owner of Shell, and U.S. Steel (USX) has entered the top ranks of Texas oil companies. These changes would not appreciably affect the average number of top investors in the major Texas oil companies.

21. In 1981, Royal Dutch Shell controlled 70 percent of the stock in Shell. I have omitted these findings because they would have distorted the pattern of average shares owned by the top twenty investors. With Shell included in the analysis the average jumps to 31 percent.

22. James W. Lamare, *What Rules America?* (St. Paul, Minn.: West Publishing Co., 1988), ch. 3.

23. Ibid.

24. Figures are from ibid.

25. Committee on Governmental Affairs, p. 12.

26. The dominant twenty-two energy firms in 1980 that could be investigated consisted of nine petroleum companies (Exxon, Mobil, Texaco, Amoco, Chevron, Gulf, Phillips, Shell, and Atlantic Richfield), three electric utilities (Texas Utilities, Houston Industries, and Central and South West), nine natural gas pipeline companies (Tenneco, Texas Eastern, El Paso Company [now Burlington Northern], Transco, Panhandle Eastern, ENSERCH, Entex, Houston Natural Gas [now ENRON], and United Energy Resources [now MidCon]), and one construction firm (Halliburton).

27. The argument is developed in Beth Mintz and Michael Schwartz, *The Power Structure of American Business* (Chicago: University of Chicago Press, 1985).

28. James W. Lamare, *What Rules America?* ch. 3.

29. Beth Mintz and Michael Schwartz, *The Power Structure of American Business.*

30. J. W. Lamare, *What Rules America?*

31. They held no stock in Shell and only .74 percent in Gulf.

32. They also possessed 1.09 percent of Central and South West.

33. They held 1.09 percent of Houston Natural Gas (ENRON), .62 percent of United Energy Resources (MidCon), .35 percent of Texas Eastern, .30 of ENSERCH, and no stock in Entex.

34. They also held .44 percent of the stock of Texas Commerce and .37 percent of Republic.

35. Texas Commerce also had a .21 percent share of First International (InterFirst), .27 percent of Mercantile (M Corp.), and .54 percent of Republic. First City owned .31 percent of First International (InterFirst) and .67 percent of Republic.

36. For a fuller discussion of the constraining influence by external institutions on the management of a company, see Edward S. Herman, *Corporate Control, Corporate Power.*

37. Dresser, *Corporate Business and Organization Philosophy* (Dallas: Dresser Industries, 1977), p. 3.

38. On these points see John Kenneth Galbraith, *The New Industrial State* (Boston: Houghton Mifflin, 1956); and Mark V. Nadel, *Corporations and Public Accountability* (Lexington, Mass.: D. C. Heath, 1976), ch. 1.

39. The concept of "privileged position" of business in the eyes of government is discussed in Charles E. Lindblom, *Politics and Markets* (New York: Basic Books, 1977), ch. 13.

PART II

Access to Political Decision Makers in Texas: Elections and Lobbying

The interests of Texas's economic elite are converted into public policy through first gaining access to political officials who make decisions in the name of the state. Political access occurs when persons or groups are able to catch the attention of political decision makers. Obtaining political access is the key step in becoming politically powerful, for without access, political power is nearly impossible.

The quest for political access is facilitated if government officials are sympathetic to one's preferences, desires, interests, and concerns. There are two principal means of achieving such a state of affairs. One is to play a predominant role in the selection of political officials. The other is to effectively pressure decision makers to act according to one's views. Chapters 4 and 5 discuss the election of officeholders in Texas. Chapter 6 investigates the techniques used to lobby officials of the state government. The importance of the economic elite in elections and lobbying is a central theme of this entire section.

4

Elections and Political Parties in Texas

In democratic societies, elections are the major means by which the public selects government officeholders. Ideally, democratic elections should counteract the ability of a few persons or organizations to dominate the lives of the many through the workings of the political system. Approaching this ideal requires elections that are open to most of the public and that present meaningful alternatives to the voters. Open and competitive elections should produce political leaders who are responsible and accountable to, as well as representative of, a wide public.

This chapter and the next assess how well Texas elections conform to the democratic ideal. Here the mechanics of the state's electoral system and the nature of its party system will be addressed. Chapter 5 probes the penetration of economic elites into electoral politics in Texas. ★

MECHANICS OF TEXAS ELECTIONS

Formally, elections in Texas provide the public the opportunity to participate with little inconvenience in the selection of a large number of officials. This feature of the state's electoral system, however, has not prevented turnout of eligible voters from being relatively low in Texas's elections. Consider the following points:

Officials Elected in Texas

A large number of state officials are selected through public elections in Texas. Every two years, the 150 positions in the state House of Representatives and, at staggered four-year intervals, the 31 Texas Senate seats are filled by election. Each legislator represents a distinct geographic district, whose lines are drawn every ten years (after the completion of the U.S. census) by the state legislature. In the past, legislative districts contained an uneven number of people, and, at times, multiple representatives. Today, after many years of legal controversy, districts are roughly equal in population size and each district is represented by only one legislator.

Hence there are 150 districts for the House (one per every representative); each has around 95,000 people in it. Also, there are 31 distinct senatorial districts, with some 458,000 Texans in each.

Texas also elects numerous executive and administrative officials. The governor is chosen every four years. In addition, the state ballot contains, at various times, candidates for the jobs of lieutenant-governor, attorney-general, comptroller of public accounts, treasurer, and the commissioners of agriculture and of the General Land Office, as well as candidates for the fifteen slots on the State Board of Education and the three positions available on the Railroad Commission.

The vast majority of state judges are also chosen by Texas's voters. Election of members of the judiciary extends from the lower courts of Texas (e.g., Justice of the Peace, and county and district courts) to the higher ones (e.g., Supreme Court and the Court of Criminal Appeals). In total, around 2,500 judicial posts are filled by election.

The statewide ballot also frequently contains amendments to the Texas Constitution and other propositions, such as bond issues. Add to this long list the electoral contests for city and county posts and it is easy to conclude that there are plenty of people and things to vote for in Texas.

Types of Elections

There are three types of elections—primary, general, and special elections—in which Texans may cast their ballots.

Primaries are utilized by political parties to determine who will be the party's candidate in the general election. If a political party in Texas collects 20 percent of the total vote in the last election for governor, it must hold a primary to select its candidates. Parties receiving fewer votes may choose their candidates either through a primary election or at a convention. In effect, only the Republicans and the Democrats are legally required to conduct primaries in Texas these days.

Primaries take place on the first Saturday in May of even-numbered years. Each party administers its own primary in Texas—a practice prevalent in only two other states. Each also selects its own sites where people may cast their ballots. On the day of the primary, Texans must go to the polling place of the party of their choice. It is not legal to vote in the primary of both parties, although incidents of double voting have been recorded in the state. It is quite likely for Republicans to vote only in the Democratic primary—usually for conservative candidates—and then to return to the GOP fold in the general election. Texas is one of only four states that allows separate party primaries. Primaries in most states are unified; that is, the parties conduct the primary jointly. Party primaries in Texas are fully funded by the state. The 1982 primaries cost the government $6.2 million.[1]

Unless a candidate receives a majority of the votes for the office he or she seeks in the primary, a runoff primary must be held. Runoffs pit the two candidates with the most votes in the first primary against each other. Runoffs are quite common in Texas. They occur within a month of the first primary. In states where one party tends to dominate electoral politics, as has been the case throughout much of the last hundred years with the electoral success of the Democratic party in Texas, the primaries are *the* important elections.

General elections occur on the Tuesday after the first Monday in November in even-numbered years. It is the time when voters select their preference from each of the parties that have contested the office. General elections for statewide races do not coincide with presidential elections. Rather, they are scheduled in even-numbered years that fall between the presidential races. State and local officials are in charge of the administration of general elections.

The secretary of state oversees elections. Among other things, he or she determines whether a person's name may appear on the ballot for the general election. County officials carry out the mechanical aspects of elections. The commissioners court of each county decides on the device to be used to cast a ballot (voting machine or paper ballot), on who will be election judges, and on how to count the votes (by hand or by computer). The county also underwrites the expense of administering the general election in its area of jurisdiction.

Special elections are called to fill unexpected vacancies, to decide the fate of constitutional amendments or bond issues, and to fill many positions in Texas local government. They are administered by the same officials who oversee the operations of general elections. One outstanding characteristic of special elections is that candidates do not declare their party affiliation. These elections are nonpartisan.

Voter Eligibility

Texas has had a checkered past where voter eligibility is concerned. Until fairly recently, certain segments of society—especially the poor and/or blacks and Mexican Americans—have been systematically excluded from voting in the state. Between 1902 and 1966, for example, Texans had to pay a poll tax to vote. Between October 1 and January 31 of each election year, depending on the county in which each potential voter resided, he or she had to pay either $1.50 or $1.75 in order to vote. In 1967 the poll tax was replaced by a very restrictive registration law: "One of the most, if not the most, restrictive among the fifty states in terms of voter convenience." [2] Before 1972, Texans wanting to vote had to register between October 1 and January 31 of each election year. In addition, severe limitations were placed on the circumstances under which a person's name could be added to the electoral rolls. Finally, the "white primary" in Texas meant that each political party could exclude nonwhites from voting in its primary. Until 1944, the Democratic party—then clearly the dominant party in the state—allowed only whites to participate in its primary. In effect, this practice denied blacks and members of other minority groups the right to meaningful participation in the electoral system of Texas.

As indicated, each of these restrictions has been eliminated. In every case mentioned the impetus for change came from outside of the state. The poll tax began to fade after the twenty-fourth amendment to the U.S. Constitution was passed by Congress and ratified by three-fourths of the states. Even though this amendment was written to eliminate the poll tax once and for all, Texas continued the levy in state and local elections. A federal court eventually ordered the state to ban the poll tax in all elections: federal, state, and local.[3] Texans finally approved an amendment to the state constitution prohibiting the tax in 1966.

The stimulus for liberalizing Texas's voter registration law also came from a federal court.[4] Under the close scrutiny of the court the Texas legislature enacted a very relaxed set of registration requirements in 1973. The changes eliminated the provisions calling for annual registration, the limitations on places where a person might register, and the short period of time during which potential voters could register. Presuming that other legal standards are met (e.g., a person is eighteen years of age or older, a citizen of the U.S., and a resident of the state), any person can register at any time, as long as it occurs at least thirty days before an election. Registration can be done through the mail or at convenient neighborhood locations, and re-registration has also been made much easier.

After many years of litigation, the Supreme Court of the United States finally ruled in 1944 that the "white primary" was an infringement of rights protected by the federal Constitution.[5] Consequently, a measure that had effectively prevented blacks and some Mexican Americans from exercising any influence through the ballot box was outlawed.

Put briefly, legal restrictions on voting in Texas elections have been eliminated. Currently, almost all citizens over eighteen can register and vote. How many do?

Voter Turnout

Relatively speaking, turnout for elections in Texas is low. Texas voters have consistently lagged behind the national average turnout in presidential elections. In the 1984 contest between Ronald Reagan and Walter Mondale, 46.7 percent of eligible Texans voted, some 7 percent below the national average. But presidential elections are the high-water mark in voting turnout. Statewide races, such as the governor's contest, rarely attract more than one-third of the eligible voters. The turnout for the 1982 gubernatorial election was a rather dismal 29.6 percent of the voting age population. And local elections fare much worse. It is not uncommon to find less than 10 percent of eligible voters turning out for school board, city council, and even mayoral contests in Texas.

Voting figures tallied in the 1982 state primaries are indicative of the typical pattern of low turnout in state elections. There were 222 contests to be decided by the voters that year in the primaries in which fully 8,200 candidates sought office. Nonetheless, only 16 percent of Texans eligible to vote bothered to cast a ballot in the first primary. Around 6 percent participated in the 1982 runoff primaries.[6] Why are these rates of voting participation so low?

To begin with, the ranks of the nonvoters are swelled by the impoverished. Poverty breeds a concern with one's own well-being and thus a lack of interest in the political world, which is perceived by most of the poor as distant and indifferent. In the case of racial minorities, this sense of alienation is often reinforced by the painful reminder that the state once, and not so very long ago, legally excluded most of them from participation in the political process. A legacy of discrimination does not die quickly in people's minds.

Moreover, as pointed out in chapter 1, the agents of political socialization in Texas do little to encourage widespread political participation, even through conventional means such as voting. Ignorance, disinterest, and apathy are major reasons for nonvoting. Some 46 percent of a sample of nonvoters in the 1982 state primaries explained their lack of participation with reference to these factors. Conversely, the minority of Texans who voted in the primaries did so out of a sense of civic duty.[7] Hence what a person thinks about his or her role in the political system has a major bearing on whether or not he or she votes. Such perceptions are largely shaped by the political socialization process.

There is also some chance that confusion and uncertainty over voter eligibility rules still linger among Texans. It took time to communicate to the voters the mechanics of the current, more liberal, registration procedures. This delay left many of the state's eligible voters somewhat unsure—at least for a while—about how, when, and where to have their names placed on the voting rolls.

The number of registered voters is now, however, continuously on the rise in Texas. In the late 1970s, for instance, less than 60 percent of all eligible voters were registered. By 1984 that number had improved to over 70 percent. Much of this increase is the result of extensive and successful voter registration drives aimed at the state's impoverished that have been carried out by various organizations, such as the Southwest Voter Registration Education Project.

Finally, nonvoting may be attributed to the lack of meaningful choices in elections. People who are not that interested in the political process in the first place, who have suffered discrimination in the past, and who might still be confused about the current voting and registration procedures may need to be jolted into participation. The presence of substantial alternatives on the ballot might light a fire under the apathetic, help destroy memories of the past, and encourage registration and actual voting. The extent of electoral choice depends much on the competitiveness of the Texas party system.

THE PARTY SYSTEM OF TEXAS

Successful political parties function at three levels. First, they play a role in the actual governing of the political system. Second, each exists as an autonomous organizational unit, much in the vein of any formally structured organization (such as a church, a labor union, a corporation, a university, and so forth). Third, they help shape the voting behavior of ordinary citizens. Each of these components of party activity as they apply to Texas will be discussed in some detail.

Party in Texas Government

The Democratic party has held the reins of government in Texas for more than a century. Only one Republican (Bill Clements) has been elected governor since 1874. Texas's judges have almost all been affiliated with the Democratic party and the legislature has overwhelmingly been comprised of Democrats. Two points, however, preclude uncritical acceptance of the conclusion that Texas government is entirely controlled by the Democratic party.

First, factors other than loyalty to a disciplined party organization affect the behavior of government officials in Texas, as well as in most political arenas in the United States. Affiliation with a political party (for instance in Texas, the Democrats) may be necessary to win an election, but party membership alone does not guarantee electoral success. The candidate's image, issue stands, social

background characteristics, fund-raising ability, and personal campaign organization can also contribute to his or her victory. Once in office a politician is not
solely indebted to a party for achieving his or her position. Indeed, at times,
elected officials will diverge from a party's policy out of respect to other factors
thought important to election.

Furthermore, political parties in America rarely possess sanctions by which
they can reward or punish a government official for his or her loyalty to the
party's program. Party discipline is difficult to enforce. Hence, although elected
officials tend to follow party lines in formulating government policy, they remain
relatively free to deviate from this norm.

Second, the strength of the Democratic party in state government has declined
in recent years. Over the last decade, the governor's office has been occupied
more by Republicans than Democrats. In 1984, according to the Republican party,
GOP candidates won 434 electoral contests across Texas, a 56 percent increase
over the 278 victories recorded in 1982.[8] The makeup of the Texas legislature has
reflected this trend. By the mid-1980s, one-third of the membership of the House
and nearly 20 percent of the Senate was composed of Republicans. Not since
Reconstruction has the GOP held more seats in the legislature.

Party Organization in Texas

The formal organization of the two major political parties in Texas—the
Democrats and the Republicans—is structured to permit close contact with voters.
As depicted in figure 4–1, the baseline of party organization forms around voters
who participate in the selection of the party leadership.[9] One becomes a member
of a political party in Texas simply by voting in the party's primary. That act
entitles the voter to attend the party's precinct convention, which is held the
night of the primary (the first Saturday of May in even-numbered years.) Texas's
254 counties are divided into around 5,500 precincts, each containing from 50 to
5,000 registered voters. As discussed earlier in this chapter, primaries attract only
a small percentage of Texas voters; primary conventions are attended by even
fewer voters. One statewide study found that only around 10 percent of Texans
who *voted* in the 1982 primaries also participated in precinct conventions held the
same night as the primary. Slightly more Republicans (5 percent) came to precinct
meetings than Democrats.[10]

The main task of the precinct meeting is to choose representatives to attend
the county convention. The precinct is allowed one delegate at the county convention for every twenty-five votes received by the party's candidate in the
precinct during the latest general election for governor.

The county convention is held within a few weeks of the party primary. The
larger counties of Texas, for example, Tarrant, Harris, Dallas, and Bexar, contain
so many people that, for organizational purposes, they are divided into districts.
These districts coincide with the geographical boundaries of the state senatorial
lines in the county, and each district holds what is the equivalent to a county
convention. The major function of the county or district convention is the selection of delegates to the party's state convention. The number of delegates to
represent each county or district is again dependent on the votes received in the
latest governor's race in the area by the party's candidate.

FIGURE 4–1 Party Structure in Texas

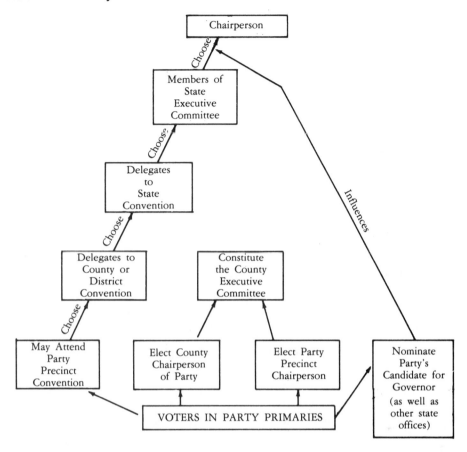

The state convention (of the Democratic party) meets twice in years during which there is a presidential race. The first meeting is in June at which time the convention selects: (1) delegates to attend the party's national presidential nominating convention, (2) electors to cast a vote in the electoral college should the party's presidential candidate emerge victorious after the general election, and (3) a committeeman and a committeewoman to serve on the party's national committee. The second meeting commences in September. Its concern is state matters. At this time, the state party platform is written, the party's nominees for inclusion on the general election ballot are certified and forwarded to the secretary of state, and the members of the State Executive Committee are chosen. Only the September meeting occurs in election years when no presidential contest is at stake.

Voters are hence in a position to affect party leadership and policy. However, low turnout in primaries and, especially, at the precinct conventions seriously weakens the linkage between leaders and the public. Not unexpectedly, a very small minority of leaders actually runs party matters. At the lowest level, the precinct chairpersons emerge as leaders. The chairperson is elected at the precinct convention and is charged with conducting party business at the precinct level.

How active and effective he or she is depends on personal motivation and environmental pressure. For instance, these leaders are generally more energetic in competitive party areas.

The next level in the party hierarchy is the county or district executive committee, composed of all precinct chairpersons in the area. This group administers the county convention and the party's primary. The single most important leader at the local level in the party organization is the county or district chairperson, who is elected in the primary for a two-year term. Recruitment of candidates, mobilizing the vote, and securing campaign donations are among the more important jobs of this leader.

The State Executive Committee, which is chosen at the September meeting of the state convention, is the highest organizational tier in the party. The committee is composed of sixty-two people—two from each of the state's thirty-one senatorial districts. The principal party office is the chairperson of the State Executive Committee, who is selected by the party's candidate for governor. It is the responsibility of the committee and its chairperson to guide the party through all its functions: raising funds, selecting candidates, getting out the vote, shaping issue stands, and coordinating the multiple levels of party organization from federal to local.

In short, party structure in Texas is organized formally in a democratic fashion; the public can influence party operations. However, the actual performance of the party is in the hands of its leaders. In turn, the leadership, lacking a strong backbone of public support to assist in carrying out party functions (such as raising funds, recruiting candidates, and turning out the vote), is vulnerable to forces external to the party that can provide these assets. Candidates of the parties are also constantly searching for campaign assistance from outside the party structure. Given the narrow band of resources (e.g., funds and personnel) at the disposal of the major parties in Texas, "most candidates prefer creating their own political organizations and thus having a personally tailored vehicle for their political ambition." [11] As shall be discussed in the next chapter, economic interests become valuable sources of commodities essential to electoral success for both the party and the candidates in state campaigns.

Parties in the Texas Electorate

Political parties also reach out far into the electorate. Part of this connection is forged through the organizational activities of the party. Parties in Texas expend some resources in attempting to rally voters to support their candidates, for instance. In recent years, the Republican party, both nationally and in Texas, has expanded its base through monitoring, and influencing, the thoughts and intentions of potential voters. The GOP has raised and spent a great deal of money on public opinion polls, media advertisements, and canvassing citizens over the phone.[12] In Texas, for example, the Republicans have developed an extensive computer data bank that contains the names of all of Texas's nearly eight million registered voters.[13] With this information readily at hand, the party can easily contact Texans to collect more data, and thus be well situated to assist candidates in their campaigns.

Party influence in the electorate goes beyond organizational endeavors. It extends into the psychological and social milieu enveloping many voters. Party attachment molds perceptions of candidates and actual voting behavior.[14] Partisan affinities are learned and reinforced through many nonpolitical socialization experiences, such as those that occur in the family, the workplace, and among peers.[15] A person without any identification with a party is unlikely to vote.

The end of Reconstruction in the 1870s left Texas firmly in the grip of the Democratic party. Republican rule after the Civil War, to be discussed further in chapter 7, was characterized by an unpleasant mixture of corruption, tyranny, ineffectiveness, and violence. Most white Texans were quick to reject it. With the imposition of state laws barring nonwhites from meaningful political participation in Texas, Republicans were denied a natural constituency among black Texans to build a support-base for the party of Abraham Lincoln.

Loyalty to the Democratic party soon became ingrained in Texas's political culture. Identification with the party was transmitted from generation to generation until one-party dominance became a trademark of the state's social and political landscape. To this day, there are complete loyalists to the party who are known as "yellow-dog Democrats," out of their ability to trace their ancestral electoral commitment to the party back to the days of the Civil War.

Some pockets of Republican strength remained in Texas. Migrants from Germany who settled near the San Antonio area in the nineteenth century were resolute in their opposition to the slave system sanctioned by the Democratic party. Hence they chose to identify with the Republicans, a commitment that persists to this day. Likewise, the Panhandle area was first settled by people who brought their Republican affiliation into the state with them.

The economic and population explosions that Texas has experienced during this century have somewhat altered the status quo of the party system. The widespread discovery of oil in the Midland-Odessa during the 1930s, for instance, attracted people to the area who were disposed to Republican virtues of free enterprise economics. The recent surge of migration has brought into the state a large number of people with staunch Republican backgrounds. Many have moved into urban centers, especially Dallas, Fort Worth, Amarillo, Austin, Beaumont, Lubbock, Wichita Falls, and Houston. In each case, to varying degrees, these cities have become more Republican over the years.

The Republican party is making significant inroads into state politics. As mentioned earlier, the 1980s have witnessed the election of the highest number of Republicans in Texas since Reconstruction. The extent to which the GOP shows signs of becoming an autonomous, full-functioning political unit is illustrated in the growing popularity of its primary. Recall that in the past many Republicans voted in the Democratic primary, since, for all intents and purposes, that was *the* election. Times have changed. More and more Texans are voting in the Republican primary these days. In 1978, for example, only 158,403 people voted in that party's primary. By 1982, the number had increased to 262,865. Fully 543,172 Texans participated in the 1986 GOP primary, a doubling of the turnout recorded four years earlier. Moreover, the number of voters casting ballots in the Democratic primary is receding. In 1982, 1.3 million Texans voted in the Democratic party primary. Four years later the figure had dropped to 1.1 million, the lowest number registered since 1946.[16]

Furthermore, there has been a significant rise recently in identification with the Republican party label. Whereas in 1983, 22 percent of Texans considered themselves Republicans, the percentage had improved to 32 percent in 1985. During this same period the proportion of Democrats fell from 38 percent to 34 percent. Viewed somewhat differently, the gap between the number of Texans calling themselves Democrats and those preferring the Republican tag has closed dramatically. A 16 percent difference between the two existed in 1983; a couple of years later the distance had been reduced to 2 percent.[17]

The future of the Republican party looks equally bright. The party is drawing its followers disproportionately from prosperous younger, urban, white (non-Hispanic) segments of the Texas population—a goodly share of the state's growing number of "yuppies" is Republican.[18] Meanwhile, the strength of the Democratic party more and more lies in the state's minority population, especially among Mexican Americans. As noted by one commentator, "Mexican Americans are now the dominant faction in the Democratic party."[19] To be sure, the party still retains support among older Texans, in particular those living in nonurban settings. However, this is not a strong population base for the party to rely on in the future. Among other things (such as mortality), there is every indication that the traditional rural constituency of the Democrats is eroding as the party increasingly becomes aligned with the interests of minority groups in the state.[20]

Hence the transformation of the party system in the Texas electorate suggests the emergence of party competition. Republicans and Democrats now appear to be more evenly matched in electoral contests than has been the case in the state's recent history. However, the extent of meaningful competition in Texas's elections can still be questioned. Doubt persists over whether substantive differences are yet available to the state's voters. The lack of third-party alternatives and the ideological similarity between the successful candidates of the two major parties converge to suggest that "competition" has only gone so far in Texas's elections. Each of these points requires some elaboration.

Third Parties in Texas.   Texas has had a rich history of third-party activity. In the past, the Greenbacks, the Populists, the Prohibitionists, States-Righters, Communists, Socialists, Progressives, and members of George Wallace's American Independent party have found room on the Texas ballot. The life span of these parties has generally been brief, however. There are several reasons for this state of affairs.

First, it is fairly difficult to get—and stay—on the state ballot. In order for a third party or independent candidate to gain access to the ballot, a number of steps must be taken. Initially, voters must sign a petition to support putting the name of a new person or party on the ballot. The number of signatures to be affixed on the petition must equal 1 percent of the *total* vote count in the latest governor's race. If, for instance, 2 million votes were cast in the preceding gubernatorial election, then 20,000 signatures would be the minimum number required on the petition. Only registered voters are eligible to sign. The petition is then sent to the secretary of state's office for verification. Here it is checked to see if the correct number of signatures has been reached, whether the petitioners are registered voters, and whether the signees voted in the primary of an established party. If one casts a ballot for an extant party in its primary, then he or she cannot petition for the name of a new party or independent candidate to appear on the ballot in the general election. In order for a party to retain its name on the ballot, its candidate must receive at least 2 percent of the total vote. Inability to reach this figure means that the petition process must begin anew.

Second, Texas's elections are based on the "winner take all" principle. That is, the victor is the candidate who amasses the highest vote count in the general election. Losers receive no rewards for their efforts. Since third parties rarely win when they first appear on the ballot, it becomes very discouraging for their supporters to stick with the party. Many people are unwilling to waste their votes and they soon abandon (or never affiliate with) the new party. In electoral systems with proportional representation—where offices are allotted on the basis of the percentage of votes won in the general election (instead of on the basis of "winner take all")—the life of third parties is ordinarily prolonged.

Third, if a third party is successful in gaining a place on the ballot and in winning votes, then the established parties frequently will adopt its issue stands. For instance, the Populists in Texas attracted a great deal of popular support by advocating stricter governmental controls over business, especially railroads and banks. The Democratic party responded by absorbing many of the Populists' views into its platform. This process, often referred to as co-optation, frequently (as was the case with the Populists) spells defeat for the third party. Interestingly, when an established party co-opts the ground of a third party, it usually dilutes the issue stance of the latter. Whereas Populists, for example, encouraged government takeover of some businesses, the Democratic party softened the message to one of government regulation.

Fourth, successful third parties that resist co-optation might find themselves being repressed by entrenched authorities. Repression is the actual or threatened use of coercion (physical force, harassment, intimidation, or manipulation) by those in government. Consider the case of *La Raza Unida* party in Texas.

La Raza Unida began in the late 1960s in South Texas, principally in Crystal City (Zavala County). This part of Texas contains a large number of impoverished residents, especially poor Mexican Americans. Zavala County's per-capita income in 1982 was $4,326, about one-third the statewide average.[21] One estimate puts 87 percent of the ownership of land in the county in Anglo hands, even though Anglos constitute only 15 percent of the county's population.[22]

Raza Unida took a stand against the conditions of poverty; inadequate services for the poor in the areas of housing, health, police, sanitation, and education (among others); and the inordinate power exercised by Anglos—frequently in a highly discriminatory manner.[23] The party, under the leadership of Jose Angel Gutierrez, took its battle to the polling booth. In local elections for school board positions and for city and county offices, the party scored impressive wins. Gutierrez himself served as the elected county judge of Zavala until the late 1970s.

At the state level, the party did not win any offices, but it played a role in the statewide electoral fortunes of both Democrats and Republicans. For instance, in 1972, *Raza Unida* 's candidate for governor, Ramsey Muniz, won 6 percent of the total vote, drawing enough support away from Democrat Dolph Briscoe to almost give the Republican candidate, Henry Grover, the governor's chair. In 1978, even though *Raza* 's Mario Compean received less than 1 percent of the vote, this percentage helped Bill Clements overcome John Hill to become the state's first Republican governor in more than one hundred years.

Once in local office, *Raza Unida* rectified some of the conditions facing poor Chicanos. In Crystal City, health care facilities were drastically improved. New schools were built. The school curriculum was reoriented to be more relevant to impoverished Mexican Americans. In the aftermath of the education changes, "the dropout rate plummeted . . . [and] more than 80 percent of Crystal City High School graduates—better than twice the statewide average for Chicano youth— were going to college." [24]

In its most ambitious project the party attempted to establish a cooperative farm in Zavala County. County Judge Gutierrez and his associates sought to purchase, as a start in this direction, 1,000 acres of farmland. The land would have been jointly operated by farm workers who would have shared any profits made from agricultural sales. To effectuate this plan, Gutierrez secured a $1.5 million grant from the federal government (under the auspices of the Ford administration).

From its inception, *Raza Unida* was plagued with problems, some of which were repressive in nature. After Ramsey Muniz's relatively strong showing in 1972, Governor Briscoe asked the state legislature to pass a bill requiring any political party to obtain 20 percent of the statewide vote in order to have its name continue to appear on the Texas ballot. The measure failed but the intent was clear. After the announcement of the $1.5 million federal grant to establish a farm cooperative, strong measures were employed to stop distribution of the funds. A farm cooperative composed of former farm workers, many of whom were migrants, constituted a distinct challenge to traditional agricultural practices in South Texas. Governor Briscoe, a major ranch and farm owner in this area, led the forces against *Raza Unida*'s farm plan. His sentiments about the project were clearly stated in a speech supporting Democratic candidates against Republicans in the state's 1976 elections:

> So I say to you . . . fellow Texans, if you want your tax money used to establish a Little Cuba in Texas—to establish a communal farm in Texas—to promote Socialism in Texas—if you want federal dollars to finance efforts to destroy the free enterprise system, the capitalistic system that has built this state and nation of ours, then you want a continuation of power of an administration that makes such grants to the *Raza Unida* party. [25]

Briscoe put much effort into blocking the grant. He convinced Washington officials that authorization releasing the money should only be granted if the governor of the state agreed in writing. No governor ever accepted the farm cooperative and the funds never came to Zavala County.

With some of its plans thwarted, *Raza Unida* found it difficult to expand into a viable political force in Texas. Compounding the external political pressure brought to bear on the party, internal disintegration occurred. Its former gubernatorial candidate, Ramsey Muniz, was sentenced to prison after pleading guilty to drug charges. Much discord among party officials over the leadership style of Gutierrez came into the open. [26] Electoral defeats mounted. By the mid–1980s the party was a fading memory.

In short, third parties have existed throughout most of Texas's history. Moreover, many have offered a wide range of options—some of which could be considered radical—to the state's voters. However, their tenure has usually been short. Texas voters, like voters in most of America, have at best a choice between the candidates of the Republican and the Democratic parties. In actuality even that choice is limited given the fact that candidates most likely to be elected—regardless of whether they are Democrats or Republicans—are much alike in their thinking.

Ideological Similarity.   The conservative arm of the Democratic party of Texas has exerted the most muscle in electoral and party politics in the state. Almost without exception, candidates elected by the voters for state offices have been identified with this faction. The occasional—albeit increasing—election of a Republican has not meant a deviation from conservative thinking. Indeed, "the Republican party can best be described as having a conservative wing and a more conservative wing." [27]

To a large extent the two major parties reflect the ideological leaning of most of the state's voters. A 1982 survey conducted among a representative sample of 1,441 registered voters in Texas found that 70 percent considered themselves at least "somewhat conservative" politically. Almost all Republicans were in this ideological camp and nearly 62 percent of Democrats were likewise disposed.[28] Consequently, electoral "victory is gained by trying to convince the electorate that a candidate is more conservative than his opponent." [29]

This presents an ideal political climate for business. Conservatives virtually never challenge the preemptive position to be granted to the business community by government. They raise hardly any objection to specific policies, such as no corporate profit taxes or right-to-work labor laws, which are quite beneficial to business. The pervasiveness of a pro-business ideology throughout Texas greatly inhibits the possibility that a critique of business will be an issue in the state's elections. It is possible for candidates to conflict over which business interest (say, petroleum versus high tech) should be given the highest priority by state government. But a challenge to the privilege to be accorded to business in general is rarely a focal point of electoral dispute.

For most of the 1970s, for instance, Texas's governor was the Democrat Dolph Briscoe. Governor Briscoe was first elected in 1972. He held the governor's position until 1978 when he was beaten in the Democratic party primary by John Hill, former chief justice of the Texas Supreme Court. Briscoe was well accepted by people in the conservative circles of the party and his background was deeply grounded in the rancher/business community of Texas.

Briscoe owns more than 400,000 acres of land in Uvalde County. He also is an important stockholder of banks in Uvalde, Pearsall, and Dallas. For instance, in the early 1980s he possessed 70,270 shares (nearly 1 percent of the total) in Dallas's Mercantile Bank (now called M Corp).[30] Subsequent to his stint as governor, Briscoe has sat on the boards of directors of some the state's leading financial institutions, namely, M Corp (number three bank in the state), Lomas and Nettleton (the country's leading mortgage banker), and Southland Financial Corporation (a major Texas-based insurance company). The privilege of business in Texas government was never in doubt while Briscoe was governor.

Briscoe's successor in the governor's chair was William P. Clements, Jr. Bill Clements's business credentials are impeccable. In 1947 he founded SEDCO. Over the years he built SEDCO into one of the world's largest oil services companies. By the early 1970s Clements's asset worth was well over $100 million and SEDCO had an asset value of $1 billion in the early 1980s. He served as chief executive officer of SEDCO until 1973, when he (temporarily) left business to become undersecretary of defense in the Nixon/Ford administrations. As undersecretary of defense, Clements's major area of responsibility was the Middle East, with a concentration on policy toward Iran. Incidentally, although Clements had no formal connection with SEDCO during this period, the company entered into a lucrative business arrangement with the shah of Iran during the mid–1970s. By the time Clements returned to head SEDCO in 1977 his firm's stock market value had increased substantially.

Bill Clements sought and won the governor's chair in 1978. He was defeated in his reelection bid in 1982. After his loss he returned to SEDCO. In 1986 he negotiated the sale (for some $1.1 billion) of his company to Schlumberger, a major oil services firm located in the Netherlands. At various times he has held a seat on the board of directors of one of Texas's leading banks—InterFirst. He also has served on the board of trustees of Southern Methodist University as well as the national executive board of the Boy Scouts of America. Indeed, Clements chaired the board of trustees of SMU when that school became embroiled in the major athletic scandal that led to the elimination of the university's football program for two years. Before his reelection to governor of Texas in 1986, Clements was a member of the Kissinger Commission, established by President Reagan to report on the political situation in Central America.

Bill Clements, to a large degree, epitomizes the success of the self-made man. He has strong beliefs in the fundamental virtues of patriotism, individual freedom, and private property and private enterprise. Many of the interests of Bill Clements are the interests of business.

Hence the conservative similarity of the leading candidates from the two major parties in Texas guarantees business a lofty standing in state government, no matter which party's candidate wins. Granted, Texas has produced some elected politicians who appear to run against the grain of big business. Two examples—one drawn from the past, the other from recent times—stand out. In each case the elected official has experienced great difficulty countering the privilege of big business in the state.

W. Lee "Pappy" O'Daniel: A Case Study.   The first example is drawn from Texas's past. It covers the case of W. Lee "Pappy" O'Daniel who in 1938 became governor of Texas. O'Daniel's election is intriguing because he ran a campaign attacking business privilege. It was during the Depression and economic times were not good. O'Daniel is also interesting because he ranks as one of the most colorful figures to hold office in the state's history.

Ohio born and Kansas reared, W. Lee O'Daniel first came to work in Texas as the manager of a flour mill company. Within a decade, he had started his own flour company and his own hillbilly band, appropriately named "The Light Crust Doughboys" (which featured among its members the legendary Bob Wills). Pappy, which soon became O'Daniel's nickname, took to the radio to sell his wares. On his daily radio broadcast, he played music, recited poems, honored Texas heroes, read from the Bible, and counseled Texans on their personal problems: "Erring husbands were advised to correct their behavior, school children were given good advice on thrift and conduct, traffic safety was emphasized, childless couples were advised to adopt babies, and religious and humanitarian movements and organizations were supported." [31]

On Palm Sunday, 1938, O'Daniel asked his radio audience if he should seek the office of governor of Texas. Armed with an overwhelming vote of confidence (54,499 messages for him, 4 against—according to O'Daniel's tally), he embarked on the campaign trail. His platform was extremely interesting, to say the least. He opposed the poll tax, "saying that no politician was worth $1.75." [32] Indeed, he never paid the poll tax and thus was not eligible to vote in his own election. During the campaign, O'Daniel—usually accompanied by his band—spoke in favor of the Ten Commandments and pensions of $30 per month for the elderly, and against imposing a sales tax on the consumers of Texas. Without a campaign manager or headquarters, he beat a field of thirteen other candidates in the Democratic primary and, given the lack of much Republican competition in the general election, in effect, became governor right then and there. He easily won reelection in 1940.

In 1941 the United States senator from Texas died. In such cases the governor appoints an interim senator and calls a special election to fill the vacated position. Pappy had his own eyes on the Senate seat, but decided to wait until the special election to run rather than appoint himself. Faced with the prospect that the person whom he selected might be his chief opponent in the forthcoming election, O'Daniel "resolved the dilemma," according to V.O. Key, "by probably the most ingenious appointment in senatorial history." [33] On the 105th anniversary of the Battle of San Jacinto, he appointed General Andrew Jackson Houston, son of Sam Houston—the hero of battle. The "younger" Houston was 87 at the time of his appointment and not in the best of health: "He managed to make the trip to Washington in the care of a nurse, took the oath of office, fell ill, and died in a Baltimore hospital while the campaign to determine his successor was at its height." [34] O'Daniel won the special election—his closest rival was Lyndon B. Johnson. In 1942, Pappy was elected to the Senate for a full six-year term.

His tenure while in Washington was not well evaluated by most of the public, his financial backers, or his colleagues. The last were not at all flattered by some of his disparaging remarks, such as "Washington is the only lunatic asylum in the world run by its own inmates." [35] He did not seek reelection in 1948, although he did make an unsuccessful bid, running as an avowed segregationist, to win the governor's chair in 1956.

O'Daniel cultivated an image of being a "good ol' boy"; a man of the people; a friend of the farmer, the downtrodden, and the elderly. Beneath that image, however, there was another side to Pappy. His financial backing came mostly from wealthy sources in Texas. For example, his major benefactor in his initial race for governor was the chairman of the board of the Fidelity Union Life Insurance Company, then one of the state's largest. When the river of money ran

Governor W. Lee O'Daniel and the appointed senator from Texas, General Andrew Jackson Houston.

Photo courtesy of the Texas State Archives.

dry, O'Daniel's political career came to an abrupt halt. Moreover, once in office, he did little to ease the plight of less fortunate Texans. While governor, his old-age pension plan never was pushed very hard. His campaign promise not to opt for a sales tax was quickly forgotten when he introduced just such a measure to the Texas legislature, although he called it a "transaction tax."

Listening to O'Daniel, one might have thought that one were hearing a candidate challenging the rich in the name of the poor. Certainly his listeners were captivated by his words. V.O. Key says of O'Daniel: "Backed by a few wealthy men, he won the votes of many poor men [and women]. He talked the language of the lesser people, but on the whole he acted and voted [like] a *Chicago Tribune* Republican." [36]

Jim Hightower: A Case Study.   It could be argued that Pappy O'Daniel was simply a bit of a huckster. That is, he was engaging in the age-old political gimmick of telling voters one thing and doing the opposite once in office. What happens when candidates who sincerely do oppose corporate interests win election in Texas?

The 1982 general election featured several important contests waged by candidates identified with the liberal wing of the Democratic party. The party's left-leaning arm has always operated in the shadow of the conservative body of the party. Nonetheless, there has been a persistent, active, and vocal liberal minority

among the Democrats for some time. Although Texas's liberals have never rejected business entirely, they have supported populist and New Deal ideas that
promote the regulation of business practices and the expansion of social programs
designed to aid people in social, economic, or political need of help. Liberal
strength geographically lies mostly in some major urban centers (Houston, for
instance), in southeastern portions of the state, and in regions along the Mexican
border, especially in West Texas. It also rests on the personal attributes of liberal
candidates, many of whom have been articulate, witty, and energetic. In 1982,
liberals scored impressive and unusual victories in the state elections. Standing
out ideologically from this crowd is the populist Jim Hightower, who was elected
to the post of commissioner of agriculture.

Jim Hightower was born in Denton in 1943.[37] After graduating from North
Texas State University where he was president of the student body, he enrolled in law school at George Washington University. His career in the law
lasted only a week. He subsequently entered a two-year postgraduate program
in international affairs at Columbia University, but withdrew after completing
half the course. In the late 1960s he first dabbled in the real world of politics
by assisting Texas's liberal senator, Ralph Yarborough. In 1970 he became
associated with the Washington-based Agricultural Accountability Project.
With the help of a $65,000 grant given to the project, Hightower began his
analysis of, and attack on, corporate influence in society generally and in agriculture specifically. His research, insight, and denouncement of the alleged
corporate capture of American agriculture were cogently presented in two
books.[38]

In 1976, Hightower was the unpaid campaign manager for Fred Harris in his
unsuccessful attempt to win the Democratic party nomination for president.
Hightower subsequently returned to Texas to become editor of the state's foremost liberal newspaper, *The Texas Observer.* Here he continued in print his assault
on the impact of corporations on politics and society, especially in Texas. With his
farewell editorial noting that "there comes a time when writing about the bastards
isn't enough," [39] Hightower resigned his position at the *Observer* to become director
of the Texas Consumer Association.

Hightower formally entered politics in 1980 when he announced his candi-
dacy for the Democratic party nomination for the Texas Railroad Commission.
During this campaign he refused to accept any donation in excess of $100. He
also rejected contributions from persons or groups that might have interests
regulated by the commission. After all the primary votes were counted, Hightower barely lost to Jim Nugent, who went on to win the general election.

Hightower's 1982 campaign for the position of commissioner of agriculture
fared much better. He beat the incumbent commissioner, Reagan Brown, in
the Democratic primary. By committing several faux pas during the campaign,
Brown virtually destroyed his electoral chances. At one point, Brown referred
publicly to educator, reformer, and author Booker T. Washington as that
"great black nigger." [40] During a speech delivered at North Texas State University, Brown commented that Texas's manufactured articles of clothing had
become so popular that "you couldn't tell the Jews and the Texans apart." [41]
On another occasion he attempted to demonstrate that the fire ants then
plaguing Texas were harmless by placing his hand in an anthill outside the

state capitol building. The reporters present carefully noted the pain suffered by Brown after being bitten thirty-seven times.[42] Hightower beat Brown by a comfortable majority in the primary; he was a convincing winner in the subsequent general election.

Between the electoral defeat of 1980 and the win in 1982, Hightower had a change of mind concerning campaign contributions. The ban against donations in excess of $100 was lifted for the second contest. Gone too was the prohibition on acceptance of money from interests that might be affected by the Department of Agriculture. Although the sums were not terribly large, Hightower's campaign received contributions from corporate sources with substantial interests in agribusiness in Texas.[43]

After his election, one of Hightower's first actions was to reassure agribusiness and chemical firms that he would operate the Department of Agriculture in a sound, reasonable way. For instance, he communicated to Harry Whitmore, director of the Texas Chemical Council, the following message:

> Look, I want to get along with you. I want agriculture in Texas to be improved, and I realize that you fellas have a big stake in it. You don't need to worry about me doing anything crazy.[44]

Apparently, at least Mr. Whitmore was convinced, for, in his words, "I don't see him [Hightower] as carried away with liberalism. He wants to do a good job. I don't think he'd let beliefs get in the way." [45]

To be sure, Hightower has not sat quietly at his post as commissioner of agriculture. He has attempted to aid family farmers by establishing markets through which they can sell their produce directly to the public. He also expanded the work force at the agriculture department and, in so doing, increased the percentage of Hispanics hired.[46] His most far-reaching action has been the imposition of new rules on the spraying of farmland with pesticides.

More than half of Texas's farms are doused in such sprays each year. In the late 1970s some 100 to 150 million pounds of pesticides were used on agricultural units. Evidence suggests that field-workers often paid an extreme physical price for the sake of controlling weeds and pests through chemical sprays.[47] Although the new regulations do not ban any pesticides, they do require (1) warnings to accompany any spraying, (2) intervals between application and continuation of farm work in the field, (3) adequate labeling of the chemicals in agricultural pesticides, and (4) concerted efforts to collect and disseminate information about the effects of chemicals.

The new pesticide rules angered some agribusiness and chemical interests. Since their announcement, the Department of Agriculture has had difficulty with the legislature in securing staff and funds. Hightower faced some fairly stiff opposition in his 1986 reelection bid. To the chagrin of his opponents he was able to ward off his challengers.

Thus far, while in office, Hightower has only mildly rebuffed the corporate structure of Texas agriculture. When he has tried such action, he has met with some antipathy and resistance. This might account for some of his hesitancy. Even without such a reaction he fully realizes that constantly to confront big business in Texas is to court political suicide. This is not the rational strategy for an ambitious politician who has let it be known that "as much good as I could do as agriculture commissioner, I could do more good as governor."[48] As noted by one close observer,

> Hightower's desire to succeed has promoted him to recant past writings, cozy up to legislators he once ridiculed, and grub for contributions from lobbyists. He is not selling out, but he is learning to play the game. His path—first as unconventional outsider, then as maverick candidate, and finally as officeholder—is a study of what happens when a skilled critic of the system becomes a skilled practitioner within it.[49]

CONCLUSION

Mass voter participation and vigorous competition among candidates are not hallmarks of Texas elections. Most voters, especially the poor and the economically marginal, simply do not cast ballots come election time. Choice among officeseekers is limited through similarity between leading candidates of the two major political parties and third parties are not viable electoral forces in the state. It is a favorable electoral and party environment for the business community. Low voter participation, vulnerable party organizations, lack of sustained party competition, and a general pro-business perspective among contenders for political office offer economic notables a terrific opportunity to elect sympathetic politicians. The next chapter details the prevalence of the dominant economic community in Texas elections.

NOTES

1. *1982 May Primary Election Analysis* (Austin: Office of the Secretary of State, 1982).

2. Janice C. May, "The Texas Voter Registration System," *Public Affairs Comment*, 16 (July 1970): 2.

3. *United States v. Texas*, 252 F.Supp. 234, Affirmed 384 U.S. 155 (1966).

4. *Beare, et al. v. Preston Smith, Governor of Texas*, 321 F.Supp. 1100 (1971).

5. *Smith v. Allwright*, 321 U.S. 649 (1944).

6. These figures are drawn from the Office of the Secretary of State's report, *1982 May Primary Election Analysis*.

7. Ibid.

8. *Texas Almanac and State Industrial Guide: 1986–1987* (Dallas: A.H. Belo, 1985), p. 646.

9. This discussion outlines the party organization of the Democratic party, since it is the dominant political party in Texas. Republican organization is very similar.

10. *1982 May Primary Election Analysis*, table 11.

11. Anthony Champagne and Rick Collis, "Texas," in *The Political Life of the American States*, eds. Alan Rosenthal and Maureen Moakley (New York: Praeger, 1984), p. 139.

12. For national efforts by the Republican party, see David Adamany, "Political Parties in the 1980s," in *Money and Politics in the United States*, ed. Michael J. Malbin (Chatham, N.J.: Chatham House Publishers, 1984).

13. Dave Denison, "Are We There Yet?" *Texas Observer*, June 13, 1986, pp. 6–8.

14. The classic study of the impact of party identification on political orientations is Angus Campbell, Philip E. Converse, Warren E. Miller, and Donald F. Stokes, *The American Voter* (New York: John Wiley and Sons, 1960).

15. David O. Sears, "Political Behavior," in *The Handbook of Social Psychology,* eds. Gardner Lindzey and Elliot Aronson, 2d ed. (Reading, Mass.: Addison-Wesley, 1969), Vol. 5.

16. Dave Denison, "Are We There Yet?" and Paul Burka, "Primary Lesson," *Texas Monthly,* July 1986, pp. 104–5.

17. Figures presented in the *Texas Poll* of April 1985. People not identifying either with the Republicans or the Democrats fell into the independent category.

18. Ibid.

19. Paul Burka, "Primary Lesson," p. 104.

20. Discussed in ibid.

21. Figures computed from the *Texas Almanac,* p. 376.

22. "Energy, Land and Natural Resources," *Texas Observer,* December 26, 1975, pp. 4–5.

23. The rise of *Raza Unida* in Crystal City is well covered in John Shockley, *Chicano Revolt in Texas Town* (Notre Dame, Ind.: University of Notre Dame Press, 1974).

24. Tom Curtis, "Raza Disunida," reprinted in the *Texas Monthly's Political Reader* (Austin: Texas Monthly Press and Sterling Swift Press, 1978), p. 40.

25. Quoted in John Muir, "La Raza's Community Farm Plan," *Texas Observer,* October 15, 1976, p. 1.

26. See Curtis, "Raza Disunida."

27. Anthony Champagne and Rick Collis, "Texas," p. 142.

28. *1982 May Primary Election Analysis,* table 3.

29. Champagne and Collis, p. 142.

30. *CDE Stock Ownership Directory: Banking and Finance* (New York: Corporate Data Exchange, 1980), p. 147.

31. Seth Shepard McKay, *W. Lee O'Daniel and Texas Politics* (Lubbock: Texas Tech Press, 1944), pp. 22–23. Quoted in V.O. Key, Jr., *Southern Politics in State and Nation* (New York: Vintage, 1949), p. 266.

32. William Earl Maxwell and Ernest Crain, *Texas Politics Today* (St. Paul: West Publishing Co., 1978), p. 26.

33. Key, *Southern Politics,* p. 268.

34. Ibid.

35. Maxwell and Crain, *Texas Politics Today,* p. 27.

36. Key, *Southern Politics,* p. 271.

37. Many details about Jim Hightower's life appear in Peter Elkind, "Cosmic Plowboy," *Texas Monthly,* December 1983, pp. 152–154 and pp. 236–247.

38. Jim Hightower, *Eat Your Heart Out: How Food Profiteers Victimize the Consumer* (New York: Crown Publishers, 1975); and *Hard Tomatoes, Hard Times: The Failure of the Land Grant College Complex* (Boston: Schenkman, 1977).

39. Quoted in Elkind, "Cosmic Plowboy," p. 238.

40. *Texas Observer,* May 7, 1982, p. 2.

41. Quoted in Elkind, p. 242.

42. Reported in *Texas Observer,* May 7, 1982.

43. Monsanto, Anderson Clayton, Temple-Eastex (then a subsidiary of Time, Inc.), and Fulbright and Jaworski, a major law firm representing several corporations with business in agriculture, made contributions to Hightower.

44. Quoted in Elkind, p. 154.

45. Quoted in ibid.

46. Nina Butts, "Four Fresh(men) Sing Hiring Improvements," *Texas Observer,* January 13, 1984, pp. 4–5.

47. For information presented above, see Dan Kelly, *New State Rules on Agricultural Pesticide Use* (Austin: House Study Group, # 114, May 20, 1985).

48. Quoted in Elkind, p. 154.

49. Ibid.

5

Economic Elites and Texas Elections

Persons and institutions in control of Texas's economic resources intercede in elections in two ways. First, economic influentials help screen candidates for suitability to hold political office in the state. Second, they are chiefly responsible for financing the campaigns of chosen candidates. This chapter investigates each of these processes. ★

CANDIDATE RECRUITMENT

The direct recruitment of political candidates by economic elites begins with a process of screening those with aspirations for elected office. Auditions for the screening usually occur far in advance of party primaries. They also mostly occur in informal settings, beyond the public's eyes.[1] Unless a person has social characteristics favored by the gatekeepers, he or she need not apply:

> The acceptable candidate must be born or educated into the middle or upper classes, displaying the linguistic and social styles of bourgeois personage. This requirement effectively limits the selection to business and professional people.[2]

If a potential candidate has the requisite background, he or she must then convincingly "express opinions of the kind that win the support of ... established interests."[3] An informal cadre of economic notables in Texas known as the "8F Crowd" and the three major law firms in the state have each conducted screening tests of potential candidates for many years.

The 8F Crowd

For more than forty years, a group of Texas economic influentials informally met in a suite of rooms numbered 8F in Houston's Lamar Hotel. The rent for the suite was paid by Brown and Root (a subsidiary of Halliburton) to the hotel on a permanent basis. The occupant of the rooms was the late George Brown, founder of Brown and Root. Over the years, Brown, who "was once widely recognized to be the most powerful man in Texas," was regularly joined in his habitat by other influential Texans. Together, they "called the shots on the most major business and political developments in Texas during the Thirties, Forties, Fifties and much of the Sixties." [4]

The list of those who met in 8F constituted a Who's Who in Texas economic development. In addition to Brown, Jesse H. Jones's name appears. Jones amassed great wealth as a builder, publisher, and banker and was instrumental in, among other things, the creation of Texas Commerce Bancshares and Tenneco. Gus Wortham was a charter member of the 8F Crowd. Wortham founded the American General Company—now the largest insurance company in the South. Judge James A. Elkins, Sr., frequented 8F. Elkins formed one of Texas's leading law firms, Vinson, Elkins, Searls, Connally, and Smith, as well as what came to be the First City Bancorporation, formerly headed by his son James, Jr. Over the years, the 8F Crowd groomed a distinguished stable of political warhorses, including Lyndon B. Johnson, John Connally, and Sam Rayburn (former speaker of both the Texas and the U.S. House of Representatives).

The importance of the 8F Crowd had reached its peak by the 1970s. With the death of George Brown in 1983, most of the founding members are now deceased. Even though the group has recruited new members in the last few years (such as Walter Mischer, chairman of Allied Bancshares in Houston) and has dabbled in screening candidates as recently as the 1978 state races, its influence has waned. The growth of Texas alone has hindered the ability of such a small group to effectively control candidate selection. Giant corporations have turned to other, more formal, institutions to recruit suitable candidates. The state's leading law firms serve this purpose well.

Law Firms

Houston is the home of the three largest law firms in the state: Vinson, Elkins, Searls, Connally, and Smith; Fulbright and Jaworski; and Baker and Botts. In terms of staff size these three rank among the top ten law firms in the U.S. More important than size, these firms have acquired as their clients many of the major companies of Texas. Anderson Clayton, Mobil Oil, and Coastal States turn to Fulbright and Jaworski for general counsel. Included among the clients of Vinson, Elkins, Searls, Connally, and Smith are First City Bancorporation, American General Insurance, Texas Eastern, and Halliburton. Baker and Botts represents the interests of Houston Lighting and Power, Zapata, Entex, Pennzoil, Mesa Petroleum, and Tenneco, among others. In 1980, Baker and Botts collected almost $3 million from the nine corporations on whose board of directors one of its lawyers sat.[5]

These law firms link the interests of their clients to the fortunes of those seeking political office in Texas. One writer pictures the mediating position of the three legal entities as follows: "To the outside observer the role of the big Houston firms in state politics is a masterwork of subtlety. In essence it is a screening system that approves candidates and enables them to tap the great resources of established wealth." [6]

This screening process affects potential candidates for most elected state offices in Texas, including the positions of governor, attorney-general, state treasurer, and members of the Texas Supreme Court and the Railroad Commission. A former state legislator says of the process:

> All the state officials go down and see them [the big three legal firms of Houston] hat in hand. . . . You have to go through the firm before you can get to the client. . . . In the old days you went to see Judge Elkins. . . . Now it's one of the other partners, but the routine is the same. If the firm approves, you got access to the client. Unless you could get their blessings, you couldn't get the money from the client.[7]

Overall, it is estimated that these firms, acting for their corporate clients, have had a major hand in the recruitment of many eventual winners of key electoral contests in Texas: "The last Texas governor who was not the candidate of the big firms (or substantially acceptable to them) was James Allred [1935–1939]."[8]

Hence the 8F Crowd and the electoral activities of the major law firms in Houston illustrate some of the informality in screening candidates—a process that occurs long before Texans have an opportunity to choose at the polls. These examples also show the primary role of corporate interests in the selection of candidates for state office. More of this type of recruiting probably happens throughout Texas in meetings and discussions (in both group and personal settings) than is generally known to the public; other examples in the local electoral context will be presented in chapter 16. Failure to be invited to the screening test, or to pass it, places potential candidates at a severe disadvantage in seeking political office against those who are supported.

CAMPAIGN CONTRIBUTIONS

The major reward awaiting a person who is validated through the screening procedures is money and the campaign amenities that it purchases. Money in Texas electoral politics has become a precious commodity. To run a viable statewide campaign is a costly proposition. The leading contenders in the 1986 race for governor spent around $20 million; in 1982, the campaign for the governor cost about $25 million.[9] The drop-off in cost may reflect the condition of the state's economy. With the recession in full swing there simply was not as much money available for campaign contributions in 1986 as there had been four years earlier. Houston oilman Robert Mosbacher, who unsuccessfully sought the Republican nomination in the 1984 U.S. Senate contest, noted in 1986:

> It has never been tougher to raise political money. The oil industry, particularly the independents, has represented a disproportionate share of high dollar contributors, especially for Republicans. They continue to be players but not in amounts they used to because they have less disposable income to invest in politics.[10]

A large endowment does not guarantee victory, as incumbents in the last two campaigns for the governorship have discovered. In his 1982 loss, Governor Bill

Courtesy of Ben Sargent, *The Austin American—Statesman*.   Reprinted by permission.

Clements had expenses in excess of $13 million; likewise, Mark White was defeated in his attempt to retain the governor's post in 1986 after spending nearly $10 million. Nonetheless, without a great deal of money, the chances of running a competitive race are nil.

Where Does the Money Go?

The high cost of Texas campaigns is a result of trying to reach all of this geographically vast state in the most expeditious manner possible. In statewide races, and also in many local campaigns, the quickest route to the electorate is through the media. As noted by three political scientists: "In a state as populous and large as Texas, and with the bulk of residents (over 80 percent) residing in well-scattered, highly urbanized centers, serious candidates for statewide office find it necessary to raise and spend large sums of money for advertising in the ten major media markets of the state." [11]

Media costs, especially for television, are very high. Money must be allocated for hiring advertising firms and for the production of messages, as well as for distribution of the campaign pitch over the airways. Production costs for a thirty-second television spot alone cost around $5,000. To air a one-minute message over television in the most populated markets, for instance in Dallas/Fort Worth or

Houston, runs about $6,000. Placing a campaign advertisement in a large-city newspaper costs around $4,000 for a full page. All told, media expenses account for most of the money exhausted in campaigns.

Who Pays the Bills?

Accurate answers to this question are made difficult because of incomplete information about who gives what to whom in campaigns. Public records of campaign contributions are not always required. Even when contribution records are mandated, there are many ways to avoid disclosing the names of actual donors. Money can be contributed in other people's names, or under an organizational title, or through mediating institutions. Sometimes contribution money remains hidden from public view by design. Nobody is sure how often this happens or what sums are involved. Enforcement of laws requiring disclosure of contributions is difficult to accomplish and is frequently lax when requested.

The Texas Election Code, as amended, has established a number of guidelines for campaign donations since 1973. The highlights of the contribution regulations include the following:

1. All candidates on the ballot must file reports on campaign contributions to the secretary of state's office. No donations may be accepted until the name of a campaign treasurer has been registered with the secretary by the candidate. All contributions and expenditures over $50 each must be disclosed, as well as the name and address of donors and recipients of these funds.
2. Any group or organization contributing more than $100 to a candidate or political party must report this to the secretary of state. Corporations and labor unions are prohibited from giving money directly out of their funds to candidates. However, they are not barred from creating committees, commonly referred to as political action committees (PACs), to collect and distribute funds. All donations to these committees are to be voluntary. PACs may also register voters and help mobilize the vote on election day. A PAC must be composed of at least ten people before it can be registered. After registration it must wait sixty days before contributions can be solicited for and distributed to candidates.
3. All reports, whether by candidates or donors, are to be filed either on a monthly or an annual basis with the secretary of state. They must be recorded no later than thirty days before and again thirty days after an election—primary or general. These files are to be open to public scrutiny.
4. Violation of these regulations may result in civil or criminal penalties. For instance, if a candidate receives money illegally, he or she may be compelled to pay any opponent twice the amount involved; three times the sum is also to be paid the state of Texas. Complaints of violations are to be made to the secretary of state. The Texas Election Code places no restriction on the amount that a candidate may spend. Nor is the contribution by any person or group limited in Texas. Finally, there is no provision for public funding of state elections.

The Corporate Connection

Campaign contribution reports reveal an extensive flow of money from the corporate sector of Texas. Banks, corporate political action committees, and company executives or stockholders are vital sources of donations.

Banks are important to candidates who must borrow money to finance their campaigns. Bank loans played a major role in the 1978 Texas governor's race. In the primaries of that year, incumbent Dolph Briscoe and challenger Bill Clements each had nearly $900,000 of credit extended by various state banks.[12] About 90 percent of this money came from banks that were members of the largest bank holding companies in Texas. Playing no favorites, one large bancorporation (Republic of Texas) lent $300,000 to each candidate.

The 1982 statewide electoral contests saw less reliance on bank loans by candidates than was the case in the prior race.[13] Mark White, elected governor in 1982, secured a $50,000 loan from the American Bank of Austin. Ann Richards, in her successful race to become state treasurer, received a $130,000 credit from the Austin National Bank. Each of these financial institutions is affiliated with large bank holding companies. Many candidates in 1982 borrowed heavily from friends. White's campaign contribution files note personal loans of around $200,000 and a loan of $500,000 from sources unknown. Ann Richards borrowed around $100,000 from other people. South Texas rancher and entrepreneur Clinton Manges guaranteed a $95,000 loan for state comptroller Bob Bullock. Attorney-General Jim Mattox reported a $125,000 personal loan.[14]

Loans again were a major source of campaign funds, especially for challengers, in the 1986 state elections. Bill Clements, who struggled to raise money in his quest to win the Republican primary, had to depend on loans to get his campaign started—over one-third of the $2.9 million spent by Clements in his primary victory. Almost all of this credit was extended by InterFirst—the state's leading bank holding company.[15] Clements served on InterFirst's board of directors; moreover, InterFirst's chairman, Robert H. Stewart III, was Clements's chief fundraiser. Kent Hance, in his unsuccessful bid to become the Republican gubernatorial candidate, raised nearly two-thirds of his money by borrowing from twenty Texas businessmen; one of Hance's foremost creditors was H.R. "Bum" Bright, owner of Bright Banc savings and loan and the Dallas Cowboys.[16]

The number of political action committees registered in Texas has increased steadily in recent years. In 1982, 950 PACs existed in the state.[17] Three years later, 1,287 PACs were counted.[18] As campaigning began for the primaries of 1986, 1,760 political action committees were on the electoral scene in Texas.[19] The largest proportion of PACs are ad hoc organizations composed of friends or supporters of a particular candidate. Many of the most important sources of campaign contributions, however, are PACs established by companies, banks, law firms, and, especially, professional people—such as doctors, teachers, and realtors. For instance, the leading political action committees in the 1982 state elections were the Texas Medical Association's PAC (TEXPAC) and the Texas Real Estate Political Action Committee (TREPAC), the fund-raising arm of the 35,000–member Texas Association of Realtors (TAR). Each of these groups distributed over $800,000 to candidates. Again in 1986, the Texas Medical Association was a major source of funds: during the primary season of that year TEXPAC gave $650,000 to various candidates. Trial lawyers raised $354,000 in the 1986 primaries. Dentists donated $374,000.[20] The Texas State Teachers Association collected over $250,000 for campaign purposes from its 97,000 members.[21]

The importance of special interest PACs to the financing of elections in Texas varies according to electoral contest. They assume a high profile, for instance, in races for legislative office. Common Cause of Texas contends that legislators are becoming increasingly dependent on PAC money to underwrite their campaigns. In 1985, for example, Texas's thirty-one senators received $1.1 million from special interest PACs. Almost half of the funds raised by senators in that year came from these groups; comparatively, in 1983 less than one-third of each dollar they received was PAC money.[22] Around 37 percent of the money raised by Senate leader Bill Hobby in his buildup for the 1986 lieutenant-governor's race came from special interest groups. The Texas Medical Association's TEXPAC alone provided Hobby with $30,000 by early 1986.[23]

Correspondingly, between 1983 and 1985 there was a 64 percent increase in PAC donations to members of the Texas House of Representatives. Half of the $1.8 million contributed to House members in 1985 stemmed from the beneficence of special interest PACs; in 1983, only 26 percent of legislative contributions represented PAC money.[24] Well over 80 percent of the estimated $418,238 contributed to House Speaker Gib Lewis in his 1986 primary reelection bid came from the coffers of special interest groups, mostly from PACs representing utilities, banks, builders, developers, insurance companies, and transportation concerns.[25] According to John Hildreth (director of Texas Common Cause):

> When PACs dominate the financing of political campaigns, our concept of representative government is mortgaged to the highest bidder. When the public believes that legislative decisions are no longer made in the public interest because of the competing interests of PAC contributions, our government loses its most important asset: public confidence.[26]

Similarly, the three contested 1986 races for seats on the bench of the Texas Supreme Court attracted a great deal of special interest money. Altogether, around $2 million was raised in the primaries for these posts.[27] Over 25 percent of this money came from groups composed of lawyers.[28] Indeed most of the contributions from the legal fraternity were provided by law firms with cases pending before the Supreme Court.[29] Oscar Mauzy, for example, received over $1 million in contributions by the time he was elected Supreme Court judge in the 1986 general election.[30] Most of Mauzy's funds were supplied by lawyers, in particular groups representing trial lawyers.[31] Trial lawyers have much to gain financially from a court that makes it easier to successfully sue businesses for negligence and damages. Conversely, in another contest for a place on the Supreme Court incumbent Raul Gonzalez was given $900,000.[32] A large portion of Gonzalez's funds came from corporations, physicians, and defense lawyers trying to stem the tide toward awarding substantial monetary awards to persons who bring suit against businesses.[33] As noted by Common Cause's John Hildreth, "the public certainly can't have much confidence that a judicial system is going to be objective and fair when you have all the financial support for the candidates coming from [plaintiffs'] trial lawyers for one group of candidates, and the defense bar and corporations and insurance companies and doctors financing the other side."[34]

Some administrative officials have also financially benefitted from groups affected by their offices. Candidates for the Texas Railroad Commission with the greatest prospect for success, for instance, are ones who as a rule receive large donations from petroleum and trucking interests—interests that are regulated by the commission.[35] Attorney-General Jim Mattox secured a great deal of his campaign funding from special interests; around 22 percent of Mattox's primary finances came from the Teamsters Union, law firms, utilities, banking groups, developers, and beer and liquor concerns.[36] Interestingly, even though Mattox had been engaged in a bitter court battle with Fulbright and Jaworski, this leading law firm still bestowed a $10,000 donation on the behalf of his campaign.[37]

Contributions from political action committees have not been overly important in the financing of the governor's race in Texas. In the 1986 primaries for the gubernatorial election, Republican challengers Kent Hance and Tom Loeffler received donations of 13 percent and 4 percent, respectively, from special interest PACs. Bill Clements' primary bid drew financial support from only one special interest group. Meanwhile, Democrat incumbent Mark White obtained 16 percent of his primary campaign contributions from special interest groups.[38]

The campaigns of leading candidates in the governor's race, especially incumbents, are financed mostly through contributions made by wealthy individuals and families. In 1982, for instance, both White and Clements gained most of their funds from individual contributions. White collected about $1 million from donors contributing over $5,000 each. Included in this elite group were the late George Brown (Brown and Root, Halliburton, First City Bancorporation, Texas Eastern, and the 8F Crowd), Walter Mischer (Allied Bank and 8F Crowd), James Elkins, Jr. (First City Bancorporation), B. K. Johnson (First City Bancorporation, AT & T, Tenneco, and Campbell Soups), Jess Hay (Lomas and Nettleton and Exxon), Bill Mead (Campbell-Taggart), Richard Wortham (American General Insurance Company), Dolph Briscoe (former governor and board director at Southland Finance and M Corp), W.E. Dyche (Allied Bank), grocery magnate Charles Butt, and oil independents Clayton Williams, Jack Dahlstrom, and Edwin Cox, Jr., whose father was a major Clements benefactor in 1978 and 1982. Bill Clements also received extensive personal donations. George Mitchell (Mitchell Energy), Eddie Chiles, John and Anne Armstrong (she has served on the boards of First City Bancorporation, General Motors, Halliburton, General Foods, and Boise Cascade), James Elkins, Jr. (First City), John Stemmons (Republic of Texas Bancorporation), Harlan Crow (of Tram Crow Developers and Texas Commerce Bank), and Michel Halbouty (independent oil producer) were major financial supporters of Clements.

Again in 1986 the bulk of campaign contributions for the leading gubernatorial candidates came from individuals and families. Former Governor White raised nearly 91 percent of his funds to conduct his primary victory from individuals contributing $500 or more to his campaign. Indeed, over one-third of this money came from donations in excess of $10,000 apiece.[39] Lawyers, real estate developers, oil and gas men, bankers, and people involved in transportation were White's major contributors.[40] White also secured a substantial portion of his campaign war chest from people whom he had appointed to administrative posts during his term of office. An analysis of contributions made in amounts of $500 or more to the White campaign between July 1985 and June 1986 revealed that 20 percent of the money raised from these donors came from White's appointees. In total, 348 of the 2,000 or so of his appointees contributed. The average donation made by persons selected to serve on the ten most important administrative boards in Texas was $9,477. All members of the Highway Commission contributed. Only one regent of the University of Texas system did not financially aid White's campaign. Led by Royce Wisenbaker's personal gift of $79,200, all but one (Mayor Henry Cisneros of San Antonio) of the board of regents of Texas A & M contributed to the White effort.[41]

The 1982 election presented a striking example of the importance of wealthy campaign donors. Rancher and farmer Clinton Manges alone contributed $2.5 million to various races. Commissioner of Agriculture Jim Hightower received $27,500. Bob Bullock, state comptroller, picked up $30,500. The commissioner of the General Land Office, Garry Mauro, was allocated $65,000. Attorney-General Jim Mattox secured $100,000, half of which was later returned to Manges. Over $1 million of Manges's dollars were spread among numerous candidates running in judicial contests: over $300,000 went to candidates seeking election to the Texas Supreme Court.[42] Why did Manges spend so much?

In a nutshell, Manges sought financial gain through investment in campaigns. For example, Manges believed that oil companies that held drilling leases on his 140,000–acre ranch in South Texas were not paying enough in royalties. He estimated underpayments to be costing him and the state of Texas—another recipient of royalties paid on the Manges land—millions of dollars. He spent millions on geologists, lawyers, and politicians to prove his claims and to carry forth with government action to change the status quo. The office of attorney-general and the General Land Office are important agencies in resolving royalty squabbles. Within months after the 1982 general election, Manges began to see some profit from his efforts. Exxon agreed to pay the state $4 million for its past drilling on the Manges land. Manges earned around a million from the agreement and much more in his future dealings with Exxon.

The large amount spent on judicial races was a blatant attempt by Manges to elect sympathetic judges. Manges is constantly involved in cases that reach the courts of Texas. It has been his belief that judicial favoritism can be bought through campaign donations and that, prior to his attempt to finance judicial elections, judges in Texas were financially beholden mostly to corporate benefactors.[43]

Most campaign contributions do not result in direct policy payoffs. Some donors give money in the hopes of electing officeholders who have beliefs that are in concert with their commitment to free enterprise and the importance of private property. The aim of the political action committee of the Texas Realtors Association (TAR), according to its former president, is to elect officials sympathetic to the needs of property owners:

> [TAR] could be and will be the most powerful organization there is in Texas. . . . If we do our part in building a fund for TREPAC, the politicians in Texas will look to TAR and they will become our friends very quickly, and we will be able to progress as

realtors should progress. . . . These people we want elected to run this great state of ours would protect . . . the realtor and the property owner of Texas.[44]

Other contributors hope that their donations to successful candidates will at least guarantee access to policymakers. Gene Fondren, lobbyist for the Texas Auto Dealers Association, succinctly notes that his organization "supports candidates who at least will give us an ear in terms of industry issues." [45]

Legally Questionable Campaign Contributions in Texas

In the aftermath of the break-in at Watergate in 1972, the federal government carried out a series of investigations into corporate contributions to political campaigns. These probes uncovered widespread violations of laws regulating the transfer of money from the business world into the political system. In corporate reports filed with the Securities and Exchange Commission, the Phillips Petroleum Company admitted illegal contributions to political candidates across the United States, including officeseekers for state posts in Texas. The company disclosed that it had given a relatively small sum of money, never in any case exceeding $200, to candidates for state elections held throughout the 1960s and into the 1970s.[46] During the same period of time, the Houston-based Tenneco company maintained a fund of $40,000 to be distributed annually to political candidates in Louisiana and Texas by high-level executives of the company.[47] Neither Phillips nor Tenneco revealed the names of Texans receiving these campaign contributions.

Gulf Oil admitted in another federal government inquiry that it had doled out a substantial amount of money illegally to a large number of candidates seeking office in Texas. Former Governor Preston Smith was given a total of $20,000. A lawyer for the company, Ira Butler, distributed illegal payments from Gulf to all but one of the elected officials on the Texas Railroad Commission between 1960 and 1974. The *Texas Observer* claimed that "Butler usually gave five grand to railroad commissioners".[48] Mr. Butler represented Gulf in cases pending before the commission during the period of illegal campaign contributions. In addition, Gulf money was funneled into the campaigns of an attorney-general of Texas (Crawford Martin, 1970, $2,500), persons seeking positions on the state's Supreme Court, and, overall, "several hundred candidates" running for office in the Lone Star State.[49]

State officials in Texas took virtually no action in any of these cases. State inaction is partly attributable to the Texas Election Code's statute of limitation of three years on prosecuting campaign contributions violations. Unless the offense occurs within three years of its allegation, the state cannot pursue conviction. However, it was possible to prosecute in some of these matters and the state simply chose a course of nonaction.

The legal question was again raised in the aftermath of the 1982 election. A grand jury in Travis County (Austin) undertook an investigation of the campaign finances of Attorney-General Jim Mattox. At issue was a $125,000 loan secured by Mattox during the course of his campaign. Mattox's disclosure statement was unclear about the source of the money. One possibility was that Mattox's sister supplied the funds. In turn, it was alleged that she received the money from a

Seattle bank, a bank that had financial connections with Clinton Manges, a Mattox benefactor. Within a week after Mattox noted in his disclosure report that he had repaid the loan, his sister sent a check to the Seattle bank to cover her loan, plus interest. It is illegal to fail to report accurately the source of campaign funds. Mattox claimed that the money did not come from his sister and that he had violated no laws.[50] His story was eventually supported by a Texas court.

Problems with the Texas Election Code

On the surface, Texas appears to have adequate regulations to prohibit extensive abuse in corporate financing of the state elections. However, there are two problem areas: enforcement and loopholes.

The enforcement difficulty is best illustrated by example. The court case of *Farenthold v. Briscoe* serves this purpose well. On the day that she announced her intention to unseat Governor Dolph Briscoe in the Democratic primary of 1974, Frances "Sissy" Farenthold also declared that she had filed suit against her opponent for allegedly receiving campaign contributions in violation of the Texas Election Code. She contended that Briscoe's campaign organization had committed three violations.

First, Briscoe received campaign funds for his 1974 race prior to the naming of a campaign treasurer as called for in the election code. Farenthold alleged that Briscoe supporters had plotted a two-pronged strategy to raise finances some two months before a campaign treasurer was announced. The suit argued that hundreds of thousands of dollars had been raised before a campaign treasurer was appointed. This violation could have cost the Briscoe camp double the funds raised to Farenthold and triple the sum to the state as a penalty.

Second, Farenthold contended that Briscoe had collected money allocated directly from corporate funds. Corporations cannot donate from the financial resources of the company. It was alleged that some companies had contributed money under the guise that it was collected voluntarily from employees, when, in actuality, the funds either came directly from corporate accounts, or were reimbursed to employees by the company, or were coerced from employees. Some of the evidence was as follows:

1. The OKC Company of Dallas disclosed that one hundred employees had each contributed $10,000 to Briscoe. None of the employees, however, was a resident of Texas: "Many of them claimed to have no knowledge of their contributions and no interest in Dolph Briscoe." [51] Did the contributions come from sources other than the OKC employees? Jess Hay (Lomas and Nettleton, M Corp, and Exxon), the manager of Briscoe's statewide finance committee and a party to the Farenthold suit, conceded that the chairman of OKC, Cloyce Box, "actually advanced the $10,000 to the employees as an exercise in democracy." [52] Hay also noted that 20 percent of the contributors listed showed little or no interest in reimbursing Box; apparently, the other OKC employees did pay him back.

2. Through its then vice-president, J. Fred Bucy, Texas Instruments (TI) contributed more than $10,000 to Briscoe, again in the names of company employees. Most of the contributors listed were not residents of Texas. Some asserted that they were coerced by TI into making donations, whereas others claimed that TI

reimbursed them through juggling expense accounts. A member of Jess Hay's legal defense "acknowledged that the Farenthold team had gathered some testimony indicating that systematic reimbursements took place through expense accounts." [53]

3. As the Farenthold suit progressed a few employees of Glenn Public Relations, a Dallas-based advertising firm, came forth and told her lawyers that their company had done work for the 1972 Briscoe campaign that was charged to the account of Lomas and Nettleton, which was (and still is) chaired by Jess Hay. An accountant for Glenn Public Relations subsequently assumed full responsibility for the irregular and illegal billing.[54]

The *third* charge raised in the Farenthold suit was that Briscoe had received a $15,000 contribution from rancher Clinton Manges in May of 1972 and had not reported it, as required by law. The Briscoe team countered that the money was not reported because the governor never intended to use it. Indeed, "Briscoe finally returned it to Manges in the Brownsville airport coffee shop," some nine months after the charge had been made.[55]

A month before trial, *Farenthold* v. *Briscoe* was settled out of court. Farenthold accepted $125,000 in damages, apparently out of Jess Hay's pocket. No guilt was to be inferred from the settlement and no aspects of the case were to be discussed by the litigants. Finally, the then attorney-general of the state, John Hill (formerly chief justice of the Texas Supreme Court), did not take the legal issues any further.

The handling of the Farenthold suit indicates several enforcement problems with the Texas Election Code. It is extremely difficult for private individuals, such as Farenthold, to legally pursue allegations of violations. The cost of vigorously tracking down and proving illegal payments and practices is prohibitive. According to published reports, Farenthold agreed to settle because she simply did not have enough money to continue the legal battle. The reluctance on the part of Attorney-General John Hill to move forward on the case underscores that prosecutors who themselves receive substantial and sometimes controversial campaign contributions are not the best people to have as enforcement officials. Former state legislator Ben Byrum, author of some reforms of the election code, argues:

> The trouble with the present law is that it is unenforceable. It has to be enforced by elected judges and elected D.A.s and elected Attorney-Generals. Until we have an Election Commission [composed of nonelected personnel], there will be no meaningful enforcement of the Election Code. The Farenthold suit is a perfect example of that.[56]

Beyond the enforcement problems raised by *Farenthold* v. *Briscoe,* the existing regulations on campaign finance are beset with additional difficulties. The sheer volume of material now disclosed to the secretary of state inhibits meaningful investigation into patterns of donations. Candidates, especially for the major statewide offices, report thousands of pages of detail. None of the material is readily accessible through high-speed computer processing. What the public has available to it is a mountain of information that only the most dedicated climber would attempt to scale. It costs a small amount of money to have the secretary of state's office photocopy a single page of a candidate's financial statement. In 1986,

Jim Mattox submitted each name of his backers on a separate sheet of paper, thus making it relatively expensive to secure a list of his benefactors: "At 1,101 pages, it would [have] cost an opponent or reporter $165.55 to get a copy from the secretary of state." [57]

In addition, the reports filed by donors can be tricky. Political action committees, for instance, may use any name they choose. Hence it is easy to disguise the actual affiliation of a PAC. For example, the law firm of Fulbright and Jaworski christened its PAC the Southwest Public Affairs Committee in 1982. Vinson, Elkins, Searls, Connally, and Smith's alias is the Texas Good Government Fund. Baker and Botts collects and distributes funds under the name of the Acme PAC. As noted by an employee of the Texas Business Political Action Committee, "I thought that's what PACs were for—to keep from knowing who's giving the money." [58]

Finally, several loopholes exist in the Texas Election Code's rules on contributions. For instance, many skeptical eyebrows have been raised over the methods employed by candidates to repay personal or bank loans; win or lose, many contenders find themselves facing vast postelection debts. The usual practice for winners is to hold dinners or other fund-raisers. This scheme opens the door wide for wealthy interests to gain effective access to an official without the nuisance of electoral loss. As pointed out by columnist David Broder with specific reference to Texas:

> The people or groups that give money after an election, when there is no risk, are almost always people who have a particular interest in ingratiating themselves with an officeholder. Giving a 'campaign contribution' to the winner for the last election, who instantly uses the money to repay himself [blurs] . . . the distinction between a campaign contribution and a personal payoff.[59]

Other than requiring disclosure of payment and receipt of this type of "contribution" the Texas Election Code has no special procedure covering this form of exchange.

Candidates in Texas can enter a statewide race, name a campaign manager, collect contributions, immediately withdraw from the election, and still keep the money under the Texas Election Code. Billy Clayton, former speaker of the Texas House of Representatives, did just this in the early 1980s. In so doing, his income was bolstered by about $400,000.

Along a similar line, unspent campaign contributions until 1985 could easily become the personal property of a candidate. In a way, they represented supplemental income to officeholders. Tati Santiestaban, state senator representing El Paso, used $16,000 of money originally donated to his campaign to make home-mortgage payments and to cover the costs of educating his two daughters. When asked about this practice, Santiestaban defended his action by saying: "I have a very expensive Anglo wife and I enjoy the good life. I have a nice car. I like cocktails and I like good wine and I certainly am not wealthy." [60]

Lastly, law firms distribute corporate funds to candidates without undue worry over disclosure of the source of the money. Three political scientists, one a former member of the U.S. House of Representatives, discuss this process in length:

> It is the key . . . whereby money is channeled, normally anonymously because of the hallowed lawyer-client relationship, to those seeking or holding public office. The fee or retainer for 'services rendered' is simply increased by an amount earmarked previ-

ously for a particular candidate, party, or fund-raising committee. Some individual member of the firm, frequently a new and relatively unknown member, through his (and the firm's) 'sense of public spirit,' then makes the money available to the candidate by a direct contribution, frequently, and certainly most preferably in the past, in cash. There are few successful politicians (or their employees) who have not endured the lunch, small talk, and obscenity of this transaction. If the state has a provision for public disclosure of campaign contributions that requires filing the name of the donor, the records probably will indicate the name of the lawyer and not of the actual source of the funds.[61]

Such practices are not precluded by the Texas Election Code. Some hint as to the source of part of the money disbursed by law firms in Texas is available from a close look at disclosure statements. The legal firm of Bracewell and Patterson, for instance, spent about $47,000 in the 1982 state elections, a substantial portion of which was collected from the Political Action Committee of Texas. The contributing members of the Political Action Committee of Texas were Robert Stewart III (InterFirst and Atlantic Richfield), Richard O'Shields (Panhandle Eastern and First City Bancorporation), Walter Mischer (Allied Bancshares), Alfred Glassell, Jr. (First City Bancorporation and formerly of the El Paso Company), Jackson Hinds (Entex), John Harbin (Halliburton), Babe Fuqua (First United Bancorporation of Fort Worth), Robert Folsom (ENSERCH and M Corp), and the late George Brown (Brown and Root, Halliburton, Texas Eastern, ITT, First City Bancorporation, and the 8F Crowd).

CONCLUSION

The thrust of this chapter has been that economic elites influence elections in Texas through screening candidates and providing the chosen few with monetary resources. The high economic standing of some Texans allows them a tremendous role in the selection of political officials. These few not only transfer capital necessary for a viable campaign, they also can swing other resources such as their media contacts, employees, social comrades, and voluntary associations behind the favored ones. Considering the fact that the active electorate in the state is mostly drawn from the middle to upper classes, it is likely that voters in Texas follow cues from the economic elite, either consciously or not, almost naturally. Such behavior has a significant impact on politics in Texas, and four of these patterns stand out.

1. *The vast majority of candidates with a good chance of electoral victory are closely tied to the stalwarts of the economic community.* Most choices presented to the public are those already acceptable to the state's dominant economic interests, regardless of which candidate ultimately wins.

2. *The importance of money in influencing electoral outcomes undermines the democratic principle that votes, equally weighted, should be the main factor in choosing officials.* Those who command economic resources have an untold advantage in the electoral process. The point is made well in the following passage penned by three political scientists:

Although all votes are presumed to be equal, the expenditures of vast sums of money in political campaigns is purposely designed . . . to provide large contributors . . . more influence than the average voter. . . . The rich and the poor might be theoretically equal at the ballot box; but, in any ultimate controversy, the rich will win and the poor will lose.[62]

3. *The major role played by economic interests in campaigns weakens political parties.* When money was not the prime mover in campaigning, candidates relied more on parties to mobilize voters. Party loyalists solicited votes through personally contacting members of the electorate. Now, in most elections, it is more effective to communicate with voters through the media. This is an expensive process. Party organizations are usually short on cash, thus candidates turn to peripheral sources for necessary funds. To the extent that well-functioning party structures rest upon citizens drawn from a near cross-section of the public, avoidance of, or less dependence on, party organizations distances both the candidate from the public and the electoral system further from democracy.

4. *Once in office, candidates assisted by economic elites are highly accessible to backers.* At the very minimum, candidate recruitment and campaign contributions mean that most elected officials have social and psychological traits closely akin to their economic benefactors. Such similarity assures a common approach to political decision making and reduces the necessity of economic elites exerting much energy to pressure officials once in office. Nevertheless, economic notables do communicate directly with elected and appointed political leaders to insure that the everyday business of government works to their benefit.

NOTES

1. See David F. Prindle, *Petroleum Politics and the Texas Railroad Commission* (Austin: University of Texas Press, 1981), pp. 170–204.

2. Michael Parenti, *Democracy for the Few,* 2d ed. (New York: St. Martin's Press, 1977), p. 203.

3. Ibid.

4. Harry Hurt III, "The Most Powerful Texans," *Texas Monthly* 4 (April 1976): 73. Emphasis in the original.

5. *Texas Observer,* October 1, 1982, p. 16.

6. Griffin Smith, Jr. "Empires of Paper," reprinted in *Texas Monthly's Political Reader* (Austin: Texas Monthly Press and Sterling Swift Co., 1978), p. 34.

7. Quoted in ibid.

8. Ibid.

9. Figures presented in *The Texas Observer,* December 19, 1986, p. 7.

10. Quoted in Virginia Ellis and Arnold Hamilton, "Economy Squeezes Election Fund Raising," *Dallas Times-Herald,* February 16, 1986.

11. Charles W. Wiggins, Keith E. Hamm, and Howard Balanoff, "The 1982 Gubernatorial Transition in Texas: Bolt Cutters, Late Trains, Lame Ducks, and Bullock's Bullets," in *Gubernatorial Transitions: The 1982 Elections,* ed. Thad L. Beyle, (Durham: Duke University Press, 1985), p. 379.

12. "The High Cost of Campaigning," *Action,* April 18, 1978; and David Guarino, "Buying into Briscoe," *Texas Observer,* April 26, 1978, p. 6.

13. Unless otherwise indicated, all the information on campaign contributions in the 1982 statewide races in Texas comes from reports on file in the secretary of state's office, Austin, Texas.

14. The loan information on Manges and Mattox comes from Geoffrey Rips and Joe Holley, "Manges, Mattox, Mauro, Mobil, and Money," *Texas Observer,* August 19, 1983.

15. Information reconstructed from reports found in William Slater and George Kuempel, "Donors Hedge Bets with Campaign Gifts," *Dallas Morning News,* April 20, 1986; Virginia Ellis, "$1.7 Million Cash Edge Boosts White Campaign," *Dallas Times-Herald,* June 3, 1986; Virginia Ellis, "Hance Leads Foes in Funding Race," *Dallas Times-Herald,* April 3, 1986; and "White Apparently Raises $5 Million," *Houston Post,* April 4, 1986.

16. "White Apparently Raises $5 Million"; and Slater and Kuempel, "Donors Hedge Bets."

17. Interstate Bureau of Regulations, *State Political Action Legislation and Regulation: Index and Directory of Organizations* (Westport, Conn.: Quorom Books, 1984).

18. Mike Snyder, "PACs Flex Their Muscles in City and State Politics," *Houston Chronicle,* January 13, 1986.

19. Jim Warren, "PACs Throwing Their Weight Around in Austin," *Laredo Morning Times,* March 23, 1986.

20. Lee Jones, "Insurance Crisis Aids Lobbyists," *Fort Worth Star Telegram,* June 22, 1986.

21. Jorjanna Price, "Educators Learning How to Play Political Game," *Houston Post,* April 6, 1986.

22. Figures reported in George Kuempel, "PACs Hike Funding to State Senators, Citizens Group Says," *Dallas Morning News,* July 12, 1986.

23. Linda Anthony, "Hobby, Lewis Fill Political War Chests with $1.5 Million," *Austin American Statesmen,* January 17, 1986.

24. Figures reported in Edward M. Sells, "Group Cites 'PAC-ed' House," *San Antonio Light,* July 24, 1986.

25. Patti Kilday, "Lewis Re-election Fund Showing Hefty Reserve," *Dallas Times-Herald,* July 8, 1986. Also see Edward Sells, "Group Cites 'PAC-ed' House"; and Anne Marie Kilday and Pete Stover, "Officials Release Finance Reports on Campaigns," *Houston Chronicle,* January 17, 1986.

26. Quoted in Debbie Graves, "Legislators Draw Fire for Gifts from Special Interests," *Austin American Statesman,* July 24, 1986.

27. Lee Jones, "Judge Candidates Raise $2 Million," *Fort Worth Star Tribune,* May 2, 1986.

28. Lee Jones and J. Lynn Lunsford, "Attorneys Give 25 Percent of Money in Judicial Races," *Fort Worth Star Telegram,* April 27, 1986.

29. Ibid.

30. Amy Johnson, "Court Reform?" *Texas Observer,* February 7, 1986, p. 8.

31. Wayne Slater and George Kuempel, "Lawyers Donating Big Sums," *Dallas Morning News,* April 25, 1986.

32. Amy Johnson, "Court Reform?"

33. Slater and Kuempel, "Lawyers Donating Big Sums."

34. Ibid.

35. David Prindle, *Petroleum Politics and the Texas Railroad Commission,* p. 170.

36. Wayne Slater and George Kuempel, "Mattox Leads in Funding," *Dallas Morning News,* April 26, 1986.

37. Ibid.

38. Slater and Kuempel, "Donors Hedge Bets."

39. Wayne Slater and George Kuempel, "White's '86 Run Fueled by Large Contributions," *Dallas Morning News,* March 23, 1986.

40. Slater and Kuempel, "Donors Hedge Bets."

41. Figures compiled by Wayne Slater and George Kuempel, "Key State Appointees Big Donors to White," *Dallas Morning News,* August 10, 1986. Also see Wiggins, Hamm, and Balanoff, "The 1982 Gubernatorial Transition in Texas," p. 401.

42. The figures for Manges's contributions to the 1982 races come from the secretary of state's office.

43. For an extensive look at Manges's contributions to the 1982 races see Rips and Holley, "Manges, Mattox, Mauro, Mobil, and Money"; and Paul Burka, "The Man in the Black Hat, Part II," *Texas Monthly,* July 1984, pp. 122–25, 175–87.

44. Quoted in Rod Davis, "The Sessions's Worst Lobby," *Texas Observer,* June 17, 1977, p. 22.

45. Quoted in Slater and Kuempel, "White's '86 Run Fueled by Large Contributions."

46. The Phillips case is discussed in Robert Engler, *The Brotherhood of Oil: Energy Policy and the Public Interest* (Chicago: University of Chicago Press, 1977), p. 71.

47. The information about Tenneco is reviewed in the *Texas Observer,* February 27, 1976, p. 8; and in Saralee Tiede, "Texas' Corporate Santas," *Texas Observer,* October 21, 1977, p. 3.

48. Molly Ivins, "Gulf's Slush Fund," *Texas Observer,* January 11, 1976, p. 5.

49. Ibid. The quote is from the *Texas Observer,* February 27, 1976, p. 8.

50. See Rips and Holley, "Manges, Mattox, Mauro, Mobil, and Money."

51. Harry Hurt III, "Under the Rug," *Texas Monthly* 3 (May 1975): 102.

52. Kaye Northcott, "Anatomy of a Settlement," *Texas Observer,* August 22, 1975, p. 7.

53. Hurt, "Under the Rug," p. 103.

54. Kaye Northcott, "The Glenn Connection," *Texas Observer,* August 22, 1975, pp. 3–5.

55. Northcott, "Anatomy of a Settlement," p. 7.

56. Quoted in Hurt, "Under the Rug," p. 104.

57. Lee Jones and R.G. Ratcliffe, "Politicians Raise $5 Million to Pay Bills," *Fort Worth Star Telegram,* January 17, 1986.

58. Quoted in Slater and Kuempel, "White's '86 Run."

59. David Broder, "Congress Should Address Campaign Funding," *El Paso Times,* November 20, 1978, p. 6–A.

60. Quoted in Anthony Champagne and Rick Collis, "Texas," in *The Political Life of the American States,* ed. Alan Rosenthal and Maureen Moakley (New York: Praeger, 1984), pp. 140–41.

61. Larry Berg, Harlan Hahn, and John R. Schmidhauser, *Corruption in the American Political System* (Morristown, N.J.: General Learning Press, 1976), p. 118.

62. Ibid., pp. 54–55.

6

Access to Political Decision Makers: Lobbying in Texas

Once in office, political officials are constantly subjected to attempts at persuasion. Groups and persons expend much time and, if they have it, money to pressure decision makers. The process of applying pressure to policymakers is commonly called lobbying. Lobbying occurs both in the informal milieu of a social gathering or a personal conversation and in the formal setting of a legislative committee hearing, administrative session, or judicial trial. Lobbying can be quite instrumental in fashioning a democratic political system if two conditions are met: first, the interests of most people must be communicated through the lobbying process to political leaders; and second, policy formulated by decision makers must reflect the views of a majority of citizens, or at least a widely based coalition of minorities.   ★

LOBBYING IN TEXAS

This chapter illuminates the lobbying techniques employed in the Texas political system. Before proceeding further, it should be said that most Texans are not effective in pressuring state decision makers. Observers of Texas politics do rank the lobbying efforts of the business community quite high, however: "Business groups and associations . . . tend to dominate the lobbying scene and command unmatched influence in the policy-making process." [1] The national director of the Baptist church's joint committee on public affairs bluntly told the Texas Conference of Churches in 1981: "Texas legislatures have been held hostage by the corporate lobby for decades." [2]

There are four types of major organized economic interest groups actively engaged in lobbying in Texas.

1. Some of the formal groups represent the overall interest of the entire corporate community in the state: the Texas Association of Business and the Texas Research League are examples.

2. Other organizations represent entire industries or professions: chemical, oil, and natural gas corporations, for instance, have industry-wide interest groups; medical doctors, trial lawyers, teachers, and bankers also have professional associations active in lobbying.

3. Additional interest groups bring together distinct economic sectors that share a common concern over a public policy matter in Texas. The Texas Good Roads Association, for example, is composed of oil, automobile, insurance, and construction representatives (among others), all of whom have a vested interest in a strong government commitment to highways as a major means of transportation in the Lone Star State.

4. Finally, a specific business firm might establish its own formal organization to lobby for the interests of the company.

Of course, it is very likely that a giant economic entity will be represented in or by more than one formal interest group. For example, Exxon, U.S.A., has a hand in several organized interest groups that lobby the Texas state government. Exxon maintains a fully staffed office in Austin to oversee the state's political process from the company's perspective. It also participates in organizations founded for the purpose of influencing policy in a specific area, such as the Texas Association of Taxpayers, a group that links many of Texas's largest property holders to governing authorities. The company has also been instrumental in the founding and continual success of the Texas Research League, an organization to be discussed more extensively later in this chapter. Finally, Exxon is the major force in industry-wide petroleum associations. For instance, Humble (now Exxon) traditionally has been the "dominant factor in the Texas Mid-Continent Oil and Gas Association," [3] a group with three thousand members dedicated to the protection and expansion of the interests of oil producers in Texas. With such an elaborate network of lobbying within its corporate empire, it is no wonder that "Exxon is [considered] most active in the politics and economy of the state." [4]

The core of the effectiveness of economic lobbying groups lies in their organization. These groups are permanent structures that are a part of the everyday business of the members or clients of the group. They are not temporary groups that disband after an issue is aired. In addition, they have a clear purpose. Primarily, they pursue the economic interests of their members through political action. Finally, these groups have paid, full-time personnel who work diligently to carry out the goals and strategies of the group.

With permanence, purpose, and personnel, the dominant economic interest groups perform two functions crucial to being effective in the lobbying process. First, much effort is devoted to the internal task of politically activating their members (doctors, lawyers, corporate employees, etc.). Second, the external function of linking the preferences of the interest group to the political system is rigorously effectuated.

Internal Function of Interest Groups

In order to be politically influential, an interest group must be aware of all political matters affecting its members. It must further be able to achieve a modicum of cohesiveness among all the constituent parts of the group; an internally divided group is easily dismissed or neutralized by political officials. Finally, it must be able to politically mobilize members or clients virtually on call. This usually involves requesting members to write letters to political officials and having them attend or testify at governmental hearings.

The government affairs division of the Houston-based Tenneco company is a good example of a corporation able to rally its forces to lobby effectively in Texas. The government affairs section solicits other departments of the company for advice on which political matters are to be monitored and addressed. It keeps the company fully informed of the status of pending political matters and analyzes the positions of government officials who might affect the corporation. The interoffice memorandum issued by the government affairs division to other sections of Tenneco captures the flavor of the internal operations of an effective interest group.

External Functions of Interest Groups

Dominant economic interest groups carry their messages to the political system by utilizing a variety of techniques. Three of the most effective tactics used by lobbyists are the following: keeping in contact with the target political officials, supplying decision makers with research on which public policy might be based, and persuading the public to support the interest group's political desires.

Keeping Contact With Political Officials. One key to effective lobbying is maintaining continuous personal contact with political decision makers. People are hired by interest groups to cultivate close connections with government officials and to be in near proximity to the ongoing business of the political system. The work of these paid professional lobbyists is most evident at the legislative level of government.

The opening of legislative sessions is usually marked by scores of lobbyists flocking to state capitols across the United States. Texas requires that persons who attempt to influence legislation must register as lobbyists if they are employed by others to persuade legislators (and administrators) and spend over $200 during any three-month period in their efforts to win the votes of lawmakers. In 1983, 1,975 persons were registered as lobbyists in Austin. An overwhelming number of these registrants represented big business or major economic interests; in 1979, for instance, 80 percent of legislative lobbyists had ties with businesses.[5] In 1986, almost all of the state's major banks, agribusinesses, utilities, insurance firms, and oil, natural gas, and chemical companies had lobbyists working the Texas legislature.

Texas legislators think that business lobbyists carry considerable weight in the state's legislative process. Nearly two-thirds of those interest groups that lawmakers rated as being powerful influences in the Texas legislature represented big business.[6] Big business lobbyists are perceived to be important in the legislatures of other states as well, but not to the degree apparent in Texas.[7]

The lobbyists employed by dominant economic interests are people who can command the attention of lawmakers. Former legislators are well qualified for this position. Ex-legislators are familiar with the ins and outs of the formal and informal procedures of the legislative process and know most current members of

INTER-OFFICE COMMUNICATION
TENNECO INC.

DATE JANUARY 31, 1973

TO:

FOR: **MR.**   AUSTIN OFFICE

FROM: **MR.**   STONE WELLS, GOVERNMENTAL AFFAIRS

RE: DISTRIBUTION OF TEXAS LEGISLATIVE BILLS

The 63rd Legislature of the State of Texas convened on Tuesday, January 9, 1973, and is required, by law, to adjourn in 140 calendar days. The House of Representatives has 150 members (24 from Harris County) and 21 Standing Committees with subcommittees. The Senate has 31 members (6 from Harris County) and 9 Standing Committees with subcommittees. Generally speaking, this session the make-up of the House is considerably more liberal and the Senate more conservative. A roster is enclosed for your information and convenience.

This is going to be a busy and important session of the Legislature and much of the legislation will have a direct affect on Tenneco. In order to better serve your department and the interests of our company, please give prompt attention to any bills referred to you. In the last regular session, 2,932 bills were introduced, so you see it is impossible to keep up with all of them without your help.

The Governmental Affairs Department subscribes to the Texas Legislative Service, and through this service we receive copies of all House and Senate Bills, Resolutions and Journals which contain all daily proceedings. We also receive House and Senate Daily reports listing all action taken by that chamber, such as: author of bill introduced, caption of contents and committee to which it was referred; Favorable or Unfavorable Committee reports; Passed, Failed; Postponed; Sent to the Governor for Signature.

We receive two copies of all bills introduced. One copy is filed numerically and permanently retained in our department. The second copy is routed to the department which is directly affected. If you have any interest in the bill whatsoever, detach the routing slip, fill in the Bill No. and Comments, and return to Room 845. Retain the copy of the bill for your files. Subsequent amendments to that bill will be sent to you automatically as they are introduced.

As you know, we maintain an office in Austin and I spend most of my time there during the session. All requests for status of bills and pertinent data are referred by Governmental Affairs to me in Austin. Please look over the attached "Company Distribution of Legislative Bills" and advise if the coverage we are giving you is satisfactory.

This session looks like it is going to move fast so time will be of the essence.

SW:ebt
Enclosures 2

this political institution. Table 6–1 contains the names of business lobbyists with prior legislative experience in Austin.

In addition to their familiarity with the legislature and its personnel, lobbyists for big business channel contributions (as discussed in the last chapter) to favored legislators. Legislators contend that big business has political clout in Austin because it plays such a crucial role in financing campaigns. In the words of one

TABLE 6–1 Some Former Legislators Serving Economic Interests as Lobbyists in Texas During the 1970s and 1980s

Legislator Turned Lobbyist	Economic Interest Represented
Bill Albington	Texas Mid-Continent Oil and Gas Assoc.
Don Adams	Texas Association of Business, Monsanto, Mobil, Valero, banking interests
Searcy Bracewell	Oil, natural gas, utilities
Buck Buchanan	Beer
Frank Calhoun	Texas Commerce Bank, Burlington Northern, Pan Am, banking interests
Walter Caven	Railroads, insurance
Billy Clayton *	Texas Utilities, telephone interests, education, agribusiness
Dean Cobb	Oil and natural gas, Entex, Temple Eastex
Richard Cory	Beer, Central and South West Co.
George Cowden	Insurance
Richard Craig	Cable T.V., drug stores, insurance
Gene Fondren	Auto dealers
Jeb Fuller	Beer
Claude Gilmer *	Southwestern Bell
Dewitt Hale	Texas Association of Builders, Association of American Publishers, education
Robert Hughes	Auto dealers, Tenneco
Jim Kaster	Texas Utilities, Southwestern Bell, health care, agribusiness, education
James Presnal	Associated Credit Bureau, State Farm Insurance
Rayford Price *	Agribusinesses, Texas Utilities, Southwestern Bell, Six Flags
Ace Pickens	Texas Medical Association
Johnnie B. Rogers	Insurance, oil marketers, retail grocers
Gerhardt Schulle	Texas Association of Realtors, Society of Professional Engineers
Reuben Senterfitt *	Texas Utilities
Jim Slider	Lone Star Steel, beverage distributors
Wade Spilman	Exxon, Houston Natural Gas, beer, insurance, stock and bond dealers
A.R. Schwartz	MCI Telecommunications, Mitchell Energy, Searle Optical
Terry Townsend	Trucking
Byron Tunnell *	Tenneco
Ralph Wayne	Oil and natural gas
Jack Welsh	Texas Retail Federation
James B. Wood	Texas Association of Taxpayers

* Former Speaker of the Texas House of Representatives

SOURCES: Richard West, "Inside the Lobby," in *Texas Monthly's Political Reader* (Austin: Texas Monthly Press and Sterling Swift Publishing, 1978), pp. 112–19; Jim Hightower, "The Pecans Belong to the People," *Texas Observer*, February 2, 1979, p. 8; and 1983 and 1986 list of registered lobbyists, Secretary of State Office, Austin.

representative: "The need for funds at elections leads to influence from wealthy groups."[8]

Observers of the Texas legislature are divided over the propriety of the tactics used by lobbyists to apply pressure to legislators. One school of thought portrays the typical lobbyist as a conscientious, public-spirited citizen who approaches the legislators in an aboveboard, low-keyed, businesslike manner.[9] According to this view, the effective lobbyist is one who provides legislators with correct answers to political questions. State legislators, including those representing Texas, say that the most successful lobbyists are those who perform this information service.[10]

Another group of observers paints a picture of the Texas lobbying process that contains much darker colors. This camp contends that money—and the things that it can buy—flows without much legal or ethical restraint between some business lobbyists and a few state legislators. According to this perspective, votes in the legislature are for sale, with legislative victories generally going to the highest bidder.[11] The following pieces of evidence lend some plausibility to this unfavorable view.

A Texas senator once remarked that one of his colleagues openly hailed the opportunity to vote on a bill as "the best day in the world . . . [because] you get paid $1,000 to vote the way you're already committed to vote anyway."[12] Personal gifts from lobbyists to legislators are also cited as important links in the chain of business influence. A lobbyist for Gulf Oil admitted that he curried favor with Texas lawmakers by supplying the staff of legislators with small gifts (coffee pots, office equipment, clocks, and so forth).[13] Free meals, drinks, and companionship have been provided to legislators by kindly lobbyists. During the 1971 legislative session, members could eat a daily lunch at the expense of Texas Trial Lawyers Association, change their diet on Wednesday by attending a fish fry sponsored by the Texas Brewers Association, and dine out every night courtesy of the Texas Restaurant Association; on each of these occasions, the liquor flowed freely. One representative had this to say about the many invitations tendered to him during the session.

> I couldn't believe it. I marked them all down on my calendar and discovered that if I wanted to, and could somehow find the energy, I could attend one dinner and two receptions a night. I tried for a week and on Saturday I collapsed. I don't know if I was exhausted or bored to death.[14]

After the 1981 session of the Texas legislature, lobbyists reported expenses of $1 million, 92 percent of which went to entertaining legislators.[15] Finally, lobbyists offer some legislators economic opportunities in the form of investment tips, loans, and partnerships in surefire business deals.

The seamy side of lobbying in the Texas legislature became publicly visible with the revelations uncovered in the Sharpstown Bank scandal. In 1969, Houston banker-financier Frank Sharp sought legislation in Texas to establish a private program to insure Texas bank deposits. Sharp apparently believed that a private state-backed insurance scheme would free him from enrolling in the deposit insurance program offered by the federal government. A new method of insuring

Courtesy of Ben Sargent, *The Austin American-Statesman.* Reprinted by permission.

deposits would also deter the federal government from inspecting the operations of Sharp's financial empire.

In an apparent attempt to smooth passage of the private insurance bill, Sharp offered key state officials an opportunity to invest in a business deal. Included among the politicians were the then speaker of the Texas House of Representatives (Gus Mutscher), his chief legislative aide (Russ McGinty), his major legislative ally (Representative Tommy Shannon), the chairman of the Texas House Appropriations Committee (Bill Heatly), the governor of Texas (Preston Smith), and a member of the State Banking Board (Elmer Baum).[16] Political officials were encouraged by Sharp to purchase stock in a life insurance company with money loaned—collateral free—from his Sharpstown Bank. Within a short period of time, the state officials sold their stock, reaping handsome profits in the process. The governor pocketed more than $60,000, while the speaker garnered some $75,000.[17]

Sharp's insurance bill was quietly and quickly whisked through the legislature during a special session called by Governor Smith in the summer of 1969. After the intervention of other bankers, however, Governor Smith refused to sign the bill and thus prevented it from becoming law.

A federal government investigation of Sharp's business practices uncovered that the passage of the bank insurance bill was most likely a direct result of the money made by key legislators in Sharp's stock investment schemes. An Austin grand jury decided that this arrangement constituted accepting a bribe, and indicted four persons (Speaker Mutscher, his legislative aide, Representative Shannon, and former member of the State Insurance Board, John Osorio). Other state officials, for instance Governor Smith, were not indicted because there was no conclusive evidence that they had helped the bill get through the legislature in exchange for profits. The four charged with accepting bribes were later found guilty. For their crime, they were placed on probation. Gus Mutscher is now county judge of Washington County.

Skeptics contend that the Sharpstown scandal revealed only a small tip of a very deep and murky iceberg of political corruption in Texas. Defenders of the integrity of the state's politics counter that the scandal was an exception to the usual practices of lobbying and, moreover, that the Sharpstown experience would put an end to the use of unsavory and illegal tactics to pressure political officials in Texas.

A cloud reappeared over the legislature, however, in 1980 when it was revealed that the then speaker of the House, Bill Clayton, allegedly received $5,000

Courtesy of Ben Sargent, *The Austin American-Statesman.* Reprinted by permission.

as partial payment of an estimated $600,000 in the form of a bribe. In a plan masterminded by the FBI, Clayton was indicted by a Houston grand jury for taking the money in exchange for using his influence over legislation that would supposedly have benefited the Prudential Insurance Company. Clayton claimed that he never intended to keep the money even though it sat in his office for three months before news of the budding scandal surfaced. Subsequently, a Houston jury exonerated Clayton of any crime, even though some rather incriminating conversations between Clayton and his "benefactors" were taped by the FBI and entered as evidence. Billy Clayton now is a major lobbyist representing several important business interests in the Texas legislative process.

Banks and the Policy–Making Process: A Case Study.   The year 1986 was not a good one for Texas's banks. As discussed in chapter 2, nonperforming loans to petroleum companies, farmers, ranchers, developers, and real estate interests were a severe blow to the financial status of many banks, including some of the largest bank holding companies in the state. By October, thirteen banks had closed their doors.[18] Earlier in the year Attorney-General Jim Mattox had added to the banks' woes by declaring that electronic transfer outlets not on the immediate premises of a bank contravened the constitutional ban on branch banking.

Banking interests were very evident during the regular and special sessions of the 1986 Texas legislature. They came to Austin looking for legislative relief. The large banks principally sought two new policies. First, they favored an amendment to the Texas Constitution that would legalize branch banking. Second, they requested that legislation be enacted that approved the entry of out-of-state banks into Texas. Ironically, in the immediate past—when economic conditions were more favorable—Texas banks strongly resisted any suggestion that outside banks should be allowed a charter to do business in the state or the right to take over local banks. With financial insolvency a real possibility, large Texas banks, however, lobbied for legislation in 1986 that might give any white knight the chance to rescue the state's struggling financial institutions.

The large-scale banks mounted a major lobbying campaign to effectuate these changes in policy. First, they induced most independent banks to drop their traditional opposition to outside banks and to branch banking in light of the threat posed to the general banking interest by depressed economic conditions in Texas. Second, personal visits by leading bankers such as Ben Love (chairman of Texas Commerce's board) and Walter Mischer (chairman of the board of Allied Bancshares) to Mark White helped win the governor's endorsement of new banking proposals. Third, the banks convinced State Treasurer Ann Richards and members of the State Banking Board of the desirability of these new laws. Finally, the state legislature was won over. In persuading the legislature it perhaps helped that one-third of the state's senators owned stock in banks, and that six senators sat on the boards of directors of banks, and that five of the nine members of the influential House Financial Institutions Committee were shareholders of banks, and that House Speaker Gib Lewis was a director and stockholder of the Worth Bancorporation, and, last, that forty-three House members and twelve senators (along with Senate leader

Bill Hobby) received campaign contributions from political action committees representing bankers. All told, banking interests spent some $400,000 to change financial policy in Texas.[19]

Their efforts were well rewarded. The 69th Texas Legislature voted approval of a constitutional amendment to be placed on the November 1986 ballot to allow branch banking. It also cleared the path for out-of-state banks to come into Texas. The voters subsequently supported the branch banking amendment. Moreover, Chemical Bank of New York—one of the nation's premier banks—acquired the financially troubled Texas Commerce Bancshares at the end of 1986.

Supplying Research to Political Officials. Officeholders frequently find themselves without sufficient technical information about a policy matter. This is especially true in Texas where many decision makers lack adequate staff and money in order to conduct sound independent research. Interest groups that can gather information and present it to policymakers are thus in an advantageous position in any attempt to influence public policy in the state.

The most interesting example of a private interest group that achieves access to the Texas governing circles through providing information is the Texas Research League (TRL). In its own image and words:

> The Texas Research League is a nonprofit educational corporation, engaged in objective analyses of the operations, programs and problems of Texas Government. The League makes no charge for its services which are financed by public-spirited citizens through annual contributions.[20]

The Texas Research League was organized in 1953. The original charter of the league allows it to do research only after state government makes an official request for information. These requests must then be approved by both the executive committee and the board of directors of the TRL. The actual collection of data is carried out by a full-time paid staff. Occasionally, the TRL contracts with other organizations for research assistance.

Over the last quarter century, the TRL has studied and made recommendations in a large number of policy areas affecting Texas, including economic development; primary, secondary, special, and higher education; vocational rehabilitation; medical care for the poor and elderly; hospitals; the state library; the Railroad Commission; the park board; the fish and game commission; the overall administration of state government; local and county government; the state retirement system; housing; law enforcement; and roads and highways. The main focus of the work of the TRL, however, is tax policy in Texas. The heart of much of the league's analyses centers on the question of who is going to pay what for which state services. In 1986, for example, the league studied student access to institutions of higher education in Texas; the current status of the state's highways, bridges, waterways, and sewage disposal plants; financing of the state's university and college systems; and overall taxation in the state.

Quite obviously, the Texas state government has taken extensive advantage of the "free" information services offered by the Texas Research League: "The TRL's staff has turned out enough reports to fill no less that seven shelves—floor to ceiling—in the Legislative Reference Library."[21] Indeed, in observing the relationship that has developed over the years between the TRL and the legislative branch of the Texas state government, one authoritative source has argued that "in effect, the league functions as a research arm of the state, and its staff will often sit at the right hand of the committee chairman in the legislature." [22]

The executive committee and the board of directors of the Texas Research League decide which studies the organization will undertake. Since its inception, the executive committee has been composed primarily of representatives drawn from the largest companies, firms, and agribusiness interests with extensive hold ings in Texas. The major push for creating the league came from big business, with Hines Baker, former chairman of Humble Oil (now merged into Exxon), acting as one of the driving forces in the league's establishment.[23] The current 15–person executive committee contains prominent persons associated with oil and natural gas companies, public utilities, industrial firms, and bank holding companies; the committee includes important officials from ENSERCH, Texas Eastern, Halliburton, Southwestern Bell, General Telephone, Xerox, M Corp, InterFirst, and First City. In 1985, the chairman of the league was T. Boone Pickens, chairman of the board of Mesa Petroleum. W. C. McCord, chairman of ENSERCH, assumed the position of the chair of the league in 1986. The remaining 150–plus members of the league's board of directors constitute much of the honor roll of the economic elite in Texas. The board can be a common forum for most of the major industries, financial institutions, and agribusinesses operating in the state.

The Texas Research League employs about fifteen people to carry out the studies commissioned by state government and approved by the executive committee and board of directors. At various times, the staff "enlists the voluntary services of executives and technicians recruited from Texas business and industry." [24] The annual operating budget of the league is nearly a million dollars. Where does the money come from?

No one knows for sure. Since it is designated as a nonprofit, nonpolitical educational corporation, the Texas Research League is not legally bound to disclose its sources of operating funds. The TRL has consistently refused to volunteer this information. At the minimum, some of the money comes from fees paid by the 1,000 or so members of the TRL. A business membership (and fully 90 percent of the league's members are businesses) entails an annual fee of $150; individuals contribute $100 per year for membership. Some observers contend that the lion's share of the league's funding comes from corporations, especially the giant petroleum companies engaged in business in Texas.[25]

Because of the business affiliation of the Texas Research League, some people, including a sprinkling of political officials in Texas, have questioned the objectivity of the organization's work. One critic, for instance, says the following of the league's studies:

> At its best the TRL is a valuable source of well-organized and carefully refined information on Texas state and local government finance. The problem is that what public officials, private individuals and the general public get to see of that information is selected, manipulated and presented to the beat of the League's drummers—the elite of Texas business and industry. Except for rare occasions of outright misrepresentation, . . . TRL tells the truth and nothing but the truth—but seldom tells the whole

truth. Indeed, some of their most insidious works exhibit an ingenious combination of relevant, irrelevant and omitted truths.[26]

Others, including the recent governors of Texas, have heaped bouquets of praise on the work of the league. Dolph Briscoe, when governor, told league members in 1975:

> For many years this organization has made important contributions to the future progress of our State through its in-depth studies of the pressing problems which have faced State government. The programs you have undertaken, and the resulting evaluations, have led to a better understanding of the functions and effects of government operations.[27]

Regardless of allegations of bias in its work, the Texas Research League has gained a great deal of access to the governing circles of Texas. At the very least, its reports draw attention; some have been fully accepted. In addition, personnel serving on the staff of the league have later joined state administrative agencies.[28] Through providing information, the league links the interests of its members to the operations of the state government. Commenting on its political and economic power, one observer argues that "it is through . . . organizations like the TRL that the modern corporation exercises its domination of the political as well as the economic arena." [29]

Mobilizing Public Support.   When an organization attempts to influence political decision makers, one of the most valuable assets it can have is popular support for its cause. To help meet this end, interest groups deliberately attempt to shape public opinion at the grass roots, as it were. Organizations with a large surplus of money are in the best position to mobilize favorable public sentiment, since persuasion on a mass level is an expensive endeavor. This mobilization of mass sentiment occurs along two fronts.

First, an attempt might be made to instill in the public *general values* conducive to the group's interests. Business groups, for instance, would like the public to favor a society in which private enterprise controls economic matters. Some Texas companies, through their public relations departments and the coordinating efforts of local branches of the chamber of commerce, have embarked on a program aimed at persuading schoolchildren (and teachers) of the overall virtue of living in a society where the economic means of production and distribution are firmly in the hands of big business. Aided by the Texas legislature, which in the late 1970s mandated the teaching of free enterprise economics in classrooms but did not allocate funding to the schools for this purpose, dominant economic interests have offered to teach this topic for free. Houston Natural Gas (before it became ENRON), for instance, bought for distribution audiovisual kits that extolled the societal value of big business. Some fifty employees of the company were trained to teach economics in the Galveston and Harris County public schools.[30]

The corporate version of the American economy presented to the school-age population of Texas is a select one. Although it applauds the achievements of giant companies, it declares the government of the United States guilty of creating most of today's economic ills. According to one critic of the materials utilized in the classrooms:

> The lessons . . . are conveyed in narratives that are long on theory but highly selective on fact, and they all but impel the conclusion that the existing concentration of wealth and power in the corporate world is the logical and justifiable result of free enterprise. . . . In almost every image and assertion presented in the . . . audio-visual program, one encounters the claim that government is the culprit to blame for most of the consumer complaints against America's producers.[31]

The second occasion prompting grass-roots lobbying on the part of interest groups is when a *specific* issue is being politically contested. Frequently, the most expedient (and expensive) means of mobilizing favorable public opinion is through the mass media. Financially healthy organizations at times engage in advertising campaigns designed to convince wide segments of the public that the group's viewpoint is the one that should be attended to by the government.

In Texas, the Texas Good Roads Association (TGRA) has utilized the mass media of the state to persuade the public of the worth of the organization's goals. The TGRA is committed to highways as the major means of transportation in the Lone Star State. Its more than 2,000 members are primarily from economic interests (for instance, petroleum, insurance, and road construction firms, as well as the trucking, bus, and automobile industries) that share the view that state government should implement this highway commitment.

Among the members of the Texas Good Roads Association are representatives of the mass media in Texas; in fact, the presiding officers of the TGRA have frequently been media people. Media members are quite a useful asset if the political and economic priorities of the TGRA are called into question. Such an occasion occurred in 1974 when a special convention was called to revise the Texas Constitution. Delegates to the constitutional convention were confronted with the proposition of transferring funds that were constitutionally dedicated for highway purposes to support other modes of transportation (for instance, bus and rail systems). Faced with a challenge to its position, the TGRA unleashed its media members on the public. After reviewing the events surrounding this issue, a journalist noted the following about the media component of the TGRA:

> When the dedicated fund is threatened, as it has been in this year's Constitutional Convention, the TGRA can expect prompt and vigorous editorial support for its viewpoint—sometimes by the very next morning in certain member newspapers. But the media can be even more cordial. A set of six TGRA advertisements praising the highway network and defending the dedicated fund was published 150 times last year [1973] in Texas newspapers as a "public service announcement," free of charge. Radio and television stations give free air time to its 20– and 60– second spots.[32]

Not surprisingly, given the strength of opposition, as we shall see in the next chapter the entire effort to revise the constitution faltered.

CONCLUSION

The theme of this and the previous chapter has been that gaining entrance into the political system of Texas requires having a hand in the selection of officeholders and being able to exert pressure on the everyday activities of political officials. The most frequently used means of securing political access are giving campaign contributions to candidates, having formal organizations that communicate with politicians, and effectively lobbying policymakers. Money is the key to doing all of these well. Making campaign donations, creating and maintaining formal organizations, and exercising effective lobbying tactics are extremely difficult without sufficient funds. In Texas, the dominant economic interest groups have spent a great deal of money for political reasons. From candidate selection to bringing pressure on officeholders, the financial presence of prevailing economic interests is quite evident.

This is not to say that all political officials in Texas are beholden only to dominant economic interests. Some politicians hold office without debts to economic concerns. Nor is it to say that all economic perspectives are similar. Conflict in economic viewpoints—even within the community of business—is sometimes present. On such occasions, every effort is usually made to soften the dispute and reconcile differences, lest the conflict spill over into public arenas and leave a factious business community vulnerable to outside demands.

What is suggested in these chapters is that many officeholders—enough to have a major impact on the governing of the state—are deeply indebted to dominant economic concerns. Further, it is argued that, even when conflict arises, it is economic issues that dominate the agenda of business put before the political institutions of Texas. Other interests—for instance, those of the poor, workers, and consumers—operate in the long shadow of governmental attention given to the concerns, desires, and preferences of those who own and run the principal economic means of production and distribution operating in the state.

NOTES

1. James E. Anderson, Richard W. Murray, and Edward L. Farley, *Texas Politics: An Introduction,* 2d ed. (New York: Harper and Row, 1975), p. 93.

2. James Dunn quoted in "Baptist Director Criticizes Lobby," *El Paso Times,* February 8, 1981, p. 4–C.

3. Hart Stillwell, "Texas: Owned by Oil and Interlocking Directorates," in *Our Sovereign State,* ed. Robert S. Allen (New York: Vanguard, 1949), p. 322.

4. Harry Hurt III, "The Most Powerful Texans," reprinted in *Texas Monthly's Political Reader* (Austin: Texas Monthly Press and Sterling Swift Publishing, 1978), p. 15.

5. Jim Hightower, "The Pecans Belong to the People," *Texas Observer,* February 2, 1979, p. 3.

6. Bryan Jones, "Why the Texas Legislature Is the Way It Is," in *Texas: Readings in Politics, Government, and Public Policy,* ed. Richard H. Kraemer and Philip W. Barnes (San Francisco: Chandler Press, 1971), pp. 136–37.

7. Ibid.; and see John C. Wahlke, et al., *The Legislative System* (New York: John Wiley and Sons, 1962).

8. Quoted in Jones, "Why the Texas Legislature Is the Way It Is," p. 137.

9. This is the conclusion presented in most standard textbooks on Texas politics. A recent assertion of this view may be found in Richard West, "Inside the Lobby," reprinted in *Texas Monthly's Political Reader* (Austin: Texas Monthly Press and Sterling Swift Publishing, 1978), pp. 112–19.

10. For data about the feelings of legislators in Utah, Massachusetts, Oregon, and North Carolina, see Harmon Zeigler and Michael Baer, *Lobbying: Interaction and Influence in American State Legislatures* (Belmont, Calif.: Wadsworth, 1969), p. 191. Similar comments by Texas legislators can be found in West, "Inside the Lobby."

11. This cynical view of lobbying is found in many journalistic accounts of the Texas legislative system. Perhaps the most vehement denouncement of the lobby in Austin is found in Harvey Katz, *Shadow on the Alamo* (Garden City, N.Y.: Doubleday, 1972).

12. Quoted in Sam Kinch, Jr., and Ben Procter, *Texas Under a Cloud* (Austin: Jenkins Publishing Co., 1972), pp. 110–11.

13. Molly Ivins, "Portrait of a Lobbyist," *Texas Observer*, December 26, 1975, p. 11 and p. 16.

14. Former Representative Lane Denton quoted in Katz, *Shadow on the Alamo*, p. 123 and chapter 7; also, see Lee Clark, "May the Lobby Hold You in the Palm of Its Hand," in *Texas: Readings in Politics, Government, and Public Policy*, pp. 148–53.

15. *Texas Observer*, July 23, 1982, p. 12.

16. Many others were involved in some way with Frank Sharp. From the political world two former attorneys-general of Texas (Waggoner Carr and Crawford Martin), an ex–state insurance board member (John Osorio), another former legislator (Sonny Shulte), and former State Treasurer Jesse James had contact with him. Key lobbyists such as Jake Jacobsen were also involved with Sharp. In addition, the cast of characters surrounding Sharp (in most cases unwittingly) included astronauts, Jesuit priests of Houston, the Pope, and Houston Baptist College. All of the major actors in this drama appear in Katz, *Shadow on the Alamo*, chaps. 3 and 4; and in Kinch and Procter, *Texas Under a Cloud.*

17. Figures are from Katz, p. 64.

18. Reported in Dave Denison, "Banking on Bigness," *Texas Observer*, September 26, 1986, pp. 7–11.

19. Ibid.

20. *Annual Report, 1978,* Texas Research League.

21. *Texas Government Newsletter,* November 24, 1975, p. 2.

22. Clifton McCleskey, Allan Butcher, Daniel E. Farlow, and J. Pat Stephens, *Government and Politics of Texas,* 6th ed. (Boston: Little, Brown, 1978), p. 176.

23. The origins of the Texas Research League are discussed in the following: Ronnie Dugger, "Researching the Researchers," *Texas Observer*, February 7, 1963, pp. 3–9; and John Muir, "Information Is Power," *Texas Observer*, August 9, 1974, pp. 14–16.

24. Quote of James W. McGrew, former executive director of the TRL, found in Dugger, "Researching the Researchers," p. 4.

25. Ibid.

26. Personal communication from Craig Foster, executive director of the Public Education Resource Equity Center, Austin, Texas. Reprinted by permission.

27. Quoted in the *Annual Report, 1978,* p. 6.

28. Briefly discussed in Molly Ivins, "The Texas Research League," *Texas Observer*, February 1, 1974, p. 3.

29. Muir, "Information Is Power," p. 15.

30. This example appears in Matthew Lyon, "Buying into the Public Schools: And Now a Word from Our Corporate Sponsor," *Texas Observer*, November 3, 1978, pp. 2 and 9.

31. Ibid., p. 5.

32. Griffin Smith, Jr., "The Highway Establishment and How It Grew, and Grew, and Grew," reprinted in *Texas Monthly's Political Reader*. Reprinted with permission from *Texas Monthly's Political Reader*. Copyright 1978 by *Texas Monthly*.

PART III

Political Institutions in Texas

Access to political decision makers depends on the permeability of the political institutions in a society. Easy penetration of governing bodies sets the stage for citizens to catch the attention of policymakers. Formidable barriers around political structures decrease the likelihood that decision makers are representative of, and accountable to, a wide public. Political institutions in a democratic society should be readily accessible to the general society. If only a relatively few social interests are able to crack the institutional walls around decision makers, democracy is weakened.

This part of the book investigates the political institutions established to govern Texas. Chapter 7 begins by analyzing the Texas Constitution, the document that creates the major governing offices of the state. Chapter 8 outlines the legislative system in the state. Chapter 9 focuses on the chief executive officers and administrators in Texas. Finally, Chapter 10 covers the state's judiciary. Beyond simple description, each chapter probes its topic for the seams that open the inner workings of state government to the stalwarts of the Texas economic community.

7

The Texas Constitution

A thorough look at the political institutions of Texas requires some analysis of the state's constitution. In general, constitutions perform two functions: they establish the organizational framework of the institutions that govern society, and they delineate the fundamental principles upon which the political system rests. The constitution is the supreme law of the land. It is usually quite difficult to change. Further, it guides, constrains, and legitimates the actions of political officials. Groups (or persons) seeking privileged status in society would naturally prefer to have their interests protected by such a powerful document.

Citizens in the United States live under two constitutions: the national Constitution, written in Philadelphia in 1787, and the constitution of the state in which they reside. The U.S. Constitution does a number of things: it outlines the basic form of government for the country, it authorizes the federal government to make public policy in specific areas (such as regulating the currency and declaring war), it restricts government intervention in the private affairs of individuals (such as the right of a person to speak or worship freely), and it commits the political system to the preservation and expansion of private property.[1]

State constitutions exist under a shadow cast by the national Constitution. The general values and form of government created by the latter are emulated in the former. The national document denies states the authority to abridge individual rights and retains an exclusive voice in some policy areas. Each state is still left with the right to fashion its own political institutions and engage in a wide range of policy matters unique to its population. ★

BACKGROUND OF THE TEXAS CONSTITUTION

Six constitutions have been written for the state of Texas since its independence from Mexico in 1836. The present-day constitution went into effect in 1876. It is basically a product of the political and economic discontent that swept across the state in the aftermath of the Civil War.[2]

At that time, an intense struggle ensued over who was to rule the Lone Star State. The battle pitted Radical Republicans against secessionist Democrats. The Radicals were committed to political equality for blacks and the punishment of Texans who aligned with the Confederacy. The Democrats were reluctant to improve the status of freed slaves and adamantly opposed any recriminations for Texas's participation on the losing side of the Civil War.

By 1870, Radical Republicans had gained the reins of state government through electoral victories. Republican Edmund J. Davis became governor. A majority of the legislators were Republicans, and Governor Davis, with the consent of the Texas Senate, appointed Radicals to fill most of the state's judicial posts.

While in office, Radicals enacted laws that profoundly affected the lives of most Texans. In the name of preservation of law and order, a state militia and police force were established and placed under the direct command of Governor Davis. All male citizens between the ages of eighteen and forty-five were ordered to serve in the militia (military duty could be avoided by paying the state $15). The governor was empowered to send the militia or police into any part of the state. Further, he could declare martial law in cases of emergency and thus suspend individual rights. The governor was also authorized to fill vacancies of *any* political office in the state (even local positions) by appointment; during his tenure as governor Davis filled 8,500 local offices. In order to vote, Texans had to register in person before judges appointed by the governor. The judges could deny the right to vote as they saw fit. Voting was permitted only at the county seat and it usually occurred in the presence of armed militiamen. The government promoted economic growth in the state by subsidizing (with tax money) corporations, especially railroad companies. Personal taxes rose dramatically during Republican rule—one historian estimates that about one-fifth of the personal income of Texans went to the Radical government in the form of taxes.[3]

A litany of complaints was aired against Republican rule. Tyranny, fiscal irresponsibility, and outright corruption were some of the general charges leveled at the so-called "obnoxious acts" of the Radicals. More specifically, many of these acts were passed only after ten legislators who opposed them were placed under house arrest and prevented from casting an unfavorable vote. Civil liberties were frequently denied by the governor, the police, and the militia.[4] Taxes were biting into the already financially burdened citizens, yet even with high taxes, the state was on the verge of bankruptcy because of its generous outlays of cash to political officials and corporations. A few legislators who favored giving financial aid to railroad companies were accused of accepting bribes: "Some of the Democratic papers expressed wonder at the fact that certain members of the ... Legislature, whose only visible income was their per diem [$8], should be able at the end of the [legislative] session to invest in fine horses and expensive furniture and make long trips north on vacation."[5] While Governor Davis appears not to have been corrupt, his adjutant-general, James Davidson, "absconded with $37,000 in state funds in 1872."[6]

By 1872, a plurality of Texans had had enough of Radical state government. In the election to fill the seats of the state legislature, Democrats scored a decisive victory. The new legislature—over the objections of holdover Radical Governor Davis—repealed most of the "obnoxious acts" and called for a general statewide election in 1873. In that election, Democrats again won most state offices, including the governor's chair. But the defeated Republicans refused to abide by the electoral results, charging that the Texas Election Code was faulty. The Radical

Texas Supreme Court upheld this objection and denied Democrats their apparent success. When the Democrats came to Austin to claim the fruits of their victory anyway, they were met by the state militia. The troops, under orders from Governor Davis, had sealed the doors of the capitol building and stood guard inside. Unfortunately for the Radicals, the militia let its guard slip and the Democrats gained entrance to the building. An eminent Texas historian describes the scene as follows:

> While the . . . troops were asleep early one morning Democrats used a ladder to secure admission to the legislative halls on the second floor, organized the legislature for work, counted the votes and declared Coke [the Democrat] elected governor. Governor Davis appealed to President Grant for aid and additional troops as soon as the Democratic plans were apparent, but the president telegraphed his refusal to interfere; the governor then withdrew from his office and from Texas public life.[7]

Once secure in office, the Democrats undertook to sweep out of Texas politics all remnants of Republican rule. The most glaring reminder of Radical control was the Texas Constitution of 1869. Many felt that the 1869 constitution had directly or indirectly authorized the "obnoxious acts." Mainly, however, it symbolized all that was wrong with Radical government. To rid the state of past memories and the possibility of future repetition of Radical unpleasantries, the Democratic state government called for a new constitutional convention. Three delegates from each of thirty geographically separate districts of the state were elected to accomplish the task. The ninety delegates began work in Austin on September 6, 1875, and completed the writing of the new (and present) constitution over the next sixty-eight days.

SOCIAL BACKGROUND OF THE FRAMERS OF THE TEXAS CONSTITUTION

About 80 percent of the delegates who assembled to write the new Texas Constitution were Democrats. By occupation, most were farmers and lawyers. Only four had been born in Texas, although the vast majority were from Southern states. The average age of the delegates was forty-five. No women were present. Five (all Republicans) of the ninety were blacks.[8]

The one formal organization that was well represented at the constitutional convention was the Grange. The Grange movement, composed mostly of farmers, had begun in 1867 and had spread like prairie fire across the agricultural sections of the United States, reaching Texas in 1873. Within a year, hundreds of local Granges had cropped up in the state and the organization counted 50,000 Texans as members.

The Grangers were deeply disturbed about the declining economic standing of farmers throughout the United States. Farm prices had been plummeting since the cessation of the Civil War. Grangers placed the blame on railroad companies and the banks, with state governments as accused accomplices. Railroads were singled out for arbitrarily overcharging farmers to transport agricultural products.

Delegates to the Constitutional Convention of 1875.
Photo Courtesy of the Texas State Archives.

During this time major banks were failing, thus making money very difficult to obtain. State governments resisted controlling the banks and railroads, and seemed more intent on protecting them—at a great expense to farmers. Thirty-eight delegates at the constitutional convention in Texas were Grangers, and their views were reflected in the new state constitution.

CONTENTS OF THE TEXAS CONSTITUTION

From the moment the first gavel jarred the delegates to order, the watchwords of the convention were "retrenchment and reform." Retrenchment mostly translated into fiscal constraint on the spending capability of state and local governments. As a direct response to the excessive expenditures of the Radical government, the new constitution limited the spending and tax-raising authority of the state's governing units. For instance, salaries for state employees were cut and delineated by the document, the state could only borrow up to $200,000 unless it was facing imminent danger of attack, and revenue for the public school system was greatly restricted. Taxes were also lowered and limited.

Reform meant weakening the power of state government and strengthening the rights of individuals in their potential interactions with political authorities. The duties, procedures, and power of government institutions in Texas were spelled out and confined by the document. In fact, about one-half of the fifty original provisions contained in the section pertaining to the legislature constrained the activities of this political institution. The constitutional delegates believed that the executive branch of government possessed the most potential for abuse. To counter this possibility, the executive was fragmented into distinct offices, each office being independent of the other and, more importantly, of the governor. Executive officials were to be elected. The governor was deprived not only of the opportunity to centralize executive business but also of the authority to appoint many members of this branch of government. Even judges of the state courts, including the highest courts, were to be elected.

In addition to retrenchment and reform in state government, the framers of the Texas Constitution were intent on plans that would further and protect their economic interests through the fundamental law of Texas. One of their prime interests was the creation of a complete transportation system that would link Texas farmers with consumers both inside and out of the state. To accomplish this, expansion of the railroad was urged. Texas only had around 1,500 miles of track at the time of the convention and most of the rails were laid in the central and eastern sections of the state. Yet however much the delegates wanted growth of the railroad, many still had a basic distrust of and hostility toward the companies. This ambivalence was reflected in the constitution. It, on the one hand, gave the state the right to regulate rail operation (especially rates charged to customers), while, on the other, it distributed large tracts of land to companies for the building of track across the state.

Other big businesses didn't fare as well in the new constitution. For instance, the antipathy the Grangers felt toward banks was clearly evident in the document: the delegates simply prohibited banks from ever incorporating in the state.

In short, the current Texas Constitution was written in reaction to political and economic events that beset the state's population more than a century ago. The delegates were mostly of an agrarian mind and wrote a document designed to remedy the misfortunes that had befallen their lot. At its core, the constitution sought to weaken state government; keep it firmly under popular control; and harness for small, independent farmers the potential and feared power of corporations.

THE TEXAS CONSTITUTION TODAY: HELPING THE BUSINESS COMMUNITY

Since the writing of the Texas Constitution, the state has experienced tremendous economic expansion and change. Giant industries, major financial institutions, and large agribusinesses (as discussed in chapter 2) have replaced the family farmer to form the backbone of the state's economy. Obviously, the original anticorporate bias contained in the constitution has done little to stunt the state's economic growth. In fact, Texas's economic elites are among the major defenders of the document. Recent attempts to revise the state constitution clearly indicate this favorable disposition.

In 1972, Texas voters authorized the state legislature to totally rewrite the constitution. The legislature created a thirty-seven person constitutional revision committee that was to study the document and offer recommendations for change. In 1974, the state legislature acted as a constitutional convention and deliberated the fate of the 1876 Constitution. After more than half a year (and $5 million in tax revenue), the convention (legislature) fell three votes shy of approving a new constitution for the state. In its next regular session, however, the legislature approved eight amendments to the old constitution; these amendments fundamentally restructured and updated the document. They were placed on the Texas ballot in November 1975 for voter approval, and the voters overwhelmingly rejected all of the proposals. The upshot of these events: the constitution of 1876 lives on.

Major opposition to constitutional revision came from the heights of the business community. Attempts to alter some of the privilege guaranteed a few economic notables were effectively thwarted. At one stage, for instance, the constitutional revision committee entertained the idea of deleting from the document a provision that dedicates tax monies to the construction and maintenance of highways. As mentioned in chapter 6, the highway lobby successfully blocked this change. Corporate owners of property intervened in the committee's proceedings to stop any changes in the methods of collecting the property tax that would have increased the tax bite of major companies. Finally, the committee's thoughts about changing the basis of funding the University of Texas, especially the Austin branch, and Texas A & M were resisted by business-oriented Texans. One key source of money for these institutions is the Permanent University Fund, a pool of money generated from revenue earned on Texas's oil-rich public lands. It was suggested that the new constitution should make this fund available to all colleges and universities in Texas. The corporate-dominated regents of the University of Texas system, and of the Texas A & M system, lobbied to defeat this notion. (More about the Permanent University Fund appears in chapter 11.)

The 1975 election held basically to rewrite the Texas Constitution found some pillars of the economic community actively leading the opposition. The late George Brown (Brown and Root, Halliburton, First City Bancorporation, ITT, Texas Eastern, and the 8F Crowd), for instance, apparently spearheaded a drive to defeat the proposed change in the constitution. After discussing with Brown the upcoming 1975 election, Searcy Bracewell (a lawyer as well as a current member of the board of directors of Houston Lighting and Power) created the Committee to Preserve the Texas Constitution. The committee raised around $15,000 to rally electoral opposition to the proposed amendments. Almost all of the money came from Brown, executives of Brown and Root, and 8F Crowd members, including: Walter Mischer (chairman of Allied Bancshares), A. J. A. Bryan (former director of Great Southern insurance and of First City Bancorporation), the late Gus Wortham (founder of American General Insurance), and James A. Elkins, Jr. (former chairman at First City Bancorporation). When Brown was asked why he favored retaining the old constitution, he bluntly responded: "I never argue with success and we have been pretty successful doing it the way we have been doing it." [9]

Hence, a century after the Texas Constitution was adopted to curtail and regulate corporate activities in the state, the corporate sector has become the document's major proponent. How did this ironic state of affairs come about? Put simply, economic leaders discovered that having a weak state government was conducive to their goals—they changed the original document only when such alteration suited their interests.

It has been relatively easy to amend the Texas Constitution. Amendment is accomplished if two-thirds of the state legislature recommends a change and a majority of voters opt for the alteration. Between 1876 and 1986, only one legislative session has concluded without any attempt to amend the constitution. The voters have been busy with 441 (as of 1986) proposals during this period, and in 65 percent of the cases have consented to constitutional change. What has emerged is an extremely detailed and lengthy document. The state charter has about 60,000 words, some six times as long as the United States Constitution. Most of the state amendments have been effectuated by organized groups,[10] with major economic interests benefiting most from the amendment process. Three examples stand out.

In the first few years of the twentieth century, a major discovery of oil was made in Texas. Petroleum brought a great deal of money into the state, but without state-chartered banks (prohibited by the 1876 Constitution) financial transactions were hampered. Economic interests affected by this burden successfully amended the constitution in 1904 to allow establishment of banks and thus facilitate the smooth flow of money. However, banks were still precluded from opening branches across the state. As was seen in chapter 2, the bank holding company movement emerged as a means to circumvent the ban on branch banking. As mentioned in previous chapters (2 and 6), the 1986 legislature endorsed an amendment to allow branch banking across Texas and in the November election of that year the voters approved this alteration. Hence Texas has gone from a state whose suspicion of financial institutions first led to prohibition of chartered banks, then to restriction of banking activities, to one that now fully provides an environment in which growth and concentration among banks are quite likely.

Automobile companies and petroleum firms throughout the twentieth century have had a common interest in the sale of cars with gas-combustion engines. The construction of roads for travel, however, was too costly a project for these corporations to fund. Yet, without paved surfaces to drive on, consumers might not find cars an attractive means of transportation. The problem was resolved in Texas by having the state government use taxpayers' dollars to build highways. The highway lobby (chapter 6) secured passage of an amendment to the state constitution that permanently dedicated revenue for the building and maintenance of roads and highways (see chapter 12 for details).

Finally, in 1978 voters were presented a package of propositions designed to bring tax relief to Texans through constitutional amendment. This omnibus measure offered at least some modicum of savings for most taxpayers and was, not unexpectedly, approved by an overwhelming majority. But the major beneficiaries of the amendment are the wealthy property holders in Texas. The owners of large tracts of farm-, ranch-, and timberland, for instance, stand to gain significant reductions in their property taxes. This is because agricultural land is now taxed on its revenue-generating capacity and not, as was formerly the case, on its fair market value. In other words, if the land, or any piece of it, is not producing a salable item, it is not subject to property taxes. In addition, intangible property (such as stocks, bonds, and certificates of deposit) are not considered taxable

Courtesy of Ben Sargent, *The Austin American-Statesman.* Reprinted by permission.

property under the new amendment. Intangibles are mostly in the possession of the wealthy.

Furthermore, the corporate community has found that constitutional restrictions on the authority of the state government are much to its liking. The legacy of the 1875 constitutional convention is a fragmented, weak set of political institutions in Texas. The core of Article III, for example, is to constrain the authority and the governing capabilities of the legislature. Section by section, it spells out who is qualified to be in the legislature, when it will meet, how it will operate, and how much its members are to be compensated. As will be detailed in the next chapter, the rules of procedure are rigid, legislative sessions are infrequent and short, and the pay is poor—all by constitutional mandate. Attempts to strengthen the government have been strongly resisted by economic elites. For instance, they as a rule oppose raising the salaries of Texas's legislators, because, according to one viewpoint, "it is much easier to pressure poorly-paid legislators than well-paid ones." [11] In order to understand more fully how the structure of government in Texas is useful to the business community, the next three chapters focus on the operations of the state legislature, the executive and administrative system, and the judiciary.

CONCLUSION

The present-day Texas Constitution is more than one hundred years old. It was originally designed to curtail concentration of both economic and political power,

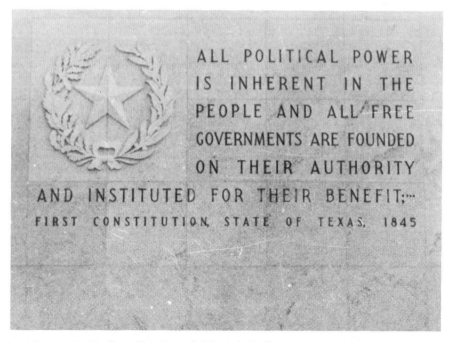

Inscription on wall of the Texas State Library Building in Austin, Texas.

but, in effect, the constitution has been only half-successful. On the one hand, the state government remains a weak and fragmented governing body. On the other hand, economic elites have become more powerful over the last century. The very nature of the state government has strengthened the economic sector. Attempts to shore up the power of the government through constitutional amendment have been thwarted by economic notables. Meanwhile, amendments to the advantage of these influentials have been incorporated into the fundamental law of Texas.

NOTES

1. A concise summary of the property orientation of those who wrote the U.S. Constitution may be found in Michael Parenti, *Democracy for the Few,* 2d ed. (New York: St. Martin's, 1977), ch. 4; and in Thomas Dye and Harmon Zeigler, *The Irony of Democracy,* 4th ed. (North Scituate, Mass.: Duxbury, 1978), ch. 2.

2. Much of the material contained in this section on the background of the Texas Constitution is drawn from Seth McKay, *Seven Decades of the Texas Constitution of 1876* (Lubbock: Texas Tech University Press, 1943).

3. T. R. Fehrenbach, *Lone Star: A History of Texas and Texans* (New York: Macmillan, 1968), p. 422.

4. Some of the violations of civil liberties are reported in A. J. Thomas and Ann Van Wynen Thomas, "The Texas Constitution of 1876," *Texas Law Review* 35 (October 1957): 907–18.

5. McKay, *Seven Decades of the Texas Constitution,* p. 34.

6. Mike Kingston, "A Concise History of Texas," in the *Texas Almanac and Industrial Guide: 1986–1987* (Dallas: A. H. Belo, 1985), p. 209.

7. McKay, *Seven Decades,* p. 46. Reprinted by permission.

8. At first, six black Republicans were present. A few days after the convention began, one resigned and was replaced by a white Democrat. There is some discrepancy about the social background of the ninety delegates. I have followed the portrait drawn by J. E. Ericson, "The Delegates to the Convention of 1875: A Reappraisal," *Southwestern Historical Quarterly* 67 (July 1963): 22–27.

9. The quote and the details about the Citizens to Preserve the Texas Constitution may be found in Kaye Northcott, "New Charter Foundering," *Texas Observer,* October 31, 1975, pp. 1 and 7–8.

10. States with much-amended constitutions are generally ones containing powerful interest groups, according to Lewis Froman, "Some Effects of Interest Group Strength in State Politics," *American Political Science Review* 60 (December 1966): 954–62.

11. Hart Stillwell, "Texas: Owned by Oil and Interlocking Directorates," in *Our Sovereign State,* ed. Robert S. Allen (New York: Vanguard Press, 1949), p. 330.

8

The Texas Legislature

The chief function of any legislative body in the United States is to enact policy that is binding for the population within its boundaries. State legislatures are mostly involved in formulating policy in the areas of education, transportation, welfare, regulation of social and economic behavior, and raising revenue to cover these activities. In addition, state legislatures play a key role in establishing administrative agencies, overseeing their operations, choosing their personnel, and terminating their existence. On rare occasions, legislatures judge the improprieties of their own members and of officials in other branches of state government (for instance, the governor). Finally, the process of amending the state constitution usually begins in the legislature. Put briefly, legislatures are important cogs in the machinery of the fifty state governments.   ★

COMPOSITION OF THE TEXAS LEGISLATURE

The Texas legislature is composed of 181 people: 150 members of the House of Representatives and 31 senators. Representatives are elected every two years from 150 distinct geographic districts, each nearly equal in population size (one representative per 95,000 Texans). Senators serve four-year terms, with half of the Senate chosen in each general election. Each senator comes from a unique geographic area. Senatorial districts contain around 458,000 Texans, although the Supreme Court of the United States has tolerated close to a 10 percent deviation (plus or minus) from this population standard in drawing the district lines for both the state senate and lower house.[1]

On the surface, most Texans are eligible to hold legislative office. To be a member of the House of Representatives, one must be at least twenty-one years old and a Texas resident for two consecutive years prior to election. Prospective senators must have reached their twenty-sixth birthday and have been Texas inhabitants for five continuous years before their election. United States citizenship and a one-year residency in the House or senatorial district are the only additional major formal requirements.

In reality, however, only a select few can afford to hold a seat in the Texas legislature. As noted by John Hildreth of Texas's Common Cause organization, "we might as well point out in the Constitution that to run for the Legislature you must first be wealthy, be in a business or a law firm where your partners will cover for you while you're gone because they feel it's in the best interest of the firm, or be owned lock, stock and barrel by the [business] lobby." [2] The principal reason for this state of affairs lies in the high cost of waging an effective campaign for legislative office in Texas and in the low salary paid to legislators.

Campaign costs have escalated in recent years. Hard-fought contests in the primary and general election for a representative's post run around $50,000; senatorial campaigns are at least, on average, double that figure. Salaries for state representatives and senators are constitutionally set at $7,200 a year. Compared with other states (especially industrialized ones), legislative salaries in Texas rank near the bottom. For instance, in the early 1980s state legislators in California were paid an annual salary of $33,732; in New York, they earned $43,000 per year. A supplemental daily payment of $30 is made to each Texas lawmaker every day of a special legislative session, and also $30 per day to cover expenses during the legislative session. By almost a three-to-one ratio, voters in 1984 defeated a constitutional amendment to raise the per diem to around $75 each day. Finally, there is reimbursement for some travel expenses incurred by legislators traveling between their district and Austin. Financial constraints hence severely restrict opportunities to become a legislator.

The membership of the House in the mid–1980s was composed primarily of males (90 percent), non-Hispanic whites (86 percent) engaged in business (36 percent) or law (31 percent) with an average age of forty-four. Only one woman and one black held a Senate seat in 1985, and four senators were Hispanic. Twenty-eight of the 31 senators were either lawyers or businessmen. The average age of Texas senators was forty-eight.

Once elected, most of Texas's legislators, especially House members, find it financially difficult to hire full-time, competent staff to assist in the performance of their legislative roles. In 1983, representatives in the House received $7,500 each for the operation of their offices during the month of January. For each remaining month in the legislative session of that year, they were granted $6,500, and $5,500 to meet monthly costs during the interim between sessions. Senators were allocated more money, but the amounts were not appreciably higher. At best, legislators can hire two, perhaps three, full-time aides.

In order to stretch their allocations for staff assistance further, some members of the legislature pool their expense accounts and hire aides shared by all participating representatives. The House Study Group is one example of a pooling arrangement. In 1986, 133 representatives and 15 senators subscribed to the services offered by the House Study Group. Legislators can also draw on the technical and legal expertise of organizations especially created by the legislature to provide information to its members. One of the most utilized organizations is the Legislative Council. The council is composed of fifteen legislators (ten from the House and five from the Senate) who appoint an executive director and a permanent staff. Legislators solicit the council for advice and assistance in drafting laws. Indeed, around three-fourths of all bills introduced in the legislature each term are prepared by the council. Finally, the Legislative Reference Library, located in the state capitol building, is a vital source of information to legislators and their aides.

The library contains more than 30,000 items, most dealing with public issues facing Texas.

Even with institutional assistance and pooling arrangements, individual legislators are hard-pressed to be fully informed about all issues that pass before the legislature. One result is that legislators welcome outside interest groups that provide research services. The success of the Texas Research League (chapter 6) in legislative matters, especially those involving taxation, is a well-documented example of a group obtaining access to the legislature through providing free facts and figures to Texas's lawmakers.

PROCEDURES OF THE TEXAS LEGISLATURE

Texas legislators confront a complicated maze of formal and informal rules and procedures as they attempt to make laws. Some of these procedural obstacles are established by the Texas Constitution; others are formulated by the legislature itself. Figure 8–1 presents a thumbnail sketch of the legislative path a bill must follow in order to become law in Texas.

The first step in enacting laws is the introduction of a bill. Only members of the Texas legislature can officially offer proposals. Most bills may be introduced either in the Senate or in the House of Representatives (or in both chambers simultaneously); however, bills that ask for new raises in revenues must first be considered solely by the House. A member ordinarily provides thirteen copies of his or her proposal to the clerk of the House or to the secretary of the Senate in order to begin the legislative process. Before being forwarded to the presiding officer of the legislative chamber, the caption of the bill is read to the Senate and House membership by the chief clerk of each institution.

The presiding officers of the House and Senate then assign the bill to a standing committee. In the Senate, the lieutenant-governor is charged with the task of forwarding bills to committee; this duty lies with the speaker in the House. Each presiding officer has some discretion in choosing the appropriate committee. If, for instance, the speaker of the House is dissatisfied with the work of the committee that first received the bill he can shift the measure to another committee. A majority of the House membership can overrule the speaker's choice of committee, but this rarely occurs.

During 1985–1986, there were thirty-four standing committees in the House: twenty-eight were structured around substantive topics (for example, appropriations, business and commerce, agriculture and livestock, criminal justice, energy, or transportation) and six were organized to facilitate the business of the House. The Senate had nine standing committees and two special committees. Table 8–1 lists the House and the Senate committees in operation during the sixty-ninth regular and special sessions (1985–1986) of the state legislature. Observers peg Appropriations, State Affairs, Ways and Means, and Calendars as the most important House committees. Finance, State Affairs, and Jurisprudence rank as the top three Senate committees.

The standing committees are composed of a relatively small number of legislators who wield a great influence over the fate of legislative proposals. Standing

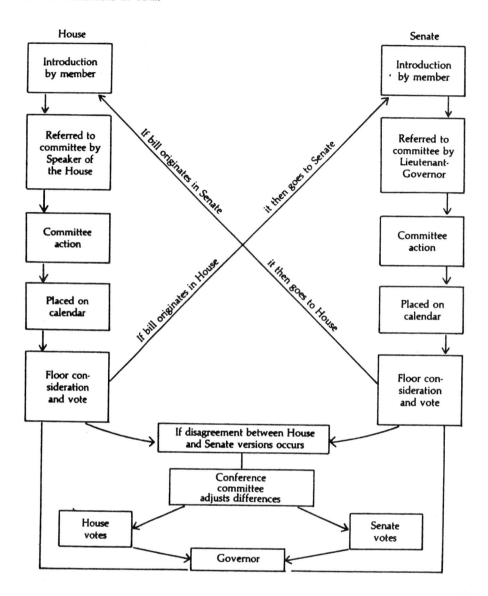

FIGURE 8–1 How a Bill Becomes Law

committees ordinarily range in size from five to twenty-nine members. The average committee size in both the House and the Senate is usually ten. In recent years virtually all substantive committees in the House have had at least one subcommittee; none of the House's procedural committees have had subcommittees. Subcommittees have been formed recently in only two Senate committees—Natural Resources and Health and Human Resources.

Each full committee has almost complete control over matters brought before it. It may approve of a measure (either unchanged or with amendments), disap-

TABLE 8–1   Standing Committees in the 1985–1986 Texas Legislature

House Standing Committees	Number of Members
House Substantive Committees	
Agriculture and Livestock	9
Appropriations	29
Business and Commerce	9
County Affairs	15
Criminal Jurisprudence	9
Cultural and Historical Resources	9
Elections	9
Energy	9
Environmental Affairs	9
Financial Institutions	9
Higher Education	9
Human Services	9
Insurance	9
Judicial Affairs	9
Judiciary	9
Labor and Employment Relations	9
Law Enforcement	9
Liquor Regulation	9
Natural Resources	9
Public Education	9
Public Health	9
Retirement and Aging	9
Science and Technology	9
State Affairs	15
State, Federal, and International Relations	9
Transportation	9
Urban Affairs	15
Ways and Means	13
House Procedural Committees	
Calendars	9
General Investigating	5
Government Organization	9
House Administration	9
Local and Consent Calendars	9
Rules and Resolutions	9
Senate Standing Committees	
Criminal Justice	7
Economic Development	11
Education	11
Finance	13
Health and Human Resources	9
Intergovernmental Services	11
Jurisprudence	7
Natural Resources	11
State Affairs	13
Senate Special Committees	
Administration	9
Nominations	9

prove of the proposal, or let it die from neglect. During its 1983 term, about 26 percent (1,024) of the 4,021 bills introduced during the regular session of the legislature were enacted into law; most of these measures were laid to rest at the committee stage of deliberation. Generally, only bills approved by a majority of the committee go beyond this step of the legislative process. It is possible for the full membership of the House or of the Senate to force a measure from a recalcitrant committee. For instance, in the House a committee can be ordered to discharge a bill if (1) it has held the measure for six working days and (2) two-thirds of the House members in the first seventy days of the session and a simple majority after that vote to have the item removed from the committee's jurisdiction. It is difficult to invoke these procedures, however, and hence committee control over legislative matters is rarely interfered with.

The chair of each committee is the most influential person in the committee's deliberations. The chair has several powers that might affect the prospects of a bill. Chairs can, for instance, decide if a hearing on the bill will be held. If a hearing on a bill is conducted, five days notice must be posted. Unless the hearing involves a quasi-judicial matter or deals with impeachment of a government official, it is ordinarily open to the public. The chairs of full committees also appoint the chairmen and chairwomen and other members of virtually all subcommittees; the only exception occurs in selection of the members of the House subcommittees on budget and oversight that make the initial recommendations for the general appropriations bill. They further can decide whether a bill is to be sent to a subcommittee. The committee chair may also request fiscal information if a bill involves additional expense to the state.

Bills that are favored by a majority of the committee proceed to the full membership of the House or Senate. Before, however, debate on any measure ensues, it must be scheduled for discussion on the floor of the House or Senate. Because of the larger size of its membership, the scheduling of floor debate in the House is done in a much more formal manner than in the smaller Senate. The rules of the House state that the Calendars Committee is to channel the flow of legislation from the standing committee to the full membership of that legislative body. Normally it has seven days to place a bill on a calendar; during the last ten days of the legislative session Calendars has seventy-two hours to act. Table 8–2

Table 8–2 House Calendars

Name of Calendar	Legislative Subject Matter
Emergency	Measures designated as emergencies and all revenue and appropriations bills
Major	State nonemergency matters not involving money but of major or statewide importance
General State	Nonemergency matters not involving money and not of major or statewide importance
Constitutional Amendments	Bills designed to amend the Texas Constitution
Local	Bills pertaining to particular counties in the state
Consent	Measures without opposition in the House
Resolutions	Measures that do not alter or add to existing Texas laws

lists the names and nature of the seven possible calendars by which a bill can get to the floor of the House.

A bill's position on the calendar is usually determined by when it emerges from the standing committee. Theoretically, the earlier a bill is reported out of committee, the sooner it is scheduled for debate. The Calendars Committee, however, can exercise some discretion in selecting the appropriate calendar for the bill and in placing it on the calendar. Because of its leeway, the Calendars Committee is one of the most important committees in the Texas House.

In the Senate, bills are simply scheduled for discussion on the floor in the order in which they appear out of the standing committees. This sequential arrangement can, however, be altered by suspension of Senate rules. A senator must notify the presiding officer of the chamber (the lieutenant-governor) of his or her intention to change the calendar. Assuming the presiding officer concurs, the call for suspension must be approved by four-fifths of the Senate in the first sixty days of the legislative session or by two-thirds in the remaining days of the term.

Once on the floor of the House or the Senate, discussion of the bill's merits is open to the full body of Texas legislators. Debate is more restricted in the House than it is in the Senate. House members are accorded ten minutes to present their viewpoints, but the floor leader of the bill is allocated twenty minutes for introduction and again for summation. More time can be allotted with majority approval, except during the always hectic last ten days of the session. Senators may talk as long as they wish (or are able)—a few have held the Senate floor for more than forty hours. Unlimited discussion opens the door for attempts to filibuster a bill. The term *filibuster* refers to the deliberate effort to kill or seriously impair a bill through endless discussion of the measure. It is a tactic usually employed by opponents of a bill who are in a minority. Filibustering is limited in the Texas Senate, however, by one rule: once a member has finished talking he or she must yield the floor to the presiding officer and thus cannot turn the debate over to a like-minded colleague. The presiding officer may then recognize a supporter of the measure and consequently short-circuit the filibuster attempt.

Approval of a bill requires a simple majority vote in both the Senate and the House. As in most states (Nebraska is the sole exception), the Texas legislature is bicameral: all bills require the consent of both legislative chambers in order to become law. It is quite likely, however, that each legislative body will pass a different version of the same bill. These differences must be reconciled, and a special committee known as a conference committee is established each time this type of conflict occurs. Every conference committee contains ten legislators: five from each chamber.

Since 1973, conference committees have been denied the right to substantially rewrite any bills approved by the House and Senate. A majority of the delegation sent from each legislative unit must agree on a common version of the bill and then the conference committee's report is presented for consideration in both the House and the Senate. Legislators may approve, reject, or return the report to the committee for further work. They cannot amend it. Considering the fact that most legislation is actually written in the waning days of the legislative session, there is little time for the full membership to do anything but accept the conference committee's version of a bill. Hence the conference committee is extremely important in the formulation of laws in Texas. Finally, after the legislature approves a bill, it is sent to the governor for consideration (a topic to be discussed in the next chapter).

Overall, the passage of legislation in Texas requires clearing a large number of hurdles. Moreover, the legislature is constitutionally authorized to exist in session for only a short period of time. A regular legislative term occurs once every two years; Texas is one of only seven state legislatures with biennial terms—the rest meet on an annual basis. A regular session of the Texas legislature lasts for 140 consecutive days. The governor may call special 30–day sessions, but only items specifically designated by the governor may be placed on the agenda of the special session. On the average, at least one special session is called in every two-year period.

During the regular legislative session the flow of business must conform to a fixed time schedule. The first 30 days are set aside for the introduction of bills, the approval of the governor's recess appointees (by the Senate only), and action on emergency appropriations and emergency matters requested by the governor. The second 30–day period is devoted to committee hearings on legislative proposals and consideration of emergency items. What remains of the 140–day term is left for legislative action on pending bills. No bills are supposed to be introduced after the first 60 days of the session. These constitutionally set rules may be suspended in each legislative chamber if four-fifths of its membership favor a change of procedure. Recently, the Senate has followed the practice of suspending the rules on a bill-by-bill basis. The House routinely suspended the rules between 1930 and 1980. In the legislative sessions of 1981 and 1983 the rules were strictly adhered to, but 1985 saw the House again suspend the rules by a 137–7 vote.

All in all, converting an idea into legislative policy is a cumbersome, taxing, often frustrating exercise. The probability that any bill will be passed is enhanced greatly, however, if the leaders of the House and Senate favor and push the measure. The dominant figure in the House is the speaker; the equivalent in the Senate is the lieutenant-governor.

POWERS OF THE LEGISLATIVE LEADERSHIP

The speaker is elected by the 150 members of the House of Representatives at the beginning of each regular session; selection requires majority support. Traditionally, speakers have served for two terms. Representative Bill Clayton, however, broke with custom and held the speaker's post for the four legislative sessions between 1975 and 1982. Clayton did not stand for reelection in 1982 and his successor as speaker is Gib Lewis, a representative from Fort Worth. The lieutenant-governor is elected every four years by the voters of Texas; Bill Hobby has held this position since 1973.

Each legislative leader has a number of resources at his or her disposal to build a strong power base in the Texas legislature. The speaker and lieutenant-governor are the presiding officers of their respective legislative chambers. In that capacity they have a great deal to say about the day-to-day process of legislation. To begin with, as mentioned before, they assign bills to a committee. In the House, that means, in the words of a former speaker, that the leader "can do much to pass a

Courtesy of Ben Sargent, *The Austin American-Statesman.* Reprinted by permission

bill he favors by sending it to a 'friendly' committee, one in which it is likely to receive favorable treatment by the chairman and a majority of the members."[3] The legislative leaders also make, and rule upon, procedural matters and, in so doing, they exercise some control over legislative proceedings. House Speaker Gib Lewis, for instance, began his stint as leader by announcing a set of rules that the sixty-eighth legislative session (1983) was to follow. He shuffled around the number, names, and size of the standing committees. The Calendars Committee was instructed to only schedule for House debate bills that were guaranteed to pass; the sponsor of the measure was obliged to prove the vote count. Lewis also reintroduced sexist language into legislative deliberations by doing away with the use of non-gender-specific words, such as *chairperson.*

As presiding officers, the legislative leaders can choose to recognize members for participation in legislative discussion, or not. Thus, they can prevent a legislator from securing the floor of the House or Senate to offer amendments, to propose suspension of the rules, or to raise unwanted views. If the speaker, for instance, "knows that a certain member is going to say something on the floor of the House and he does not wish to have it said, [he or she] can simply fail to recognize that member."[4]

Another source of power for the lieutenant-governor and speaker is their right to appoint members to the standing committees of the Senate and House, respectively. In the House, under Gib Lewis's leadership, almost 80 percent of all committee assignments are selected by the speaker; the remainder are determined on the basis of seniority. In the 1983 session, Lewis delayed his appointments until members signed pledge cards proclaiming support for him for the leadership post in 1985. Failure to pledge loyalty meant poor committee assignments.[5] The lieutenant-governor appoints about two-thirds of the Senate committee members; the other third is allotted on the basis of seniority. Chairpersons of all committees within each chamber are selected by the leader of each body. Gib Lewis went one step further in 1983 when he claimed the right to terminate the chairperson at any time during the session. Lewis also effectively gained total control over the important House Appropriations Committee by restricting membership to legislators who chaired the twenty-eight other substantive committees. He also appoints all members of the subcommittees on the budget that submit budgetary recommendations to the Appropriations Committee. Last, the legislative leaders choose from within their respective chambers the five-person contingent to serve on the conference committees. The leadership can stack legislative committees with personnel who are supportive of its views.

In addition, the lieutenant-governor and speaker play a major role in staffing organizations or agencies established to aid the legislature in its work. The four major legislative agencies are the Legislative Council, the Legislative Audit Committee, the Sunset Advisory Commission, and the Legislative Budget Board. The Legislative Council assists legislators in drafting bills and researching topics. The Legislative Audit Committee investigates the expenditures of any state administrative agency. The Sunset Advisory Commission recommends to the legislature, as appropriate, the cessation of operations of most state administrative agencies. The ten-member Legislative Budget Board (LBB) prepares a version of the state budget. It recommends to the legislature what the state should fund and at what price.

The principal members of these four legislative organizations are appointed by the speaker and the lieutenant-governor. The latter also serve as the chief officers in each of these agencies, the most important of which is the Legislative Budget Board. The lieutenant-governor chairs the board; the speaker is the vice-chair. Each can make two appointments to the LBB. Some eighteen months before each legislative session begins, the board prepares its version of an operating budget for the state. After the legislature commences, these recommendations are forwarded to the Senate Finance Committee and to the Appropriations and Ways and Means committees of the House. As will be seen in chapter 9, the governor and his or her office have some voice in the budgetary process, but the legislative leaders have greater say in how much money the state spends, and for which projects.

Thus the legislative leadership possesses many resources that can be easily converted into political power. Indeed, legislative leaders are quite aware of their power base. Current Lieutenant-Governor Bill Hobby notes, "Today, the office of lieutenant-governor is one of the most important in Texas government."[6] Former House Speaker (and former lieutenant-governor) Ben Barnes bluntly asserts that "a Speaker who uses the office fully can virtually *determine* what does and what does not become law in Texas."[7]

Political influence in the Texas legislature is thus distributed along hierarchical lines. The presiding officer of each legislative chamber exercises the most influence over legislation. A team composed of committee chairpersons and legislative aides surrounds the leadership. Other legislators who desire to curry the favor of the leadership "go along to get along" in the legislature. The minority of legislators not on, or wishing to join, the leader's team are relegated to positions of secondary importance. According to former Speaker Barnes, "House members who have opposed the Speaker are likely to get assignments on the least active committees and be placed in roles where they can do him the least harm."[8]

The powers of the legislative leaders are so formidable that legislators who oppose the leadership must sometimes resort to dramatic and extreme tactics in their quest to influence legislation. An example of this type of confrontation emerged near the end of the sixty-sixth legislative session (1979).

One of the items favored by the legislative leaders during that session was a measure to set a separate election date for the 1980 Texas presidential primary. Normally, the presidential primary and primaries for statewide offices are held on the same day. It is illegal for voters to vote in two different party primaries when the elections occur on the same day. If the primary dates were separated, however, voters would have been able to vote in both primaries and thus cross party lines in the process, if they so desired. Most observers contended that the bill was designed to assist John Connally in his quest to win the presidential nomination of the Republican party in 1980 without hurting the electoral chances of conservative Democrats seeking offices in state government that year.

In the Senate, bills traditionally appear on the floor for debate and subsequent vote only after two-thirds of the senators agree to consider them. But the required number of senators did not support the leadership's presidential primary bill. Facing this stumbling block, Lieutenant-Governor Hobby juggled the calendar of the Senate so that the presidential primary bill could be considered with the consent of a simple majority of members. Opponents of the bill were angered by Hobby's procedural ruse and promptly walked out of the Senate, thus depriving it of the quorum necessary to conduct any business. Hobby ordered the Department of Public Safety and the Texas Rangers to arrest and return to the Senate its twelve missing members, dubbed the "Killer Bees." Eluding the state police, the dissidents hid for five days, returning only after Hobby agreed to withdraw the primary bill from Senate consideration.

ECONOMIC ELITES AND THE LEGISLATIVE LEADERSHIP

There are clear signs that the legislative leadership is directly connected to wealthy individuals and corporations in Texas. The need for campaign contributions links aspirant leaders to the pocketbooks of well-heeled financial backers. Candidates for lieutenant-governor run a statewide race for that office. The minimum cost necessary for an effective campaign exceeds $1 million. A candidate for the speaker's position must first be elected in his or her district. Then the successful candidate must be selected by a majority of fellow legislators. It is estimated that this latter election costs in the neighborhood of $100,000. As a consequence, in the words of former Speaker Barnes, "A candidate for Speaker must be acceptable to lobbying interests, especially those representing clients who are a prime source of political contributions in the state." [9]

Ben Barnes knows of what he speaks. Barnes was born in the West Texas town of Comyn, located in Comanche County. His ancestors were farmers who had experienced many hard times on the land. Barnes sought and won a seat in the Texas House of Representatives in 1960 at the tender age of twenty-one. In 1965 he became the youngest person to be selected speaker of the Texas House. In 1968, and again in 1970, he was elected lieutenant-governor.

Prior to his entry into politics, Barnes had no steady source of income. When he held legislative office, his monthly salary was $400. Yet by 1971, "Barnes had business interests in radio stations at Grand Prairie and Abilene, several Holiday Inns, a multi-million-dollar shopping center, and an apartment complex in Brownwood, numerous stock investments, and 863 acres in valuable farmland." [10] Obviously, once in office he had made friends with people of capital.

Barnes's first legislative victory (in 1960) was financially backed by a lobbyist for the Texas Manufacturers Association. During his political ascent in Texas, Barnes developed close contacts with persons doing business in banking, oil, real estate, and other corporate activities. Banker Walter Mischer (now chairman of Allied Bancshares in Houston and a member of the 8F Crowd) lent him money to buy into the radio station in Abilene. Barnes's interest in the Holiday Inn at Marshall was a joint venture with "Walter Caven, a railroad lobbyist, and Peter Gilvin of the Texas Good Roads Association." [11] Two Dallas banks extended loans to Barnes totalling $165,000—loans granted on collateral worth much less money.

His chief benefactor, however, was multimillionaire realtor-contractor Herman Bennett. While in the legislature, Bennett provided Barnes with a $4,800 yearly income, the use of a very comfortable home on the shores of Lake Brownwood, and a houseboat on Lake Travis. Moreover, Barnes purchased 10 percent of Bennett's construction firm with an interest-free personal loan from Bennett. Barnes was to repay the loan with profits from the firm's business. In 1967, Bennett's contracting firm received a financial boost from the Barnes-led Texas legislature. In that year, Texas enacted a law requiring auto license plates to use materials that reflected light. The only company in the state producing reflective material was the 3M (Minnesota Mining and Manufacturing) Company whose plant was in Barnes's district. Bennett's construction firm had built the 3M plant and "was to do the further construction work on the plant expansion, made necessary by the new legislation." [12] Reflecting on his friendship with Bennett, Barnes once noted, "I owe everything to Herman Bennett. I couldn't have done any of this without him." [13]

The financial story of Ben Barnes is not an isolated example of a close relationship between legislative leaders and members of Texas's business community. Gus Mutscher, Barnes's successor as speaker (1968–1972), had cultivated many ties with economic interests long before Frank Sharp (see chapter 6) offered a stock deal in exchange for favorable legislation. Mutscher too had been born into a poor Texas farm family. Like Barnes, he entered the legislature in 1960 at a relatively young age (28). Furthermore, he found that his $400 monthly legislative salary did not go very far. Among the economic interests that came to Mutscher with financial aid was the beer lobby.[14] Mutscher apparently didn't forget his contributors: "According to those who financed the sailing of the Mutscher ship ..., he never failed to serve his angels—from small things such as intervening with state agencies to larger matters such as passing crucial pieces of legislation."[15]

The more recent legislative leadership also is financially linked with dominant economic interests. Lieutenant-Governor Bill Hobby is from a politically and economically prominent Texas family. His father, Will Hobby, once was governor of the state, as well as owner of the *Houston Post.* His mother, Oveta Culp Hobby, continued at the helm of the *Houston Post* until 1984 and extended the family's media holdings to television (KPRC in Houston and a station in Nashville). Mrs. Hobby also has held political positions. She was the parliamentarian of the Texas House of Representatives, commander of the Women Army Corps (WACs), and the first secretary of the Department of Health, Education, and Welfare in the Eisenhower administration. The Hobby family has close ties to other economic influentials of the state. A bank in which it owns substantial stock is a member of the Allied Bancshares holding company (whose chairman is Walter Mischer). Mrs. Hobby became one of the few female visitors to her friend George Brown's 8F Suite in the Lamar Hotel (in Houston).[16]

Lieutenant-Governor Hobby was president of the *Houston Post* until 1984. He was first elected to his present political position in 1972 and was handily reelected in 1978, 1982, and 1986. On the surface, he appears not to be close to economic lobbyists, perhaps because, as a former Texas senator put it, "He doesn't have to—after all, they (the lobbyists) already work for people like the Hobbys."[17] Yet there is some clear evidence that shows a more manifest relationship between economic interests and Hobby.

In 1975, Hobby pushed a bill through the legislature that permits a legislator to accept outside contributions to pay his or her "office expense account." In 1976–77, Hobby had amassed slightly more than $85,000 to cover his expenses, which included his apartment ($17,413), food and drink ($15,596), Christmas cards to his supporters ($3,037), and travel ($40,732). A large proportion of the money came from the political action committees of large corporations (such as Brown and Root), banks (First International—now InterFirst—and Republic of Texas), law firms (including Baker and Botts; Vinson, Elkins, Searls, Connally, and Smith; and Fulbright and Jaworski), professional associations (doctors and dentists for example), and real estate groups (Texas Association of Realtors, for one).[18]

In the same vein as Hobby, Bill Clayton, when speaker of the House, accumulated $62,000 from outside contributors to reimburse his expense account in 1976–77. Much of the money went to pay the rent of an airplane from a company in which Clayton owned 100 percent of the stock, to entertain, and to hire aides and staff, including the pilot of the plane. As with Hobby, Clayton's benefactors included people and institutions of property, such as James A. Elkins, Jr. (former chairman of First City Bancorporation), the Aluminum Company of America (Alcoa), major beef packers, and insurance and oil executives, as well as the ever-present leading law firms of Texas.[19] On leaving the Texas legislature, Clayton and his wife became lobbyists. During the 1983 session they represented the interests of eighteen clients, including the state's largest electric utility (Texas Utilities) and communication interests.

Current speaker of the House of Representatives, Gib Lewis, also has been assisted by economic notables. Large contributions from wealthy Texans have financed his efforts to win the speaker's post. For instance, independent oil producers Perry Bass, Clint Murchison, and Edwin Cox have given Lewis thousands of dollars in support of his quest to assume the House leadership position. Business lobbyists apparently rounded up a substantial majority of legislators to vote him in as speaker in 1983.[20] Lewis clearly told the Texas Association of Business his convictions:

> What is good for business is good for Texas. And I think that's why you see that we're one of the few states in this nation that does not have a corporate profit tax.... We're one of the few states in this nation that maintains a right to work law.[21]

A large portion of Lewis's campaign contributions, as pointed out in chapter 5, have come from special interest groups, especially "from utility, banking, builder, developer, insurance, health care, and transportation interests." [22] Some of it landed in his office expense account. In 1985, Lewis spent $30,000 of this money to remodel his apartment. An additional $32,000 paid for dues to private clubs, charter fees for airplanes, flowers, and food and beverages.[23]

CONCLUSION

The Texas legislature is largely a weak political institution. Legislators are poorly paid, understaffed, and forced to resolve a mammoth amount of business in a very short period of time. These limitations not only restrict the activities of the legislature, they also make it open to influence from resourceful external interests. In effect, well-organized economic interests are able to exert a great deal of pressure in the legislative process. These factors may partially account for the fact that the legislature is not very well received by the Texas public, a majority of whom rate the performance of the legislature no better than fair.[24]

The bridge between economic elites and the legislature is most easily crossed through the legislative leadership. The leaders orchestrate much of the business accomplished by this institution. Through financial connections or similar social background, the leadership is usually closely tied to economic stalwarts in Texas.

NOTES

1. *White* v. *Regester*, 412 U.S. 755 (1971).
2. Quoted in Jim Warren, "PACs Throwing Their Weight Around in Austin," *Laredo Morning News*, March 23, 1986.
3. Ben Barnes, "The Speaker's Office Seat of Power," in *Governing Texas: Documents and Readings*, 3rd ed., ed. Fred Gantt, Jr., Irving O. Dawson, and Luther G. Hagard, Jr. (New York: Crowell, 1974), p. 135.
4. Ibid.

5. "Lewis and Company Protect the Status Quo," *Texas Observer,* June 24, 1983, pp. 12–14.

6. Bill Hobby, "The Lieutenant-Governor's Job: An Incumbent's View," in *Governing Texas,* Gantt, Dawson, and Hagard, p. 131.

7. Barnes, "The Speaker's Office," p. 134 (emphasis added).

8. Ibid., p. 135.

9. Ibid., p. 138.

10. Sam Kinch, Jr., and Ben Proctor, *Texas Under a Cloud* (Austin: Jenkins Publishing Co., 1972), p. 84.

11. Harvey Katz, *Shadow on the Alamo* (Garden City, N.J.: Doubleday, 1972), p. 102.

12. Ibid., p. 92.

13. Quoted in ibid., p. 106.

14. Discussed in ibid., p. 106.

15. Kinch and Proctor, *Texas Under a Cloud,* p. 66.

16. Harry Hurt III, "The Last of the Great Ladies: Oveta Culp Hobby," *Texas Monthly* 6 (October 1978):230.

17. Quoted in Paul Burka, "The Other Hobby," *Texas Monthly* 6 (October 1978):149.

18. This information is from Jaime Murphy, "An Audit of Accounts Receivable," *Texas Observer,* September 9, 1978, pp. 9–10.

19. Ibid.

20. "Lewis and Company Protect the Status Quo," *Texas Observer.*

21. Ibid., p. 12.

22. Linda Anthony, "Hobby, Lewis Fill Political War Chests with $1.5 Million," *Austin American Statesmen,* January 17, 1986.

23. Ibid.

24. *Texas Poll,* July 1985.

9

The Governor and the Administrative System of Texas

Public policy rarely becomes effective automatically; administrative units are established to carry out policy directives. Frequently, administrators have some discretion in implementing policy. Beyond simple application of a policy or law to a specific case in a more or less mechanical way, administrative agencies have the latitude to add new rules and to adjudicate disputes. Rule implementation, rule making, and rule adjudication are thus usually within the legitimate authority of an administrative body.

The administrative branch of government has grown tremendously in the last half century. In Texas, there are so many administrative units that it is difficult to find agreement on their exact number. One reliable source has counted roughly 160 administrative units in the state; [1] another equally trustworthy estimate places the number nearer to 180. [2] All told, more than 185,000 Texans are employed by state agencies, including colleges and universities.

There is great variation among Texas's administrative agencies. Differences are rooted in their origin, importance, and autonomy from the federal government. Less than 10 percent of the state's administrative units were established by the Texas Constitution; the legislature and the governor created the rest. A few agencies are virtually inactive, others operate only sporadically, and the remainder are continuously involved in administration. Federal assistance, usually in the form of money, supports some of these bodies whereas others are funded solely by state resources. In the 1986–87 budget the state legislature authorized money for 140 administrative boards, commissions, departments, and agencies, including state colleges and universities.

It would be a mindless (and perhaps impossible) exercise to describe all the activities of every administrative official and agency in Texas. Instead, a brief discussion of the major administrative positions, beginning with elected officials and then appointed ones, follows. ★

ELECTED ADMINISTRATIVE OFFICIALS

The statewide electorate chooses some of the key administrative personnel in Texas. The state constitution authorizes the election of the governor, the attorney-general, the comptroller of public accounts, the treasurer, and the commissioner of the General Land Office.[3] State law has further called for the election of the commissioner of agriculture and the members of the Railroad Commission and the State Board of Education.

Governor

Among the individual executives elected, the governor is the most visible: "To most citizens of Texas, the office of governor of Texas more than any other office is the epitome of state government."[4] Reflective of this perceived importance, the governor in 1985 received an annual salary of $94,350—only the governors of New York and North Carolina made a higher salary.[5] Yet, regardless of high compensation and public recognition, the chief executive of Texas has been rated the weakest of all state governors.[6]

The governor's major position of strength lies in his or her relationship with the legislature. By constitutional mandate, the governor is to address the legislature and inform it of the condition of the state. The chief executive usually takes this opportunity to present the legislature with a program for its consideration. The constitution also empowers the governor to call for and set the agenda of special sessions of the legislature. The governor's most impressive legislative weapon is the veto power.

Every bill passed by the legislature must be sent to the governor's office for approval. The governor has the option of affixing his or her name to the bill and making it the law of the state or of refusing to sign the measure and thereby vetoing it. With respect to the appropriations bill (the state budget), the governor may choose to veto any item in it. The governor has ten days during the legislative term (twenty days if the session ends) to act; failure to do anything within the time period results in the bill becoming law automatically. The legislature, if it is still in session, can override the governor's veto by a two-thirds vote of the members of each chamber. Compared with most states, the votes needed to overrule the governor's veto in Texas are quite high.

Since statehood, the governor has exercised the veto more than 1,200 times. In 1981, Governor Clements rejected 27 pieces of legislation. During his four-year term, Mark White vetoed 96 legislative measures, including 86 bills, 6 concurrent House and Senate resolutions, and 4 line items in the legislative budget. The governor's decision is usually final. For more than a century, the legislature has been able to muster enough votes to override the veto in only 50 instances. Only one veto—Governor Clements's rejection of a minor point in 1979—has been overcome by legislative action in the last forty-five years.

The constitution names the governor the chief executive officer of the state, but fails to provide many resources to achieve this lofty position. One of the foremost executive powers is the ability to appoint most of the state's administrators—during any four-year period in office, a governor can expect to make around 4,000 appointments. Yet, a number of factors undermine the governor's potential control over administrative behavior through appointments.

First, many appointments require the consent of two-thirds of the Texas Senate. For instance, about half of Governor Clements's nominations during his first term of office had to be confirmed by the Senate; the senators rejected four of his nominees.[7] Moreover, when the governor makes an appointment, the senator from the prospective appointee's home district must personally approve of the nomination or the Senate will usually refuse confirmation. Such deference to an individual senator is called "senatorial courtesy."

Second, many appointed officials serve six-year terms. Vacancies occur at staggered intervals, with only a few administrators leaving an agency every two years. The four-year term of the governor makes it impossible to fill *all* positions on a board unless he or she is reelected. Until recently, many administrative appointments were done at the end of the calendar year. A newly elected governor would not start his or her term until the beginning of the next year. In effect, a governor, even after defeat or retirement from office, could still make appointments, thus depriving his or her successor of these selections. Governor Clements, *after* losing to Mark White in 1982, nominated people for 171 positions, though the Texas Senate rejected about one-third of these choices.[8] Interestingly, Mark White subsequently appointed to administrative posts 11 of the people rejected by the Senate.[9] The 68th (1983) Texas Legislature enacted a law that stopped the practice of "lame duck" appointments. Governors no longer may make new appointments after November 1st in an election year. In addition, the terms of many appointed positions now expire in February of odd-numbered years.

Third, the governor often has a small pool of people from whom to select his or her appointees. Special requirements for administrative positions are sometimes set by Texas law and thus limit choices. Moreover, the informal pressure of the clients of an agency at times constrains the discretion of the governor in the selection process. (Both of these points will be discussed later in this chapter.)

Fourth, it is not easy for a governor to remove people from administrative office. Until 1980, the chief executive could only terminate members of his or her personal staff (some 500 people). The voters approved an amendment to the state constitution in 1980 that entitles the governor to remove members whom he or she has appointed to state boards and commissions. Still, the governor has to show cause for termination. Moreover, the removal suggestion must be approved by two-thirds of the Senate, if this action involves a person who was originally confirmed by this legislative chamber.

Beyond making appointments, the governor has few resources with which to coordinate the disparate activities of the administrative branch. The governor's constitutionally authorized involvement in the state's budgetary process—a feature found in only five states including Texas—potentially gives him or her an important say in administrative matters. Agencies and officials are required to submit financial reports to the chief executive twice a year, which are to contain detailed information about the activities of each administrative unit. Furthermore, the governor is given access to the accounts and financial records of all agencies, boards, and commissions. None of these practices, however, results in much administrative control by the governor.

To be sure, each administrative unit must have its financial requests to the legislature first approved by the governor. Furthermore, every two years the governor does prepare a state budget for legislative consideration. However, the legislature (as pointed out in the last chapter) tends to overlook the governor's budget. Consequently, each administrative agent is free to approach the legislature on its own. In reality, the governor achieves very little administrative integration or control through his or her budgetary authority.

Finally, the governor may directly call on the Texas Rangers, the Department of Public Safety, and the state militia if some form of police action is necessary to carry out public policy. In cases of emergency, he or she may declare martial law.

The governor of Texas is without some powers that his or her counterparts in other states possess. For instance, the chief executive has no authority to reorganize the executive branch of the Texas government. Basically, the governor must live within an administrative system designed by the framers of the constitution to severely constrain the ability to govern. The fact that nine of the key executive offices in the state are elected means that there is a major structural barrier to coordination within this branch; each elected administrative official is able to build a power base quite independent of the governor. Texas, compared with other states, ranks among the upper echelon of states with elected administrators.

Furthermore, the transition between governors in Texas is a rather haphazard process. A newly elected governor is not formally given any office space during the transition. Nor is any money provided from the state treasury. No institutional attempt at acquainting him or her with government procedures or important information is made. Consequently, "gubernatorial transition can best be described as a free-lance affair, with most of its components at a given time stemming from a mixture of tradition and the personal predispositions of the key actors in it." [10] The governor-elect, in other words, must mostly fend for himself or herself in preparing to take the highest office in the state.

In his preparations, Mark White brought together a transition team composed of 200 people, most of whom were on White's campaign staff or were formerly in Texas government.[11] The group was divided into nine subcommittees, each structured along an issue or policy position raised in the campaign. The entire team formally convened on two occasions to hammer out the goals, objectives, and strategies of Mark White's governorship: a 200–page report was forthcoming from these efforts. Most of the expense and effort that went into the transition were borne by White's campaign organization.

In short, the Texas governor lacks much formal authority to execute and influence the laws of the state. This is not to underestimate the powers this officeholder does possess, especially through the veto. In the administrative system, the governor's power of appointment and command over the coercive arm of the state cannot be discounted. His or her position of power is enhanced by public popularity, aggressive style of leadership, and a gift for the art of persuasion. As noted by one commentator, "a Texas governor . . . occupies an office with little inherent strength and must earn whatever power he hopes to exercise. . . . A governor has only one power really—the power to persuade." [12]

To assist him in being an effective governor, Mark White established a hierarchic organization within his office. Two major wings—one to attend to programs, the other to carry out administrative tasks—were institutionalized in the White executive office. The programmatic division was headed by an executive assistant and composed of six offices, including the Office of Management and Budget, Office of Planning and Intergovernmental Affairs, Department of Community Affairs, the Texas Film Commission, the Criminal Justice Division, and the Office of State-Federal Relations. The administrative section had an executive assistant in charge and eight composite officials, including a deputy assistant for administration, a special assistant for appointments to public office, a special assistant for internal affairs, a director of scheduling, a director of accounting and personnel, a director of staff services, an assistant to attend to security, and a crew to fly the governor's airplane.[13]

On the surface, White's executive organization appeared efficient and effective. However, in practice it was marked by disorganization, with very little direction or clear chain of command. In the early stages of White's administration, the governor's office had "the atmosphere . . . close to the chaos of a political broiler room."[14] Near the end of his term, it had become "weak on substance and strong—too strong—on appearance."[15]

Part of the problem appears to have stemmed from White's overall style of leadership. A fair amount of indecisiveness (for instance, on competency tests for teachers, taxes, pari-mutuel betting on horses, a state lottery) characterized policy proposals and administrative approach. According to one observer, "White . . . rarely says what he is going to, and when he does, he doesn't stick by it."[16] He, moreover, depended greatly on opinion polls to provide ideas and issues to promote. Consequently, "relying on polls . . . made White a follower, not a leader."[17] Over time, ironically, polls in Texas revealed a growing loss of confidence among Texans in White's ability to handle his job.

By contrast, the structure of Bill Clements's governor's office during his first term "was more horizontal and diffuse."[18] Clements's office was run in a businesslike manner, more like a corporation than a political institution. By most accounts, he was judged an effective administrator. Among other things, Clements appointed some quite capable people to administrative posts. Nonetheless, Clements's first administration was hampered by some poorly conceived ideas. Moreover, his abrasive, opinionated style of leadership was quite controversial, often interfering in the initiation and implementation of his programs.[19]

Attorney-General

The attorney-general of Texas has three primary responsibilities:

First, he or she acts as the state's lawyer in legal matters. In civil cases, whether the state is the plaintiff or defendant and regardless of which governmental unit is party to a case, the office of the attorney-general provides legal counsel. In criminal proceedings, the attorney-general can coordinate investigations, assist in the preparation of cases, and seek civil sanctions (fines, for example) against those who commit offenses, but he or she cannot prosecute criminal law violators.

Second, the attorney-general may issue advisory opinions to state and local officials throughout Texas and is authorized to answer questions about state law submitted by these officials. Although the opinion delivered is not legally binding, in the absence of a court ruling the attorney-general's view carries great weight and it is usually the final interpretation.

Third, the constitution and state law authorize the attorney-general to investigate activities of corporations and to guard against the rise of monopolies in Texas. This office is empowered to search corporate records, gather any information that shows illegal corporate action, and submit it as evidence in a civil case against the company. The attorney-general's investigatory power over companies is without much legal inhibition: "The Attorney-General has full, unlimited, and unrestricted right to examination of corporate books at any time and as often as deemed necessary." [20] A corporate executive who refuses access to company books can be fined or imprisoned. Yet, throughout the history of Texas, "there is a strong tradition of cautious and restrained use of these powers by the Attorney-General." [21]

Comptroller of Public Accounts

The comptroller of public accounts is deeply involved in the receipt and distribution of the state's money. He or she is the chief tax collector for the state, although this function is shared with other agencies and officials. The comptroller has the ultimate responsibility for the collection of the general sales tax, the severance tax on oil and natural gas produced in Texas, the motor fuels tax, the inheritance tax, and many occupational taxes (as well as other minor taxes). As the principal accountant for the state, the comptroller keeps a complete record not only of all revenue received by the state but also of all the state's expenditures. Requests for payment of state funds must first be made to this office; once approved, warrants (checks) are issued to the appropriate party. Since 1942, the comptroller has been constitutionally authorized to certify that the appropriations bill passed by the legislature is in accordance with present or incoming revenue. If, in his or her judgment, funds are or will not be sufficient to cover appropriated costs, the budget is void—unless four-fifths of all legislators vote to override his or her objections. Over the last decade the comptroller's office has underestimated revenue by, on the average, about 10 percent.[22]

Treasurer

All money collected by the state is the custodial responsibility of the treasurer. Checks written to pay for financial obligations of the state that have been approved by the comptroller must be countersigned by the treasurer. He or she also sits on other administrative agencies, the most important of which is the State Banking Board, whose responsibility includes the licensing of new banks in Texas.

Commissioner of the General Land Office

Texas holds title to about 12 million acres of land. Some of the land is suitable for agriculture, but the most profitable acreage contains petroleum products. The commissioner of the General Land Office administers the use of the state's land. At times the land is sold outright, but most of it is leased. This official is responsible for collecting proceeds from rental or sale of public land.

Commissioner of Agriculture

The office of the Department of Agriculture was established by the legislature in 1907. The commissioner enforces regulations pertaining to the growth of plants; the marketing of fruits, vegetables, and eggs; the sale, use, and disposal of pesticides; and the accuracy of weights and measures such as meters, pumps, and scales. In addition, the department disseminates information to farmers and ranchers through its market news service.

State Board of Education

Until 1984, the State Board of Education consisted of twenty-seven members, each chosen from one of the state's congressional districts. In 1984, as part of a major overhaul in the administration of educational policy in Texas, the board was totally restructured. The legislature created an eight-person board—the Legislative Education Board (LEB)—to study educational issues and oversee the implementation of school policy in the Texas schools. The Legislative Education Board is composed of the lieutenant-governor, the speaker of the House, the chairman of the House Appropriations Committee, the chairman of the Senate Finance Committee, and four officials to be selected by the speaker or the lieutenant-governor. The former State Board of Education was replaced by a new fifteen person board. The state was divided into fifteen districts, each to have one representative on the board. The LEB nominated three candidates from each district; the governor appointed one of the trio to the State Board of Education. In 1988, the fifteen seats on the new Board of Education will be elected.

The board, along with the LEB, establishes policy for the state's primary, secondary, and vocational schools. Among other things, it prepares a budget for the public schools, approves textbooks for classroom use, sets general policy for all school districts, evaluates achievement of policy goals, reports to the legislature on progress toward these goals, oversees financial performance of local school districts, and appoints (with the consent of the Senate) the commissioner of education. In the past, the commissioner acted fairly independently of the board; the 1984 revisions placed the commissioner squarely under its control. He or she implements the policies of the board and makes recommendations for its consideration. The commissioner is aided by the Department of Education (composed of professional and clerical employees appointed by the commissioner). Together, the State Board of Education, the commissioner, and the Department of Education constitute the Texas (or Central) Education Agency, the umbrella administrative unit responsible for public education below the college level in Texas.

Railroad Commission

The final major administrative agency whose members are elected statewide is the Railroad Commission. Usually, however, the three commissioners are appointed by the governor (and Senate) to serve out former commissioners' unexpired terms. The newly appointed commissioner then seeks a full six-year term via election. Over the years, the commission has been given regulatory jurisdiction over railroads, buses, trucks, and energy firms doing business in Texas.

Its authority with respect to petroleum production makes the commission extremely important not only in Texas but in the nation as well. The Railroad Commission supervises many technical and substantive aspects of oil production, such as the spacing of wells and the amount of oil that can be removed from a field. These regulatory powers not only promote conservation of petroleum, they also affect the market price of oil and its by-products. Rate hikes for natural gas fall within the commission's jurisdiction, as do setting policy for the transportation and distribution of natural gas throughout the state and for the mining of coal, lignite, and uranium. Finally, the commission is the state watchdog on the environmental impact of exploration of Texas's natural resources.

The organizational structure of these offices is basically similar. Each administrative agency is divided into sections. These divisions are usually grouped around specific policy matters that fall within the agency's jurisdiction. For instance, the attorney-general's office is composed of fifteen units that cover areas of litigation such as antitrust suits, consumer protection, state and county affairs, natural resources and energy, taxation, and labor.

APPOINTED ADMINISTRATIVE OFFICIALS

Officials appointed to their positions of administrative power abound in Texas. Table 9–1 lists the key administrative posts filled in this fashion. The functions of

TABLE 9–1   Major Appointed Administrative Agencies in Texas

Administrative Unit	Functions	Number of Members
A. Higher Education		
1. Boards of Regents	Supervises senior-level colleges	nine [a] (on each board)
2. Boards of Trustees (49 distinct boards)	Supervises junior or community (two-year) colleges	depends [b]
3. Coordinating Board, Texas Colleges and Universities	Coordinates the senior and junior college systems	eighteen [a]
B. Highways		
Highway Commission (heads Department of Highways and Public Transportation)	Oversees construction and maintenance of state roads	three [a]
C. Public Welfare		
Board of Human Services	Supervises state participation in aid to families with dependent children and medical aid to the elderly programs	three [a]
D. Health		
1. Board of Department of Health Resources	Oversees a broad spectrum of programs relating to disease prevention and providing health services	eighteen [a]
2. Board of Department of Mental Health and Mental Retardation	Supervises mental health and mental retardation services, including hospitals, centers, and clinics	nine [a]
3. Health Facilities Commission	Coordinates building of health care facilities	three [a]
E. Regulation of Economy		
1. Public Utility Commission	Regulates activities of (especially rates charged by) telephone and electric companies.	three [a]
2. Financial Institutions		
a. Finance Commission: banking section; savings and loan section	Oversees state-chartered banks; Oversees state-chartered savings and loan firms	(nine in total) [c] six [a] three [a]

Administrative Unit	Functions	Number of Members
b. State Banking Board	Charters state banks; supervises the closing and reopening of state banks; regulates employer-employee relations in banks	three [d]
c. State Insurance Board	Charters, examines, and sets policy for insurance companies	three [a]
d. State Securities Board	Regulates the sale of stocks and bonds in the state	three [a]
3. Licensing Occupations (more than 30 boards)	Certifies a person for an occupation (such as lawyer, doctor, teacher, accountant, architect, water well digger, pharmacist, mortician, new car salesperson, lie detector operator, or local tax assessor)	depends [e]
4. Control over Labor		
a. Texas Employment Commission	Sets standards for receiving unemployment benefits	three [a]
b. Industrial Accident Board	Determines compensation for injured workers	three [a]
c. Occupational Safety Board	Promulgates rules and regulations for safety at the work place	three [f]
d. Commissioner of Labor and Standards	Enforces most of the state's labor laws	one [a]
F. Property Tax		
1. State Property Tax Board	Gathers information on market value of property in state and coordinates local property tax assessment and collection	six [a]
G. Natural Resources		
1. Air Control Board	Implements air quality standards and monitors air for violations	nine [a]
2. Water Development Board	Establishes general policy and rules for water development	six [a]
3. Water Commission	Issues water permits and settles water disputes	three [a]
4. Low-Level Radioactive Waste Disposal Authority	Oversees disposal of radioactive materials in Texas	six [a]

[a] All members are appointed by the governor with Senate approval for staggered six-year terms.

[b] Members of the Boards of Trustees are elected from the community college district; the length of term in office varies.

[c] There are nine appointed members of the Finance Commission: six serve in the banking division; three are on the savings and loan board. All nine are appointed by the governor with Senate consent for six-year staggered terms.

[d] The State Banking Board is composed of the treasurer, the banking commissioner, and a third person appointed by the governor and Senate for a six-year term.

[e] Most of the members of licensing boards are appointed by the governor and Senate.

[f] The Occupational Safety Board is composed of the commissioner of health, the commissioner of labor, and a third person appointed by the governor and Senate for a six-year term.

these boards and commissions cover a wide spectrum of activities, including higher education; highway construction and maintenance; financial aid to children of impoverished families and medical assistance to the elderly; the physical and mental health of Texans; the delivery of electricity, phone service, and water; regulation of banks, savings and loan firms, insurance companies, and the sale of stocks and bonds in the state; the licensing of persons to engage in certain occupations; payment of unemployment benefits and compensation for injuries sustained while working; the establishment of safety standards in work places; oversight of local property tax collection; and, finally, abating the pollution of air and water. The governor—with Senate confirmation—appoints at least one person to each of these administrative agencies; in most cases, all the positions are filled by gubernatorial appointment. The usual length of appointment is six years.

These administrative agencies are independent of each other. Even within a common policy area autonomy is frequently to be found. For instance, the fifteen boards of regents that supervise the senior colleges in Texas are distinct agencies. The Coordinating Board of Texas Colleges and Universities was established in 1965 to oversee the operations of the entire system and to prevent duplication, but the board has had a difficult time contending with the centrifugal tendencies of the various sets of regents, especially the regents of the University of Texas system. Control over the administration of water policy falls into the hands of numerous boards and commissions. For instance, until 1985 the Public Utilities Commission set rates for water utilities, the Water Development Board established the general overall water policy of Texas, the Water Commission settled water disputes, and river authorities such as the Lower Colorado River Authority regulated the development of major rivers in the state. Other examples of many agencies performing in the same general administrative area are evident in the regulation of banking and the implementation of labor policy.

The results of the independence and autonomy granted to these agencies are duplication and fragmentation of services, hazy lines of authority, and confusion (especially among the general public) over who is to do what in the administration of policies.

In their organizational structure, most of the boards and commissions resemble each other. Many of the appointed members are nonsalaried, part-time administrators, meeting as a group to oversee the agency only on occasion. The heaviest burden of administrative duties is placed on the shoulders of a full-time, salaried commissioner or executive director appointed by the board or commission (with Senate confirmation in most cases). For instance, a board of regents for a college or university system appoints (in this case without Senate approval) a chancellor or president (the title varies with the school system) to preside over the institutions of higher learning. The Coordinating Board of Colleges and Universities has a full-time commissioner of higher education. The Highway Commission selects a state engineer to supervise its policies and programs. In similar fashion, the Department of Health Resources, the Department of Mental Health and Retardation, the State Insurance Board, the State Securities Board, the Department of Labor and Standards, the Air Control Board and the Water Development Board each appoints (with Senate confirmation) a commissioner or executive director. The nine-member Finance Commission chooses, along with the Senate, three commissioners—one for banking, another for savings and loans, and the last for consumer credit regulation.

Many of the administrative agencies listed in table 9–1 are organized into divisions or sections (as are the departments headed by elected administrators or executives in Texas). Subdivisions within a department are usually created to implement specific policies or to serve geographic areas of the state. The usual result is decentralization in the implementation of public policy, with the actual responsibility of administration resting in the hands of a relatively obscure official or bureau of the agency. The Texas Department of Highways and Public Transportation provides a good example of the decentralization process.

A three-person commission appointed by the governor and the Senate establishes the general policy of the highway department. Its chief administrative officer is a state engineer who is selected by the commission (with the consent of the Senate). Two assistant engineers work under the state engineer. One of the assistants supervises a division with eight component sections—Highway Design, Bridges, Maintenance Operations, Secondary Roads, Construction, Right of Way, Materials and Testing, and Planning and Research. The other assistant is in charge of a division composed of seven separate administrative sections—Finance, Motor Vehicles, Automation, Insurance, Travel and Information, Equipment and Procurement, and Personnel. In addition, the department has an office and staff in twenty-four geographically distinct areas of the state. A district engineer is in charge of each office. Indeed, he or she assumes most of the responsibilities for highway construction and maintenance in Texas. Specialization and decentralization leave day-to-day decision making in the hands of persons positioned deep within the structure of the highway department.

One consequence of administrative decentralization is that the general public has great difficulty in monitoring the activities of the agency. With decision making so far removed from large segments of the population, most people hardly know the name of the agency and its subdivision, let alone what actually occurs where. Without sufficient knowledge about the operation of an agency, the general public is in no position to hold an agency responsible or accountable for its actions.

PENETRATION OF THE ADMINISTRATIVE SYSTEM BY DOMINANT ECONOMIC INTERESTS

Fragmentation, specialization, and decentralization in a multi-agency executive branch of government facilitate an administrative climate of mutual accommodation between special interests affected by regulation and the official regulators. Far inside the maze of the administrative process (and outside the view of the general public), a close symbiotic relationship between administrators and private interests is frequently forged. In state governments that are marked by a multitude of uncoordinated administrative units, "this accommodation has amounted to parceling out of public authority to private groups." [23]

Texas fits this pattern well. Administrative agencies and their clientele—especially if the clients are from the corporate community—are tightly knit together. McCleskey and his associates, for example, argue that the financial institutions of the state (such as banks, insurance companies, savings and loan firms, stockbrokers) are affected by administrative agencies (such as the Finance Commission, State Banking Board, State Insurance Board, and State Securities Board) that have a "history of undue sensitivity to the wishes of the group being regulated." [24] The Department of Highways and Public Transportation has a smooth working relationship with the highway lobby (primarily petroleum companies, automotive concerns, and road construction outfits): "In a real sense the interests of the highway bureaucracy and the highway lobby have become identical." [25] A government report found that "there is considerable evidence that the Texas Liquor Control Board [now called the Alcoholic Beverage Commission], insofar as its administration is concerned, has been, in a large measure, controlled by the very industry it was designed to regulate." [26] A probe of the Parks and Wildlife Department concluded that "from the beginning, the commission that rules the department has been oriented toward the firmly held belief that big men owning ranches are its principal constituency." [27] A detailed study of the Railroad Commission and its primary clientele group—the oil and natural gas industry—described the close nexus that has developed between the two as follows:

> Railroad Commissioners and members of the industry engage in a series of mutual applications of influence that mute conflict and preserve harmony. Furthermore, members of the industry interact with one another in a manner that suppresses hostility and creates consensus. The Railroad Commission has to be thought of not as a discrete governmental body outside the industry but as an integral part of that industry. This means not that the Commission is a "captive agency" but that [it] and .... the industry have a reciprocally dependent relationship.[28]

And so on throughout the labyrinth of the Texas administrative process to the point that "interests that are regulated carry so much weight among so many agencies that they have, in effect, become their own regulators." [29]

A common outlook between agency and regulated interests develops mainly through the exchange of personnel. It is not uncommon for former administrators to land on the payroll of major economic entities in Texas. For example, Byron Tunnell left the Railroad Commission to become a vice-president at Tenneco, a company regulated by the commission. Likewise, Joe Foy went from the Railroad Commission to chair Houston Natural Gas and become a board member of Central and South West. Jon Newton served on the commission and then as a regent of the U.T. system before becoming a member of the board of Texas Commerce Bancshares and a director of Lomas and Nettleton, the country's foremost mortgage banker. Former Secretary of State George Strake shifted from public office to the board of directors of Republic of Texas Bancorporation. Ex-Governor Briscoe holds a seat on the board of another large bank (M Corp), an insurance firm (Southland Financial), and Lomas and Nettleton. Similarly, former Governor Alan Shivers had a place on the board at InterFirst, Texas's largest bank, and John Connally, chief executive of the state during most of the 1960s, was a director at First City Bancorporation. After Bill Clements was defeated in 1982, he assumed the chairman's position at SEDCO, the company he founded; he also was a director at InterFirst and Shulumberger, the Holland-based company that bought SEDCO in 1985.

Moving in the opposite direction, many elected and appointed administrators come from, or are heavily supported by, dominant economic interests. Elected officials sometimes emerge directly from the higher circles of the business community—Governors Briscoe (with extensive agricultural holdings) and Clements

(SEDCO) are examples. So too, Railroad Commissioner Buddy Temple is heir to the Temple family fortune, which includes a major share in Time, Inc., as well as extensive land-holdings in East Texas. One-third of the members who formerly sat on the now-extinct State Board of Education were "from oil, chemical, or banking industries; half of them [were] presidents, vice-presidents, owners or manager of important businesses in Texas." [30] Chapter 5 documented the ties forged between many elected administrators in Texas and vested interests through campaign contributions. Table 9–2 lists people with affiliations to major corporations in Texas who have recently been appointed to state administrative agencies, boards, commissions, or departments.

Business interests frequently prevail in the appointment of administrators in three ways. First, qualifications for appointment to an agency are at times written expressly to favor industry representatives. For instance, four of the nine members of the Finance Commission (which has jurisdiction over banks and savings and loan institutions) must be active bankers with not less than five years' executive experience; two other commissioners must be building and loan executives with similar experience. Boards that examine and license occupations in Texas are mostly composed of members from the very professions to be certified. Usually, the chief administrative officers of these state boards double as executive directors of professional associations of the groups they regulate.

Second, the conditions of the office itself often limit membership on these boards. Most of the boards, commissions, and agencies in Texas are composed of part-time, unsalaried officials. Only those people who can afford to engage in administrative service as an avocation, not a job, are, in effect, eligible. Obviously this means people with some affluence.

Finally, business groups lobby intensely and quietly (with the governor and the Senate) to influence the appointment of key administrators. For example, over the last three decades the Texas Good Roads Association has sponsored virtually all the eventual appointees to the three-person commission that heads the Department of Highways and Public Transportation. About 87 percent of the railroad commissioners have first been appointed to their position by the governor. The oil and natural gas industry seldom nominates people for these posts, but it always can effectively veto the governor's recommendation. [31]

At times it appears that campaign contributions are the key to securing or maintaining an appointed position. A former commissioner of the Parks and Wildlife Department has observed that "if a man is a big contributor, he can be appointed. All of the commissioners I know of have been big contributors. . . . All have been big landowners with extensive ranches; their allegiance is with the landowners." [32] In the administration of Mark White, it was not uncommon for appointed administrators to also be major campaign contributors. Almost 68 percent of White's ninety appointees to the top seventeen boards and commissions in Texas contributed to his campaign; all but three gave over $1,000. [33] In his bid to be reelected governor in 1986, White collected $43,000 from six of the nine members of the University of Texas Board of Regents; $110,948 from six of the nine regents of Texas A & M; $36,038 from six of the nine regents of Texas Tech; $30,800 from seven of the eighteen members of the Coordinating Board, Texas College and University System; $45,500 from the three-member Highway Commission; $40,615 from six of the nine-man board of the Parks and Wildlife

TABLE 9–2   Corporate Affiliations of Some Recent Appointed Administrators in Texas

Name	Corporate Affiliation	Administrative Position
T. Louis Austin	President, Brown and Root	Former Chairman, Board of Corrections
Perry Bass	Bass Enterprises	Former Chairman, Parks and Wildlife Commission
Robert Bass	Bass Enterprises	Highway Commission
Louis Beecherl	Director, Texas Oil and Gas (now part of USX)	Chairman, Water Development Board; U.T. Board of Regents
Jack Blanton	Director, Texas Commerce and United Energy Resources (now MidCon)	Chairman, U.T. Board of Regents
H.R. Bright	Bright Banc; East Texas Motor Freight; Republic of Texas	Former Chairman, Texas A & M Board of Regents
J. Fred Bucy	Texas Instruments	Board of Regents, Texas Tech
Charles Butt	Chairman, H.E.B. Stores; Director, Texas Commerce	Coordinating Board; Advisory Council, U.T. Marine Science Institute
Edwin Cox, Jr.	Owner, Swift & Co.; Director, InterFirst–Dallas	Chairman, Parks and Wildlife Commission
Harlan Crow	Trammel Crow developers; Director, Texas Commerce	Coordinating Board
Trammel Crow	Trammel Crow developers (largest in U.S.)	Board of Architectural Examiners
Hal Daugherty	Director, M Corp.	Coordinating Board
Charles Duncan	Director, Texas Commerce and Texas Eastern	State Board of Education
Lucien Flournoy	Director, Central Power and Light	Economic Development Commission
Jess Hay	Chairman, Lomas and Nettleton; Director, M Bank and Exxon	U.T. Board of Regents
Mary L. Kleberg	King Ranch	Board of Directors, University System of S. Texas
Thomas McDade	Director, Texas Commerce and Houston Industries	Board of Corrections and Investment Advisory Committee, Texas A & M
Mary Moody Northern	Director, American National Insurance Co.	Commission on the Arts
James R. Powell	Director, Texas Commerce	Former Chairman, U.T. Board of Regents
Tom Rhodes	Director, SEDCO	U.T. Board of Regents
Gerald Smith	Chief Executive Officer, Allied Bancshares	State Banking Board
B.A. Steinhagen	Director, InterFirst and Gulf States Utilities	Board of Regents, Lamar University
Harvey Weil	Director, M Corp	Vice-Chairman, Coordinating Board

Commission; and $79,630 from one-third of the fifteen-person Economic Development Commission.[34]

This pattern prompted John Hildreth of Common Cause to note that "it's a time-honored tradition in Texas politics that if you expect to receive one of the plum appointed positions you should expect to be a hefty contributor." [35] Not so, counters Joe Bill Watkins, chief fund-raiser for White's 1986 campaign: "I think there are a whole lot of factors that go into the selection of somebody for a board or agency. But the suggestion that they're out there being bought and paid for is absolutely wrong and unfair." [36]

With so much cross-fertilization between regulators and the regulated, it is not surprising that each would begin to identify with the other. Mutual identification is furthered by tangible rewards available through interdependence. The administrative agency, if it keeps its most important constituency satisfied, is assured of political support. Supportive clients can help the agency with such essential matters as improvement of its budget or prevention of legislative elimination of the agency or some of its functions.

Private groups also realize that regulators can serve their interests. Favorable administration often results in the distribution of state funds to private parties. Or it might mean that the state will perform services essential to the growth of the industry—services that would be financially prohibitive if a company had to absorb the costs itself. Regulation might curtail competition and thus keep prices high for the goods offered by the established industries. Or it might channel the activities of conflicting interests into the peaceful confines of an administrative boardroom and out of the violent potential of street confrontation. Finally, the existence of administrative agencies generally appeases a restless public when it desires control over unpopular corporate practices—even if, as the case has sometimes been, the regulation is purely symbolic.[37]

Needless to say, many corporations have found administrative regulation to be a positive phenomenon. Indeed, instead of opposing government regulation as unwanted outside interference, numerous industries have avidly sought it—public exhortations to the contrary.[38]

CONCLUSION

The executive branch of government in Texas is composed of hundreds of administrative offices. Some of the people holding these positions are elected, but most are appointed. Administrative agencies, regardless of the means of selecting key officials, are largely autonomous from each other and from centralized coordination. Within an agency, operations are usually highly decentralized. Because of the organizational structure of executive offices, it is very difficult for people and groups not directly and immediately affected by the administrative system to evaluate decisions made there.

Conversely, groups with a stake in the administrative process are keenly aware of the policies of executives and agencies. In many instances, this means economic groups, especially those associated with economic notables. These outside organizations are very instrumental in the selection of administrative personnel. Indeed, at times, they have greatly assisted in the creation of these agencies. Through supplying research, expert testimony, and general support for executive units, economic elites have a major effect on the everyday business of the administration of public policy in Texas.

NOTES

1. *Guide to State Agencies,* 5th ed. (Austin: Lyndon Baines Johnson School of Public Affairs, 1978).

2. Texas Research League, *To Make Texas Government Modern, Viable, Responsive* (Austin: Texas Research League, 1975).

3. Officially the position of lieutenant-governor is listed in the constitution as an executive office. The importance of this position, however, lies in its legislative functions.

4. Fred Gantt, Jr., *The Impact of the Texas Constitution on the Executive* (Houston: Institute of Urban Affairs, University of Houston, 1973), p. 1

5. *Book of States: 1986–87,* vol. 26 (Lexington, Kentucky: Council of State Governments, 1986), p. 35.

6. Joseph A. Schlesinger, "The Politics of the Executive," in *Politics in the American States: A Comparative Analysis,* 2d ed., ed. Herbert Jacob and Kenneth N. Vines (Boston: Little, Brown, 1971), p. 232. Another study ranks the powers of the Texas governor next to last in comparison to chief executives of other states: Thad L. Beyle, "The Governor's Formal Powers: A View from the Governor's Chair," *Public Administration Review* 28 (Nov./Dec.1968): 540–45.

7. This does not include the "midnight appointments" made by Governor Clements after his 1982 electoral defeat, many of whom were rejected in the 1983 session of the Texas Senate.

8. Charles Wiggins, Keith E. Hamm, and Howard Balanoff, "The 1982 Gubernatorial Transition in Texas: Bolt Cutters, Late Trains, Lame Ducks, and Bullock's Bullets," in *Gubernatorial Transitions: The 1982 Elections,* ed. Thad L. Beyle (Durham: Duke University Press, 1985), p. 387.

9. Ibid.

10. Ibid., p. 403.

11. The details of the White transition effort are found in ibid.

12. Paul Burka, "The Strange Case of Mark White," *Texas Monthly,* October 1986, p. 136.

13. Details of the governor's office of Mark White are in Wiggins, Hamm, and Balanoff, "The 1982 Gubernatorial Transition in Texas."

14. Paul Burka, "Mark White's Coming Out Party," *Texas Monthly,* May 1982, p. 394.

15. Paul Burka, "The Strange Case of Mark White," p. 213.

16. Ibid., p. 212.

17. Ibid.

18. Wiggins, Hamm, and Balanoff, p. 392.

19. Paul Burka, "The Strange Case of Bill Clements," *Texas Monthly,* October 1986, pp. 136–37.

20. James G. Dickson, Jr., *Law and Politics: The Office of the Attorney General in Texas* (Manchaca, Texas: Sterling Swift Publishing, 1976), p. 19.

21. Ibid.

22. Gary Keith, *Revenue Estimating and Spending Limits* (Austin: House Study Group, 1983), calculated from table 3, p. 9.

23. Grant McConnell, *Private Power and American Democracy* (New York: Knopf, 1967), p. 189.

24. Clifton McCleskey, Allan Butcher, Daniel E. Farlow, and J. Pat Stephens, *The Government and Politics of Texas,* 6th ed. (Boston: Little, Brown, 1978), p. 359.

25. Griffin Smith, Jr., "The Highway Establishment and How It Grew, and Grew, and Grew," reprinted in *Texas Monthly's Political Reader* (Austin: Texas Monthly Press and Sterling Swift Publishing, 1978), p. 157.

26. *Attorney-General's Report Concerning Investigation of Texas Liquor Control Board* (Austin: Attorney General of Texas, 1968), pp. 15–16. Quoted in James Anderson, Richard W. Murray, and Edward L. Farley, *Texas Politics: An Introduction,* 3d ed. (New York: Harper and Row, 1979), p. 196.

27. Richard Starnes, "The Texas Fat Cat Game," *Outdoor Life,* February 1980, p. 59.

28. David F. Prindle, *Petroleum Politics and the Texas Railroad Commission* (Austin: University of Texas Press, 1981), pp. 144–45.

29. William Earl Maxwell and Ernest Crain, *Texas Politics Today* (St. Paul: West Publishing Co., 1978), p. 430.

30. Ibid., p. 542.

31. Prindle, *Petroleum Politics,* pp. 156–59.

32. Bob Burleson, quoted in Starnes, "The Texas Fat Cat Game," pp. 134–35.

33. Figure cited in Geoffrey Rips, "Gov. White's Algebra," *Texas Observer,* October 25, 1985, pp. 4–5.

34. Calculated from Wayne Slater and George Kuempel, "Key State Appointees Big Donors to White," *Dallas Morning News,* August 10, 1986.

35. Quoted in ibid.

36. Quoted in ibid.

37. On the point of the symbolic function of administration to assuage public discontent with the practices of private interests, see Murray Edelman, *The Symbolic Uses of Politics* (Urbana: University of Illinois Press, 1964), ch. 2.

38. For national examples see Gabriel Kolko, *The Triumph of Conservatism* (New York: The Free Press, 1964).

10

The Texas Judiciary

In a society in which formal law regulates social conduct, courts are indispensable. Disputes among people and between the government and its citizens are frequently resolved in the thousands of state, local, and federal courthouses across the United States. Courts can simply apply laws derived from the legislature, administrative agencies, constitutions, or other courts. They can modify, create, or, at times, nullify legal codes. The judicial branch of government ranks as an extremely important institution in the political system.

In Texas, the state has established a large number of diverse courts. Judges, usually elected by the voters, preside over these institutions. Lawyers lend a guiding hand to the parties of a legal dispute. Ordinary citizens enter into the judicial drama either as jurors or litigants.

This chapter first outlines the structure of the Texas judicial system. It then discusses the major participants in the legal process. Throughout, a constant eye is focused on how the operation of the state judiciary might work to the benefit of dominant economic elites.   ★

THE TEXAS JUDICIAL SYSTEM

The court system in Texas is marked by great diversity and complexity in its organizational structure. These features are most evident in viewing the various types of courts in the state and the jurisdiction exercised by different courts.

Types of Courts

The Texas judicial system includes three distinct yet overlapping types of courts: constitutional, statutory, and municipal. The state constitution designates six different courts: the Supreme Court, the Court of Criminal Appeals, Courts of Appeals, District Courts, County Courts, and Justice of the Peace courts. The legislature is constitutionally authorized to establish additional courts and has responded by creating special statutory courts at the county level (for example, county probate courts, county civil courts, and county criminal courts) and at the district level (for example, domestic relations courts, juvenile courts, and criminal district courts). Finally, each incorporated city in the state may have its own municipal court as well as a small claims court.

The result is a judicial system with a multitude of courts and judges. There is only one Supreme Court and one Court of Criminal Appeals; each is composed of nine justices. There are fourteen courts of appeals in Texas, each located in a distinct district. The number of judges sitting on a court of appeals varies: in Houston, for instance, there are nine, whereas there are six on the Austin court, thirteen on the Dallas one, and seven on the Fort Worth and San Antonio courts, respectively. As of 1986, there are 374 district courts in Texas. Each has one presiding judge, although a constitutional amendment approved in 1985 allows the legislature to designate more than one judge for a district court. The constitution establishes a court for each of Texas's 254 counties. Constitutional county courts (usually called commissioners courts) are mostly authorized to govern the county: they have limited judicial responsibilities. In addition, the legislature is empowered to install courts in counties to hear both civil and criminal matters; by 1986, 138 such courts have been created. Each of Texas's counties also has a justice of the peace court. Up to eight of these courts can be established in any one county; in total (in 1986), there are 948 in the state. Finally, there are 839 municipal courts spread across the state. One judge sits on the bench of each county, justice of the peace, and municipal court. All told, "Texas reputedly has more judges than any geographic unit in the English-speaking world, including all of Great Britain." [1]

The Texas courts also have a heavy work load.[2] Municipal courts handle almost 7 million cases a year, most of which involve traffic violations. Justice of the peace courts render verdicts in nearly 2 million cases annually. At the end of 1985, over 600,000 cases were pending before the state's district courts; even though these courts had disposed of some 470,000 cases during the year, nearly 500,000 cases were added to the dockets in 1985. The figures for the county courts parallel those for the district courts; nearly one-third of the matters facing county courts involve driving while intoxicated (DWI) offenses. The fourteen courts of appeals decided nearly 8,000 cases in 1985, over half of which were criminal in nature; still, at year's end, 5,692 matters were pending. The Court of Criminal Appeals had 4,558 items of business on its 1985 calendar. In any one year, it reverses judgment in around 10 percent of the appeals involving criminal convictions in lower courts. Some critics score the court for reversal on trivial technicalities that have virtually nothing to do with the preservation of the rights of the individuals.[3] The Supreme Court of Texas disposed of 1,970 cases—217 involving written opinions—in 1985; both figures were well above average for the court.

Jurisdiction

There is a great deal of variation in the jurisdiction of Texas's courts. Basically, a court's jurisdiction is determined by the nature of the case heard before it and by the order in which it is asked to decide the case.

There are two types of court cases: criminal cases and civil cases. Criminal cases involve alleged violations of laws thought by the government to be crucial for harmonious social relations. Offenses falling into this category include murder, robbery, assault, public drunkenness, smoking marijuana, and illegal parking (among many, many possible examples). Civil cases generally involve disputes where one party accuses another of inflicting damage to him, her, or it. The complainant seeks financial compensation for the alleged harm. In many civil matters, business practices (such as fraud, deception, making harmful products, dangerous workplaces, physical damage to the environment, price-fixing, and monopolistic actions) are at issue.

There are also two different time frames during which a case may reach a court. Some courts are the first to decide a case. When this occurs, the court has *original jurisdiction* over the dispute. At other times, courts try a case on appeal from another court. This is a situation of *appellate jurisdiction*

Table 10–1 presents the actual jurisdiction of Texas's courts in terms of types of cases heard (civil or criminal) and time of presentation (original or on appeal). There is very little symmetry to the jurisdictional pattern of the state's courts. It would be cumbersome (and probably only add to the confusion) to attempt to sort out all the details of court jurisdiction; instead, a few general points about the intricate network are offered.

TABLE 10–1   Jurisdiction of the State Courts in Texas

| Court | Criminal Cases | | Civil Cases | |
	Original	Appellate	Original	Appellate
Supreme Court	None	None	Writs to remove political officials from office	Cases involving conflict among judges of the Courts of Appeal, cases where a trial court or a Court of Appeal has declared a legislative act or an administrative decision unconstitutional; cases involving the Railroad Commission; and cases where a Court of Appeal may have made an error in applying the law
Court of Criminal Appeals	None	All cases from county, district, and Courts of Appeal where a person is to be jailed or fined over $100	None	None
Courts of Appeal	None	Cases from county and district courts	None	All civil cases from county and district courts where litigant has been fined $100 or more

TABLE 10–1—Continued

Court	Criminal Cases		Civil Cases	
	Original	Appellate	Original	Appellate
District Courts [a]	All felonies, and, in some counties, misdemeanors	None	Cases involving over $500; cases involving $500 to $5,000, concurrent with county courts; special cases such as slander and libel, divorce, land titles, and state suits for recovery of penalties	Probate appeals from county courts and some special cases involving detention for mental illness and alcoholism
County Courts [b]	Misdemeanors involving fines over $200 and/or jail	All cases from jp and municipal courts (de novo) [c]	Cases involving $200 to $500; cases involving $500 to $5,000 concurrent with district courts; probate cases	All cases from jp involving $20 to $200 (de novo) [c]
Justice of the Peace	Misdemeanors not involving a jail term and fines less than $200	None	Disputes involving less than $200; concurrent jurisdiction with county courts in disputes involving $200 to $1000 and district courts in disputes involving $500 to $1,000	None
Municipal	Violation of city laws; misdemeanors involving fines less than $200, concurrent jurisdiction with jp	None	None	None
Small Claims	None	None	Claims under $200	None

[a] Most of the district courts are courts of general jurisdiction; that is, they hear both civil and criminal cases. The legislature, however, has created special district courts with jurisdiction limited either to civil or criminal matters.

[b] Most of the county courts are courts of general jurisdiction; that is, they hear both criminal and civil cases. The legislature, however, has created special county courts with jurisdiction limited either to civil or criminal cases and restricted to appeals.

[c] A case appealed to a county court from most justice of the peace and municipal courts must be completely retried because these latter courts, in most instances, do not record their proceedings.

First, some of the state's courts (i.e., district courts, some county courts, and justice of the peace courts) have original jurisdiction in both criminal and civil disputes; other courts (i.e., municipal, small claims, statutory district, and some county courts) exercise original jurisdiction over one type of case or the other, not over both. Second, the first court to hear a case is usually determined by the severity of the crime (in criminal cases) or the amount of money sought as compensation (in civil cases); but, in many instances, more than one court has original jurisdiction over the same criminal or civil matter. Third, the Supreme Court, the courts of appeals, and the Court of Criminal Appeals function basically as appellate courts. The Supreme Court only hears civil appeals. The Court of Criminal Appeals is only involved in criminal matters. The courts of appeals, thanks to a 1980 amendment to the Texas Constitution, now render decisions in both criminal and civil disputes. Finally, constitutionally authorized county courts have both original and appellate jurisdiction over both criminal and civil cases, although in any case the matters in question are usually not terribly serious.

PENETRATION OF THE COURT SYSTEM IN TEXAS BY ECONOMIC ELITES

There are two major features of the Texas judiciary that make it very amenable to the influence of economic elites. First, the structure of the court system is most conducive to penetration by people and organizations from the higher economic circles. Second, the people most responsible for the functioning of the judicial branch are generally of a social background similar to members of the economic elite or they are somewhat indebted to economic notables for their position.

The Structure of the Court System

As previously noted, the one word that best describes the organization of the Texas court system is *complexity.* Mastering the court system requires a full understanding of the complicated nuances of the judiciary. Legal expertise is a purchasable commodity. Those with an abundance of financial resources are in the best position to buy the knowledge necessary to successfully traverse the intricate pathways of the Texas court system.

Social Background of Court Personnel

There are three groups of people who play starring roles in the Texas judicial drama: judges, lawyers, and, in some cases, jurors. People with a social and economic background in a vein similar to that of the higher economic elites of the state predominate in each of these groups.

Lawyers.   Most of the state's 40,000 lawyers are white, male, and largely from upper- to upper-middle-class families.[4] Lawyers who represent firms with corporate clients are even closer in class standing to their business customers.[5] Needless to say, the very opulence and success of corporations are responsible for the high status position of many of the state's attorneys.

Jurors.   Citizens of the state of Texas have a hand in the judicial process through their selection as jurors. There are two types of juries operative in the state: grand juries and trial (petit) juries.

Grand Juries.   The state constitution guarantees that no person shall be charged with a serious (felony) criminal offense without first being indicted by a grand jury. An indictment is made if, in the opinion of nine of the twelve members of the grand jury, there is sufficient evidence to warrant a trial. In its proceedings, which generally last from three to six months, a grand jury can investigate any suspected criminal activity within its geographic jurisdiction (usually the county).

The twelve members of a grand jury are officially chosen by a district court judge. The judge is aided in his or her selection by a jury commission, which is composed of three to five citizens also appointed by the district court judge. The commission compiles a list of fifteen to twenty residents of a county from which the district judge selects the final twelve members of the grand jury.

Available evidence shows that most of the jury commissioners in Texas "are upper-middle-class Anglo Saxon males."[6] Not unexpectedly, the jury commission selects people with similar social and economic backgrounds to be potential members of the grand jury. Hence a district judge makes the final twelve choices from a panel of persons atypical of the general population. Studies corroborate the fact that an overwhelming number of grand jurors in Texas are from high-status positions. Most of the grand jury members in Harris County (Houston), for instance, come from the upper to upper-middle classes.[7] Even in Texas's poorest county, Hidalgo, almost every grand juror is drawn from the ranks of the area's wealthy.[8] Moreover, there is some indication that the social background of jurors influences the indictment process, with upper- to upper-middle-class, male-oriented values guiding the deliberations of the grand jury.[9]

Trial Juries.   The fate of persons accused of felony crimes in Texas is usually in the hands of a trial jury. Criminal offenses of a lesser nature and civil cases also can, at the choice of the defendant, be adjudicated by trial juries. The size of the jury and the number needed to reach a verdict depend on the case.

On the surface, most Texans are eligible for jury service. A juror must be at least eighteen years old, a citizen of the state (and of the United States), a person of sound moral character, and someone who is able to read and write (unless an insufficient number of literate people exists). Many factors, however, significantly reduce the population from which the jury is actually chosen.

First, jurors are selected at random from voting registration lists; failure to register to vote excludes a person from jury duty. Texas, unlike most other states, does not use any other means of jury selection to supplement the electoral rolls. Considering that almost one-third of voting age Texans—mostly to be found among the state's poor, racial minorities, and young—fail to register, jury duty is somewhat restricted. Second, people over sixty-five, men or women who have custodial care of children under ten years old, and full-time students are automatically exempted from being jurors. Third, judges can excuse otherwise qualified persons for compelling reasons; for instance, if economic hardship would result from missing work. Finally, lawyers have a number of peremptory challenges that they can use to strike prospective jurors from the final jury.

The pool of potential jurors thus becomes ever smaller and ultimately results in juries where "professionals, managers, and proprietors are vastly over-represented."[10] Even with this distinct class bias existing on a jury, it nonetheless contains people more representative of the wider community than are either lawyers or, as will be discussed shortly, judges. Indeed, there is some suggestion that juries will, at times, rule against wealthy persons and corporations in civil judgments because of the very affluence of the parties.[11] This may be one of the reasons why civil cases are mostly tried by judges alone and often only after administrative agencies have first heard the case.

Judges.   Many of the courts in Texas (specifically, the Supreme Court, the courts of appeals, the Court of Criminal Appeals, and the district courts) stipulate that an aspirant judge must be an attorney licensed to practice law in the state. Most of the legislatively created county courts are open only to lawyers; about five out of every six judges presently serving on these courts are licensed attorneys. Commissioners of county courts and justices of the peace need not be lawyers. In fact, in 1976 only about 30 percent of the county judges and 7 percent of the justices of the peace were attorneys. Municipalities vary in requiring legal training of judges. Cities with populations over 5,000 generally do specify that a municipal court judge be a licensed lawyer.[12]

Most of the lawyers who become judges in Texas, especially on the state's higher appellate courts (i.e., Supreme Court, Court of Criminal Appeals, and courts of appeals) come from a social background near the heights of the economic ladder.[13] Judges are even more akin to the corporate wealthy than are other lawyers. There is scattered evidence that shows social background to be a good predictor of judicial behavior.[14]

The transmission belt between economic interests and the judiciary is tightened through the process of selecting judges. Formally, almost all of Texas's judges (the sole exception occurs at the municipal court level) are elected. Campaign contributions have always been a possible point of linkage between donors and judges. In the past, however, practical obstacles generally prevented judicial races from becoming an auction, with justice possibly going to the highest bidder. Judges in Texas were frequently appointed initially by the governor to their posts in order to complete a term of office conveniently vacated by a retiring judge. The governor's appointments were often influenced by well-established corporate interests, usually as represented by the leading law firms (such as Fulbright and Jaworski; Baker and Botts; and Vinson, Elkins, Searls, Connally, and Smith) in the state. Consequently, "incumbent" judges—even recently appointed ones—rarely faced serious opposition at election time. If a judicial race was seriously contested, the results of a poll conducted among members of the state's bar association usually became a guide to media endorsements and, in almost all cases, candidate selection. This pattern of appointment-then-election of judges suited the corporate community of the state well. As noted by one observer:

> In effect, the legal and political establishment begat generations of justices who reflected the assumption of their progenitors that preservation of a "good bidness [business] climate" is the highest aim of government. Part of that climate was a legal system in which oil companies, hospitals, insurers, and other enterprises didn't have to live in constant fear of lawsuits.[15]

Things began to change in 1982, however. In the judicial elections of that year, rancher Clinton Manges poured a substantial amount of money—some

$350,000—into judicial campaigns, usually those of challengers. Manges saw an opportunity to influence the selection of judges. His intent was to assist in the election of judges who might be more sympathetic to the economic plight of landowners in their dealings with oil companies that held leases on their property. Manges appears to have met with much success in his effort to elect the "right" court personnel.[16]

The 1986 judicial contests attracted even greater sums of money. As pointed out in chapter 5, the three competitive races for places on the Supreme Court, for instance, were very well financed: nearly $3 million was donated to leading contenders. More important, contributors could be divided into two opposed camps. One side was composed of trial lawyers, while the other consisted of large corporations, doctors, hospitals, and insurance companies. The first group supported candidates who might sympathize with plaintiffs damaged by the malfeasance or negligence of companies or professionals, in particular physicians. The second group hoped for a court containing justices for the defendants fighting such claims. On balance, the Supreme Court now is firmly in the hands of the plaintiff/trial lawyer contingency.[17]

Charges have also been aired that some judges—including ones sitting on the highest courts of Texas—are violating the law in order to help campaign benefactors.[18] As might be expected in this type of climate, the public's opinion of the Texas judiciary is not very sanguine. When Texans were recently asked whether "the courts in this state dispense justice fairly or . . . favor the rich and influential," 32 percent answered "fairly" and 54 percent said that the judicial advantage went to the wealthy.[19]

Also, as one might predict, there have been concerted attempts made to alter the selection process of Texas's judges. The leading "reform" would establish a nominating committee to present three names to the governor for vacated judicial posts. The governor, with Senate confirmation, would appoint one of the trio to the bench. After a year on the court, the judge would run unopposed in an election.[20]

THE CLASS BIAS OF THE CRIMINAL JUSTICE SYSTEM IN TEXAS

For the poor of Texas the legal system, especially the criminal justice system, can be very harsh. The lower one's economic standing, the greater the chance of arrest, conviction, imprisonment, and death at the hands of the state. The legal machinery begins with arrest.

In recent years the arrests of some poor Texans have been chilling experiences—fraught with the dangers of harassment, beatings, and even death at the hands of the arresting officers. Between 1973 and 1978, one source lists twenty Texas cases in which "a law enforcement officer killed a civilian under questionable circumstances." [21] Sixteen of the twenty cases involved young, male, impoverished Mexican Americans. Consider the following examples.

A Dallas policeman in 1973 arrested a twelve-year-old Mexican American boy, Santos Rodriguez, and his brother for allegedly stealing money from a soft drink vending machine. While driving the boys to the police station, the officer

Courtesy of Ben Sargent, *The Austin American-Statesman.*   Reprinted by permission.

placed a .357 Magnum to Santos Rodriguez's head in an attempt to extract a confession. Thinking that the gun was not loaded, the policeman spun the cylinder and pulled the trigger. The boy died in the police car. At a later time, the brothers were cleared of any involvement in the burglary.[22]

In the summer of 1975, the Castroville police chief, Frank Hayes, arrested Ricardo Morales, a part-time day laborer, on suspicion of stealing televisions and stereo sets. The chief drove Morales to a dirt road in an isolated area outside of Castroville. Along the way he told his prisoner, "You're a thieving bastard and I'm gonna kill your ass."[23] Once stopped, Hayes took Morales out of the car. A blast from the chief's shotgun killed the prisoner at point-blank range. Later, Hayes's daughter and sister-in-law transported Morales's body hundreds of miles away and buried it at a farm owned by the chief's brother-in-law.

On a warm spring night in 1976, a Houston man, Joe Campos Torres, was arrested by six city patrolmen for drunk and disorderly conduct. Words were exchanged between the police and Torres and five of the officers beat him. At the station house, the duty sergeant refused to book Torres and instructed the cops to take him to a hospital for emergency treatment. Instead, they offered to release Torres, who responded by cursing them. The angered officers then took Torres to Buffalo Bayou to "see if the wetback can swim." [24] Three days after the police threw him into the water, Torres's body washed ashore.

In 1978, Larry Lozano, suffering from mental depression, got drunk and caused a disturbance in Odessa. When police came to arrest him, a scuffle broke out. After Lozano was restrained, he was booked into the Ector County jail. Later Lozano's bruised and battered body was discovered on the floor of his cell. The police claimed that he had gone beserk and killed himself by repeatedly banging his head against the bars of the jail. A report issued by the coroner of El Paso County, called in by the family of the deceased to determine the actual cause of death, ruled out suicide and noted that the victim had died "from extensive blunt trauma, such as beating, hitting, kicking, as well as possible small wounds made with sharp instruments." [25] Law enforcement officials subsequently admitted that force had been used to control Lozano, but denied killing him.

In McAllen, police routinely used physical coercion on prisoners as they were being booked into the local jail. In fact, for five years (until 1979) they filmed this treatment! One of the videotapes—some of which were shown on national television in 1981—was of "a prisoner who was thrown against a wall, kicked, punched, and then grabbed by officers who smashed his head against the booking desk." [26] Virtually all of the ill-treated prisoners were poor Chicanos.

The sheriff of San Jacinto County admitted in 1983 that he operated a speed trap in his area and that his men were authorized to stop and search indiscriminately anyone they suspected of anything. Mostly young persons were detained. In addition, "confessions" from arrested suspects were coerced through water torture administered by the local police. [27]

Police charged with using unnecessary force to arrest Texans, especially the impoverished, do not usually receive harsh punishment. In Houston, for instance, a grand jury investigated twenty-five cases between 1974 and 1977 involving police shootings of civilians and issued an indictment in only one instance. [28] The Ector County law enforcement officers accused of beating Larry Lozano to death never were prosecuted. When police have been convicted of misconduct by courts, especially state courts, their sentences have been light. The Dallas patrolman who played Russian roulette with the Rodriguez boy received a five-year prison term. Only two of the five Houston policemen were tried in state court for their role in the drowning death of Joe Campos Torres. For their guilt, each of these officers received a one-year probated sentence and a fine of $2,000. [29] (Ironically, a short time later Torres's parents were booked for resisting arrest after they came to the aid of a young Chicano being taken into custody. They had to pay $1,900 to be released on bail. [30]) Frank Hayes, the police chief of Castroville, was convicted of aggravated assault in a state court and was sentenced to the penitentiary for ten years. His wife was given a one-year probated sentence and a fine of $49.50 for her part in the burial of Ricardo Morales; the other two women who participated were not prosecuted by state authorities. [31]

Of course, these cases of police mistreatment of the poor are extreme examples and do not necessarily reflect the everyday interactions between the two groups. But the high rate of such incidents in Texas has raised many eyebrows. Among others, Percy Foreman, famed criminal lawyer who has previously represented policemen in litigation, expressed outrage at the behavior of the Houston police force during the recent past. Commenting on this city, he has complained: "We are in a police state. . . . This is the case here more than in any other city in the United States, and I've practiced in just about all of them. It even transcends the police-state situation that prevails in some of the totalitarian countries." [32] Lately, after the appointment of a black as chief of police in Houston, the city's police force has not been involved in the unsavory incidents that marred its reputation in the past. [33]

Once in court, poor defendants are frequently not provided the best of legal representation. Legal aid in Texas is not widespread. The quality of the public defender system varies from city to city. In some locales it is quite good, providing indigents with conscientious attorneys who spend a great deal of time preparing a thorough defense. In many other areas, however, the public defenders are inexperienced and not encouraged to become fully engaged in the trial of a poor person. Frequently, the public defender instructs his or her client to plead guilty and forgo a trial. A study of the Travis County (Austin) jail found that court-appointed attorneys did not even see their clients until ten to twenty-one days after booking. [34]

Not surprisingly, the state jails and prisons are filled with impoverished Texans. Table 10–2 lists a number of social characteristics of the prison population serving time in the state penitentiary system. The typical inmate in Texas is a young, black, urban male with a rather low IQ. Not mentioned in the table, but nonetheless an overall trait of Texas prisoners, is the low social standing of those in jail. Most of them are at the bottom of the income ladder; as economic conditions in society grow worse, the prison population increases.

Being behind bars in Texas is an unusually unpleasant experience. Most poor people are forced to stay in jail while awaiting trial. Without sufficient funds to finance bail and with judges not usually willing to release them on their personal recognizance, the impoverished languish in confinement. Mostly they are kept in county jail houses to await trial. A study completed in 1975 by the Texas Commission on Jail Standards discovered that only 6 of the state's 254 county jails met *minimum* criteria for facility management and living conditions. [35] In 1987, a federal court in Houston found the sheriff of Montgomery County in East Texas had abetted in the beating of prisoners in the county jail; damages of $30,000 were awarded against the sheriff. [36]

After conviction, the treatment of prisoners and the quality of penal institutions do not necessarily improve. In 1973, for instance, a federal district court branded the state's youth correction centers, which house juvenile offenders, as brutal and inhumane. [37] Recently, the twenty prisons that compose the adult penitentiary system in Texas have come under legal attack.

Nearly 36,000 prisoners—more than in almost any other state—are confined in these prisons. Since these institutions were built to accommodate 19,000, the Texas prison system is greatly overcrowded. In the late 1970s, a number of state prisoners brought suit against prison authorities, basically claiming that the peni-

TABLE 10–2   Social Characteristics of Inmates in Texas State Prisons

Characteristic	Percent	Number
Ethnicity		
Black	43.1	13,211
Anglo	37.4	11,494
Mexican descent	19.4	5,608
Sex		
Male	95.4	34,120
Female	3.7	1,652
Age		
Under 25	52.2	11,914
26 to 34	23.4	12,701
35 to 49	18.4	5,770
Over 50	6.2	1,407
IQ		
Below 80	31.2	10,213
81 to 109	56.2	20,368
110 to 129	6.5	2,138
Above 130	.04	13
Prior Residence		
Houston	26.8	9,308
Dallas/Fort Worth	25.6	8,897
San Antonio	5.8	2,005
Beaumont	3.1	1,082
Austin	3.4	1,170
Other cities in Texas *	18.4	6,602
Other counties in Texas	12.1	4,221
Other state or country	4.1	1,459

* Includes Abilene, Amarillo, Brownsville, Bryan, Corpus Christi, El Paso, Galveston, Laredo, Lubbock, McAllen, Midland, Odessa, San Angelo, Sherman, Temple, Texarkana, Tyler, Waco, and Wichita Falls.

SOURCE: Texas Department of Corrections, *1983 Fiscal Year Statistical Report* (Huntsville, Texas: Texas Department of Corrections, 1984).

tentiary system violated their constitutional right (Eighth Amendment of the U.S. Constitution) not to be subjected to cruel and unusual punishment. After the longest prison trial in U.S. history, a federal district court agreed and ordered Texas to make sweeping changes in its prison system. In the words of the presiding judge:

> It is impossible for a written opinion to convey the pernicious conditions and the pain and degradation which ordinary inmates suffer within TDC [Texas Department of Corrections] prison walls—the gruesome experience of youthful first offenders forcibly raped; the cruel and justifiable fears of inmates wondering when they will be called upon to defend the next violent assault; the sheer misery, the discomfort, the wholesale loss of privacy for prisoners housed with one, two, or three others in a forty-five foot cell or suffocatingly packed together in a crowded dormitory; the physical suffering and wretched psychological stress which must be endured by those sick or injured who cannot obtain adequate medical care; the sense of abject helplessness felt by inmates arbitrarily sent to solitary confinement or administrative segregation without proper opportunity to defend themselves or to argue their causes; the

bitter frustration of inmates prevented from petitioning the courts and other government authorities for relief from perceived injustices.[38]

The state has responded by appealing some of the points of this decision and
by embarking on a major construction program to relieve the problem of overcrowding. By the mid–1980s, the principal state prison, Huntsville, had developed
some of the best educational programs to be offered prisoners in America. It also,
however, had experienced an upsurge of inmate violence, perhaps as a result of
stiffer sentences that have tended to keep prisoners in jail for longer periods of
time than in the past.[39]

Finally, the death penalty is a probable sentence for a poor person, especially
if nonwhite, convicted of murder, especially if the victim is white. As of March
1987, Texas held 247 prisoners on death row; only Florida had more waiting to be
executed. Since the U.S. Supreme Court lifted the embargo on capital punishment
in 1976, Texas with 22 deaths has led the nation in the number of prisoners
executed.[40] Three-fourths of Texans approve of capital punishment.[41]

To summarize: the poor in Texas are more likely than any other group in the
state to be arrested for a crime, convicted, imprisoned, and executed. Their treatment by police, courts, and jails often ranges from coldness and indifference to
hostility and victimization. To those who might think that only the poor are
disposed toward crime, and therefore receive what any system of justice would
deliver to its incorrigibles, examine the following.

A look at corporate violations of the law during the first half of the twentieth
century uncovered widespread offenses.[42] A more recent examination of corporate
illegality concurs.[43] Some of these breaches are of great magnitude. For instance,
when executives at General Electric conspired to fix the price of light bulbs in the
early 1960s, it cost the American people $2 billion in artificial charges, "a sum far
greater than the total losses from the 3 million burglaries in a given year." [44]
Punishment, however, is usually light. In one year (1975–76), sixty-one corporate
officials were convicted of breaking the law but only 8 percent were imprisoned.
In that same year the federal government laid some 1,500 charges against companies. But, as noted by one expert in this area, "for the crimes committed by the
large corporations the sole punishment often consists of warnings, consent orders
or comparatively small fines." [45]

Why do rich corporations and individuals receive preferential legal treatment?
Three reasons emerge. First, people with an abundance of economic resources, as
discussed in chapters 6 and 8, have a strong voice in writing the laws that define
crime and outline punishment. Legislation is mostly geared, especially in Texas, to
the protection of those with property. For many years, for instance, industrial
pollution was not against the law, even though it was quite harmful to people's
health. Corporate interests successfully staved off environmental controls thought
to be threatening to their property (and profits).

Second, many legal issues pertaining to large companies have been diverted
from the court system into administrative agencies. Here, as shown in chapter 9,
corporations exert a great deal of influence over the course of administration.
Harsh penalties for corporate violators of administrative rulings are rare. About 90
percent of the enforcement actions imposed against corporate breaches of the law

Courtesy of Ben Sargent, *The Austin-American Statesman*.   Reprinted by permission.

are done through administrative rulings and, in most instances, the punishment meted out is extremely light.[46]

Third, if legal matters are brought to the attention of the courts, the affluent, through their penetration of the court system (discussed in the preceding section of this chapter), are better able to cope with judicial proceedings than are the less fortunate. Money buys legal talent. Courtrooms are filled with people generally sympathetic to the plight of the wealthy. The case of multimillionaire T. Cullen Davis underscores these points.

Davis is a very wealthy Fort Worth industrialist who once sat on the board of directors of one of the larger bank holding companies in Texas, Texas American Bancshares. His legal troubles began the night of August 2, 1976, when a man shot and killed his stepdaughter and a house guest, and seriously wounded his estranged wife and a family friend. Three eyewitnesses claimed that Davis was the gunman. Some two years later, Davis was charged in another courtroom with attempting to hire a "hit man" to kill the judge who was presiding over his divorce trial. In this instance, the FBI had audio- and videotapes in which Davis apparently discussed the assassination with the liaison for the contracted killer.[47]

Davis hired a first-class legal team, headed by celebrated criminal attorney Richard "Racehorse" Haynes, to defend him. All told, Davis was tried three times for his alleged offenses. Over $12 million of his money went to his defense. His first trial cost him more than $3 million—ten times the amount spent by the state.

Haynes alone gained another $3 million of Davis's money for the second trial. The legal team utilized the money in instructive ways.

Part of it was spent on a detailed analysis of the background and character of all potential witnesses. The first trial, held in Amarillo, involved the charges of killing Davis's stepdaughter. Before it began, $30,000 was allocated to conduct a scientific study "to determine what sort of jurors would likely be sympathetic to [Davis]." [48] All potential jurors were investigated thoroughly by a former judge of Potter County hired by the defense. A public relations expert was employed to court the press covering the Amarillo case. This expert was paid to have people write favorable letters about Davis to local newspapers, plant stories in the media, and provide inside information to reporters considered friendly to the defense. (Later he was relieved of his duties when charges of trying to buy a favorable press surfaced.) To help win over the citizens of Amarillo, the defense brought a local attorney, Dee Miller, on board. Miller, the brother of the then secretary of the treasury, G. William Miller, did nothing but sit at the defense table, lending credibility to the Davis team, since "all twelve jurors knew [Miller] either personally or by reputation." [49]

The Amarillo trial dragged on for thirteen weeks. When the jury announced its verdict, Davis walked out of the courtroom a free man. The second trial, conducted in Houston, raised the charges of attempted murder of the Texas judge hearing Davis's divorce case. It lasted eleven weeks, and after deliberating for forty-four hours the jury still could not reach a decision. The judge declared a mistrial and Davis, after posting $30,000 in bond money, was again free. He was retried in late 1979 in Fort Worth and a jury cleared him of trying to arrange to have the judge killed. Subsequently, Davis became a born-again Christian. During the throes of the economic recession that struck the state in the 1980s, Davis's company, KenDavis, declared bankruptcy. After the verdict of the first trial was announced, the state prosecutor in the case—conservative former state legislator Joe Shannon—had this to say about justice: "I never thought I'd hear myself say this, but it appears that we *do* have two systems of law in this country. One for the rich and one for the poor." [50]

CONCLUSION

The Texas judicial system is composed of a multitude of distinct courts. Knowledge of the court system is made difficult by the intricate and confusing lines of jurisdiction. Legal experts are necessary to successfully maneuver through the state's judicial maze, but the price of obtaining top-flight legal assistance is high. Consequently, wealthy individuals and corporations have a distinct advantage in legal disputes with ordinary citizens or with the government.

Moreover, the key figures in the state judicial process are similar in background to the Texas economic elite. Jurors, especially those serving on the grand jury, lawyers, and judges are socially akin to the economic notables of the state. The knot is tightened through campaign contributions to Texas judges. Little wonder that when asked if the defendants in the Watergate affair would have fared better if their cases had been tried in Texas courts, the late Frank Erwin (former chairman of the University of Texas Board of Regents) reportedly replied: "Hell yes. We own the judges down here." [51]

NOTES

1. Allen E. Smith, *The Impact of the Texas Constitution on the Judiciary* (Houston: Institute for Urban Affairs, University of Houston, 1973), p. 19.

2. Figures from Texas Judicial Council, Texas Judicial System, *Annual Report, 1985.*

3. Paul Burka, "Trial by Technicality," *Texas Monthly,* April 1982, pp. 127–31, 210–18, and 241.

4. T. C. Sinclair and Bancroft Henderson, *The Selection of Judges in Texas* (Houston: Public Affairs Research Center, University of Houston, 1965), pp. 51–68; and Douglas C. Harlan, "New Lawyers View the Profession in the System of Justice," *Texas Bar Journal* 37 (1974): 57.

5. See Griffin Smith, Jr., "Empires of Paper," in *Texas Monthly's Political Reader* (Austin: Texas Monthly Press and Sterling Swift Publishing, 1978), pp. 20–36.

6. Robert A. Carp, "The Behavior of Grand Juries: Acquiescence or Justice?" *Social Science Quarterly* 55 (March 1975): 862.

7. Ibid.

8. David G. Hall, "Trial by Money, Power and Race," *Texas Observer,* February 25, 1977, p. 25.

9. Carp, "The Behavior of Grand Juries," p. 865.

10. Herbert Jacob, *Justice in America: Courts, Lawyers and the Judicial Process,* 3d ed. (Boston: Little, Brown, 1978), p. 128.

11. David W. Broder, "University of Chicago Jury Project," *Nebraska Law Review* 38 (1959): 750–51.

12. Data about the legal background of Texas judges come from a survey conducted by the Texas Judicial Council in 1975; the results are reprinted in Eugene W. Jones, Joe E. Ericson, Lyle C. Brown, and Robert S. Trotter, Jr., eds., *Practicing Texas Politics,* 3d ed. (Boston: Houghton Mifflin, 1977), pp. 402–3.

13. Sinclair and Henderson, *Selection of Texas Judges.*

14. See, for instance, Stuart S. Nagel, "Testing Relations between Judicial Characteristics and Judicial Decision Making," *Western Political Quarterly* 15 (September 1962): 425–37.

15. Paul Burka, "Heads, We Win, Tails, You Lose," *Texas Monthly,* May 1987, p. 139.

16. Paul Burka, "The Man in the Black Hat: Part I," *Texas Monthly,* June 1984, pp. 128–33, 212–23, 230.

17. See Ken Case, "Blind Justice," *Texas Monthly,* May 1987, pp. 136–38; and Amy Johnson, "Court Reform?" *Texas Observer,* February 6, 1987, pp. 8–10.

18. Details are in Ken Case, "Blind Justice."

19. *Texas Poll,* July 1985.

20. Discussed in Amy Johnson, "Court Reform?"

21. Glenn Garvin, "When Police Go Wild," *Inquiry,* January 8 and 22, 1979, p. 15.

22. Discussed in ibid.

23. Ibid., p. 15.

24. Ibid., p. 4.

25. Quoted in Mark Vogler and Eric Hartman "Inquest in Odessa," *Texas Observer,* March 17, 1978, p. 10.

26. "Videotapes of Beatings Figure in Federal Inquiry of Police Force in Texas," *New York Times,* April 4, 1981, p. 7.

27. *New York Times,* March 27, 1983, p. 38.

28. Garvin, "When Police Go Wild," p. 14.

29. These two policemen, along with another Houston officer, were later tried in a federal court for violating the civil rights of Joe Torres. The judge gave them each a ten-year suspended sentence on one charge and a one-year jail term for another.

30. Garvin, "When Police Go Wild," p. 16.

31. In 1977, a federal court sentenced Chief Hayes and his wife to ten years each; the two other women were imprisoned for three years apiece.

32. Quoted in Tom Curtis, "Houston's Blue Army," *Austin American-Statesman,* June 6, 1977, p. 1.

33. Discussed briefly in Peter Elkind, "Mayor, Council Locked in Bitter Struggle," *Texas Monthly,* February 1985, pp. 120–22, 168–76, and 182.

34. Marianne Hopper and Cliff Robertson, "Jail Overcrowding: The Search for Solutions," *Texas Business Review* 56 (January-February 1982): 19–20.

35. *Texas Observer,* December 24, 1976, pp. 14–15.

36. *Christchurch Press,* May 12, 1987, p. 16.

37. *Morales* v. *Truman,* 326 F.Supp. 677, 1971.

38. From the opinion of Justice William Wayne Justice in the case of *Ruiz* v. *Estelle* quoted in Betty Anne Duke, *The Ruiz Decision and Texas Prisons* (Austin: House Study Group, 1981), p. 3.

39. Michael Vines, "An Inmate Examines TDC Violence," *Texas Observer,* September 14, 1984.

40. *Christchurch Press,* May 22, 1987.

41. *Texas Poll,* July 1985.

42. Edwin Sutherland, *White Collar Crime* (New York: Holt, Rinehart and Winston, 1949).

43. From a study conducted by Professor Marshall Clinard. Findings reported to the Subcommittee on Crime, House Committee of the Judiciary, *LEAA Reauthorization* (Washington, D.C.: U.S. Government Printing Office, 1981), pp. 621–42.

44. Ibid., p. 631.

45. Ibid.

46. Ibid., p. 633.

47. Details about the Davis cases are found in Gary Cartwright, *Blood Will Tell* (New York: Pocket Books, 1980); and in his article "Trial by Flurry," *Texas Monthly,* May 1979; and in the same issue of the *Texas Monthly,* "How Cullen Davis Beat the Rap."

48. Cartwright, "Trial by Flurry," p. 128.

49. Ibid., p. 129.

50. Quoted in Cartwright, "How Cullen Davis Beat the Rap," p. 220. Emphasis in the original.

51. Quoted in *The Texas Observer,* June 18, 1976, p. 9.

PART IV

Public Policy in Texas

The subject of part IV is public policy in Texas and who benefits from it. The analysis unfolds in five chapters. Chapter 11 scrutinizes state and local expenditures for public education, kindergarten through university. Chapter 12 reviews transportation and welfare policy. Chapter 13 takes a detailed look at the budget, taxes, and who pays what for state services in Texas. The next two chapters concentrate on state regulation. Chapter 14 details the regulation of natural resources (oil, natural gas, coal, water, and air), electricity, financial institutions, and the sale of items to consumers. Chapter 15 discusses state policy toward labor unions and working conditions in Texas.

Throughout these chapters, the prime beneficiaries of state expenditures and regulations are identified. In most cases, the bounty of public policy directly or indirectly redounds to the economic benefit of business. The payoff of effectively gaining access to the state's political institutions is public policy favorable to the lofty position of the dominant economic interests of Texas.

11

Public Education in Texas

Responsibility for educating the public has traditionally fallen upon the shoulders of state and local governments in the United States. Economic factors have greatly influenced the degree to which states actually fulfill this obligation. In general, local educational systems have been quite sensitive to the economic needs—especially the employment needs—of their communities. In the words of one political scientist, "American education, with some notable exceptions, has been largely vocational in nature, geared to training people for available jobs in the marketplace." [1]

Public schooling in Texas has reflected the economic trends of the state. When agriculture was the mainstay of the economy, there was little call for a highly educated work force. Tending to the chores on a farm or ranch did not require much formal schooling. Consequently, throughout much of the nineteenth and twentieth centuries, the state was not urged to provide extensive, sophisticated educational services.

As the Texas economy grew and became more diversified, new job requirements demanded an education commensurate with industrial expansion. For example, Governor John Connally in 1963 initiated a study designed to find reasons for the failure of the state's higher education system to respond to the wholesale changes that were then taking place in Texas. He appointed a twenty-five person committee to investigate post–high school education and to make recommendations for improving the delivery and quality of higher education. In reading the committee its charge, Connally called for an educational system "adequate to back up a potential for the economic, industrial, political and cultural expansion necessary for the great Southwest area." [2]

To meet the current need to diversify the state's economy beyond its petroleum-base, government has again called on the educational system to be in the vanguard of this new move. During the 1980s, billionaire H. Ross Perot was entrusted by the governor to head a committee that was to analyze the primary and secondary schools in Texas and to make recommendations with regard to their improvement. The Select Committee on Higher Education established in 1985 contained a pronounced business profile with Jess Hay (Lomas and Nettleton, M Corp, Exxon), Bobby Inman (MCC, Texas Eastern), Arthur Temple

(Temple Inland, Time, Inc., Republic of Texas), and George Mitchell (Mitchell Energy, M Corp) among its members.

It should be borne in mind that the Texas economy requires a work force composed of employees with varying degrees of job skills. Professionals, technical experts, corporate managers, scientists, and engineers are needed to command the top positions in the economy; but people willing and available to fill the less prestigious job slots are also required. The education system is designed to meet these variegated requirements. Hence some students will receive an extremely sophisticated education, while others will be prepared for semiskilled or unskilled work. Public schools are not under a great deal of pressure to train all students equally, so that any one student could potentially move to the top of the occupational hierarchy. Instead, "the educational system basically helps to maintain the structure of inequality in the marketplace." [3] ★

PRIMARY AND SECONDARY EDUCATION IN TEXAS

In total, about $7.7 billion are spent each year to enhance the education of the state's three million primary and secondary school students.[4] The money comes from three sources. State government provides 64 percent of the funds. Local governments—specifically, the nearly 1,100 school districts across Texas—supply another 26 percent. The federal government is responsible for the remaining 10 percent.

Over the last decade, the Texas Education Agency has surveyed the educational achievement of the state's schoolchildren. Tests administered in 1978 were compared to nationwide scores. Overall, Texas's youngsters fared worse than students in the rest of the country and fell far short of standards deemed acceptable to education officials.[5] They were specifically below par in vocabulary, reading comprehension, understanding of mathematical concepts and their application, knowledge of the structures and functions of government, support for the political system, and writing that is expressive, persuasive, or explanatory. In comparison to the national norm, Texans wrote sentences that were awkward and paragraphs that were incomplete, short, and composed of simple sentences. By 1985, competency levels in reading, mathematics, and writing showed "substantial gains in the mastery of basic skills."[6] However, fully 44 percent of ninth graders still could not obtain a passing mark on at least one of these tests; 8 percent failed all three.[7] Moreover, as reported after testing in 1982, students were "performing lower than desired in the more complex or higher order skills."[8]

In 1984, partially in response to these testing results, the legislature instituted several sweeping changes in the state's educational system. As mentioned in chapter 9, a new fifteen-person State Board of Education was established. The board has been empowered to keep close tabs on the academic (and financial) performances of schools. Inability of a school to meet satisfactory standards could lead to a loss of accreditation. Additionally, teachers were given substantial pay raises. The minimum pay for a teacher (in 1985) was set at $15,200, a 27 percent increase above the previous year's pay. The average salary for Texas's nearly 170,000 teachers in 1983–84 was $20,170—twenty-fourth among all states.[9] With a new twelve-step pay scale now in place, the average salary should be on the

Courtesy of Ben Sargent, *The Austin American-Statesman*.   Reprinted by permission.

incline; by 1985, indeed, it had reached $22,800.[10] Teachers, however, were also required to pass a competency test or face loss of their jobs. Although the prospect of such an assessment incurred the wrath of some of the state's teachers, nearly 80 percent of the public voiced their support for these competency tests.[11] Moreover, the legislature stipulated that students would only be allowed to partake in extracurricular activities—including sports—if they passed their school subjects. Again, a large portion of Texans (77 percent) approved of "no pass, no play." [12] Finally, the legislature, in another move that was met with widespread public approval, mandated that students enrolled in odd-numbered grades are annually to be given a test (called TEAMS) measuring their minimum skills. The initial testing of eleventh graders in 1986 found that in mathematics and English language usage Texas students scored higher than the national norm.[13]

Every assessment of schoolchildren in Texas, however, has found that blacks, Mexican Americans, and the poor consistently score lower than other students. There has been some improvement among minority children in reading and mathematics performances over the decade, but they still remain below the Texas and national average. Moreover, among youngsters in higher grades, assessment discrepancies along racial, ethnic, and income lines have actually increased.

How well students do on such measures is a product of a number of influences. Most social scientists agree that the family's attitudes toward the value of education and the encouragement of reading have a major impact on educational motivation and achievement.[14] The school system, however, also plays a role in the skill levels of its pupils. The extremes in performance between low- and high-income students are partially attributable to the quality of education available to each group: the wealthier the school district the better the student performances on assessments of reading, writing, and mathematics in the third, fifth, and ninth grades.[15] Differences in educational performances among social classes are encouraged in Texas through the state's method of financing public schools.

Financing the Public Schools in Texas

There are two principal means of financing education in the state. First, the legislature, through its Foundation School Program (FSP), underwrites the basic costs of school districts. Second, each school district has the option of enriching its education program by raising local funds.

Foundation School Program. Established in 1949, the Foundation School Program provides state money to each school district according to the number of pupils in attendance. The funds are used to maintain and operate school facilities, to transport students to and from school, and to pay the base wages of administrators, counselors, and teachers. This program is designed to fund at the minimum level; that is, the basic costs of these services are to be covered by the state. Consequently, there is little room for extravagance here.

The FSP program costs around $6 billion a year these days. Until recently, the state contributed nearly 90 percent of the FSP funds. After 1984, the legislature limited the state's share to no more than two-thirds of the costs of the program; the remainder must be paid by local school districts. Each district fulfills its financial obligation by taxing property within its boundaries at a rate determined by a state formula.[16] All told, school districts contribute about $1 billion annually to FSP funds.

Enrichment. School districts are entitled to collect additional funds in order to enrich their allotments from FSP. Enrichment money is usually deployed to construct buildings (something not covered in FSP), purchase equipment, and increase salaries for administrators, counselors, and teachers. These funds come from property taxes collected within the district. In other words, a district may, if it so chooses or is able to, tax property in excess of the sum required for enrollment in the FSP. The surplus is utilized for improvement of the local school system.

Class distinctions in educational services are basically a result of the enrichment program. As noted by one group of researchers, "wealthy districts can do anything they want: pay high salaries and attract the best teachers, adopt novel programs (like computer-related courses), build new buildings, equip marvelous libraries and labs, and provide an array of special programs." [17] It is easier for a district with an abundance of valuable property to offer a quality education than a less affluent one because of the arithmetic of property taxation. For example, a school district containing $90 million in property can raise $90,000 in taxes by collecting only 10¢ for every $100 of property from its residents. Conversely, a district with only $9 million worth of property must extract $1 on every $100 from the owners in order to reach the $90,000 figure. Actually, most of Texas's school districts are below the statewide average in property value of $228,287 per student (in 1984).[18] Hence these districts are faced with the choice of charging their residents exorbitant taxes or sacrificing enriched schools: most follow the latter course of action.

Property Taxes

To understand the problems with financing public schools from the property tax requires some appreciation of the chaotic practices associated with collection of this tax in Texas. Property taxes are the major means of raising revenue to pay for local services such as police and fire protection, water delivery, hospitals, city roads, sewage treatment plants, and numerous municipal and county programs, as well as the public schools. Local taxing units, such as the school board in each district, follow three steps in the collection of the property tax.

First, property in the area must be appraised. That is, a dollar value must be placed on the property. The value is supposed to approach fair market value—the amount one could get if the property were bought in the marketplace.

Second, until recently, the taxing unit decided on an assessment ratio that was to apply to taxable property. The assessment ratio is the portion of the value of the property subject to taxes. If, for instance, a house is appraised at a value of $100,000 and the school board decides on a 100 percent assessment ratio, then the full value of the house ($100,000) is liable to the tax. If, however, the taxing unit chooses a lower assessment ratio, say 50 percent, then only that portion of the property's value is subject to the property tax. In the example above of the $100,000 home, only $50,000 would be taxable if a school district selected an assessment ratio of 50 percent.

Third, the tax rate must be set by the taxing unit. Tax rates are expressed in terms of dollars per $100 of appraised value. A tax rate of 10¢ per every $100 of appraised value means that a person would pay 10¢ in taxes on every $100 of the worth of his or her property. Property appraised at $100,000 and assessed at full value would produce a tax bill of $100 for the owner, if the effective tax rate were pegged at 10¢ for every $100 worth of property.

For many years, the uneven execution of these three steps—appraisal, and fixing the assessment ratio and the actual tax rate—resulted in near anarchy in property tax administration in Texas. Until 1981, there were 2,000 units of government that collected the property tax. Variation abounded in appraisal practices, assessment ratios, and effective rates. Uniformity, even in areas where a single piece of property was subject to the jurisdiction of multiple taxing units (such as a school board, the county government, or a municipality), was rarely the rule.

Most taxing units did not have the technical expertise to adequately appraise property on a continuous basis. In such cases, determining the worth of a piece of property was an infrequent event. Prior to 1980, for instance, the thirteen tax entities of El Paso County had not systematically reappraised property values in their area for almost a quarter of a century. Dallas County, until the late 1970s, had failed to monitor property worth for over a decade. Assessment ratios differed not only among taxing units but also on various types of property. It was not unusual to find a tax agency proclaiming one assessment ratio for agricultural property and another ratio for people's homes. Finally, tax rates differed depending on the taxing body. Unless a uniform rate were set by the legislature, one school district might set the rate at 20¢ per $100 of property, while an adjacent board might establish a 45¢-per-$100 rate. Obviously, the person living in the first school district would be paying less in property tax than a person with property appraised at the same amount in the second district.

Effect on the Wealthy.   Corporations and wealthy individuals have benefited greatly from the past methods of collecting property tax in Texas. Failure of taxing units to continuously update property values generally meant that corporate property was undervalued. Affluent property holders frequently also had the wherewithal to outmuscle taxing bodies in property tax matters. Appraisers and collectors were generally not well trained and worked without much technical assistance. A big corporation, however, usually maintains full-time staff devoted to its tax obligation. Standard Oil of Indiana (Amoco), for instance, has holdings in 99 percent of the school districts of Texas. The company has a seven-person department, complete with lawyer, accountant, tax experts, and secretaries, to monitor property tax matters in these districts. The head of this tax division is convinced that "it's been a very workable system over the years." [19]

Many local taxing units relied on the "honor system" in their attempts to determine the worth of corporate property. That is, the company itself was entrusted to calculate the value of its property. Discrepancies between the company's estimate of value and independent measures of the property's worth were commonplace. In Houston, for example, Shell Oil built its corporate headquarters at an announced cost of $35 million; the tax rolls of Harris County (Houston), however, showed the appraised value of the structure to be only $12 million. Shell had provided the lower figure to tax officials. When quizzed about the large difference between stated values, a Houston tax collector said, "We just have to take [Shell's] word for it." [20]

Attempts by conscientious tax assessors to measure corporate worth through objective means were frequently thwarted. Many companies refused to disclose vital information that would have revealed the true market value of their property. Some blatantly sought to deceive the local tax office. The following excerpt suggests how major oil and natural gas companies in Texas obstructed the administration of the property tax laws:

> To help determine the fair market value of mineral properties, . . . local taxing authorities try to assess the value of . . . gas taken at the wellhead. The companies argue that the value of gas must not be based on the going market rate (roughly $2 per thousand cubic feet) but on the long-term contract price they have with customers, which they say is as low as 16 cents per thousand cubic feet. Sun Oil will not let the taxing authorities look at its ultimate sales contracts, but the documents the company files with the state comptroller's office show that Sun Oil has been selling gas to itself at the 16–cent price. [A] Rio Grande School District attorney . . . says "These companies list themselves as buyers at the low price for taxing purposes, then they sell the gas to someone [else] at a much higher price, and no record of that sale has to be given to the comptroller."[21]

As a last resort, companies may appeal assessments that they believe are set too high. The first appeal is usually to local and county officials. The appeal, if pushed any farther, then goes to one of the state's civil courts. The following vignette that occurred in El Paso in the late 1970s illustrates a successful appeal of a tax assessment by a major corporation.

In 1978, the county tax assessor-collector increased by fourfold the property taxes to be paid to El Paso County by the American Smelting and Refining Company (ASARCO). ASARCO appealed this decision to the county commissioners, disputing the appraisal of the company's El Paso holdings made by the tax official. ASARCO presented the county a counterappraisal, one that was substantially lower than the tax assessor's. Without independently validating the true market worth of the company, the county commissioners accepted ASARCO's figure. One commissioner publicly chided the county assessor, saying that "you probably got [your] figures out of the air or out of the smokestack over there at ASARCO." When the tax assessor retorted that he had based his appraisal on ASARCO's mass media campaign, which boasted of a $20 million addition to the El Paso plant in the form of air pollution abatement equipment, the commission shot back: "Well, I don't believe those figures on TV." [22]

A side effect of the appeals is that the process usually takes time. The delay often works to the advantage of the appealing corporation since the company may withhold payment of any tax during the period of adjudication. This factor alone places tremendous pressure on assessors, especially those working in districts where the company is the most important tax source. Continued financing of public schools or other local amenities can seldom wait for the ultimate disposition of an appeal. Nonpayment frequently forces assessors to modify the tax bite to suit the corporation.

As a result of these assessment practices, the property tax burden in Texas fell mostly on small businesses and individual homeowners—not corporations. A study undertaken by the Texas Legislative Property Tax Committee in 1975 found industrial property to be, on the average, valued at 58 percent of its market worth, while single family homes were appraised at 71 percent of their true value and commercial property (much of which was in the hands of small businesses) was at 77 percent of its worth.[23]

School districts, especially in areas where a relatively few corporations have a large share of property, were also shortchanged. In extremely wealthy areas, a low corporate tax did not seriously deplete enrichment funds. There was simply so much wealth that corporate slackers could be tolerated with little harm to a high-quality education. However, poorer districts with corporate property in their midst could not provide educational services of merit under these circumstances.

Changes in School Financing

Leaving educational enrichment in the hands of local school boards resulted in unequal funding of public education across the state, since the quality of education offered depended on the financial base of the school district. In 1971, a federal district court ruled in the case of *Rodriguez v. San Antonio* that Texas must change its methods of funding schools because poor children were, under the existing approach, being denied their constitutionally guaranteed right to an equal education. Two years later, however, the U.S. Supreme Court reversed this decision, allowing Texas to continue with school financing that culminates in social class distinctions in education. Nonetheless, this legal controversy provoked the state legislature into addressing school revenue problems. Legislative action followed along two fronts: equalization and property tax reform.

Equalization.   Beginning in 1975, the state government assumed a larger share of the Foundation School Program (FSP). This alteration allowed local school boards to either reduce property taxes or add to their enrichment funds. Since, however, this shift in policy was across-the-board, it did little to close the enrichment gap that existed between wealthy and poor school districts. If anything, the chasm appeared to widen.[24]

The equalization bill of 1975 directly confronted the problem of inequitable funding. The legislature created a special fund to be distributed to school districts with property valued 25 percent below the statewide average; however, only $50 million was set aside for enrichment. In 1977, the legislature added another $135 million to the equalization fund and ruled that only districts in which property values fell 110 percent below the statewide norm were eligible for assistance. Equalization aid was increased to $457.5 million in 1984. In that year, 720 school districts (out of 1,098) received equalization funds.[25] Most of the money landed up in the accounts of the state's poorest school districts.[26] To what extent has equalization funds leveled class differences in public education?

At first, not much changed. Until 1984 the overall gulf between the finances of wealthy and poor districts actually widened considerably.[27] This mainly was because districts containing valued property could and did increase their enrichment funds and thus significantly added to the resource base of their local school system.

Consider the Edgewood School District, the principal petitioner in the Rodriguez case. In the early 1970s, when the original suit about inequitable school financing in Texas was first litigated, Edgewood had the lowest expenditure per pupil of any school district in Texas. Ten years later it still ranked at the bottom and was even farther away from the finances available to neighboring, more affluent districts in the San Antonio area.[28] Part of Edgewood's woes stemmed from a $3 million cutback in federal funds.[29] But the core problem was the inability of Edgewood, and all poorer districts in Texas, to increase local enrichment funds through the property tax.

After the legislature in 1984 significantly increased equalization funds and targeted the money for the poorest schools, some closing of the gap between financing poor and wealthy schools has occurred. An infusion of equalization money enabled the poorest school districts to increase their per student allocations. These districts are now much closer to the statewide norm in per student expenditures than they were in the early 1980s.[30] However, rich districts, given their solid propertied basis, can still financially outmatch less affluent school districts with fairly minor property tax increases.

Property Tax Reform.   Through a series of legislative bills and constitutional amendments, comprehensive changes have been made to the property tax laws of Texas. The following are the most important alterations made.

1. Each of the state's 254 counties may now have only one tax board. This board is composed of members chosen by all the taxing units in the area. The board is responsible for all property tax administration, including appraisal of property, setting of the tax rate, collection of taxes, and appeals.

2. All property in the state is to be appraised to reflect true market value.

3. Assessment ratios are to be at 100 percent of the property's appraised value.

4. If in any given year aggregate community property taxes rise more than 5 percent, the voters living in the tax district may roll back the increase. A rollback is accomplished if 15 percent of eligible voters petition for an election and if a majority of the voters approve of the rollback. In order for the rollback election to be valid, 25 percent of the registered voters in the area must cast a ballot.

5. Two state agencies have been established to oversee property tax administration. The Board of Tax Assessor Examiners registers only qualified persons as property tax appraisers. The State Property Tax Board sets minimum standards for the administration of local tax assessing offices, provides information on property tax matters, and engages in studies of taxation of property, including its own appraisal of property values throughout Texas.

These changes in the property tax laws have only gone into effect recently (1983), yet they have set in motion a flurry of activity. Local governments have busied themselves jockeying for advantage on the appraisal boards, renovating the tax rolls by establishing new values for property, and facing the wrath of angry, confused property owners who find themselves on the verge of higher tax payments.[31] In order not to precipitate a taxpayers' revolt, many taxing units have scaled down their effective tax rates. Hence, even with property valued closer to fair market value and at 100 percent assessment ratios, local tax authorities can avoid a drastic rise in property taxes by lowering their effective rate—say, from 75¢ per every $100 of property to 35¢ per $100. In addition, very few appraisal boards value property at full market value. Around 58 percent of the tax boards appraise property at 60 percent of its true market worth, or less.[32] Nonetheless, some tax districts have imposed a hike in the property tax exceeding 5 percent. In the first quarter of 1983, thirteen rollback elections occurred; only one rollback attempt failed.

The impact of these changes on school districts is still difficult to assess. Overall, more valuable property is now on the tax rolls. But school boards are not eager to confront ratepayers (voters) with higher taxes. Ironically, higher value on property probably has increased the amount that these districts must pay into the Foundation School Program, since the local share is based on the worth of property in the area. Finally, only in recent years are there any discernible signs that reform in property taxes has had a bearing on unequal school financing.

What about the effect of these changes on corporations? At first blush, not much has altered. Companies still are on the "honor system." That is, tax boards generally must rely on information provided by a corporation in order to determine its property value. In addition, the new legislation keeps these disclosures confidential. After the first round of property reappraisal, corporate property appears not to be valued near full market price. In Dallas, for instance, tax authorities in anticipation of the new property tax legislation began a systematic reappraisal of county property in the late 1970s. It was found that "while homes jumped drastically from the 1979 tax rolls to 1980 (from $3.5 billion to $8.2 billion), business inventory did not change at all from its $3.9 billion level." When tax officials were criticized for blindly accepting corporate disclosure of business property value, one responded by saying: "I don't feel like I should call a man a liar and I'm not going to." [33]

Finally, a great deal of property owned by the rich is exempt from taxes. Intangible items such as corporate stocks and bonds and certificates of deposit are free from the property tax. Nor does the state consider personal assets (art collections, jewelry, boats, tools, etc.) to be taxable property. It has been estimated that $400 billion are invested in intangibles—about one-half of the property extant in the state.[34]

In short, inequity in the finances available to school districts still exists. Equalization aid and property tax reform have not totally cemented the gap. In essence, a dual system of education at the primary and secondary level results. Wealthy districts that serve the well-to-do in the state are able to provide quality education, while poorer ones are restricted to inferior schooling.

HIGHER EDUCATION IN TEXAS

There are some 771,000 students attending institutions of higher learning in Texas. Around half are enrolled in the state's thirty-five universities; most of the other half matriculate in the forty-nine two-year community colleges. The rest attend the state's private colleges. Each year around $3 billion in tax dollars is allocated by the state government to the universities; $440 million is budgeted annually for the community colleges.

As is the case with public schools, the money allotted by government for higher education is not evenly distributed. Some colleges and universities receive more state funds than others. Table 11–1 presents the state contribution to the various senior-level universities in Texas.

The University of Texas system and the Texas A & M system garner the lion's share of the state money. Furthermore, there is marked variation in the financing of individual campuses within each of these two university systems. The Austin branch of the University of Texas receives much more than the combined total of the six other campuses in the system. Texas A & M (College Station) collects fully six times the amount of money authorized for the other two institutions in its system. Similarly, the main campus of the University of Houston has three times the total of its three branches.

Much of the inequity in funding lies in the means by which the state finances higher education. There are two primary sources of money. One is the state legislature, which appropriates funds for institutions of higher learning; the other is the Permanent University Fund, a pool of state revenue earmarked for some universities.

Appropriations

The state legislature budgets the financing of Texas's universities over a two-year period. In the 1986–87 biennium the appropriation was $2.3 billion. Most of the

TABLE 11-1   State Contributions to Universities and Colleges in Texas, 1987

University or College	State Contribution [a]
University of Texas System (Arlington, Austin, Dallas, El Paso, Permian Basin, San Antonio, and Tyler)	$376.2 million
Texas A & M System (College Station, Prairie View A & M, Tarleton State)	$200.6 million
University of Houston System (University Park, Clear Lake, Downtown, and Victoria)	$132.5 million
Texas State University System (Southwest Texas State, Sam Houston State, and Sul Ross)	$ 86.7 million
Texas Tech University	$ 78.7 million
North Texas State University	$ 59.8 million
Lamar University (Beaumont, Orange, and Port Arthur)	$ 33.0 million
Texas Woman's University	$ 32.9 million
University System of South Texas (Corpus Christi State, Texas A & I, and Laredo State)	$ 29.5 million
Stephen F. Austin State University	$ 29.4 million
Texas Southern University	$ 25.7 million
East Texas State University (including Texarkana)	$ 25.6 million
Pan American University (including branch at Brownsville)	$ 22.5 million
West Texas State University	$ 16.4 million
Midwestern State University	$ 10.8 million

[a] Only funds appropriated by the legislature are noted. Funds from other sources, such as the Available University Fund, are not included.

SOURCE: Legislative Budget Board, *Fiscal Size-Up: 1986–87 Biennium* (Austin: Legislative Budget Board, 1986), p. 71.

money is to cover salaries for school personnel (faculty, administrators, and staff) and for operating expenses.

The amount distributed to each college or university is based on a formula devised by the State Coordinating Board. The basic element in the formula is student enrollment: the larger the student body, the greater the appropriation—or so it seems. According to the formula, graduate students (especially those enrolled in health, science, business, or engineering programs) are expensive to educate. Consequently, schools with a large enrollment of graduate students in these departments are appropriated more money than are universities predominantly composed of undergraduate liberal arts majors. Among the larger universities (those with enrollment in excess of 10,000 students), the University of Texas at Austin, Texas A & M, the University of Houston (University Park), and Texas Tech University, in that order, have the most robust budgets (see table 11–2).[35]

Permanent University Fund

In 1876, the Texas Constitution set aside a substantial amount of land in the state in the hope that it would produce enough income, through sale or lease, to establish a first-rate university. Today the land mass dedicated to higher education totals 2.1 million acres, located in nineteen West Texas counties. This proper-

TABLE 11–2 State Appropriations to Universities per Full-Time Student, 1986–1987 Biennium

University	Number of Students (1986–87 Base) [a]	Appropriations (1986–87 Biennium)	Per Student Expenditure
University of Texas at Austin	43,113	$425.8 million	$9,876
Texas A & M, College Station	33,861	$329.7 million	$9,737
University of Houston, University Park	24,502	$207.7 million	$8,477
Texas Tech University	22,070	$157.7 million	$7,145
North Texas State University	17,509	$119.9 million	$6,848
University of Texas at Arlington	18,367	$116.2 million	$6,326
Lamar University [b]	11,027	$ 67.7 million	$6,140
University of Texas at El Paso	12,541	$ 71.0 million	$5,661
Stephen F. Austin State University	11,978	$ 58.8 million	$4,909

[a] Full-time equivalent students during budgetary base period for 1986–87.

[b] The student and appropriations figure include the Lamar campuses at Beaumont, Orange, and Port Arthur.

SOURCE: Legislative Budget Board, Fiscal Size Up: 1986–1987 Biennium (Austin: Legislative Budget Board, 1986), p. 71.

ty has raised a tremendous amount of revenue. Through royalties, sales, and leases the state earned in excess of $2.3 billion in 1985 alone. This money constitutes the Permanent University Fund (PUF)—the second largest university endowment in the United States. The revenue in the PUF is invested in government securities and corporate stocks and bonds, and the interest and income derived from these investments are collected into the Available University Fund (AUF). The AUF was worth about $194 million in 1985, some three times the 1978 amount.[36]

By law only a relatively few universities may receive proceeds from the AUF. Those in the Texas A & M system (including the main campus at College Station, Prairie View A & M, Tarleton State, and the agricultural and engineering services and stations administered under the A & M auspices) are eligible. Some members of the University of Texas system, namely, the branches at Austin and El Paso and the medical and dental schools, as well as the McDonald Observatory also participate in the AUF. One-third is earmarked for the A & M system, and the rest is reserved for the University of Texas system. Within these systems the principal components at Austin and at College Station have reaped most of the financial benefits. For instance, between 1958 and 1978, Prairie View A & M collected $8.2 million from the AUF while Texas A & M (College Station) gained $54.8 million.[37] In 1984, Texas voters approved a constitutional amendment that dedicates $6 million of AUF money for the next decade to Prairie View to further desegregation of higher education in the state. Most of the AUF proceeds are spent on construction of buildings, land acquisition, collateral for loans, and faculty salaries.[38]

The AUF clearly benefits the state's largest schools. Until 1985, institutions that were excluded from the earnings of the fund faced a fiscal crisis. Very little money for construction was available to non-AUF members. Before 1979, seventeen universities (U.T. Arlington, Texas Tech, North Texas State, Lamar, Texas A

& I, Texas Woman's, Texas Southern, Midwestern, Houston, Pan American, East Texas State, Sam Houston, Southwest Texas State, West Texas State, Stephen F. Austin, Sul Ross, and Angelo State) relied on the state property tax as a source for building funds. The 66th (1979) Texas Legislature effectively eliminated this tax and these schools, along with other universities not in AUF or covered by the old state property tax (such as the U.T. branches at Dallas, Permian Basin, San Antonio, and Tyler), had great difficulty financing their building programs. In November 1984, voters approved a constitutional amendment authorizing the legislature to establish an annual fund of $100 million for all nonmembers of the AUF to be used to build, maintain, or improve facilities and to buy equipment, including library books. The legislature also was empowered to create from tax revenues a Higher Education Fund for non–AUF beneficiaries; this new pool of money would parallel the Permanent University Fund.

Corporate Ties to Higher Education in Texas

There are numerous links between the economic notables of Texas and the state's universities. In the first place, many corporate executives serve on the boards, commissions, councils, and agencies governing these institutions. (Table 9–2 lists the names of corporate officials that in recent years have held positions on the State Coordinating Board and various university boards of regents.) Since the administration of higher education policy, in the words of a former chairman of the Board of Regents of the University of Texas, "comes from the top", corporate leaders play an important role in charting the destiny of Texas's universities.[39] They have a voice in all policy matters, including hiring and firing of administrators and faculty, curriculum development, student admissions, construction priorities, and investment of university funds.

Second, some university administrators and faculty are members of the boards of directors of, or consultants to, major corporations. For example, Lorene Rogers, former president of the University of Texas at Austin, sat on the boards of Texaco and Gulf States Utilities during her administrative stint. Her replacement at Austin, Peter Flawn, was a company director at Tenneco. Former chancellor of the U.T. system and current president of the University of Texas System Cancer Center, Charles LeMaistre was on the boards of Houston Natural Gas (now ENRON) and United Savings (a subsidiary of the Kaneb energy company). When Jack Williams was chancellor at Texas A & M, he also held seats on the boards of Campbell-Taggart (now owned by Anheuser-Busch) and Anderson-Clayton— two of the nation's larger agribusiness firms. The current president of the University of Houston, Charles E. Bishop, is also a director of Houston Industries.

Third, some of the state's universities have, through investments, a financial stake in the economic growth of corporations. The University of Texas, for instance, must invest proceeds from the Permanent University Fund. It carries out this policy by purchasing shares of stock in major corporations. The constitution restricts shareholdings by the university to no more than 5 percent of the total stock in any single company, and provides that less than 1 percent of the total PUF is to be invested in any one corporation. The University possesses shares in 190 companies.[40] In 1986, about 25 percent ($871 million) of the university's total corporate investments was in companies that either operate in South Africa or have loans in that country.[41] The advisory committee that suggests stock investments to the U.T. Board of Regents is mostly composed of executives from financial institutions. In 1981, for instance, its membership included representatives from Texas Commerce Bancshares, Mercantile Bancorporation (now M Corp), Southwestern Life Insurance, American National Insurance, and the law firm of Fulbright and Jaworski.[42]

Finally, through research grants and gifts, corporations have some say in university matters. The following examples drawn from the University of Texas at Austin and from Texas A & M illustrate the impact of corporate money on research at these two key institutions.

The University of Texas at Austin has received generous support from private corporate sources. The school's College of Engineering offers businesses the chance to become members of its foundation program. The donation allows the contributor to specify exactly how 40 percent of the fee is to be spent. Among the nineteen participants in the program are Exxon, Gulf (now Chevron) Texaco, Atlantic Richfield (Arco), Mobil, Shell, Dupont, General Dynamics, and Union Carbide.[43] In 1978, the Department of Chemical Engineering at the college conducted research into gasification of lignite (sponsored by Texas Utilities, Arco, Mobil, Dow, Dupont, and ENSERCH), efficient use of this form of coal (sponsored by Celanese, Dow Chemical, and ENSERCH), and conversion of algae into protein (sponsored by Kraft, General Foods [now Philip Morris], Miles Laboratories, and Amoco Foods—a division of Standard Oil of Indiana). The Civil Engineering Department featured research into uranium exploration and usage, paid for by Anaconda (now a part of Arco), Mobil, Sun Oil, Texaco, Union Carbide, and U.S. Steel (USX). Petroleum Engineering had an interest in geothermal research, thanks to the financial support of Texas Utilities, Central Power and Light, Houston Lighting and Power, and Gulf State Utilities. Limited research—virtually none sponsored by corporations—into solar energy was conducted that year at the college.[44]

The Center for Energy Studies, created on the Austin campus in 1973, coordinates research into energy questions and disseminates its findings. Private sources have contributed close to $2 million to the center's work. Included among the benefactors have been Exxon ($400,000), Texas Utilities and its subsidiaries ($181,000), Central Power and Light ($150,000), Gulf States Utilities ($75,000), General Electric ($80,000), and the Electric Power Research Institute, a nationwide consortium of private electric companies ($500,000). Although the grants are not restricted to any particular research topic that might commercially benefit the corporations, one observer notes that "the companies do in fact stand to gain from the research they support, and they know it from the start."[45] In 1985, the center received financial grants from Texas Power and Light (a part of Texas Utilities), Houston Natural Gas (now ENRON), Dupont, Arco, ALCOA, Celanese, Chevron, and a consortium of companies that included Goodyear, Monsanto, Shell, Sohio, Texaco, and Union Carbide.[46] Along a similar line, the Center for Plasma Physics and Thermonuclear Research at U.T. Austin has been, over the last two decades, developing technology necessary to generate electricity from nuclear fusion. The center has received handsome support from electric companies. The first recipients of any technological breakthroughs are the private financial backers.[47]

The university was quite active in the successful wooing to Austin of the Micro and Computer Technology Corporation (MCC), a consortium originally composed of Advanced Micro Devices, Allied, Control Data Corporation, Digital Equipment, Harris, Honeywell, Mostek (a division of United Technologies), Motorola, National Semiconductor, NCR, RCA (now General Electric), and Sperry. The university's Balcones Research Center has donated, on an interim basis, twenty acres of its land. Some $15 million for faculty positions in computer science and microelectronics, $750,000 for postgraduate fellowships, and $1 million a year to support research also have been committed by the university. Texas A & M joined in the chase for MCC and offered the incentive of "endowed chairs and completion of an engineering research building for microelectronics and robotics research." [48]

Finally, one of Texas A & M's agricultural stations experimented with growing a nonhot chili pepper at the behest of a fast-food chain. When asked about the commercial appeal of such a pepper, an A & M researcher made the following anthropological observation: "Some of those Polacks [sic] or whatever you call them really love the hot ones, but on a general market, people don't like them like that. Yankees grab their throats and fall over in a snow bank." [49]

In short, corporations exert influence over institutions of higher education in Texas. Corporate executives are in a position to give focus to some research priorities, hiring practices, and the nature of the curriculum in a college or university. Hence instead of offering alternative insights and solutions to social problems, universities in Texas often march to a corporate tune. Studies into energy, for instance, explore sources (nuclear, for example) beneficial to private companies but devote little attention to other energy forms perhaps more suitable to the general population (such as solar energy). Agricultural research is geared to the needs of agribusinesses and not to the problems facing small farmers in Texas.

CONCLUSION

The public school system of the state serves the economic needs of corporate Texas. Some students receive an exceptionally good education; they are well prepared to assume the lead positions in the state's corporate economy. Others leave school capable only of the most menial and mindless tasks. The rest fall somewhere inbetween. Schools, of course, are not the only factors that account for economic success or failure. Family background, personal motivation, and the very structure of the economy have some bearing on earnings and occupational status. Nevertheless, public schools do independently affect economic standing.

The seeds of economic inequality in Texas are firmly planted in the early years of schooling. Primary and secondary schools best serve youngsters living in affluent school districts. Here enough money is available to hire good teachers, construct new buildings, and supply the school with the most modern equipment. Ironically, considering their family backgrounds, students in these districts are probably already well advanced on the road to economic success. Districts in areas with little property or with corporations that don't pay their fair share of property taxes are hard pressed to provide a quality education. The state government has recently attempted to close the educational gap, but there still is a substantial distance to travel.

The institutions of higher education in Texas also reflect the interests of the state's wealthy. State-supported universities train the future employees of the corporate world, engage in research that is commercially beneficial to big business, and, at least at the University of Texas, infuse investment capital into the corporate sector. All these activities are under the direction of some corporate executives who serve on the governing boards of the universities.

NOTES

1. Edward S. Greenberg, *Understanding Modern Government: The Rise and Decline of the American Political Economy* (New York: John Wiley and Sons, 1979), p. 100.

2. Governor's Committee on Education Beyond the High School, *Education: Texas' Resource for Tomorrow* (Austin, Governor's Office, 1964), p. 5. Quoted in Frank Aranda, "Economic Elites in Higher Education, The Coordinating Board, Texas College and University System" (Paper delivered at the Southwestern Political Science Association meeting, Fort Worth, Texas, March 24–26, 1979), p. 4.

3. Edward S. Greenberg, *Serving the Few: Corporate Capitalism and the Bias of Government Policy* (New York: John Wiley and Sons, 1974), p. 108.

4. This figure does not include money raised from the proceeds derived from local communities issuing bonds for capital outlays. Approximately, another $2 billion in school funding is available through this means.

5. Texas Education Agency, *Texas Assessment Project: Summary Report* (Austin: Texas Education Agency, 1978).

6. State Board of Education, *Texas Assessment of Basic Skills, Report for 1985* (Austin: Texas Education Board, 1986), p. 2.

7. Ibid.

8. State Board of Education, *Texas Assessment of Basic Skills, Report for 1982* (Austin: Texas Education Agency, 1983), p. 2.

9. The average salary figure comes from Legislative Budget Board, *Legislative Budget Estimates for the 1986–87 Biennium* (Austin: Legislative Budget Board, 1986), p. III–3. The ranking of Texas teacher's salary is from Jody George, "Courts Split on School Finance," in *State Government*, ed. Thad Beyle (Washington, D.C.: Congressional Quarterly Press, 1985), p. 178.

10. LBJ School of Public Affairs, *The Initial Effects of House Bill 72 in Texas Public Schools: The Challenges of Equity and Effectiveness* (Austin: LBJ School of Public Affairs, 1985), p. 13.

11. *Texas Poll*, Winter 1986.

12. Ibid.

13. Texas Education Agency, *TEAMS: Performance by School District Categories and Individual School Districts* (Austin: Texas Education Association, 1986).

14. Christopher Jencks and Associates, *Who Gets Ahead? The Determinants of Economic Success in America* (New York: Basic Books, 1979), ch. 3.

15. State Board of Education, *Texas Assessment of Basic Skills, Report for 1985*.

16. The exact tax rate in the formula shifts at the discretion of the legislature. During much of the 1980s, local school officials either multiplied the total market value of property in the district (less legal exemptions) times .0015 or multiplied the productivity value of agricultural land in the district times .00175. The school board chooses the rate that produces the lower overall amount.

17. LBJ School of Public Affairs, *The Initial Effects of House Bill 72,* p. 1.

18. Texas Education Agency, *Foundation School Program, Fiscal Impact Model* (Austin: Texas Education Agency, 1984), p. 1.

19. Jim Hightower and Tim Mahoney, "Texas Property Taxes: The Unfair Deal," *Texas Observer,* July 21, 1978, p. 6.

20. Mitch Green, "Like to Set your Own Tax Rate?" *Texas Observer,* August 25, 1972, p. 6.

21. Hightower and Mahoney, "Texas Property Taxes," p. 11. Reprinted with permission.

22. The exchange is recorded in Gregory Jones, "Tax Increase Overturned," *El Paso Times,* June 21, 1978, p. 1,

23. Discussed in House Study Group, Special Legislative Report No. 61, *Property Taxes: Relief, Reform, . . . Revolt?* November 10, 1980.

24. Grace Garcia, *Texas School Finance,* House Study Group, Special Legislative Report, No. 45, May 8, 1979.

25. LBJ School of Public Affairs, *The Initial Effects of House Bill 72,* p. 8.

26. Texas Education Agency, *Foundation School Program,* p. 1.

27. Richard A. Gambitta, Robert A. Milne, and Carol R. Davis, "The Politics of Unequal Educational Opportunity," in *The Politics of San Antonio: Community, Progress, and Power,* ed. John Booth (Lincoln: University of Nebraska Press, 1983), pp. 152–55.

28. Ibid, pp. 154–55.

29. Geoffrey Rips, "Edgewood Still Austere," *Texas Observer,* April 8, 1983, pp. 13–16.

30. LBJ School of Public Affairs, p. 18.

31. See the comprehensive report by the House Study Group, *Property Taxes,* for details.

32. Texas Research League, *Practices of Texas School Districts and Counties, 1981* (Austin: Texas Research League, 1983), p. 2.

33. Chairman of the Board of Equalization of Dallas County, quoted in House Study Group, *Property Taxes,* p. 130.

34. Hightower and Mahoney, "Texas Property Taxes," p. 4.

35. Inclusion of smaller universities results in some changes in rankings. Start-up costs, such as at the University of Texas at Dallas, of newer universities with relatively small student populations result in higher expenditures per student. Texas Woman's University is at the top in appropriations owing to its heavy concentration of students studying scientific subjects. Finally, Prairie View A & M, with only around 4,400 students, receives almost $7,382 each biennially, probably in response to allegations that in the past racial discrimination affected its financial status.

36. Figures on the PUF/AUF are found in Board of Regents, University of Texas System, *Permanent University Fund Investments for Fiscal Year Ending August 31, 1985.*

37. Amy Johnson, "The Haves and Have-Nots," *Texas Observer,* July 10, 1981.

38. In addition, all members of the UT and A & M systems may borrow using part of the PUF as collateral to construct or repair buildings and purchase equipment and library materials. As of 1984, the value of 30 percent of the PUF can be used as a basis of collateral.

39. The late Frank Erwin, quoted in Michael Parenti, *Power and the Powerless* (New York: St. Martin's Press, 1978), p. 135.

40. Board of Regents, University of Texas System, *Permanent University Fund Investments for Fiscal Year Ending August 31, 1985.*

41. *Austin American-Statesman,* October 22, 1986, p. A12.

42. Amy Johnson, "Playing the Market with PUF," *Texas Observer,* July 10, 1981.

43. *The Texas Observer,* August 26, 1978, p. 13.

44. The College of Engineering, University of Texas, *Engineering Research* (Austin: Bureau of Engineering Research, 1978).

45. Jim Hightower, "Corporate Money in the Public Till: What Does It Buy?" *Texas Observer,* January 28, 1977, p. 15.

46. The University of Texas at Austin, *Report on Organized Research: Non-State Funded Organized Research Units,* August 31, 1986.

47. "Public Work for Private Power," *Texas Observer,* April 26, 1974, pp. 8–11.

48. Kate Jenkins, "The Wining, Wooing, and Winning of MCC," *Southwest Airlines Magazine,* September 1983, p. 82. Also see in the same issue, D. Lee McCullough, "The Day the Chips Fell on Austin."

49. Discussed and quoted in *The Texas Observer,* October 21, 1977, p. 13.

12

Highways and Welfare: Contrasting Policy Priorities

The state government of Texas allocates nearly 30 percent of its biennial budget—some $10.7 billion—for transportation (primarily highway construction and maintenance) and welfare. Overall, these policies work to the advantage of the corporate elite of Texas and do very little to improve the economic standing of the state's impoverished. This chapter first analyzes transportation policy in Texas; next, the state's welfare commitment comes under scrutiny.   ★

TRANSPORTATION POLICY IN TEXAS

Devising a systematic transportation policy suitable to cover all of Texas, both inside and outside of government, poses a very formidable problem for decision makers. The immense size of the state (267,339 square miles) makes the smooth conveyance of goods and people a difficult task. Government officials first became involved in the formulation of a statewide transportation program in the mid-nineteenth century. At that time, the state legislature subsidized the development of a comprehensive rail system for Texas through grants of land for track and cash assistance (see chapter 7). In 1917, Texas established the Highway Department and began to invest in the construction of roads and highways. Over the last seven decades, the state's highway commitment has grown considerably. Indeed, today transportation policy in Texas is actually highway policy.

For the 1986–87 biennium Texas allocated $5.3 billion on transportation, most (nearly 80 percent) of which is for the construction and maintenance of roads and highways.[1] By the mid–1980s, Texas could boast of one of the most extensive and expensive road systems in the world: 72,363 miles of highway worth an estimated replacement value of $117 billion.[2]

The state's commitment to highways is not the result of chance. Rather it has been molded by groups with a vested, usually economic, interest in the development of a sophisticated road system. Highway enthusiasts include the manufacturers of motor vehicles and their parts, petroleum companies, road construction firms, truck companies, and auto and bus drivers, as well as local chambers of commerce who hope that a road in their city or town will mean more commercial business. These interests have lobbied extensively over the years for huge annual highway appropriations. These funds are generated from two revenue sources in Texas: the dedicated fund and the general revenue fund.

The Dedicated Fund

In 1946 the highway lobby in Texas, spearheaded by the efforts of the Texas Good Roads Association (see chapter 6), persuaded state legislators and voters to amend the state constitution and establish a permanent revenue source to finance highway development. This revenue source is known as the dedicated fund. It is composed of taxes from the sale of petroleum products and motor vehicles and fees paid for the registration of cars, buses, and trucks. The constitution specifies that three-fourths of the sales tax on gasoline and oil and around 80 percent of registration fees be used only for transportation needs. Ten percent of the sales tax imposed on the purchases of motor vehicles is earmarked for the highway fund, thanks to a law enacted in the 1984 special session of the Texas Legislature. In the 1986–87 biennium the dedicated fund—officially referenced as State Highway Fund No. 006—totaled around $3.06 billion; it accounted for 57 percent of the financing of transportation policy in Texas.[3]

For nearly three decades, the highway interests were comfortable with their status in the state government. Every attempt to chip away at the dedicated fund was defeated. Moreover, the revenue from the fund was more than sufficient to construct, repair, and maintain all highways.[4] But in the mid–1970s economic events began to take their toll on the highway establishment.

In a nutshell, the dedicated fund was not raising enough money to continue the state's rich endowment of highway interests. Facing gasoline shortages and spiraling prices for fuel, Texans responded by purchasing small cars. This choice affected the dedicated fund in two ways. First, smaller cars are lighter. Since the fee to register an auto was based on the weight of the vehicle, the coffers of the highway fund declined. Second, the escalating price of a gallon of gasoline did not result in greater tax revenues from the sale of fuel. The sales tax on gas in Texas was fixed at five cents per gallon (then the lowest rate in America), regardless of the price per gallon. Fuel-efficient cars and less driving in order to conserve petroleum products curtailed the total revenue earned from the gasoline tax. Consequently, the dedicated fund was being seriously depleted.

General Revenue Funds for Highways

To offset losses suffered by the dedicated fund, highway interests sought financial help from the Texas legislature. In 1977, the legislature approved spending general revenue money for highways if the dedicated fund fell below $750 million in any given year. Moreover, to counter the effects of inflation, these expenditures were indexed to constant 1977 dollars. Between 1977 and 1984, this policy generated an average of $250 million of general revenue money for highways each year.

In its 1984 special session the legislature ended its indexed assistance to highways from general tax revenues. It instead instituted a policy of routinely transferring general funds into the highway account. The amount involved equals one-eighth of the state's tax on motor fuels. In the 1986–87 biennium $277 million were shifted into the highway fund from general taxes.[5] In addition, the legislature increased the state's tax on gasoline sales (to ten cents a gallon) and the annual cost of registering a motor vehicle (by $25). Since these tax sources form the backbone of the dedicated fund, this pool of constitutionally guaranteed money has been reinvigorated. Finally, in 1982 the federal government increased its tax on the sale of a gallon of petrol by five cents. This added sum goes directly to the states; Texas gains over $500 million yearly in additional highway revenue from this change. All told, the federal government pumps $2 billion into Texas to meet its transportation requirements.[6]

Beneficiaries of the Highway Commitment

Highways are welcomed by a large number of people. Indeed, the widespread popularity of roads is a strong justification for the continued definition of transportation policy as highway policy. Some interests, however, benefit more than others from this state of affairs.

Industries that supply the essential materials for highway travel earn large profits from highway usage. Petroleum companies, automobile manufacturers, auto parts firms, bus and trucking companies, and road construction outfits have derived untold amounts from the government subsidization of highway expansion.

The nine million owners of automobiles in Texas can ride a highway system second to none in engineering soundness and convenience. Yet drivers run some risk in highway safety. Each year about 4,000 Texans lose their lives in automobile accidents, and an additional 125,000 are injured. More than $1 billion of property damage occurs annually through highway carnage.[7] The air Texans breathe becomes increasingly poisoned by exhaust fumes.

Impoverished people find little comfort in a transportation policy that exalts the individual ownership of automobiles. Mass transportation would probably be of greater assistance to the mobility of the poor, many of whom are black, Mexican American, or elderly. Yet Texas spends very little on mass transportation. Only around $19 million was budgeted for this purpose in the 1986–87 biennium, less than 1 percent of the total transportation appropriation in Texas.[8] At times, money authorized for mass transportation goes unspent, usually because cities fail to take advantage of available state money.[9] Fully $10.5 million earmarked for mass transportation in the 1984–85 biennium went unspent.[10] All in all, Texas is a classic example of a "transportation system . . . [where] the well-to-do get the most and the needy the least." [11]

In short, there is a distinct corporate bias to transportation policy in Texas. Automobiles and highways are promoted by the actions of public decisionmakers, much to the satisfaction of automotive, car insurance, highway construction, and oil companies. This commitment, however, precludes the development of alternate transportation systems: systems that would be safer, more conserving of fuel, less destructive of the environment, and used by the public at large. Moreover, even in a tight fiscal environment, highway funding has grown. Between the biennium of 1984–85 and that of 1986–87, the total amount budgeted for transportation—primarily highways—in Texas increased by two-thirds, an achievement that no other program in the state could come close to matching.

POVERTY AND WELFARE

Poverty: The Other Texas

Amid the corporate plenty of Texas there are deep pockets of poverty. The economic boom experienced in the state during the late 1970s and early 1980s expanded the affluence of many Texans, but left others still below the poverty line. One study showed that in fact during the good times the poor in Texas suffered a decline in income.[12] In 1980, 14.7 percent of the population (or 2 million Texans) were classified as poor;[13] during the economic recession, the number of the state's poor (in 1985) grew to 2.9 million or 18 percent of all Texans.[14] More than one in ten Texas families is impoverished. These figures place Texas high among all states in the number of poor within its geographic boundaries—only two states have more poor people.[15] Who are the poor of Texas? What does the state government do to attenuate their economic status?

Characteristics of the Poor in Texas.   Poverty is a burden that weighs most heavily upon distinct segments of society. It is particularly evident among the following people.

The Young and the Old.   Poverty occurs most frequently at the extremes of the age continuum. One of every five young (under fourteen years of age) Texans is poor. Likewise, 23 percent of the state's elderly (sixty-five years or more) are impoverished. All told, 70 percent of the state's official poor are either under eighteen or over sixty-five.[16]

Blacks and Mexican Americans.   Poverty has a clear racial or ethnic bias to it in Texas. About 12 percent of the state's population is black, but nearly 28 percent of the poor are black. Similarly, Mexican Americans constitute 21 percent of the state's people, but account for nearly 40 percent of its poor. Anglos comprise the remaining two-thirds of the state's citizens and 32 percent of the impoverished. In other words, many economically destitute are Anglo; however, poverty only envelopes around 11 percent of all Anglos living in Texas. Mexican Americans and blacks do not fare as well. About 25 percent of both the black population and Mexican American population are officially categorized as poor.[17]

Dwellers of the Inner Cities and Border, Rural Areas.   The slums of the large cities in Texas are the home of many of the state's poor; nearly 85 percent live in urban centers.[18] For instance, around 21 percent of the people of both El Paso and San Antonio are officially poor. Poverty is also quite pronounced in the smaller cities and rural counties in East Texas and along the United States–Mexico border from the far west of El Paso to the deep south of Brownsville. For example, 37.5

percent of the people of the city of Pharr in South Texas's Hidalgo County are classified as officially poor. The rate of poverty in College Station is 32.3 percent; in Laredo it is 34.5 percent; in Brownsville it is 33.3 percent.[19]

Consequences of Poverty. Insufficient income has a dramatic effect on obtaining a comfortable life-style in the United States. Poverty has an especially dire impact on the housing, education, and health of the poor.

Housing. The vast majority (85 percent) of the poor in Texas rent their apartments or houses. Only 16 percent of the state's impoverished live in quarters supported through governmental subsidies.[20] Most of the rest pay rent to private landlords and live in tenements. Tenement living, overall, is cramped, uncomfortable, and dangerous considering the fact that many tenements are not in compliance with the structural specifications established by housing codes. In South El Paso, a slum where extremely poor Mexican Americans reside, 96 percent of the tenements that fill the square-mile area are officially classified as "deteriorating/ dilapidated." Under the housing code of El Paso, these buildings are designated as "unfit for human habitation." Less than 1 percent of these dwelling units have inside toilets; only 3 percent are equipped with indoor showers or bathtubs. Yet around 11,000 people still occupy these units.[21]

For the relatively few Texans who live in public housing, the internal living quarters are certainly safer and more comfortable. Yet life in public housing still brings complaints from the poor. Inadequate management of the housing units, lack of services such as transportation and police protection, and estrangement from the world outside the public housing complex are frequent targets of criticism.[22]

Education. In number of school years completed, the poor rank much lower than their more affluent fellow Texans. Only about one-third of the poor of Texas complete high school, a proportion half the statewide figure.[23] Another one-third never finish the fourth grade.[24] While in school, as shown in chapter 11, the quality of education the poor receive is substantially inferior to that offered to other Texans.

Health. The federal government's definition of poverty is based on a family's ability to purchase a nutritionally sound diet. A recent legislative inquiry into hunger in Texas revealed a substantial number of people going without much food. As noted by Texas Senator Hugh Parmer, "I assumed that there would be some people who were occasionally hungry, but I didn't really know whether there was chronic hunger in Texas. I'm convinced, absolutely, by listening to the testimony that there is."[25] Insufficient nutrition and inadequate income often give rise to chronic health problems among the poor. For example, a high incidence of malnutrition exists among low-income pregnant women in Texas. The consequences are most clearly seen in their offspring: "[An] . . . improper diet can prevent a child from reaching full height, delay bone development, cause skin ailments, increase susceptibility to disease and cause other problems."[26] Many of the state's Chicano poor who live in South Texas farming counties (Hidalgo, for example) not only face a daily scarcity of food, but also lack suitable water for sewerage, bathing, or drinking.[27]

Impoverishment also leads to substandard health care facilities and, in turn, ill-health for the poor. The health care system in this country is primarily based on the principle of "fee for service." Some 46 percent of the state's poor "are without any form of health insurance."[28] Four of every ten reside in counties that either do not have a clearly defined health care policy for the poor or public hospitals.[29] Having very little money can seriously impede receiving adequate medical care. For example, Texas's farmworkers rank well above the statewide norm in the number of reported cases of hepatitis, influenza, pneumonia, tuberculosis, scarlet fever, strep throat, and work-related diseases such as insecticide poisoning: indeed, "the life expectancy for the average farmworker is 50 years."[30]

Welfare Policy in Texas

As the Depression of the 1930s deepened, the government, after the election of President Franklin D. Roosevelt, assumed a greater role in attending to the economic hardships of many of its citizens. Public policy soon emerged to assist the impoverished, the unemployed, the elderly, and the incapacitated. Over the last fifty years, federal assistance has also been given to the hungry and to some of the ill.

From the beginning of welfare legislation, states have been encouraged to actively participate in these programs. States are persuaded to provide some financial support through the enticement of receiving matching funds from the federal government, usually of a size much greater than the state's contribution. States and local communities are on the front line in program administration. Consequently, each state maintains some control over the implementation of assistance and can shape the federally outlined programs to conform to the economic conditions that prevail within its boundaries.[31]

Texas was quite slow to join in a welfare partnership with the federal government. As of late 1940, for instance, only eighty-five impoverished Texas families with dependent children were receiving cash benefits from the federal/state assistance program.[32] Currently, the state government participates with a varying degree of financial commitment in three important federal assistance programs: Aid to Families with Dependent Children (AFDC), the Food Stamp program, and Medicare and Medicaid.[33] Table 12–1 outlines the fiscal details of these programs.

Aid to Families with Dependent Children is designed to provide income for the offspring of unemployed parents who are below the poverty line. Medicare covers some of the health costs of the aged, and Medicaid offers some medical assistance to the needy. Food stamps are issued to the impoverished to purchase items in grocery stores for the purpose of maintaining an adequate diet.

Just under $2 billion of taxpayers' money is annually spent on these programs. Medical services consume over half the funds, food stamps cost $697 million, and AFDC absorbs another $224 million. The federal government picks up about 71 percent of the tab. The state's share amounts to $491 million for medical assistance and $102 million for AFDC, but the state makes no financial contribution to the provision of food stamps to Texans.

TABLE 12–1 Welfare Programs in Texas

Program	Total Spent (1985)	Amount Spent by Federal Government (1985)	Amount Spent by State Government (1985)
Medical Services (Medicare and Medicaid)	$1.06 billion	$595.5 million	$461.1 million
Aid to Families with Dependent Children	$223.8 million	$122.0 million	$101.8 million
Food Stamps	$697.2 million	$697.2 million	
Totals	$1.98 billion	$1.41 billion	$562.9 million

SOURCE: Texas Department of Human Services, *Annual Report 1985.*

Beneficiaries of Welfare in Texas. An obvious answer to the question "Who benefits from welfare policy in Texas?" is "The poor." To a certain extent this is true, for the impoverished are assisted with cash, food, and medical care. Yet, for the three reasons that follow, this conclusion has to be tempered.

1. *Most of the poor do not receive welfare benefits.* Direct cash assistance through the Aid to Families with Dependent Children program in Texas reaches on a monthly average (in 1985) 116,582 families, or 358,479 people.[34] Since Texas is home for 2.9 million poor, only about 12 percent of the economically destitute receive proceeds from AFDC. Eligibility requirements severely limit the number of participants. Basically, only unemployed women who support families with minor children (eighteen years of age or younger) and who live alone qualify for the benefits. By law (federal and state), the poor who are single and without children, or who are in families with offspring over eighteen still living at home, with both parents in the house, or with a male as the sole parent, are excluded from the AFDC rolls. Incidentally, about two-thirds of the state's impoverished families are headed by males.[35]

Since 1982, the AFDC caseload has been on the rise, probably in direct response to the spread of the recession in Texas. The number of families receiving assistance increased 37 percent between 1982 and 1987.[36] Most recipients, however, only stay on the welfare rolls for a relatively short period of time. While a very few Texans have participated in the AFDC program for years and years, the longest tenure for most beneficiaries is twelve months or less.[37]

Food stamps don't reach all the state's poor either. With 1.3 million participants, this program covers the dietary needs of about 45 percent of the impoverished. To be eligible for food stamps in Texas a family must either be receiving AFDC assistance or have an annual income well below the official poverty level (defined at about $10,200 for a family of four in 1984). Moreover, a food stamp recipient must be without major assets, such as a car valued at over $4,500, and, in order to continue on the program, adults must register for work with the Texas Employment Commission. If a person chooses not to accept available employment or quits a job, he or she automatically becomes ineligible for food stamps. Food stamp coupons are mostly allocated to children or the elderly or the disabled.

Further, until recently state medical assistance affected only a fraction of the poor. Before 1984 it was available, through the Medicaid program, either to AFDC beneficiaries or to most low-income elderly living in nursing homes. Unlike other states, Texas had chosen not to enroll in the federal program that expands medical insurance to a greater portion of the poor. In the early 1980s, only about one-quarter of the state's poor fell under the protection of the Medicaid program.[38]

Since 1984, Texas has been in the process of implementing medical assistance programs designed to reach more of the state's poor.[39] One program, established by the 1984 Indigent Health Care and Treatment Act, offers an incentive system for Texas's counties to provide hospital care to the impoverished. A minimum level of care for the poor in each county has been prescribed by the legislature. Counties that allocate some of their money for health care are now eligible for supplemental state financial aid. A primary health care system aimed at prevention of disease and illness among the poor is also being put into operation. Pregnant women and infants can now take advantage of an array of state-supported medical services regardless of their income status. In recent years, in other words, the state has made a concerted effort to attend to the health needs of its destitute. However, it is estimated that only one-fourth of the state's poor will be eligible for coverage under these programs.[40]

2. *The benefits allocated to participants in welfare programs are not overwhelming.* In 1987, for instance, each person in a family eligible for AFDC received, on the average, $57.50 a month. Between 1982 and 1987, the monthly AFDC grant rose about 40 percent.[41] Throughout the decade Texas has, however, compared with other states ranked near the bottom in AFDC expenditures per recipient.[42]

Until 1978, food stamp recipients had to match some of the dollar value of the coupons distributed. In 1977, for instance, Texas participants paid around $34 for every $100 worth of stamps received; the federal government made up the difference. Now the entire cost is borne by the government. In 1983, food stamp benefits averaged 48 cents per meal.[43]

Medical payments generally do not cover all the health care expenses of those eligible. One nationwide study suggests that half the actual medical costs of those enrolled in government-sponsored medical programs are paid out of the patients' pockets.[44]

3. *Welfare recipients often pay an exacting psychological and sometimes physical price for participating in the programs.* Most Americans view those receiving welfare with disdain. They perceive the beneficiaries as shiftless, lazy, promiscuous, and with no one to blame but themselves for their economic condition. These negative sentiments are frequently translated into administrative policy in the implementation of the programs. Application forms are lengthy and probe into very personal areas. Long waits for processing are usual. Refusals, especially in the past, have been capricious and often times based on the whimsy of the administrator. Some people declared eligible for welfare are not informed of the full extent of their benefits. Termination from the dole is encouraged, and has, at least in the past, been arbitrary. Hostility and suspicion about the morals, motives, and integrity of applicants and recipients pervade the administrative atmosphere of the programs. In Southern states, including Texas, racial discrimination was a common barrier that kept blacks and Mexican Americans from joining or staying on the welfare rolls.[45] Now, fully 80 percent of AFDC and food stamp recipients in Texas are

black or Mexican American.[46] Even with most of these bureaucratic practices eliminated, the stigma associated with accepting welfare benefits still lingers with many administrators, legislators, the general public, and even with the participants themselves.

Physical abuse of welfare recipients has been recorded as well. Unseemly incidents have been observed in nursing homes financed through government medical assistance funds to provide care for elderly Texans. An investigation by the Texas Attorney-General's Office revealed some startling findings. The task force probed a random sample of 113 homes for a year (1978) and found that 25 percent were inadequately maintained, 20 percent were below average in cleanliness, theft was a "serious problem," fiscal mismanagement was a "significant problem," neglect of patients was "serious . . . in many Texas nursing homes," drug misuse existed in some, and, in a small number, physical abuse of residents occurred.[47] Seventy-one complaints of bodily mistreatment involving at least one-half of the homes in the study were communicated to the task force. One resident "saw the administrator [of the nursing home] hang a man on the door by his clothes and leave him there. An aide got him down five to ten minutes later." [48] A seventy-six-year-old woman told another investigating team that six employees of a home in Lufkin beat her "with belts, coat hangers and shoes." [49] Finally, three attempts have been made to indict the Autumn Hills Convalescence Home of Galveston County with the murder of eight residents. The assistant district attorney of the county feels that the home, through negligence and starvation of residents, is guilty of murder. The Texas Department of Health, in its investigation of this establishment, found an inordinate number of deaths (thirty-five in a ninety-day period). A probe into one of these deaths "showed the staff to be totally negligent in observing visible signs of congestive heart failure," according to the Health Department. The home pleaded "no contest" to one charge of involuntary manslaughter and agreed to pay Galveston County $100,000; early in 1983, however, this offer was withdrawn.[50]

Part of the cause of these sordid findings has been the "hands off" policy adopted by government officials in Texas in dealing with the day-to-day operation of nursing homes. The attorney-general's task force charged that the Department of Health, which is responsible for regulating the homes, "tend[ed] to embrace its role as a consultant to the nursing home industry and shun[ned] its role as an enforcer of the laws and regulations governing the industry. [It] . . . frequently play[ed] an endless 'compliance game' with substandard homes . . . [and] exhibit[ed] a protective attitude toward the nursing home industry." [51] Legislators, amid claims that several of them were part-owners of some of these homes and were the recipients of generous campaign contributions from nursing home administrators, have been slow to intervene in these problems.[52] In 1983, however, the legislature ordered the Department of Health to make unannounced inspections at every nursing home in the state twice yearly and to downgrade any home found in violation of any laws. Since then, given the negative publicity surrounding the plight of some patients in a few homes, standards have been more strictly enforced. Medical contracts have been cancelled with homes deficient in health care. Some 72 homes were closed by the Department of Health for impairing the health and safety of patients during 1985.[53]

In short, welfare policy in Texas does not benefit all the state's poor. Eligibility requirements keep many off of the welfare rolls. Benefits are partial, never entirely covering the income, dietary, and health needs of the poor. Recipients are, at times, abused psychologically and physically for partaking in the programs. As paradoxical as it may at first seem, the welfare system in Texas is probably more helpful to people with wealth than to those without it. This position can be supported by analyzing the direct and indirect benefits that accrue to affluent Texans through the state's welfare programs.

Welfare: Direct Assistance to the Wealthy.   Some well-established economic interests in Texas earn handsome profits from the state's welfare policies. This is most evident in the medical services and food stamp programs.

Through Medicaid and Medicare a great deal of money distributed by the state (and federal) government terminates in the bank accounts of two relatively affluent recipients: nursing home operators and medical professionals (doctors, dentists, pharmacists, and hospital administrators). In 1985, just under half of all medical funds (some $500 million) were distributed to around 1,000 nursing homes. Most (over 85 percent) of these establishments are private, profit-making institutions. Over 100,000 residents, most of whom are very poor Anglo women over the age of eighty, are in these homes.[54] Indeed, homes have an incentive to enroll additional people in order to maximize profits. Corporations have recently entered into this business in Texas. Almost a third of these institutions (around 300) are owned by ten companies.[55] The largest of the lot is ARA, a billion-dollar Northeast enterprise known more for its food concession and vending machine endeavors than its health services. Through its two subsidiaries, National Living Centers and Geriatrics, ARA has cornered 11 percent of the Texas nursing home market. In addition, through management contracts, it, in effect, operates another 5 percent of the state's nursing homes.[56]

Another third of the medical assistance money goes directly to private health insurance firms.[57] From there, after administrative costs have been deducted, most of the money is sent to hospitals, physicians, lab technicians, and dentists. The rest is used for investment purposes by the insurance company. Prior to 1978, Blue Cross/Blue Shield of Texas, the largest private health insurance company in the state, held the contract for medical services. Between 1966 and 1975, this company received $745 million to cover medical claims by the poor and elderly. It paid out $602 million for health care services, $44 million for administrative costs (essentially computer processing performed by H. Ross Perot's Electronic Data Systems Corporation), and invested the $100 million balance in interest-bearing accounts. The principal depository of medical insurance funds was Republic of Texas Bancorporation, second largest bank holding company in the state. The bank, as well as Blue Cross/Blue Shield, profited from the interest.[58] Another company of H. Ross Perot, National Heritage Insurance, replaced Blue Cross/Blue Shield in the late 1970s. In 1981, National Heritage was apparently outbid for this lucrative contract by a New York firm. National Heritage, however, managed to persuade the Texas Department of Human Resources (now called the Department of Human Services) to reopen the matter and subsequently retained its middle-man position between the health care establishment in Texas and government medical assistance funding agencies.

All in all, Medicaid and Medicare have been a major economic boon for nursing home owners and members of the medical profession, as well as some insurance companies. Each of these groups can now cater to the health needs of the poor and elderly, and largely set their own prices for their services—payment is guaranteed by the government.

In a similar vein, the ultimate beneficiary of the food stamp program is the grower, processor, and retailer of food products. As pointed out in chapter 2, in Texas this mostly means wealthy agribusinesses. The stamp program has, in effect, converted the less affluent into new food customers. The government (the taxpayer) foots the bill and the producers and distributors reap the harvest of profits.

Welfare: Indirect Assistance to the Wealthy.   There are less obvious ways in which the welfare system benefits economic elites. Foremost among them, it creates an oversupply of cheap labor and restrains the destitute from engaging in rebellious actions against the social, political, and economic structure of society.

Cheap Labor.   One of the major results of welfare in Texas is the availability of a large number of people willing to trade their welfare checks in for paychecks, regardless of how low the salary might be. A household receiving AFDC payments, food stamps, and medical assistance through Medicaid still has a usable income 50 percent below the poverty level.[59] Hence those physically able to work have a clear economic stimulus to do so. Moreover, this incentive is constantly brought to the attention of Texas's welfare recipients. By state law, all participants in the AFDC program over sixteen years of age must actively seek employment through the Texas Employment Commission in order to receive cash assistance. In 1983, the legislature directed the Department of Human Services to create a job training program in selected areas for AFDC recipients. For the first two months of training, AFDC payments continue to be paid to the recipient. During the next four months, the employer receives these funds. Failure to participate in the program means a cessation or reduction of AFDC benefits. Overall, state leaders deliberately keep welfare checks stingy because many believe, in the words of former House Speaker Bill Clayton, that this "incentive is the only way we have to break the poverty cycle."[60]

Among nonwelfare poor—many of whom are disqualified by law from securing benefits—the stigma attached to being a welfare recipient is sufficient enough incentive to seek employment. In order to avoid the social loathing that accompanies classification as a member of the dole, many of the poor seek work, even if it is in low-paying jobs.

Almost two-thirds of the state's impoverished families have at least one member who works. Three out of every ten poor families contain a person employed a minimum of fifty weeks a year.[61] The working poor are mostly employed in service occupations (for example, maids, maintenance workers, and in heavy labor) and on the farms of the state, especially the large ones. In the mid–1970s some of the working poor made less than the federal minimum wage (then only $2.40 an hour). One study found that "13 percent of Dallas' inner city workers and 12.1 percent of Houston's are employed well below the minimum wage."[62] The state was quite slow in adopting a minimum wage law that covers employees working for firms with business transacted solely in Texas. Finally, in 1970, a Texas Minimum Wage law was passed, but the in-state minimum wage is well below the federal standard and allows for a number of occupational exceptions.

The end result is that jobs open to the poor are generally of the low-paying kind. In fact, many of the state's poor remain in their impoverished condition because of their work: "Eighty percent of ghettoites in our two most 'dynamic' and 'opportunity-rich' cities [Dallas and Houston] stay poor because of the sort of jobs they have." [63] Job loss for a member of the working poor often means no unemployment benefits, since some employers are not required to deduct unemployment insurance.

Containing the Poor.   Government welfare policies also indirectly help dominant economic interests by holding in check the possible anger, frustration, rage, and violence of the otherwise totally destitute. Without some financial aid, the impoverished might turn to civil disorder out of sheer economic desperation. Any large-scale concerted attempt on the part of the poor to attack the current economic system would certainly disrupt corporate planning, stability, and profit.

One major study has amassed a great deal of evidence that links widespread public displays of discontent on the part of those on the economic fringe to increases in welfare benefits.[64] The sharp rise in the number of welfare recipients experienced by all states, including Texas, in the late 1960s has been viewed as a political reaction to the protests and urban riots of that era. Under the financial prodding of the federal government, all states and most local governments had to increase their welfare rolls. States retained the option of expanding benefits even more. Texas, as pointed out earlier, initially chose to limit its contribution to welfare, and especially to the AFDC program. Perhaps one reason for this position was that civil disorder never became explosive in the state. None of Texas's major urban centers experienced serious riots in the 1960s. Not having to face any imminent danger to political and economic stability, Texas elected not to enlarge its welfare rolls beyond what the federal government required.

In short, established economic interests across the nation and in Texas receive direct and indirect benefits from the current welfare system. Lending further strength to this contention is the fact that many of these programs were not only supported by the heads of major corporations, they were actually written by them. For more than two decades prior to the passage of the Social Security Act of 1935, a law that began the national commitment to welfare and established the AFDC program, leading corporate executives had called for some form of assistance to the needy. The Social Security Act itself was endorsed and advanced by the chieftains of several large companies and banks, including among others the Chase Manhattan Bank, General Electric, Standard Oil, and Remington Rand. These business leaders foresaw that modest government assistance to the impecunious would short-circuit radical social behavior and reinforce a stable supply of employable persons—all at a relatively low cost to major corporations.[65]

CONCLUSION

This chapter has explored the chief beneficiaries of transportation and welfare policy in Texas. In each case, wealthy individuals and institutions in the state have reaped impressive gains.

Transportation policy is a clear instance in which dominant economic interests profit the most from the expenditures of state government. The millions of taxpayers' dollars spent each year on highways directly improve the economic status of companies involved in vehicular traffic. Conversely, mass transportation, which is probably more suitable to meeting the transportation needs of the impoverished, is given short shrift by state policymakers.

Indeed, policies ostensibly designed to upgrade the overall welfare of Texas's poor mostly fall short of their mark. The state, comparatively speaking, provides very little assistance to the destitute. Moreover, the psychological cost of being on welfare is not offset by the meager benefits available.

However, welfare programs have directly aided many economically well-off Texans. Agribusinesses, medical doctors, hospitals, nursing homes, dentists, and medical insurance firms have received a healthy share of the welfare dollar. In addition, the overall business community benefits through the welfare system that guarantees the availability of a steady pool of labor for low-paying jobs and contains the potential anger of the impoverished.

NOTES

1. Figures are from Legislative Budget Board, *Fiscal Size Up: 1986–1987 Biennium* (Austin: Legislative Budget Board, 1986), pp. 101–102.

2. Ibid., p. 103.

3. Ibid., p. 105.

4. For an excellent account of the self-sufficiency of the highway establishment see Griffin Smith, Jr., "The Highway Establishment and How It Grew, and Grew, and Grew," reprinted in *Texas Monthly's Political Reader* (Austin: Texas Monthly Press and Sterling Swift Publishing, 1978), pp. 143–57.

5. *Fiscal Size Up,* p. 102.

6. Ibid.

7. Legislative Budget Board, *Fiscal Size Up: Texas State Services, 1982–1983 Biennium* (Austin: Legislative Budget Board, 1981), p. 127.

8. *Fiscal Size Up: 1986–1987 Biennium,* p. 102.

9. Susan Raleigh, *Highway Finance,* Special Legislative Report, No. 90, House Study Group, February 10, 1983, p. 21.

10. *Fiscal Size Up: 1986–1987,* p. 107.

11. Michael Parenti, *Democracy for the Few* (New York: St. Martin's Press, 1977), p. 112.

12. Julie Ardery and Bill Bishop, "Prosperity for the Few," *Texas Observer,* May 26, 1978, p. 4.

13. Bureau of the Census, Department of Commerce, *1980 Census of Population and Housing: Texas* (Washington, D.C.: Government Printing Office, 1983), p. 138.

14. Texas Department of Human Services, *Annual Report, 1985,* p. 1.

15. The Texas ranking is based on absolute numbers. In terms of percent of population poor, Texas has the ninth highest proportion of impoverished people. Department of

Commerce, *Statistical Abstract of the United States, 1982–83* (Washington, D.C.: Government Printing Office, 1982), p. 444.

16. Figures computed from Bureau of the Census, Department of Commerce, *Money Income and Poverty Status in 1975 of Families and Persons in the United States and the South Region, by Divisions and States* (Washington, D.C.: Government Printing Office, 1978), p. 227; and Bureau of the Census, Department of Commerce, *General Social and Economic Characteristics: Texas* (Washington, D.C.: Government Printing Office, 1983), p. 138.

17. Ibid.

18. Ibid.

19. Ibid.

20. Bureau of the Census, Department of Commerce, *Money Income and Poverty Status in 1975,* p. 228.

21. James W. Lamare and Mary S. Lamare, "Sociopolitical Reactions to Public Policy: Tenant Attitudes about a Relocation Program," in *Politics and Society in the Southwest,* ed. Z. A. Kruszewski, R. L. Hough, and J. Ornstein-Galicia (Boulder: Westview, 1982), ch. 11.

22. Ibid.

23. Bureau of the Census, Department of Commerce, *Detailed Population Characteristics: Texas* (Washington, D.C.: Government Printing Office, 1983).

24. Ibid.

25. Quoted in Zy Weinberg, "Hunger in Texas," *Texas Observer,* August 17, 1984, p. 10.

26. Texas Department of Community Affairs, *Still the Darker Side of Childhood* (Austin: Department of Community Affairs, 1978), p. 61.

27. Norman de Weaver, "Struggling for Water," *Texas Observer,* December 10, 1976, p. 1; and John Davidson, "A Harvest of Poverty," *Texas Observer,* February 3, 1978, p. 5.

28. Task Force on Indigent Health Care, Final Report, 1984, p. 10.

29. Ibid., p. 14.

30. Geoffrey Rips, "The Battle for Farmworker Compensation," *Texas Observer,* January 13, 1984, p. 10.

31. The economic basis of the federal/state cooperative effort in welfare policies is discussed in Frances Fox Piven and Richard A. Cloward, *Regulating the Poor: The Functions of Public Welfare* (New York: Pantheon, 1971), pp. 130–45.

32. Ibid., p. 117.

33. These are the primary welfare programs available in Texas. The state does provide a number of other services, including protection of abused children, child care centers, family planning assistance, and pursuit of parents delinquent in their child support payments.

34. Department of Human Services, *Annual Report, 1985.*

35. Bureau of the Census, Department of Commerce, *1980 Census of Population and Housing: Texas,* p. 138.

36. Calculated from *Fiscal Size Up: 1986–1987,* p. 84.

37. Department of Human Resources, *AFDC Income Benefit Study, 1978* (Austin: Department of Human Resources, 1978).

38. Task Force on Indigent Health Care Final Report, 1984.

39. These new changes in the law are well covered in Tom Whately, *Indigent Health Care Legislation: A Summary* (Austin: House Study Group, # 117, July 16, 1985).

40. *Texas Observer,* June 27, 1985, p. 3.

41. *Fiscal Size Up: 1986–1987,* p. 84.

42. Department of Human Resources, *Annual Report, 1982.*

43. Report of the Texas Senate Interim Committee on Hunger and Nutrition in *Hearings Before the Select Committee on Hunger,* House of Representatives, 98th Congress, 2nd Session (Washington, D.C.: Government Printing Office, 1984), p. 226.

44. See Edward S. Greenberg, *Serving the Few: Corporate Capitalism and the Bias of Government Policy* (New York: John Wiley and Sons, 1974), pp. 204–5.

45. These practices are thoroughly discussed in Piven and Cloward, *Regulating the Poor,* ch. 5.

46. Figures supplied by the Texas Department of Human Services.

47. Nursing Home Task Force, *Report on Texas Nursing Homes to John Hill, Attorney General* (Austin: Office of the Attorney General, n.d.).

48. Ibid., p. 46.

49. Jack Anderson, "Saddest Story Ever Written: Nursing Home Care for the Elderly," *El Paso Times,* July 24, 1977, p. 8–A.

50. Facts and report presented in Wayne King, "Nursing Home Deaths Raise Issue of Medicaid Pay System," *New York Times,* April 4, 1983, pp. 1 and 16.

51. Nursing Home Task Force, *Report on Texas Nursing Homes,* p. x.

52. William Cabin, "A Booming Industry," *Texas Observer,* August 12, 1977, p. 8.

53. Department of Human Services, *Annual Report, 1985.*

54. Profile presented in Nursing Home Task Force, *Report on Texas Nursing Homes.*

55. Ibid., p. ix.

56. Ibid., p. 19.

57. Texas State Department of Public Welfare, *Statistics 76* (Austin: Department of Public Welfare, 1976), p. 53.

58. Reported in Jackie Cox, "Blue Cross Blues," *Texas Observer,* January 31, 1975, pp. 7–9.

59. Department of Human Resources, *Annual Report, 1982,* p. 1.

60. Quoted in June Kronholz, "Texas Skimps on Aid to Poor, Saves Money; But Some Call It Cruel," *Wall Street Journal,* November 11, 1976, p. 1.

61. Bureau of the Census, *Money Income and Poverty Status in 1975,* p. 228.

62. David Perry and Alfred Watkins, "The Working Poor," *Texas Observer,* May 26, 1978, p. 6.

63. Ibid.

64. This is the major thesis presented in Piven and Cloward, *Regulating the Poor.*

65. This interpretation draws from the analysis of G. William Domhoff, *The Higher Circles, The Governing Class in America* (New York: Vintage, 1971), pp. 207–18. This is not to say that business was of one voice in its support of welfare legislation, for that simply was not the case. But among influential corporate giants with political ties, welfare was advocated.

13

Fiscal Policy in Texas

In the 1986–87 biennium the government of Texas appropriated $37.3 billion for state services. Nearly 75 percent of these funds were committed to education, transportation, and human resources, principally assistance to the needy. The overall budgetary figure is some three times the total amount allocated a decade before. However, when inflation and population increases are taken into consideration, the state budget has only expanded by 10 percent over the last ten years.[1]

Expenditures for state programs depend on an adequate supply of revenue. In 1942, the voters of Texas approved a constitutional amendment that requires government spending to be based on a "pay as you go" formula. Texas hence must balance its biennial budget: all outgoing state appropriations must be matched by an equal amount of incoming revenue. Throughout most of its contemporary history, the state has experienced little difficulty in meeting this constitutional obligation. Revenues necessary for underwriting the costs of state programs were almost always on hand. The economic decline in the 1980s, however, placed severe constraints on state funding. Not enough revenue was being generated to expand or even sustain government services. Something had to give. The state basically had two stark options. Either taxes could be raised or programs could be eliminated or trimmed.

This chapter explores fiscal policy in Texas along several fronts. First, the process of writing the state budget is discussed. Second, sources of state revenue are outlined. Third, beneficiaries of taxing policy are identified. Finally, the public's view of fiscal matters is presented.   ★

WRITING THE STATE BUDGET

The principal architect of the budget for the Texas state government is the Legislative Budget Bureau (LBB). The LBB is composed of ten legislators, including the lieutenant-governor, the speaker of the House, the chairmen of the House Appropriations Committee, the House Ways and Means Committee, the Senate Finance Committee, and the Senate State Affairs Committee, two members appointed by the speaker, and two chosen by the lieutenant-governor. The LBB employs a staff of 66 persons who assemble, prepare, and disseminate budget proposals.

The LBB forwards copies of its budget to the legislature within the first five days of its session. All other budgetary requests must be submitted to the legislature during the first week of its term. Every proposal, including the LBB's, is sent to the appropriate committee in each legislative chamber.

In the House, the Appropriations Committee is the first port of call for the budget bill. The first task of the committee is to send to each substantive committee in the House budgetary considerations that fall within the ambit of its expertise. Each of these substantive committees has a subcommittee on oversight and the budget. It is at the subcommittee level that the first serious legislative investigation of the budget occurs. The chair of each subcommittee, as of 1983, is also a member of the full Appropriations Committee and budgetary recommendations are relayed back to the Appropriations Committee.

The Appropriations Committee conducts hearings at which members of each substantive subcommittee on oversight and administrators from state agencies are invited to appear. Before the ninetieth day of the session elapses the Appropriations Committee must report its budgetary recommendations to the legislature.

In the Senate, budgetary matters are principally the province of the Finance Committee. Rarely do the Finance Committee and the Appropriations Committee agree on the budget, hence a conference committee inevitably is formed to unify the perspectives of these committees. Key members of the respective budgetary

Courtesy of Ben Sargent, *The Austin American-Statesman*. Reprinted by permission.

committees in either chamber of the legislature are appointed by the leaders to the conference committee. Only matters of disagreement are discussed by conferees these days. In the past they were able to address any fiscal issue; thus, in effect, they could write the state's budget. The common budget bill usually reaches the full membership of the legislature only in the closing days of the session.

Before the legislature can approve the budget bill, the comptroller of public accounts must certify that there will be sufficient revenue to cover the amount appropriated. Before the bill is law the governor must sign the measure. The governor of Texas is empowered with the item veto over budgetary lines of appropriations. That is, he or she can delete line by line funds that are authorized for programs, agencies, and services.

The governor ordinarily submits his or her own budget for legislative consideration. Not unexpectedly, confrontation between the executive and the legislature on finances is inevitable. A gubernatorial threat to veto items in the budget, as was proffered by Governor Clements during the 70th (1987–88) Texas Legislature, is often enough to wield some influence over fiscal proposals. At times, the legislature will attempt to veto-proof a budgetary proposal by attaching it as a rider to a substantive piece of legislation. Although the governor can veto an entire substantive bill, he or she is not authorized to nullify items in legislative measures other than the budget. Regardless of the various strategic tools available to the executive and to the legislature in determining the state's fiscal policy, both must cooperate in order for the government to have a budget.

SOURCES OF REVENUE

Table 13–1 presents the sources of revenues that supported programs in Texas in fiscal year 1985. The federal government through grants, revenue sharing, and other programs, transferred some $3.5 billion from Washington, D.C. to the state treasury in Austin. Federal assistance constitutes one-fifth of all revenue available for state services in Texas.

The burden of raising money within Texas falls heavily on consumers. The general sales tax has been the backbone of state finances in Texas. In 1985, the sales tax raised some $4.2 billion, an increase of around 25 percent since 1983. The reason for the rise in revenue from this source is that policymakers have steadily increased the sales tax rate in recent years. The special legislative session in 1984 added .125 percent to the 4.0 percent state sales tax baseline. The second special session of 1986 clipped another 1 percent on to this tax. Finally, the special session meeting in 1987 raised the sales tax to 6 percent on most items purchased in the state. As other sources of state revenue have dried up, state officials in Texas have become more and more dependent on the sales tax for funding.

Another $2.6 billion in 1985 came from taxes on the sales of specific items, namely, alcohol, tobacco, motor vehicles, gasoline, and motor oil. Again in the recent era of fiscal distress the state has accelerated the taxation on these specific items. For instance, the tax on the sale of a gallon of gasoline has increased from 5 cents to 15 cents. In 1985, general and specific sales taxes accounted for nearly 40 percent of the revenue necessary to operate state government in Texas. This

TABLE 13-1   Sources of Revenue for 1985 Expenditures by State Government

Source	Amount		Percent of Total
Federal government		$ 3.47 billion	20.2
State sources	$4.2 billion		
Sales tax			
General			
Specific			
motor fuel	$987 million		
motor vehicle	$895 million		
tobacco	$374 million		
alcohol	$333 million		
Total sales tax		$6.79 billion	39.4
Business taxes and fees			
Severance tax			
crude oil production	$1.04 billion		
natural gas prod.	$1.12 billion		
Total severance	$2.16 billion		
Insurance firms	$368 million		
Telephone	$111 million		
Utilities	$210 million		
Hotel and motel	$61 million		
Corporation franchise tax	$856 million		
Total business tax		$3.80 billion	22.1
Other sources			
Licenses and fees	$848 million		
Interest income	$1.0 billion		
Land income	$556 million		
Inheritance tax	$148 million		
Sundry sources	$594 million		
Total other		$3.15 billion	18.3
Total revenue		$17.21 billion	100.0

SOURCE: Adapted from Legislative Budget Board, *Fiscal Size Up: Texas State Services* (Austin: Legislative Budget Board, 1986), p. 10.

represents a rise of some 4 percent since 1983 and portends an even larger tax share emanating from sales in the near future.

Both large and small businesses are subject to a number of fees and taxes. Oil and natural gas companies paid (in 1985) $2.2 billion to the state in the form of severance payments. These payments are considered to be compensation for the removal of nonrenewable natural resources from Texas land. However, the total paid into the state treasury was a half a billion dollars less than what was collected in severance taxes in 1983. Herein lies the heart of the fiscal crisis in Texas. As oil prices plunged in the mid–1980s, so did severance revenue.

In 1985, insurance companies paid $368 million to ply their trade in Texas. Utilities, including phone companies, contributed another $321 million to the state budget. Most corporations (state and national banks are the major exceptions) pay the state a tax for the privilege of holding a franchise in Texas. In 1983, the franchise tax was worth $463 million in revenue; two years later, after the legislature had increased the franchise tax in 1984, it brought almost $500 million more into the tax base. About 8 percent of all revenue currently comes from this tax. Indeed, Texas now has the second highest franchise tax among all states.[2] All told, around 22 percent of state finances comes from business practices in Texas.

The final 15 percent of state money comes from a myriad of sources. Income earned from land owned by the state—income used basically to fund primary, secondary, and some university education—totaled $556 million in 1985, down by almost 25 percent from 1983. Most of the profitable state land is on oil-rich fields. Interest on investments of state money was worth $1 billion dollars in 1985, a sizable rise over interest earned in previous years. Licenses and fees transferred over $848 million from the pocketbooks of people and some businesses into the state treasury. The state continues to look to this area as one in which revenues can be increased. Fees for the registration of motor vehicles, for instance, have been on the rise lately. Likewise, students (or their parents) enrolling in the state's universities and colleges have been required to pay higher fees. The 69th Texas Legislature in 1985 increased tuition costs across the board. Most resident students saw their fees jump from $4 per semester hour in 1985 to $12. Tuition will continue to rise over the years, reaching $22 a semester hour by 1995. Out-of-state students, as well as persons enrolled in the state's professional schools (law, medical, dental, and veterinary), also witnessed substantial fee increases.

Juggling the tax base has not fully offset the financial shortfall in Texas—billion-dollar deficits have loomed large in the state's financial picture. Policy-makers have responded by cutting state services. Governor White ordered a 13 percent cutback in 1986. The number of state employees has been on the decline, and their pay has stood virtually still in recent appropriations. Education, welfare programs, and some regulatory agencies (for instance, the Air Control Board and the Water Development Board) have experienced substantial decreases in funding.

BENEFICIARIES OF THE TAX STRUCTURE

Texans pay less in state taxes than citizens of forty-two other states.[3] In the early 1980s, they contributed on average 8.4 percent of their personal income to finance state and local services, "the third lowest percentage in the nation."[4] However, the tax burden falls unevenly on the state's population. The heavy reliance on the sales tax means a regressive distribution of tax payments. That is, lower-income people pay a larger share of their wages to tax authorities than do high-income earners. Indeed, virtually every major tax used in Texas is regressive in effect.[5] Consequently, lower-income families, especially in urban settings such as Houston, pay "a state/local tax bill that [is] slightly higher than the median bill for families ... across the United States."[6] As one moves up the income ladder, one contributes a lower portion of their income in the form of taxes in Texas. In Houston, for instance, families with annual incomes over $100,000 pay only 3.08 percent of that sum in state and local taxes. This percentage is far below what the poor in Texas contribute.[7] The state's superrich pay even less. Only about 1.5 percent of their income goes to the state as taxes, even though their earnings are quite impressive.[8]

Corporations and affluent individuals in Texas benefit not only from the taxes they do pay, but also from the tithes that they need not pay the state. In the first group, businesses appear (table 13–1) to pay substantial taxes. Severance payments from petroleum firms, for example, are a crucial form of state revenue. However, these companies add this tax on to the cost of gasoline, natural gas, and other petroleum items distributed in Texas and throughout the rest of the country. As a result, this practice is "a convenient means of taxing nonresident consumers of these products." [9] Utilities and insurance companies follow the same pattern and tack their tax burden on to the cost of their services to consumers. Business franchise taxes are more troublesome for small firms than for larger ones. In the words of state Representative Senfronia Thompson, the franchise tax for "the smallest businesses was at least double the rate paid by the 80 giant conglomerates worth $100 million or more." [10] Moreover, thanks to a 1978 amendment to the state constitution, the first $200,000 of a person's estate is now exempt from any inheritance levy. One source calculates that this tax break directly benefits only around 3 percent of the state's population.[11] Finally, as might be recalled from chapter 11, the property tax—a major source of revenue for local government and school boards—has not posed much of a hardship on the affluent, especially large corporations.

The most significant benefits from tax policy in Texas for the wealthy are the taxes not paid to the state. Texas is one of but a handful of states that does not tax the personal income of its citizens or the profits of its corporations. A personal income tax, even with exemptions and deductions, tends to be a progressive tax. That is, the more money one makes, the greater the portion of income to be taxed. No corporate profits tax means that at least $33 billion in net income earned annually in Texas by companies is left untouched by the state and unavailable to finance public services.[12] One estimate suggests that a corporate income tax might generate additional revenue of $641 million each year.[13] Estimates aside, many legislators have made their antipathy to personal and corporate income taxes quite clear. Recent legislative sessions have come very close to enactment of a proposed constitutional amendment to ban, preferably forever, this form of taxation.

THE PUBLIC'S VIEW OF FISCAL POLICY

Texans are of a mixed mind in offering suggestions about the state's economic and fiscal decline. Most are aware of and concerned about the economic situation in the state.[14] Indeed, almost two-thirds profess support for an increase in taxation in order to encourage economic development. Higher education, water development, and highway construction are seen as the best means to advance economic progress. Given the choice of a rise in the sales, gasoline, personal, or corporate income tax to effectuate this goal, most opt for higher taxes on sales. Although only a few (some 14 percent) favor a tax on personal income, a slight majority approve of a levy on corporate income.[15]

However, when confronted with the reality of the revenue shortage in 1985, Texans wavered in their position on taxes. Only a few (3 percent) preferred that the legislature raised taxes to offset any deficit. Forty percent concluded that state services should be cut back; 49 percent hoped for a combination of increased taxes and trimming of state programs. Interestingly, the services that Texans would least like to see reduced are those that provide assistance to the poor. Equally intriguing, if not a bit contradictory, the state activity held in lowest esteem—at least in times of fiscal crisis—is the government's traditional (and generous) commitment to highways and roads.[16]

Spokespersons ordinarily closely associated with corporate business in Texas have also expressed concern about fiscal policy in the state. Many argue that economic well-being can only be achieved through maintaining some critical state programs, such as a top-notch university system. Some concern about state revenue sources has also been detected from the business community. Jared Hazleton, director of the business-sponsored Texas Research League (see chapter 6), offered the following comment in 1987:

> We've pushed the existing tax structure close to the limits. The more the sales tax is broadened the more it looks like an income tax in drag, but it doesn't have exemptions, so the poor pay in higher proportion. People are beginning to accept the fact that the income tax will be seriously considered.[17]

Adding to the chorus singing a song of change, House Speaker Gib Lewis, certainly no enemy of the affluent (see chapter 8), has opined recently:

> Personally I am opposed to an income tax, but at the same time I realize that I have a certain degree of responsibility for keeping this state going. You have to be realistic about this. You have to be responsible at some time in your life.[18]

To be sure, Lewis's realism is not totally delusionary. He fully recognizes that most Texans are not prepared to accept a state personal income tax at this juncture: "I think that it's going to take a few years to sell [it] ... to the citizens." [19]

CONCLUSION

State government in Texas is in the midst of a fiscal crisis: not enough revenue is coming in to underwrite the costs of its programs and services. The government has met this crisis through a patchwork of remedies. Established taxes, especially ones on sales, have been increased; some state services have been cut back. Sweeping, innovative approaches have been eschewed—at least so far.

Payment for state appropriations in Texas is not a matter of proportional equity. Most of the tax burden falls on the incomes of lower- and middle-class Texans. Affluent individuals, families, and corporations are not overly encumbered by high tax bills. They are able to avoid certain taxes, such as state income and profit taxes. Companies can also pass some tax levies on to consumers. In fact, consumers pick up most of the tab for government expenditures when they pay taxes on items sold to them. In the final analysis, it is no wonder that major corporations have heeded the call to relocate in Texas. After the books have been balanced, "only about 7.8 percent of Texas' total tax collections come from corporations." [20]

Courtesy of Ben Sargent, *The Austin American–Statesman.* Reprinted by permission.

NOTES

1. Legislative Budget Board, *Fiscal Size Up: 1986–1987* (Austin: Legislative Budget Board, 1986), pp. 3–5.
2. Nick Davsters, "Talking Sense on Taxes," *Texas Observer,* April 4, 1986, pp. 12.
3. "Eating Up the Seed Corn," *Texas Observer,* October 10, 1986, p. 3.
4. Anthony Champagne and Rick Collis, "Texas," in *The Political Life of the American States,* ed. Alan Rosenthal and Maureen Moakley (New York: Praeger, 1984), p. 134.
5. Studies reported on in Rick Plitz, *Banning the Income Tax,* Special Legislative Report, No. 54, House Study Group, February 7, 1980.
6. Kim Quaile Hill, "The Low-Tax Myth," *Texas Observer,* June 27, 1986, p. 7.
7. Ibid.
8. Estimate offered by economist Norm Glickman in "Visions of Tax Reform," *Texas Observer,* March 20, 1987, p. 13.
9. David R. Francis, "How Texas Has Gained From OPEC," *The Christian Science Monitor,* September 11, 1978, p. 10.
10. Senfronia Thompson, "Taxing Corporate Profits: A Proposal," *Texas Observer,* December 10, 1982, p. 19.
11. Jim Hightower, "Going Haywire over Tax Relief," *Texas Observer,* September 8, 1978, p. 5.
12. Senfronia Thompson, "Taxing Corporate Profits," p. 19.
13. Bob Eckhardt, "Time to Tax Corporate Income," *Texas Observer,* March 20, 1987, p. 9.
14. *Texas Poll,* Spring 1986.

15. *Texas Poll,* Winter 1986.

16. *Texas Poll,* April 1985.

17. Interview with the *New York Times,* reprinted in the *Texas Observer,* May 1, 1987, p. 17.

18. Ibid.

19. Ibid.

20. Fred Schmidt, retired member of the faculty of the UCLA Graduate School of Management, quoted in "Visions of Tax Reform," p. 14.

14

Government Regulation: Natural Resources, Financial Institutions, and Consumer Protection

The impact of a state government extends beyond the money it allots for public services. Government regulation of human behavior also affects the distribution of societal benefits. This is particularly evident with regard to economic activities. Decisions made by legislators, administrators, and judges often have a major bearing on crucial economic matters such as the availability of goods, the prices paid for items in the marketplace, and the profits allowed on sales.

This chapter investigates the regulation of key components of the Texas economy by the state government. It specifically delves into state policy toward the use of natural resources, the operations of financial institutions, and the protection of consumers from faulty products and deceptive sales practices. As was the case in the preceding chapters on public policy, the goal here is to identify the primary beneficiaries of government regulation of these economic activities. ★

NATURAL RESOURCES

As pointed out in chapter 2, Texas is blessed with an abundance of natural resources, particularly oil, natural gas, lignite, and uranium. At various times during the twentieth century, the state government has entered into the regulation not only of these resources but also of electricity generated from them, the air we breathe, and the water we drink. This section details state regulatory policy for oil, gas, lignite, uranium, electricity, water, and air.

Oil and Natural Gas

The state government of Texas became deeply involved in the petroleum business in the early 1930s. The largest oil discovery of the time was made on October 3,

1930, near Kilgore in East Texas. The great East Texas field attracted thousands of independent wildcatters hoping to make quick fortunes. The lavish crude gushing from the field immediately created intense competition among producers and refiners and a sharp decrease in the price of petroleum. By 1932, a barrel of oil was selling for around 10¢. (Compare this with the price of $32.48 for a barrel of Texas oil sold on the world market in 1982.) The profits of major oil companies such as Humble (now Exxon) and the Texas Company (Texaco) suffered as prices spiraled downward.[1]

Oilmen, especially representatives of the largest firms, insisted that the state government of Texas intervene to halt the excessive competition. Governor Ross Sterling, one of the original founders of Humble, called for legislative action to regulate the immense quantities of oil being produced in Texas. But before the legislature could act, the Texas Railroad Commission imposed quotas on oil production. Many of the producers in the East Texas field—especially the independent operators—defied the proration orders. Governor Sterling declared martial law in the area. The national guard and the Texas Rangers were sent to impose order and shut down production. Interestingly, the commander of the national guard unit was also the chief legal counsel for Texaco.

By 1935, the Texas legislature had authorized the Railroad Commission to regulate the production of oil in the state. One major power entrusted to the commission was the authority to limit how much crude could be removed from a field. As applied to the East Texas find, any proration order was supposed to affect all producers equally. In actuality, however, the decision to curtail recovery operations was much more devastating to the small independents and wildcatters because they heavily relied on their strikes in the East Texas field. The major oil companies, conversely, could continue making profit on their holdings in other parts of the world and let their East Texas claims lie temporarily dormant. As a consequence, many independents went out of business, usually selling their interests to the majors in order to make a quick, sure profit. So many leases changed hands that "by 1938 the major oil companies had gained control over 80 percent of the production in the East Texas field." [2] Refineries were affected as well. Prior to regulation some 155 refineries were operating in the area; "by 1941, there were only three . . . [all] owned by the major companies." [3]

Giant petroleum companies thus actively sought government regulation in Texas in order to harness competition, stabilize prices, and dominate oil production in the state. Their efforts have been well rewarded. Writing in the late 1940s, one author noted that, with the assistance of state government, the major petroleum companies "now control Texas oil." [4]

This pattern of corporate and government cooperation in the regulation of oil and natural gas continues today. State allowances for the amount of oil production generally follow the pricing needs of the big companies. Moreover, within Texas natural gas pipeline companies set rates without any state regulation. The rates that Texas gas companies charge are among the highest in the country, guaranteeing the corporations healthy profits. Rates charged by companies distributing natural gas to Texas consumers are set by the commission. Profit maximization again has been its policy: "The natural sympathy of the Commissioners for the industry led them to grant rates that were by national standards almost confiscatory." [5] The commission also has jurisdiction over environmental prob-

Courtesy of Ben Sargent, *The Austin American–Statesman.* Reprinted by permission.

lems arising from drilling for oil. A report issued by a committee of the Texas Legislature in 1971, however, denounced the commission for displaying a "callous disregard for the environmental damage caused by oil companies operating in Texas." [6] Specifically, the committee chided the commission for not having any equipment to inspect offshore drilling rigs for pollution violations, for never denying a permit to drill regardless of the ecological consequences, and for "never in its history tak[ing] action against any oil company in any case of petroleum pollution," although such cases have frequently occurred.[7] The commission still shies away from rigorous enforcement of environmental standards in oil recovery operations. But in 1983 it was given the authority to regulate pollution precipitated by improperly plugged or abandoned oil wells, and since 1985 some 1,000 wells have been plugged by the commission in order to prevent damage to the Texas environment.[8]

Overall, the oil and natural gas companies have been very pleased with the regulatory performance of the Railroad Commission. In 1970, for example, the companies were moved to publicly thank the Texas Railroad Commission for having "served the oil industry . . . since 1891." (See the advertisement reprinted in this chapter.)

For a brief period in the early 1970s, the Texas Railroad Commission criticized the practices of a large natural gas corporation, the Lo-Vaca Gas Gathering Company, a subsidiary of the multibillion-dollar Coastal Corporation. The ultimate outcome of the Lo-Vaca case, however, indicates the rather diffident nature of the commission's regulation of the petroleum business. Because of the intense controversy caused by this corporate-agency dispute, the case deserves closer scrutiny.[9]

Created in 1955, Lo-Vaca was a neophyte in the natural gas business of the state. Under the tutelage of its founder (and current chairman of the board of Coastal), Oscar Wyatt, Lo-Vaca began as a company that gathered gas and stored it for later distribution. Wyatt secured the natural gas rights to portions of Texas farmland that the established gas firms thought were either too small or too isolated to be tapped. With a large pool of processed natural gas and backup reserve in hand, Lo-Vaca searched for commercial markets requiring direct delivery. Fortunately for the company, the natural gas distribution contracts for three major Texas cities—Corpus Christi, San Antonio, and Austin—were open to competitive bidding in the early 1960s. Oscar Wyatt intensively lobbied officials of these (and other) cities to secure the contracts. Through the use of shrewd political and business tactics, he was mostly successful. Over the years Lo-Vaca became the gas supplier for some four hundred Central and South Texas communities.

The company's principal selling point was guaranteed delivery of cheap gas over a long term (usually twenty years). For almost a decade the deal was equally beneficial to Lo-Vaca, the cities, and their utility customers. The company grew dramatically. Municipalities were blessed with a constant supply of inexpensive gas to heat homes and businesses and to generate electricity. Consumers paid utility bills that were among the lowest in the nation. But in the early 1970s this community of interests became increasingly disintegrated.

The first public sign of trouble occurred in the winter of 1972–73. In the midst of the record cold of that season, Central Texas residents and businesses found themselves without full electric service on sixty-five separate occasions. Factories, schools, and government buildings were forced to close. Heat was as infrequent as the warm rays of the sun. Electric companies fixed the blame for the brownouts and blackouts on Lo-Vaca's sporadic delivery of the natural gas vital for production of electricity. Lo-Vaca initially contended that the irregularities were a result of faulty pipelines. Critics accused Lo-Vaca of selling off its gas—gas contractually obligated to Lo-Vaca's customers—to the highest bidders (notably El Paso Natural Gas Company and Lone Star Gas Company). Lo-Vaca argued that its contracted prices were too low and that the once-rich energy reserves of Texas were rapidly dwindling. In short, Lo-Vaca refused to honor its municipal contracts. Cities could either increase their payment for gas or switch to more expensive heating oil. Regardless, utility bills would increase dramatically. The matter soon came to the attention of the Texas Railroad Commission.

Lo-Vaca argued that the original contracts signed with its customers should be voided. The customers—including cities, industries, and electric companies—charged Lo-Vaca with breach of contract. They demanded full compliance with the original agreements and financial restitution for high costs incurred in the purchase of energy substitutes during the 1972–73 crisis. In 1973, the commission revoked the original contracts and permitted Lo-Vaca to charge whatever it cost to deliver gas plus a 5 cent profit on each 1,000 cubic feet of gas distributed. In the same year, a state court took the company out of Oscar Wyatt's control and appointed a supervisor-manager to report back to the court. Still, the parties to the dispute squabbled.

The commission reversed its field in 1977 and ordered Lo-Vaca to honor its original commitments (to deliver gas at the cheap price) and also to refund $1.6 billion to its customers. With the company facing bankruptcy and consumers coming to realize that they soon might be without a supplier of gas, new agreements were finally reached. The commission rescinded its 1977 order and in 1979 wrote the final chapter of this story. Lo-Vaca ceased operation. A new gas utility, Valero, came into existence. Valero is totally independent of Wyatt and his company, the Coastal Corporation. However, Coastal was instructed to spend $180 to $230 million in searching for gas fields for Valero.

Although the punishment meted out to Lo-Vaca surpasses any ever dealt a large oil or natural gas company by the Texas Railroad Commission, it falls far short of being severe. In effect, Lo-Vaca was allowed to ignore its contracts and increase its prices. Coastal weathered the storm well. After initially faltering at the height of the controversy, it recovered rapidly once free of the many liabilities amassed by its Lo-Vaca subsidiary. Coastal's stock value has shot up—its assets are now worth in excess of $8.2 billion and its profits continue to rise. The loss of Lo-Vaca hardly has been felt. Customers who at one time paid very little to heat and light their homes, schools, and businesses now pay very high utility bills. The late Frank Erwin, once a lawyer for Lo-Vaca and former chairman of the Board of Regents of the University of Texas, wasn't pleased with Coastal/Lo-Vaca's fate. According to him, his former clients "ought to be put in the penitentiary."[10]

Coal, Lignite, and Uranium

As pointed out in chapter 2, Texas has a bountiful supply of uranium and coal, especially lignite. Declining reserves of oil and natural gas have made lignite and uranium more attractive to producers and users of these energy sources. Indeed the Texas Railroad Commission in the late 1970s instructed factories in the state to phase out the utilization of natural gas as a boiler fuel. The federal government also encouraged utilities to generate electricity from fuels other than conventional petroleum products.

Surface mining is the principal means of extracting lignite and uranium from the land of Texas. Strip-mining is the process of digging large chunks of land (usually in sections of 1,000 by 120 feet) with huge earth movers. This technique poses significant problems for the environment. Destruction of agricultural land, release of damaging chemicals from the earth, and pollution of water and the air are major worries. Farmers and ranchers near mining sites have complained bitterly about the effects of the digs, especially the search for uranium being conducted by Conoco (now a part of Dupont) in Karnes County. One farmer in the near vicinity of the Conoco operation had this to say about the strip mining:

> It's already killed my daddy. He had a stroke. You know, they bought the land right across the road from us and right away stripped the topsoil off of about 500 acres. Well, that stuff is real fine and when it blows into your house you can hardly breathe. There's footprints all over the house. Then you walk outside and you can't tell whether the whole world is on fire or if it's heavy, heavy fog just driftin'. They have

those darned old lights and bulldozers running day and night—you don't have a moment's peace. It's not just a little old investment to us. It's our way of life—it's all we have.[11]

This advertisement appeared in the *Texas Almanac and State Industrial Guide 1970–1971* (Dallas: A.H. Belo Corporation, 1970), p. 425, and is reproduced here with permission.

Government policy on strip-mining only emerged in the mid–1970s. In 1975, the Texas legislature enacted the Surface Mining Control and Reclamation Act and the federal government followed suit two years later. (The federal law only pertains to surface mining of coal and lignite, and not uranium.) Companies seeking to mine must apply for a permit from the Railroad Commission; public hearings are usually conducted. Reclamation plans must be presented and carried out after the dig. The commission is required to pay surprise visits to the mining sites and, after inspection, issue orders to correct any faults uncovered. Failure to abide could lead to a fine or a prison term for the offending company.[12]

Although both laws aim at compelling mine operators to restore excavated land to its original state, the federal law is more stringent.[13] Congress, for instance, mandates strip miners to improve the use of the land through reclamation, whereas approximating the status quo is all that the state law requires of miners. The U.S. Department of Agriculture also designated some 70 to 80 percent of the farmland that covers Texas's lignite reserves as "prime farmland," land to be carefully restored on the completion of any strip-mining operation. Topsoil—the crucial element in enriching farm and grazing land—must be set aside from other soil during the dig and replaced intact.

In 1978, federal and state officials agreed to give the Texas Railroad Commission exclusive jurisdiction over reclamation matters. The commission has exempted lignite miners (most of which are major corporations such as Texas Utilities, Shell Oil, Phillips Petroleum, and Alcoa) from the necessity of systematically and thoroughly restoring land, including agricultural land, to its original condition. Contrary to the U.S. Department of Agriculture, the commission has argued that much of the lignite is below farmland of such poor quality that letter-perfect reclamation is a waste of time and money. Critics, however, have contended that "most of the lignite is under good farm and grazing land. . . . [T]he lignite belt runs through several counties in Texas' blackland prairie, the richest farmland in the state." [14]

Electricity

Prior to 1975, the economic activities of electric and phone companies in Texas were regulated by local governments. Generally, these private utilities outmuscled (with staff, research, and statistics) municipal governments in conflicts to determine matters such as rates to be charged customers. Consequently, many Texas residents paid utility bills that were among the highest in the nation and received utility service that was very poor, especially in rural parts of the state.[15] Texas was the last state to turn to state regulation of electric and phone utilities to correct this imbalance.

In 1975, the Texas legislature created a statewide regulatory body, the Public Utilities Commission (PUC), to oversee the operations of private and municipal electric utilities, phone companies, and water and sewage plants. The PUC has original jurisdiction over electric, phone, and (until 1986) water and sewer rates and service in unincorporated areas of Texas. Cities, however, have original jurisdiction (unless they vote to give the PUC this jurisdiction) in setting the rates of investor-owned electric utilities. Most cities have retained the right to regulate these utilities. Companies displeased with a city's rate decision can appeal to the PUC for an adjustment.

Since it first began to hear utility disputes in September 1976, the PUC has decided some 3,500 cases, most involving electric companies. The pattern of the commission's regulation is outlined in the following points:

1. In its early years the PUC decided cases very quickly. Although the commission legally could take up to 185 days to reach a decision, it ruled, on the average, in 125 days.[16] In 1983, the commission was encouraged by the Texas legislature to slow down the rate determination process. Now it usually takes months to decide on an application for a rate increase.

2. The PUC accepts on face value the information supplied to it by utility companies. The commission has exerted little effort to investigate the veracity of the facts and figures submitted in the rate proposals of the utility corporations. The PUC claims that it was ill-staffed to comprehensively check into such data.[17] In recent years, some of this problem has been alleviated through the hiring of additional personnel. In 1987, for instance, approximately 190 employees worked as staff in the PUC. The agency had an operating biennium budget of $19.8 million, including $3.8 million from the federal government, for 1986–87.[18]

3. Once a rate schedule for payments by utility customers is established by the PUC, the private corporations are entrusted with implementing it. On a few occasions, the companies have deviated from the schedule and charged customers more money than the PUC allowed. The PUC again claims that a lack of staff prevented a closer monitoring of the rate schedules.[19]

4. Overall, the PUC does not give the utilities all that they seek. The pattern of decisions reached by the PUC shows a sharp reduction in the rate increases requested by the companies. In its first two years of existence, the commission pared the original rate proposals of major electric utilities (cooperatives excluded) by an average of 62 percent.[20]

5. The utilities are guaranteed a high yearly rate of return (profit) by the PUC. PUC rate rulings allow Texas utilities to earn an average of 16 percent return on their investment, a rate some 4 percentage points higher than the national norm.[21]

6. The PUC permits rate increases to cover the costs of building new electric generating plants. Houston Lighting and Power, for example, was granted a $50 million rate increase, 70 percent of which covered the costs of construction in progress on the company's coal-generating facilities.[22] About a third of El Paso Electric Company's rate increase approved by the PUC in 1978 was earmarked for building a nuclear power plant (in Arizona).[23] In effect, the PUC obligates utility customers to pay for electricity that they do not receive in the present; the Texas PUC is one of twenty-three state utility regulatory bodies that permits this practice. Currently, the commission is facing the question of whether to permit utility companies to pass the cost overruns on nuclear plant construction on to their customers. The South Texas Nuclear Power facility, built under the supervision of Houston Industries, and Texas Utilities' Comanche Peak nuclear power plant have cost billions of dollars in excess of their originally budgeted prices.[24]

7. The PUC also allows a number of other company expenses to be passed on to the customer. For instance, the costs of advertising, even when a company is a monopoly, are tacked on to utility bills. (The commission allows an electric company to spend 0.3 percent of its annual income on ads and to pass this cost on to its customers.) Charitable contributions by the companies are actually paid by consumers of electricity. Controversy has recently engulfed the commission for allowing utilities the right to pass any increase in their fuel costs on to their customers.

8. Private citizens and small businesses have had great difficulty in presenting their views to the commission. Hearings occur only in Austin and they can take weeks to conclude. Factual information is the commodity that both staff and the commissioners value most. For the average citizen or small-scale businessperson to intervene in the hearings, he or she must endure the costs of travel, lodging, and research. Needless to say, few can afford such luxury. Hence utility companies along with municipal governments, if they choose to partake in the hearings, delivered until recently their arguments without having to face much citizen reaction. The 68th Texas Legislature in 1984 established the Office of Public Utility Council to represent the interests of individual customers and small commercial enterprises in matters before the commission. During 1984 the Public Utility Council participated in eighteen major rate cases, saving Texas ratepayers some $1 billion in the process.[25]

9. Staff of the PUC have little independence from the commissioners. The commission follows a hierarchical form of organization with the three appointed commissioners at the helm. The 190 staff members do the basic work that goes into a rate case, such as collecting technical information, forecasting future trends in use of electricity, and presenting various viewpoints about any issue in dispute. However, critics claim that staff are not free to propose positions that run counter to the commissioners'. For instance, the staff recommended that the commission hold a hearing into Houston Lighting and Power's (Houston Industries') management of the South Texas Nuclear Power Project. Construction on this plant was some seven years behind schedule and $4.5 billion beyond the original budget. In addition, a federal government investigation of the plant found numerous safety violations in its building. Houston Lighting and Power, the managing partner in a consortium with the municipal power companies of Austin and San Antonio, was cited for bungling its role as overseer of the construction and was fined $100,000, the maximum allowed under federal law. Although the PUC has no jurisdiction over safety problems in construction of power plants, the staff argued that the performance of Houston Lighting and Power should be taken into consideration when the company comes to the commission seeking rate increases to cover construction costs. The PUC, however, refused to address the issue in a hearing and, in effect, overruled its staff's recommendation.

Overall, state intervention into the activities of Texas utilities has not lowered the economic standing of private companies. Indeed, it seems that the foremost principle guiding the PUC has been the upholding of the financial integrity of businesses engaged in delivery of electricity to Texans. As a result of PUC decisions, Texas companies consistently display a high rate of return on the invested dollar and thus maintain good ratings in the eyes of investors. With such high marks, investors are willing to lend the companies money to build new facilities. For the customers, the result is continuous delivery of electricity, albeit at a fairly high price.

Water

Water is crucial to the economy of Texas. The state government is mostly interested in two phases of water policy. First, the state, with taxpayers' money, partially finances the construction of waterways, reservoirs, and dams in order to insure residents a steady supply of water. Second, the state assumes some responsibility in keeping Texas's water clean and free of damaging pollutants. This section focuses on each of these aspects of water policy in Texas.

Delivery of Water.   About three-fourths of all the water in Texas is underground, stored in seven aquifers dispersed throughout the state. Until recently, Texas contained enough water to satisfy its residential, agricultural, and business needs. But the explosive growth of population and industry coupled with the depletion of some key aquifers has cast a shadow over the future availability of an adequate water supply.

Future projections place the Texas population at about 20 million in the year 2000. With that many people by the twenty-first century, most of the state, especially the arid Panhandle and West Texas regions, will not have enough water. One study estimates that almost three-fourths of the state's forty-three zones and coastal basins will be well below adequate water levels half a century from now.[26]

The hardest hit will be farmers and ranchers living in the High Plains (Panhandle) region of the state. The water source (the Ogallala Aquifer) that has served this area well in the past is rapidly running dry. By the year 2030, only about 37 percent of the current water supply is expected to be available for softening the hard, dry High Plains soil.[27] Most of the states's irrigated farming occurs here. One-fourth of the nation's cotton, 20 percent of its sorghum, and 5 percent of its wheat are grown on the High Plains of Texas. In addition, "the highest concentration of beef cattle feeding facilities in the world" would be affected by any curtailment of the Ogallala water supply.[28] Panhandle water irrigates the land that produces the grain that fattens many of the cattle in Texas.

Urban areas of the state are also endangered by the growing water crisis. San Antonio, for instance, is rapidly depleting the Edwards Aquifer. Some parts of Houston are sinking because of overuse of underground water sources.

For more than two decades the state has been attempting to formulate a sound water plan. In the late 1960s, it pursued a very ambitious plan to import water from out of state and to transfer it to deficient regions. In 1969, the legislature proposed to the voters of Texas a constitutional amendment to issue $3.5 billion in bonds for financing the importation of water from the mouth of the Mississippi River. This plan would have drained some 6 trillion gallons of water out of the Mississippi for delivery across Texas. The eventual recipients of the water were to be the endangered High Plains farmers and ranchers, as well as agricultural interests in South Texas and, eventually, El Paso. In order to carry the water, pipelines and concrete canals were to be built along a route that extended some 800 miles—uphill. Elevating the water to the necessary 3,500 feet (by means of pump and lock systems) would have required electric plants with extensive (probably nuclear) generating capacity. In fact, this project alone would have used one-third of all electricity produced annually in the state.[29] After all the votes were counted in August 1969, the amendment was defeated by a slim 6,000 votes.

Imminent water shortages still worry state officials. A recent report by the Texas Water Development Board warned that "without water importation [from out of state] sectors and regions of the Texas economy will suffer severe economic decline." [30] In 1982, Governor Clements appointed a special task force to update the Texas water plan and make recommendations to the state legislature for future action on reviving the water supply. The thirty-one member blue ribbon panel included many persons with corporate ties. Ben Love, chairman of the board of Texas Commerce Bancshares and, until 1983, board member of the El Paso Company; Preston M. Geren, Jr., company director at ENSERCH and Gibraltar Savings, the largest savings and loan association in Texas; William McCord, chairman of ENSERCH (Lone Star Gas) and member of the board of Republic of Texas bancorporation; Edwin Cox, independent oil and natural gas producer as well as board member of InterFirst bank and Halliburton (Brown and Root); James Keay, company director at Republic of Texas; Walter Mischer, chairman of Allied Bancshares and director at the Southland Corporation; Louie Welch, member of the Texas Water Development Board and the board of directors of Gibraltar Savings; and Louis A. Beecherl, Jr., chairman of the task force and the Water Development Board and company director at Texas Oil and Gas (now a part of USX), the fifth largest producer of natural gas in the state. In its report, the task force urged the legislature to increase funding for water development and explore tapping sources of water in Texas's bordering states.[31]

During its regular session the 69th Texas legislature established a new state agency, the Multi-State Water Resources Planning Commission, to study the prospect of importing water from other states into Texas. The legislature also passed a proposed constitutional amendment on water policy in the state. In November 1985, voters approved an amendment creating a financial scheme to improve the water situation. The state was authorized to seek $400 million in bonds to build new reservoirs, water pipelines and pump stations, and wastewater treatment plans. An additional $200 million to underwrite loans to agribusinesses purchasing irrigation equipment that conserved water was approved. Almost $190 million in assistance for locales, such as the impoverished areas of South Texas, that lacked running water became policy. A year later, however, no bonds had been issued. Caught in the economic recession, the state was reluctant to borrow money for water development, lest the interest rates on the bonds would be too high. Hence the new Texas water plan has been slow to get off the starting line.

Any effort on the part of the state to deliver water amounts to a subsidy of big business. Nearly 90 percent of the state's water is used by industrial corporations, commercial feedlots, mining companies, electric utilities, energy and chemical firms, and agribusinesses. The remaining 10 percent flows into municipalities for home and business purposes.[32] Irrigated farming alone consumes three-fourths of the water. Without government aid, businesses in the most lucrative economic arenas of the state would have great difficulty staying afloat in Texas.

Water Pollution.   The first statewide regulation of water pollution began in Texas in 1961 with the enactment of the Water Pollution Control Act. The state legislature created the Water Pollution Control Board, composed of seven members, to implement the law. The board was given a new name—the Texas Water Quality Control Board—in 1967, and ten years later was absorbed into the Department of Water Resources. In 1985, this department was broken into two separate agencies: the Texas Water Commission and the Texas Water Development Board. The Water Commission oversees pollution matters, including discharging sewage and solid and hazardous waste into the state's lakes, streams, and rivers.

Businesses wishing to dump waste material into the state's waterways must receive a permit from the Texas Water Commission. This permit imposes standards designed to prevent undue damage to marine and human life. The commission is empowered with the authority to fine individuals or companies in violation of water quality laws. Conviction of water pollution may bring a fine of $10,000 a day for each count.

For many years government regulation had little effect on eradicating water pollution in Texas. During this time critics accused state administrators of neglect in dealing with the problem. For instance, in 1971 former Congressman Bob Eckhardt of Texas claimed that the Houston Ship Channel "is still a dead stream; in fact, in much worse shape than it was in mid–1955 before the state ever entered the pollution control problem." [33] Permits issued by the Water Pollution Control Board were portrayed as licenses for, not deterrents against, polluters.[34] Water quality standards were so low and irregular that they did little to hold pollution in check, and the monitoring of offenses remained basically in the hands of the polluters.[35] The board rarely sought legal prosecution of violators, preferring instead to persuade industries to cease pollution practices. The chief of the environmental protection division of the Texas attorney-general's office charged that the slow progress made in cleaning the state's water was due to "the failure of the water pollution agency of my State to utilize enforcement mechanisms of the attorney-general's office, and [its] reliance on a policy of continued negotiation and extension of deadlines." [36] The few cases that were resolved in state courts usually involved small businesses, not large corporate polluters. Penalties assessed were not usually very harsh.[37]

By the late 1970s, a major transformation in the state's water had occurred: much of the pollution had been eliminated. Between 1971 and 1976, for example, private industries in Texas reduced the amount of suspended solids discharged into the state's waterways by 85 percent.[38] The owners of cattle feedlots in the state had virtually no pollution facilities in 1969; five years later there wasn't a feedlot in the state without these facilities.[39] According to the Department of Water Resources, "Of the more than 16,000 stream miles subject to quality standards, over 87 percent currently meet the 1983 fishable and swimmable goals of federal clean water legislation, with another 4.5 percent to 5.0 percent projected to be in compliance by 1983." [40] Why the dramatic turnabout?

The impetus for change came from many sources. The federal government began to prosecute water polluters in Texas with success. For example, ARMCO Steel Corporation, which owns and operates a mill on the Houston Ship Channel, was convicted of dumping cyanide, phenols, ammonia, and sulfides on a "significant and substantial scale with results, actual and potential, deleterious and even deadly to the existence and survival of organic and marine life in the Channel." [41]

Next, financial inducements in the form of grants and tax breaks by the federal government made the installation of water treatment facilities more attractive to business. Finally, with growing water shortages, the state of Texas began to take quality improvement of what water was available most seriously and began to encourage the demise of pollution: the enforcement authority of state regulators was expanded; staff were added to the Water Commission; and penalties for pollution were substantially increased.

The one remaining large-scale water polluter in Texas is municipal government. Cities continue to lower the quality of water, primarily through the discharge of sewage. It is a financial problem that inhibits cities from stemming the tide of pollution—they are reluctant to raise taxes (and anger voters) to build water treatment facilities. The federal government stepped into this arena during the 1970s and offered municipalities funds to abate the problem. The Reagan administration, however, phased out a large portion of this federal assistance. In 1985, the Texas legislature has authorized substantial state aid to help cities improve their waste treatment facilities.

Air

In many parts of Texas the air is heavy with odor, haze, and eye irritants. During the last two decades the federal government, through the efforts of the Environmental Protection Agency (EPA), and the state government, through the Texas Air Control Board, have been authorized to regulate the quality of air that surrounds us. The EPA establishes what constitutes pollutants and how much of this matter may be permitted in the air. It has identified seven pollutants that foul the air: carbon monoxide, sulfur dioxide and sulfates, nitrogen dioxide and nitrates, hydrocarbons, oxidants (ozone), particulates, and lead. Each can have a harmful impact on health. For instance, a steady intake of carbon monoxide and sulfur dioxide may lead to respiratory problems. The EPA has designated standards that may not be exceeded for each pollutant. For example, ambient (moving) air is considered legally polluted if the amount of photochemical oxidants (ozone) is in excess of 0.12 parts per million, using an hourly average, on one day during any three-year period. The administrative function of the state government is to formulate a plan to implement the EPA guidelines and, once the program is approved by the federal agency, execute the policy.

Government attempts at cleaning Texas's air have had an uneven history. The Texas Air Control Board (TACB) was established in the mid–1960s amid criticism that it was institutionalized only as a means to dodge and delay the anticipated stronger pollution control laws from the federal government (which didn't create the EPA until 1970).[42] The TACB at first was understaffed and underfinanced. Now it has a yearly budget of $13.8 million and a staff of some 370 people working either in Austin or in twelve regional offices.

In the TACB's formative years, polluters were almost always given variances allowing them to emit harmful substances for a period of time designated by the agency. In 1969, for instance, the TACB granted a variance to the American Smelting and Refining Company (ASARCO) that allowed the company to continue to release cadmium from its Amarillo plant, even though a staff member of the agency warned that "the magnitude of the polluting generated by ASARCO was absolutely unsanctionable by any enforcement agency." [43] Staff also found a link between the company's pollutants and the high level of cadmium in the bodies of children within the vicinity of ASARCO. Cadmium is associated with hypertension and arteriosclerosis; indeed, Potter County, which housed the plant, led the state in the number of annual deaths from these diseases.[44] The variance was extended four times by the TACB contrary to staff recommendations. The last extension lapsed the day ASARCO closed its plant in 1975, an event that the TACB had fully anticipated. Today, variances are a thing of the past. The TACB stopped issuing them in 1975, a practice initiated after the EPA began to review every extension granted.

In the pursuit of pollution violators, the TACB has followed the path of persuasion, not prosecution. The first step in abating emission of a pollutant is investigation of an alleged problem: in 1983, 4,800 investigations were conducted by the TACB. Next the board can issue a notice of violation of air standards: some 6,000 notices were forthcoming in 1983.[45] Discussion then ensues between TACB staff and the offending party to correct the problem. It is only as a last resort that the board seeks a legal remedy. In 1983, for instance, only seven violations were taken to the office of the attorney-general. Staff members of the TACB must have the approval of the board before they take a case to the attorney-general, who then presents the pollution allegations to a state court, which may issue an order directing the polluter to cease its activities and, in cases of guilt, fine the violator no more than $1,000 for each day it emits pollutants into the air.

It is a rare event when legal action is sought, however. In its first decade of existence, the TACB prosecuted only 375 cases in total, most of which were done in 1973–1975. These convictions resulted in fines of $4 million dollars, the largest of which was $250,000 paid by ARMCO Steel and also by ASARCO for its pollution of El Paso.[46] Leniency toward polluters is the watchword of the agency. The deaths of nine Texans in 1975 caused by emission of harmful fumes at the Atlantic-Richfield plant near Denver City prompted former board member Joe Bridgefarmer to comment: "I realize that they [Atlantic-Richfield] were probably in violation of some regulations of ours, but I fail to see how the State of Texas has been damaged." [47]

The foremost weapon in the TACB arsenal to fight pollution is its authority to issue permits for new plant construction. Before a construction project may begin, the board is to evaluate the impact of the plant's operations on air quality. If the board feels that the company has incorporated adequate pollution abatement equipment into the building plans, a permit to start construction is granted. After the facilities are erected, the board checks the operating capabilities of the antipollution devices and certifies their effectiveness.

There has never been a case in its twenty-year existence in which the TACB has refused to issue a permit to initiate construction. The only consideration that the board entertains in its deliberations is the technical aspects of the pollution abatement equipment. As long as technology suitable to the curtailment of pollutants is to be installed, permits are granted. The effect of new construction on the surrounding environment is not a factor in the board's decision.

There have been occasions when companies have built new plants without first securing a TACB permit. Texaco, for instance, constructed new facilities in

Seminole in 1978 without the sanction of the board. After numerous citizen complaints about the hydrogen sulfide odors coming from the operation, the TACB staff investigated and found evidence of pollution. Fifteen notices of violation were sent to Texaco. A field agent for the TACB recommended that the company be sued, but the agency balked.[48] Negotiation again prevailed as a means to bring a company into compliance with the law.

The Texas Air Control Board and the Environmental Protection Agency have been at odds most of the time since their joint adventure into ending pollution began. The TACB encountered great difficulty gaining EPA acceptance of its plan to improve air quality in the state. The EPA felt that the state was being too lenient on polluters. On occasion, the EPA resorted to direct intervention in Texas in order to stop pollution that it considered the TACB had, in effect, condoned. Angry verbal exchanges, differences in philosophies about how to achieve clean air, and heated legal battles marked the relationship between the two agencies. In the early 1980s, for example, they were in conflict over the introduction of testing autos for pollution in Texas. The TACB saw little need for this practice, while the EPA thought the opposite.[49] Finally in 1983, an auto emissions inspection and maintenance program began in Harris County (Houston).

What about the goal of improving air quality in Texas? The TACB boasts of some impressive statistics in support of its view that it has contributed to a significant reduction of air pollutants. Before the board's inception, polluters emitted 32,000 tons of damaging materials daily into the state's atmosphere; by the late 1970s, this amount had been substantially reduced.[50] However, foul air persists in the state. El Paso and Houston exceeded the standard for carbon monoxide in 1983. El Paso, San Antonio, Houston, Laredo, Corpus Christi, and places in the Rio Grande valley were in violation of the standards for suspended particulates. El Paso and Dallas had excessive concentrations of lead in each city's air.[51] An EPA study found that the ozone levels were surpassed in each of seven areas tested: Austin, Beaumont/Port Arthur, Corpus Christi, Dallas/Fort Worth, El Paso, Houston, and San Antonio.[52] Houston is the smoggiest part of the state and third highest in the country in ozone.

The future of clean air in Texas does not bode well. There is still some uncertainty about what actually causes smog and haze in the state. Initially, the EPA considered hydrocarbons (such as diesel fuel, gasoline, and kerosene) the primary sources of smog and ordered a reduction of their emission into the air. But even with a 40 percent decrease in hydrocarbon deposits by 1976, "there ha[d] not been a substantial reduction of oxidants." [53] As industry grows in Texas and the number of automobiles increases with the population rise, more sources of pollution are added to the 1,500 that already exist in the state. In addition, more pollutants will be released into the air. The executive director of the TACB predicted in the late 1970s that "by the year 2000 emissions of hydrocarbons could double, particulate emissions . . . [and] nitrogen oxides could be up by a factor of 8, and sulfur dioxide could be up by a staggering factor of 24 times the present . . . rates," as industries switch to burning coal to run their factories.[54] Finally, there has been a reduction in the commitment to use exacting standards to improve the air under the Reagan administration. This change at the federal level reinforces the more relaxed administrative practices of the Texas Air Control Board.

FINANCIAL INSTITUTIONS

The state government of Texas has the authority to oversee many of the activities of the financial institutions located within its boundaries. This section explores state regulation of the banking business, insurance practices, and the policies of lending firms.

Banks

The populist framers of the Texas Constitution, it will be recalled from chapter 7, had a deep suspicion of banks. Over time, that distrust paved the way for state regulation. When, for instance, a 1904 amendment to the constitution permitted the chartering of banks in Texas, it also prohibited banks from operating branches throughout the state. State regulation of the banking world still continues, but the major beneficiaries of public policy now are the banks themselves. This has been clearly seen in the state's reticence to enforce the constitutional ban on branch banking.

Without branches, no single bank in Texas could amass a dominant share of assets or deposits. Big businesses in need of huge loans for expansion went out of state for credit since Texas banks simply could not finance large-scale notes. As late as 1973, "many of the lending corporations of this state used twice as many out-of-state banks as Texas banks and ... approximately four-fifths of their bank loan balances and outstanding lines of credit originated outside of Texas." [55]

In order to strengthen their lending position, the larger Texas banks began, in the early 1970s, to form bank holding companies. A holding company purchases other banks and consolidates the deposits and assets of all its members. By 1975, there were 35 bank holding companies in Texas with 224 affiliate members. (Table 2–7 lists the largest bank corporations.) There is little doubt that the bank holding company movement successfully circumvented the state's restriction on branch banking. A bank economist in direct reference to Texas once commented that "when branching is denied, enterprising bankers will find a way to get around [the] barrier.... The growth of multibank holding companies is proof of this." [56] Most key government officials in Texas acquiesced in this subterfuge.

A fairly recent legislative inquiry into the growth of bank holding companies, for example, completely ignored the constitutional branch banking problem altogether and "applaud[ed] the ... movement for the contributions it has made and will continue to make to the state economy." [57] Various attorneys-general of Texas, who were in a position that would have allowed them to prosecute violations of the ban on branch banking, did not block the bank holding company phenomenon. In 1952, Attorney-General Price Daniel ruled that a holding company is not illegal if it simply owns member institutions. If the parent company manages the day-to-day operations of the affiliates, however, this would constitute a transgression of the state constitution. Daniel noted that charges of illegal management would have to be handled on a case-by-case basis. [58] Subsequent attorneys-general have reaffirmed the Daniel opinion, but none prosecuted a bank holding company for managing the operations of its subsidiaries. Critics contended that the holding companies were deeply involved in the everyday business of their member banks. [59] In 1986, Attorney-General Jim Mattox broke with tradition when he issued an opinion that detached banking facilities (over 20,000 feet from the central building of a bank) violated the constitutional ban on branch banking. In effect, many remote electronic banking machines owned by large holding companies were illegal. Finally, in November 1986, the voters approved an amendment to the Texas Constitution that resolves this problem: branch banking has been legalized in the state.

State officials have been helpful to the Texas banking community in other ways as well. Generosity begins with the State Banking Board, which is authorized to grant charters to new banks in Texas. The board is composed of three members: the state treasurer, the banking commissioner, and an appointee of the governor, usually a person with close political contacts to the chief executive and not an expert on banking. Ostensibly the board scrutinizes new charter applications to assess the financial integrity of the bank's owners and the impact that the institution will have on the economy in its locale. Critics, however, argue that charters are granted more on the basis of cronyism than for financial reasons. Campaign contributions, the inclusion of politicians among the prospective shareholders of a bank, and outstanding loans to political figures are but some of the extraneous forces that appear to sway the Banking Board's decisions. "The results of all this are obvious: banks that should not necessarily exist, controlled by people who are not necessarily fit to operate them." [60]

Administrative review of established banks is entrusted to the state banking commissioner. The administrative capacity of the commissioner is hampered by a number of factors. First, the office has no authority over some of the more dubious banking transactions that occur in the state. For instance, a change in ownership of a chartered bank is not regulated by the commissioner, and when a bank holding company adds a new member, the commissioner has no jurisdiction (the Federal Reserve Board has the final say in such mergers). Second, the staff are few in number, poorly paid, and because of a rapid turnover in personnel, inexperienced. Consequently, the commissioner has great difficulty monitoring the activities of the 1,853 banks in Texas. Third, the person holding this position usually has close ties with members of the state banking community and, when problems arise, he or she tends to protect the bank. For example, former commissioner Robert Stewart was once described as an administrator who felt that "the best way to protect the public [was] to cover the slummy side of life with a smile and try to deal with it behind the scenes." [61] On his retirement after thirteen years as banking commissioner, the Texas Bankers Association presented Stewart with a $53,000 check.[62]

In this atmosphere of somewhat lenient regulation, grievous banking practices exist. Texas banks account for one-fifth of all bank closures in the country.[63] In 1976, the Federal Deposit Insurance Corporation (FDIC) counted twenty-five of the state's banks as ones with "serious problems" and listed thirty-five more in the category of "problem" banks.[64] The most drastic bank problem is insolvency—the inability of a bank to return deposits to customers. Insolvent Texas banks are noted for rapid changes in ownership. The new owners frequently buy the bank with borrowed money, then lend excessive amounts of money to themselves and others, including friends, relatives, and associates. These borrowers often live beyond the bank's legal territory. State regulatory agencies in Texas ordinarily do not catch up with such indiscretions until the deposits have nearly all been lost and the bank is unable to meet its financial obligations. Only under these circumstances is the bank closed. As noted by the current bank commissioner, James Sexton, when recently confronted with highly dubious banking practices in four West Texas banks, "I don't like closing banks. I don't feel comfortable closing banks." [65]

As a final benefit to the banking community, state officials deposit much of the government's money into select banks. Formerly, the funds earned little or no interest for the state but did produce interest for the banks. The choice of banks was often based on political friendships with members of financial institutions. During the 1970s, for instance, about one-half of the money banked annually by the Board of Regents of the University of Texas was deposited "in [banking] institutions where regents [were] major stockholders or directors." [66] The state treasurer has great discretion in designating banks as depositories for billions of dollars of state funds. For more than three decades former state treasurer Jesse James chose banks in which he had close political and financial ties. Mr. James, for example, placed slightly more than $10 million in state money in the ill-fated Sharpstown Bank (see chapter 6) just prior to its financial collapse. At the time, James was engaged in a major financial transaction with the bank's founder and owner, Frank Sharp. [67]

Insurance

State policies in Texas have also been advantageous to the insurance industry. The State Board of Insurance regulates, charters, and sets rates for the insurance companies of Texas. Before the mid–1950s, a company could issue insurance in the state with a minimal financial foundation and not worry about stringent government regulation. After a large number of failures among insurance companies and widespread scandal in the industry, the state tightened its rules and regulations. Companies are still allowed to earn high profits on policies issued to Texas ratepayers.

Auto insurance rates, for example, are consistently set by the State Board of Insurance to guarantee a substantial profit to the policycarrier. Moreover, the board has done little to counter the rising cost of insuring a motor vehicle. Most insurance claims are for auto repair and not for hospitalization, legal fees, or work missed because of an accident.[68] Auto repairs escalate in cost "not so much [as] a result of any higher rate of accidents . . . [but] as a result of shabbier construction of the automobile shell and profiteering by mechanics who raise their estimates on cars covered by insurance." [69] Instead of putting pressure on the auto industry to manufacture stronger cars and on repair shops to do better work, the board generally allows insurance companies to raise rates to cover all claims.

Lending Institutions

The state government further regulates the lending practices of institutions such as banks, savings and loan firms, and credit companies. The most visible financial transactions falling within the jurisdiction of the government are rates of interest charged to borrowers by lenders. A 1905 amendment to the state constitution limited interest rates to 10 percent on any loan. In 1963, the constitution was altered to allow the Texas legislature to decide appropriate interest rates. Since then, the legislature has been constantly pressed by financial groups to raise interest rates.

Throughout the 1970s, creditors responsible for small loans (under $2,500) continuously pushed for legislation that would have set a high upper limit on interest. The legislature responded by permitting credit companies to levy fairly high rates.[70] The amount of interest depends on the size of the loan: the smaller the loan, the higher the annual interest charged. For the lending institutions, the largest of which are giant corporations headquartered outside of Texas, favorable legislative action generally meant high profits. For the borrowers, the majority of whom are "blue collar workers with annual earnings of $15,000 or less," high interest rates served to limit purchases or the ability to pay bills.[71]

In 1979, a concerted attempt by financial institutions to persuade the legislature to increase the 10 percent upper limit on interest rates for home mortgages to 12 percent transpired. State lending institutions argued that, at the time, their money was borrowed from national financial sources at an interest rate above 10 percent; thus they could not profitably loan money to home buyers in Texas while the 10 percent ceiling existed. If a rise in interest rates were not forthcoming, lenders promised, mortgage money would simply dry up in the state. The legislature, and eventually the governor, were convinced and approved a measure permitting interest rates to rise to 12 percent. In January 1980, the federal government supplanted state control over rates charged on mortgage money, but rates have generally been over 10 percent.

In sum, state regulation has created a favorable environment for Texas's financial institutions. Establishing a bank or insurance company is not very difficult. State administration is not overly restrictive of the activities of the institutions that it reviews; under the state's laissez-faire policies, most of these firms have grown and prospered. The distrust of financial institutions displayed so vehemently in the past has been replaced by today's overwhelming government support of banks, insurance companies, and creditors.

CONSUMER PROTECTION

The actions of the state government in Texas result in consumers paying high prices for petroleum products, natural gas, electricity, insurance, and the privilege of borrowing money. In contrast, during the 1970s the state became a leader in protecting consumers from defective goods and deceptive sales practices. Under the state's laws, especially the Consumer Protection Act of 1973, customers victimized by an unscrupulous salesperson or a faulty product have a host of legal remedies to redress their grievances. Individuals are encouraged to sue businesses for fraudulent trade practices or for making defective products. The attorney-general of the state may seek civil penalties against the violators of these consumer protection laws.

Between 1973 and 1979, the attorney-general's office received almost 72,000 consumer complaints against businesses. Charges were filed in 363 cases. In all but 3 instances, the Texas courts ruled in favor of the complainant, netting consumers some $3 million as compensation for damages. In addition, during this six-year span the attorney-general extracted $5.3 million from businesses for consumers through negotiated settlements.[72]

Because of the dramatic relief it offers from the corporate bias that afflicts so much of Texas's public policy, some elaboration about the passage of the Consumer Protection Act is warranted. To appreciate the origins of the legislation, the following points must be considered. First, the Sharpstown Bank scandal (chapter 6) had a major impact on the composition of the 1973 Texas Legislature. Legislators even remotely associated with the scandal were not returned to office by the voters, and among the foremost casualties were the leaders. Without the well-entrenched leadership cadre, the corporate conduit to the legislature was (temporarily) blocked. Second, the ranks of the business world were split over consumer protection legislation. Trial lawyers in Texas, with visions of earning large legal fees in consumer cases against manufacturers, supported the act. In this atmosphere of major turnover in legislative officerholders, disarray in legislative leadership, and a fissure within the business lobby, the consumer protection bill became law. This was a very unusual set of simultaneous occurrences.

Many business interests have become displeased with Texas consumer protection laws. They argue that these laws have swung too far to the advantage of the consumer. Businesses, it is claimed, have suffered great financial losses incurred from the legal expense of consumer suits, the compensation awarded to customers by generous juries and judges, and the increasing cost of product

Courtesy of Ben Sargent, *The Austin American-Statesman.* Reprinted By Permission.

liability insurance for some enterprises and individuals, including doctors, hospitals, day care centers, newspapers, and small businesses.[73]

Others dispute this viewpoint with the following arguments: in individual suits, consumers win only one out of every four cases against companies; the financial awards to consumers are not very high—in 1979, for instance, the mean award granted by juries was around $69,000; and the rise in insurance costs is more a result of the practices of the insurance company than the consequences of losing damage suits.[74] Insurance companies underwrote product liability insurance in the late 1970s for a relatively cheap price because they were earning handsome profits from making commercial loans at a high rate of interest. When interest rates fell during the 1980s, the companies had to raise liability insurance premiums to compensate. Thus economic trends, not court awards, have led to problems in affording insurance.[75]

Recently, businesses and insurance companies have attempted to whittle away at the consumer protection laws of Texas. In recent legislative sessions many bills have been introduced to curtail the liability of companies and certain individuals. These bills aim at creating new legal defenses, effectively freeing businesses at fault in cases of fraud and product defects. They additionally would restrict the amount that a court could award consumers, define who could sue, designate the state and county in which a suit must occur, limit plaintiff's attorney's fees, and delineate financial culpability on the part of those guilty of liability.[76] Efforts to curtail product liability suits and awards through legislation show little sign of abating. Many of the consumer gains made in the Consumer Protection Act of 1973 appear in jeopardy.

CONCLUSION

The regulatory policies of the state government of Texas have been, overall, to the economic advantage of giant corporations. Financial institutions, electric companies, and petroleum firms find a favorable regulatory environment in Texas. Legislative, administrative, and judicial decisions mainly permit these enterprises to go about the business of earning profits without undue interference on the part of the state government.

For consumers, government regulation of financial matters and the use of the state's abundant natural resources have resulted in stiff interest rates; costly insurance premiums; insecurity over the integrity of some financial institutions; high prices for oil, natural gas, and electricity; and, finally, dirty air and water, with the average Texan footing the bill for most cleanup efforts. Conversely, the state has sufficient penalties to compensate for negligence and to prevent the production of faulty goods and deceptive trade practices, although signs point to some future dismantling of this protective shield for consumers.

NOTES

1. See Warner E. Mills, Jr., *Martial Law in East Texas*, Inter-University Case Program, No. 53 (University, Alabama: University of Alabama Press, 1960).

2. William Earl Maxwell and Ernest Crain, *Texas Politics Today* (St. Paul: West Publishing Company, 1978), p. 25.

3. Hart Stillwell, "Texas: Owned by Oil and Interlocking Directorates," in *Our Sovereign State,* ed. Robert S. Allen (New York: Vanguard Press, 1949), p. 322.

4. Ibid.

5. David F. Prindle, *Petroleum Politics and the Texas Railroad Commission* (Austin: University of Texas Press, 1981), p. 113.

6. Joint Report of the Interim Committee on Pipeline Study and Beaches, *Pollution vs. the People,* 62nd Legislature of the State of Texas, 1971, p. 1.

7. Ibid., pp. 8–9.

8. Legislative Budget Board, *Fiscal Size Up: 1986–87 Biennium* (Austin: Legislative Budget Board, 1986), p. 178.

9. For an excellent account of the troubles surrounding Lo-Vaca, see Paul Burka, "Power Politics," *Texas Monthly,* May 1975, pp. 69–97. Also see Prindle, *Petroleum Politics,* pp. 114–19.

10. Quoted in Burka, "Power Politics," p. 77.

11. Quoted in House Study Group Special Legislative Report No. 28, *Strip Mining in Texas,* June 1, 1978, p. 18.

12. The act is discussed in ibid., pp. 38–40.

13. Betty Anne Duke, "Texas Lignite: Stripping Away Illusions," *Texas Observer,* August 11, 1978, pp. 10–11.

14. Ibid., p. 11.

15. Discussed in Jack Hopper and Eric Hartman, "Rating the PUC: An A-minus from Wall Street, A D-minus from Consumers," *Texas Observer,* July 29, 1979, pp. 2–8 and 18–21.

16. Ibid., p. 20. Also Rick Piltz, *The Public Utility Commission,* House Study Group Special Legislative Report No. 80, March 22, 1982, pp. 35–42.

17. Hopper and Hartman, "Rating the PUC," p. 6.

18. *Fiscal Size Up,* p. 193.

19. Hopper and Hartman, pp. 19–20.

20. Calculated from Daniel T. Dougherty, "Electric Utility Regulation in Texas: The Case of the El Paso Electric Company" (Master's thesis, University of Texas at El Paso, 1979), pp. 138–39.

21. Rick Piltz, *The Public Utility Commission,* p. 50.

22. Hopper and Hartman, "Rating the PUC," p. 5.

23. *El Paso Times,* special section on the El Paso Electric Company, October 5, 1979, p. 5.

24. Discussed in Kaye Northcott, "The Bonehead Business of Nuclear Power," *Texas Observer,* February 20, 1987, p. 1 and pp. 5–7.

25. *Fiscal Size Up,* p. 170.

26. Texas Water Development Board, *Continuing Water Resources Planning and Development for Texas* (Austin: Texas Water Development Board, 1977), vol. 1, pp. 111–38.

27. Ibid., pp. 111–39.

28. Ibid., pp. 111–38.

29. For a detailed account of the Texas Water Plan, see the entire issue of *The Texas Observer,* August 1, 1969.

30. Texas Water Development Board, *Continuing Water Resources Planning,* pp. 111–38.

31. *Recommendation of Governor's Task Force on Water Resources Use and Conservation,* September 2, 1982, Austin, Texas.

32. Clint Winters, "Texas Water Problems: Work Begins on a New Plan," *Fi$cal Note$,* September 1982, p. 2.

33. Testimony before the Committee on Public Works, *Water Pollution Control Legislation—1971,* 92nd Congress, 1st Session, House of Representatives (Washington, D.C.: Government Printing Office, 1971), p. 803.

34. The point is made in Joint Report of the Interim Committee on Pipeline Study and Beaches, *Pollution vs. The People,* pp. 10–11.

35. Ibid.; and Kaye Northcott, "Hugh Yantis Is a Scare Word," *Texas Observer,* February 28, 1975, pp. 6–7.

36. Testimony of Troy Webb before the Subcommittee on Environmental Pollution of the Committee on Environment and Public Works, 95th Congress, 1st Session, U.S. Senate (Washington, D.C.: Government Printing Office, 1977), p. 28.

37. See Northcott, "Hugh Yantis Is a Scare Word."

38. Presented in testimony of Dick Whittington, acting deputy director of Texas Department of Water Resources, before the Committee on Public Works and Transportation, *Federal Water Pollution Control Act Amendments,* 95th Congress, 1st Session, House of Representatives (Washington, D.C.: Government Printing Office, 1978), p. 95.

39. Ibid.

40. Texas Department of Water Resources, *Water for Texas: Planning for the Future* (Austin: Department of Water Resources, February, 1983), pp. 1–2.

41. *U.S. vs. ARMCO Steel Corporation,* reprinted in Hearings before the Subcommittee on Public Buildings and Grounds of the Committee on Public Works, 92nd Congress, 1st Session, House of Representatives (Washington, D.C.: Government Printing Office, 1971), p. 466.

42. A thorough discussion of the controversy surrounding the inception of the Texas Air Control Board is in G. Todd Norvell and Alexander W. Bell, "Air Pollution Control in Texas," *Texas Law Review* 47 (June 1969): 1086–123.

43. Quoted in Gary Keith, *Air Pollution Control in Texas,* House Study Group, Special Legislative Report No. 65, February 3, 1981, p. 46.

44. Paul Stone, "TACB Won't Close Amarillo Smelter," *Texas Observer,* September 8, 1972, p. 10.

45. These figures are found in Texas Air Control Board, *Annual Report, 1984.*

46. Gary Keith, *Air Pollution Control in Texas,* p. 43.

47. Quoted in ibid.; p. 45.

48. Ibid., p. 46.

49. Discussed in ibid.; pp. 9–12 and pp. 33–37.

50. Susan Reid and Becky Moon, "How Much Pollution Is Safe?" *Texas Observer,* May 6, 1977, p. 4.

51. Texas Air Control Board, *Annual Report, 1984.*

52. Environmental Protection Agency, *Hydrocarbon/Photochemical Oxidant Control Strategy for the State of Texas,* reprinted in the Hearings before the Subcommittee on the Environment and the Atmosphere of the Committee on Science and Technology, *Special Urban Air Pollution Problems: Denver and Houston,* 95th Congress, 1st Session, House of Representatives (Washington, D.C.: Government Printing Office, 1978), pp. 456–675.

53. Statement of former Representative Bob Eckhardt of Texas, ibid., p. 323.

54. Testimony of Bill Stewart, ibid., p. 282.

55. Interim Report of the Committee on Financial Institutions, Texas House of Representatives, *Bank Holding Companies,* 65th Legislative Session (1976), p. 9.

56. Testimony of Jerome C. Darnell before the Subcommittee on Financial Institutions of the Committee on Banking, Housing, and Urban Affairs, *Federal Bank Policy,* 94th Congress, 2nd Session, U.S. Senate (Washington, D.C.: Government Printing Office, 1977), p. 293.

57. Interim Report of the Committee on Financial Institutions, *Bank Holding Companies,* p. 11.

58. The Daniel opinion is discussed in Tim Mahoney, "Bankholding Companies," *Texas Observer,* July 29, 1977, p. 5.

59. See, for instance, Tim Mahoney, "Bank Holding Companies Keep Branching Out," *Texas Observer,* December 2, 1977, p. 18.

60. Harvey Katz, *Shadow on the Alamo* (Garden City, N.Y.: Doubleday, 1972), p. 181.

61. Ibid., p. 190.

62. *Texas Observer,* May 18, 1984, p. 11.

63. Noted in Kaye Northcott and Jo Clifton, "Texas Rent-a-Bank, etc.," *Texas Observer,* December 24, 1976, p. 1.

64. Kaye Northcott, "Problem Banks," *Texas Observer,* March 11, 1977, p. 24.

65. Presented in hearings conducted by a subcommittee of the Committee on Government Operations, House of Representatives, 98th Congress, 2nd Session (Washington, D.C.: Government Printing Office, 1984), p. 2008.

66. *The Texas Observer,* October 1, 1976, p. 8.

67. Katz, *Shadow on the Alamo,* pp. 176–78.

68. For an example of the profit orientation of the state insurance board, see the report issued by Texas state senator Charles Wilson, *A Consumer Viewpoint on Automobile Liability Insurance,* December, 1970, pp. 1–9.

69. Ibid., p. 9.

70. See Paul Sweeney and Jim Hightower, "Consumer Finance Companies, Again," *Texas Observer,* February 11, 1977, pp. 3–4.

71. Ibid., p. 3.

72. Figures cited in Jim Hightower, "Have We Got a Deal For You," *Texas Observer,* March 16, 1979, p. 3.

73. For a rundown of business complaints about consumer protection laws, see the statement of Gerald Dorsey, staff attorney of the Texas Association of Business, presented to the Select Committee on Small Business, *Impact on Product Liability,* 94th Congress, 2nd Session, U.S. Senate (Washington, D.C.: Government Printing Office, 1976), pp. 1430–35. Also see Tani Adams, "The Lawsuit 'Crisis' and the Justice Issue," *Texas Observer,* May 16, 1986, pp. 9–12.

74. These arguments are summarized in Tina Lam, "Making the State Safe for Unsafe Products," *Texas Observer,* April 13, 1979, pp. 2–7 and Tani Adams, "The Lawsuit."

75. Rebecca Lightsey, "The Insurance Crisis," *Texas Observer,* May 2, 1986, pp. 9–11.

76. See Tina Lam, "Making the State Safe," and "The Tort Reform Package," *Texas Observer,* April 17, 1987.

15

The Regulation of Labor in Texas

Prior to the industrial age the relationship between employer and employee was an intimate one, based on mutual dependence. In that atmosphere, controversies over wages and working conditions were discussed and settled through interpersonal contact and exchange. Industrialization impersonalized the interaction between manager and worker. As corporations became highly organized, the employer-employee relationship became dominated by the economic prowess of big business. In the wake of industrialization, workers (including women and children) found themselves toiling long hours in unsafe jobs for little pay. Unemployment and work-related accidents were as common as they were unpredictable. There was no financial compensation during periods of unemployment, no matter what the reason for losing one's position.

In time, pressure mounted to alter the low status of employees. Workers organized into unions. Demands for higher pay, greater job security, safer working conditions, and compensation for unemployment and injury were emphatically made to industrial employers. For the most part, corporate managers and executives balked at the workers' pleas for change. An intense economic conflict featuring wildcat strikes, work slowdowns and stoppages, and deadly violence ensued. Government at the federal and state levels ordinarily allied with employers in these disputes, although on occasion laws improving the lot of workers were enacted. The balance was tipped in favor of comprehensive labor legislation during the New Deal period of the 1930s.

Surprisingly, the impetus for government intervention in labor matters came not only from organized workers but also from corporate sources. As early as the year 1900, executives of large corporations and banks evinced great concern over labor unrest in the United States. Strikes, slowdowns, stoppages, and protracted litigation over industrial accidents, as well as growing dissatisfaction among more and more workers, stimulated big business to counter the trend.[1] Even during these early days of corporate development, it was advantageous to have a stable political, social, and economic environment to nurture the primary mission of business: maximizing profits.

Corporate input into government policy toward labor came through business-sponsored civic groups such as the National Civic Federation (1900–1939) and the American Association for Labor Legislation (1906–1945). These and other business groups played a major role in the drafting and enactment of many labor laws, including compensation for both unemployment and injury and the recognition of a labor union as the workers' bargaining agent with employers.[2]

Federal law permits states to regulate many labor activities. Workers in jobs that produce goods used only within the state, for instance, are under the jurisdiction of the state. Labor activities not covered by federal laws also remain open to state control. Finally, some federal labor statutes invite state participation in the regulation of the work force.

Labor policy in Texas, overall, parallels national trends with one clear exception: the treatment of labor unions. This chapter focuses on the state policies that regulate working conditions, wages, and labor union activities. It concludes with a special look at the status of legal protection offered the state's farmworkers and a brief investigation of the plight of undocumented immigrants in Texas.   ★

WORKING CONDITIONS AND WAGES

Throughout this century, the Texas legislature has enacted a variety of laws affecting the status of workers in the state. This section probes into four areas of legislative concern: the protection of laborers against work-related accidents, compensation available to unemployed Texans, regulation of the employment of women and children, and the minimum wage to be paid employees.

Workman's Compensation and Safety at the Workplace

Texas joined the parade of states enacting policy to improve the status of workers in 1913 with the passage of the Workman's Compensation Act. This law, modeled after legislation written by the business-sponsored American Association for Labor Legislation, created procedures for paying compensation to workers injured on the job. Under the law, employers contribute money to an accident insurance fund, and insurance companies issue policies covering work-related injuries. Injured workers apply for compensation payments to the State Industrial Accident Board, a three-person panel appointed by the governor.

The workman's compensation program insures quick decisions on an employee's claims. The worker also stands a good chance of receiving at least some compensation for injuries sustained at the workplace. For these reasons, the program benefits employees. Prior to passage of accident compensation laws, workers found it extremely difficult to secure payment for injuries even though, in most instances, company practices caused the injury.

Employers also benefit from the law. Businesses participating in the Texas compensation program may argue to the Industrial Accident Board that the worker was partially responsible for his or her injury, or that a fellow employee contributed to the cause of injury, or that the worker was plainly aware that his or her job was risky from the beginning date of employment. If accepted, any of these defenses may free the company from at least some liability. Further, there is a limit to the monetary compensation that the worker may receive and the company must pay. Instead of facing the possibility of a financially ruinous settlement in a liability case, a company can rest assured that, no matter what the administrative decision, it will not be financially drained. Finally, having state administrators decide compensation matters saves companies the expense of lengthy court battles.

The 1913 Texas compensation program solely applies after a worker suffers an accident. Legislation to *prevent* industrial accidents has only recently been added

WORKERS! Demonstrate
on
INTERNATIONAL FIGHTING DAY—FEB. 25th. 1931
at the
STATE CAPITOL at 12 NOON

Demand Unemployment Insurance and Inmmediate Relief for the Unemployed

NEGRO, MEXICAN, WHITE WORKERS; WOMEN and YOUNG WORKERS:

Come to the demonstration before the State Capitol Building, on Feb. 25th at 12 noon to demand of the Governor and the State of Texas and the City of Austin the right to work, demand work or wages.

Demand unemployment insurance for all workers and poor farmers of Texas.

Demand inmmediate relief in the form of cash for all unemployed.

10.000.000 workers are without a job in United States, over 1000 a day die from starvation, 40 000.000 are hungry and sick from lack of food, clothing and shelter in the richest country in the world.

Women, young workers and children of the working class join your fathers and mothers, your brothers and sisters and husbands in the fight against this deplorable condition of the working class.

Negro workers, join the demonstration and fight for full social, political and economic equality for the Negro workers.

Governor Sterling turned down our demands on Feb. 10th.

Demonstrate on Feb. 25th with the workers of the entire world and again tell the Governor or Texas, the workers and farmers of Texas will not starve.

Auspices: Trade Union Unity League and Unemployed Councils Add of Texas.

For information of these organizations write:
T. U. U. L. 404½ Nebraska St. San Antonio, Texas

Courtesy of the Texas Archives.

to state and federal law books. Texas passed an occupational safety measure in 1967 and the federal government followed in 1970. Yet these laws do not contain stringent safety codes nor are they comprehensively and/or rigorously enforced. Part of the problem is establishing a causal link between conditions in the workplace and injuries, potential or actual, to employees. For instance, workers in Texas's petrochemical plants appear to contract diseases, such as brain cancer, that might be attributable to the chemicals in the factories.[3] Yet, since many of these illnesses are invisible in their formative stages, or take their toll outside of the workplace, or may be related to factors other than industrial climate, proving beyond a shadow of a doubt that a firm is responsible for the injury is almost impossible.

In addition, the Reagan administration has targeted the federal agencies—principally the Occupational Safety and Health Agency (OSHA)—charged with keeping places of employment safe as prime examples of unwanted government regulation. Budgetary cutbacks have resulted in staff reductions and even less enforcement of occupational safety codes. During the early 1980s some 654 workers were killed on construction sites in Texas, 200 more than construction deaths recorded in any other state. It is estimated that fewer than half of the contractors in the state were in compliance with federal safety standards. Indeed, 75 percent of the deaths occurred on sites where the employer was in violation of these standards. Yet OSHA exacted on average only a $350 fine from offending parties.[4]

Hence, although workers now have a government forum to seek compensation for work-related injuries, they are not automatically guaranteed a favorable decision, nor can they be completely sure that their workplace is free of unnecessary hazards. Texas, with nearly 1,000 fatalities yearly in the workplace, leads the nation in such deaths.[5] In recent years, workers sustaining injuries on the job site have been turning to state courts for compensatory damages. Lawyers offer their services in such cases on a contingency fee basis. That is, a legal fee—usually set at 30 percent of the financial damages sought—is forthcoming only if a court victory for the plaintiff results. Successes are on the rise. Judges on the state courts deciding liability cases have been more inclined in recent years to grant financial awards to workers injured during the course of their employment.[6] As noted in chapter 10, a great deal of money has been poured by trial lawyers into the election of judges who manifest sympathy for the plight of injured workers.

Unemployment Compensation

Since the mid-1930s, Texas has also provided a compensation program for workers who lose their jobs. Unemployment compensation is available to most out-of-work persons who had previously held a steady job, who didn't quit voluntarily or to attend school, who weren't fired for misconduct, and who actively seek work during the period in which they receive benefits. Through a fairly complicated formula, most employers in the state pay fees into an unemployment compensation fund. These fees are usually tacked on to the price that consumers pay for the business's product or service. In recent years the rate of unemployment has been steadily increasing. Between 1984 and 1985, for instance, some

115,000 Texans were added to the rolls of the unemployed. Those eligible for benefits receive an amount that is in line with their prior earnings, although the the 1985 average stipend was $140.52 weekly.[7] Generally, compensation may not extend beyond twenty-six weeks in any calendar year.

Protection for Women and Children

Since 1915, Texas has regulated the hours that women and children are allowed to work. Young children (under fifteen years of age) are barred from working in heavy industries, laundries, or as messengers. Youngsters may work in other occupations, but for no more than forty-eight hours each week. (Special dispensation from these restrictions may be granted by the state.) Women, until 1971, were to work no more than nine hours per day and no more than fifty-four hours each week. The nine-and-fifty-four law was amended in 1971 to allow women who are professionals, executives, administrators, salespersons, or who simply want to work longer to do so. This change was enacted to end state-authorized sex discrimination in employment.

State Minimum Wage

Texas passed a minimum wage act in 1970. In addition to being one of the last states to legally establish the minimum a person must be paid, the Texas hourly wage has always been far below the federal standard. Since the inception of this law, the state rate has been $1.40 an hour, compared with, in 1985, the federal minimum of $3.35 an hour. Of the forty-one states with a minimum wge, Texas's hourly rate of pay is the lowest.[8] Persons working for firms whose market lies entirely in Texas generally earn at most the low state hourly wage.

LABOR UNIONS

After the industrial revolution, workers began to organize into labor unions in order to bargain collectively for better pay and working conditions. Businesses, with some notable exceptions, resisted the union movement. Until the New Deal, government officials had disagreed over whether or not workers would be allowed to form unions. At times, governments approved of union activities. For instance, in 1899 the Texas state government permitted workers to join unions, although employers were not legally required to accept unions. Mostly, however, public policymakers, especially judges sitting on state and federal benches, thwarted the organizational efforts of unions. Finally, in 1937, with the passage of the Wagner Act, the federal government recognized the right of unions to mobilize and represent workers in disputes with management. The law also established the administrative machinery to hear labor complaints and enforce labor agreements.

Ironically, some of the most influential backers of the Wagner Act were from the corporate world. For years business was deeply divided over the desirability of labor unions. Most businesspeople adamantly opposed unionization and worked steadfastly to eradicate the labor movement in the United States. Conversely, other business leaders, including executives from the major banks and corporations of the country, actively supported the recognition of labor unions. To this pro-labor wing of the business community, the benefits of having labor unions were several: "Greater efficiency and productivity from labor, less labor turnover, the disciplining of the labor force by labor unions, the possibility of planning labor costs over the long run, and the dampening of radical doctrines." [9]

The federal government allows states to control many activities of labor unions. Section 14(b) of the Taft-Hartley Act of 1947, for instance, empowers states to decide if employers must *only* hire union members as employees. Texas, primarily because of its late entry into the industrial age and the lack of widespread discontent within its work force, has traditionally enacted legislation that restricts unionization in the state. Texas labor law closely regulates and monitors the internal operations of union organizations and their efforts to recruit new members and to pressure employers.

Labor Union Regulation in Texas

In 1943, the Texas legislature established a set of rules to guide the internal activities of labor unions in the state. The Mumford Act requires a union to file an annual report with the Texas secretary of state. This report is to include the union's affiliations, its property, its constitution, its bylaws, and its finances. Union records must be open for inspection at any time by any member. The union cannot expel a member without just cause and a formal hearing. Reinstatement may be ordered by a state court. No union fees may be automatically deducted from the paychecks of employees without their prior written authorization. Union organizers—unless they are national organizers—must register with the state and obtain a card to solicit funds or recruit new members. The union cannot contribute money to political candidates or parties, although it may establish a political action committee for this purpose.

Other laws prohibit certain workers from joining unions. For instance, domestic servants are not only denied the benefits of unemployment and workman's compensation, they are also not allowed to bargain collectively to change the status quo. Since 1973, all state and local government employees may form unions, but their right to collective bargaining with their employers is limited. Police and fire department personnel can enter into collective bargaining only if a majority of local voters approve of this action. By the late 1970s, elections to establish this practice were held in about 25 of Texas's 1,000-plus municipalities. In most cases the voters turned down the union. Three cities repealed through election the authorization of collective bargaining after initially endorsing it.[10]

The tactics a union may use in dealing with employers are greatly circumscribed by state law in Texas. Businesses may hire workers regardless of their union status. Texas is one of twenty states with this "right to work" rule.[11] Without the necessity of joining a union in order to work, employees are discouraged from swelling the ranks of labor organizations. During disputes with management, unions may not do any of the following: threaten or actually use violence; insult, slander, libel, or obscenely speak against the business; harass workers; block entrances to the workplace; engage in mass picketing (defined as two or more pickets within fifty feet either of the entrance to the firm or to another picket); or involve parties not primarily salient to the labor dispute, such as another company doing business with the original target. Union actions that result in a breach of contract with an employer are in violation of the state's antitrust acts. Strikes aimed at forcing business management to recognize a union must cease if a majority of workers vote not to join the union. Conversely, if a majority of workers approve of the union, it is thereafter certified to be their bargaining agent. Finally, union strikers and sympathizers are denied unemployment compensation benefits.

Overall, union efforts in Texas are hampered by many legal obstacles. Only about 12 percent of the state's work force is unionized.[12] This is 6 percent below the estimated national average.[13] For the last two decades, the state has ranked in the bottom ten in percent of employees in unions; among industrialized states, Texas is dead last. Union membership is mostly concentrated among workers in the industrial plants located in southeastern Texas, along the Gulf Coast. The country's leading labor organization, the AFL–CIO, launched a massive campaign in Houston in 1981 to unionize more of the state's workers. After spending $2 million dollars over two years, however, only around 8,000 new recruits were added to the membership ranks of the union. Moreover, as economic hard times struck Texas, many of the leading unions, such as the Oil, Chemical, and Atomic Workers (OCAW), lost members. Only the state's United Food and Commercial Workers union has experienced growth in its membership base in recent years.[14] The lack of union strength probably accounts for the lower wages and per-capita income earned by Texans in comparison to other Americans, especially those who reside in large industrial states. Overall, labor policy in Texas "has heavily been weighted in favor of management."[15]

Moreover, organized labor is not a strong influence in the politics of the state. Lacking a large membership, unions don't have much say in the selection of candidates or in political decision making. Very few elected or appointed officeholders in Texas are drawn from the ranks of labor. Consequently, unions are not an important political counterweight to big business in the state.

LABOR LAWS AND TEXAS FARMWORKERS

Although only 3 to 4 percent of the Texas work force is composed of farm laborers, almost two-thirds of them are earning below poverty-level incomes. The average family income of Texas's farmworkers is $7,200. Fully 200,000 of the farm laborers are migrants; that is, they work part of the year in Texas, part outside the state, and, at other times, they don't work at all. The average yearly wage for the migrant farm laborer is $3,500. Most work less than half a year.[16] When unemployed, benefits from the state are few. Many don't qualify for AFDC (welfare) payments (see chapter 12) because their families are intact and thus ineligible. Others who might otherwise qualify for cash assistance don't apply out of a keen sense of self-respect: "People willing to travel thousands of miles a year, suffer great indignities, and do backbreaking work for very low pay are not the sort eager to take government handouts."[17]

Until quite recently, Texas farmworkers hardly benefited from the state's labor laws. Before the mid-1980s, they were not covered by either workman's or unemployment compensation. In March 1984, a Texas district court ruled that farmworkers injured on the job must receive compensatory benefits. The legislative special session held in 1984 put this program into place. A state court declared in 1985 that unemployment benefits must also be extended to out-of-work farm laborers. The 69th Legislature established the machinery to implement this verdict. In 1985, the Texas Department of Agriculture implemented sweeping regulations on farmworker exposure to the spraying of pesticides. Prior to these rules, farm laborers risked illness and death from pesticide exposure. The new regulations, endorsed by the Texas legislature, require due caution in pesticide application, notification that spraying is to occur, an appropriate interval between spraying and returning to work, and the collection and distribution of information about chemicals contained in the sprays.[18] Finally, in 1987 the Texas legislature increased the minimum hourly wage for farmworkers from $1.40 to $3.35.

Efforts by unions to organize Texas's farmworkers, however, are still resisted by the state officials. In the past, state opposition to unionization of farm laborers has been manifested in the form of repressive police action.

In the spring of 1966, for instance, the Independent Workers Association, an affiliate of Cesar Chavez's National Farm Workers Association, initiated a plan to organize farmworkers in Starr County, located in the fertile Rio Grande valley of South Texas.[19] Most of the laborers were of Mexican descent, and, at the time, were paid about 25 cents an hour for their work. The union rallied some 700 workers and instituted a strike against the large agribusiness firms of this area. The immediate goals of the union were to improve the wages of the workers and to become the bargaining agent for laborers in disputes with growers.

In the fall of 1966, local authorities requested that the Texas Rangers be sent into Starr County. The rangers are a small state police force that has been romanticized in literature and in movies as a group of frontier heroes. Some of their critics, however, denounce them as being the major means for "the State [political and economic] establishment and local political machines . . . to harass and terrorize Mexican Americans."[20]

During their eight-month stay in Starr County, the rangers arrested strikers, union officials, and sympathizers, including members of the clergy. Most of those arrested were accused of violating the state's laws against labor activities, including mass and secondary picketing, illegal organizing, using obscene language, damaging the property of growers, and impeding the economic operations of agribusinesses. Many observers claimed that the rangers brutalized some of those arrested, denied them due process of law, manufactured charges against them, and systematically harassed union sympathizers, strikers, and officials.[21] Indeed, critics asserted that the actual motive behind the rangers' actions was twofold: to protect the economic interests of the growers of Starr County and to destroy the union through breaking the strike—a feat accomplished in June 1967. In 1974, the United States Supreme Court agreed with the rangers' detractors. In the case of *Allee v. Medrano,* the Court chastised the rangers for engaging in "a persistent pattern of policy misconduct" in Starr County.[22] Further, the Court, in the words of Justice William O. Douglas, damned the fact that "because of the intimidation by state authorities, [the union's] lawful effort was crushed."[23]

UNDOCUMENTED IMMIGRANTS IN TEXAS

Undocumented immigrants, the vast majority of whom are from Mexico, occupy jobs that are among the lowest paying in Texas. It is extremely difficult to accurately gauge the number of undocumented in the state. There is a constant fluctuation in this population since many depart from Texas for other locales in the United States or to return to Mexico. Counting the undocumented is made more formidable by their illegal status. Statewide estimates place their number anywhere from 284,450 to 1.8 million.[24]

Profile of the Undocumented

Nationally, undocumented immigrants from Mexico tend to be young, predominantly married men. They speak little, if any, English, and, especially if they are far from the Mexican border, evince a strong desire to return to their homeland. Most have less than a third-grade education and very little money on arrival in this country, although they are generally not from the lowest economic strata in their community or origin. In terms of attitudes, the undocumented laborers, as compared to nonmigrant Mexicans, are more work-oriented, more disposed to think about and plan for the future, less fatalistic about their lives, less submissive to authority, and more likely to condone the practice of birth control (although just as likely not to use preventive measures that are largely unavailable to them).[25]

A sample of undocumented migrants living in Texas finds that among those not in detention most are married and have resided in the state for, on the average, 4.3 years: "This suggests that a large proportion of the sample population has established permanent residence in the U.S." [26] Nearly two-thirds came to the state in search of jobs. Just over 40 percent are employed in service jobs working for restaurants and hotels. Another 22 percent work at construction sites. Some 12 percent are employed as domestics. An equal number work in factories. Only 6 percent are farm laborers. For their work, they are usually paid around $4.13 an hour. On average they are employed for 39 hours a week, generating a gross yearly income of approximately of $8,500.[27] Describing the jobs available to the undocumented worker, one observer notes that "they involve dirty, often physically arduous tasks, . . . low social status, low job security (often due to the short-term or seasonal nature of the work), and little chance for advancement." [28] These are not jobs aspired to by most U.S. citizens, especially in light of the fact that wages paid in these positions are somewhat below the poverty line.

Undocumented Workers and Employers

For employers, the undocumented worker is usually a cheap source of labor. As noted by a student of this subject, "the hiring of the illegal alien is generally a profitable business which contributes to the widening of [employers'] profit maximization margins." [29] This pattern is especially evident on the farms and ranches owned by large agribusiness outfits in South Texas where "wage exploitation of Mexican workers seems to be practiced on a far wider scale . . . than in any other sector of the U.S. economy where large numbers of Mexican illegals are still employed."[30]

In addition to working cheaply, undocumented workers raise few complaints, present their employer with negligible disciplinary problems (although historical examples of undocumented workers rebelling against their employment status have been recorded), and are available to replace striking workers. Until recently, the working conditions of the undocumented placed them at the mercy of employers who have been known to hand them over to immigration authorities in lieu of payment for work done. This practice has been declining since immigration policy now compels employers to compensate the undocumented for work accomplished even if the boss turns them in. Nevertheless, fourteen of seventeen recent cases of this unsavory tactic have occurred in the state of Texas.[31] With passage of the Simpson-Rodino immigration bill Congress now makes it illegal for employers to knowingly hire an undocumented worker.

Giving More Than They Take

Undocumented immigrants pay more for services offered by federal, state, and local governments than they receive. A study of a sample of Texas's undocumented discovered that very few of them received welfare, food stamps, rent and utility supplements, unemployment and workman's compensation, or senior citizen services: "The use of social services by the undocumented sample was quite low given the generally low income status of this population."[32] Some 40 percent of their households contained school-aged children who attended public schools. Around half received legal aid and utilized public transport systems.[33]

The undocumented do pay taxes. Federal taxes such as social security and personal income are in many cases deducted from their wages. The state receives revenue through the sales tax that doesn't discriminate on the basis of the citizenship status of buyers in Texas. Property taxes are included in rent charged for lodging. They help finance local government policies, including the public education system. Consequently, "the undocumented aliens in Texas contribute more revenue to the state than the cost to the state to provide them with public services."[34]

In addition, a fair share of the earnings of the undocumented worker ultimately boosts the U.S. economy. About two-thirds of the money they earn stays in this country to cover the expense of housing, food, transportation, and other necessities.[35] In San Antonio, less than a majority of the undocumented immigrants sampled send money to relatives in Mexico. When they do, the amount is usually around $15 a week.[36] Interestingly, the recipients of this money in Mexico—assuming it reaches them—are likely to spend it on goods made in this country or produced by U.S. corporations operating south of the border.[37]

In short, undocumented migrants from Mexico constitute a hidden work force in the Texas economy. They pick a great deal of the food we eat, clean many of the establishments in which we shop, serve us in restaurants and hotels that we patronize, construct some of the houses in which we live and the buildings in which we work, keep a goodly number of our houses neat and tidy, raise a fraction of our youngsters, and engage in sundry activities that result in profit for their employers. For this they are paid little and incur the wrath of a large segment of the public who resent their presence in this country. Not to be overlooked is the fact that most of their earnings stay here. Finally, even though they usually pay taxes, the undocumented only rarely receive benefits from services offered by the government.

CONCLUSION

Many of Texas's labor laws have improved the general working conditions and wages of employees. These advancements, however, have not undermined the lofty position of large businesses in the state's economy. Indeed, state regulation of labor fosters a more stable environment in which corporations can plan rationally for future profit. Further, the cost of these programs is not fully borne by companies. Instead, the costs of higher wages and unemployment and accident compensation insurance are passed along to consumers in the form of higher prices for products. Comparatively, labor policy in Texas is not as advantageous to workers as it is in other states, especially industrialized ones. This is particularly true in the case of laws affecting labor unions.

NOTES

1. This argument is presented in G. William Domhoff, *The Higher Circles* (New York: Vintage, 1970), ch. 6.

2. Ibid.

3. Paul Sweeney, "Life-and-Death on the Job in Texas City," *Texas Observer,* November 6, 1981, pp. 1 and 10–18.

4. Reported in the *Texas Observer,* July 11, 1986, p. 7.

5. Paul Matula, "Texas Leads Nation in Job-Related Deaths," *The Daily Texan,* October 16, 1986, p. 9.

6. See, for examples of recent cases, Paul Burka, "Heads, We Win, Tails, You Lose," *Texas Monthly,* May 1987, pp. 138–39 and p. 206.

7. Figures from the Texas Employment Commission, *Annual Report, 1985.*

8. *Book of States, 1986–1987* (Lexington: Council of State Governments, 1986), pp. 377–78.

9. See the discussion in Domhoff, *The Higher Circles,* p. 225 and pp. 218–50, passim.

10. "Local-Option Fire/Police Collective Bargaining in Texas," *Texas Town and City,* August 1977, pp. 10–11.

11. In 1950, only 12 states, including Texas, were "right to work" states. By 1964, the number increased to 20. In 1978, it remained at 20. Winthrop Quigley, "Right to Work: The New Mexico Lesson," *National Review,* February 3, 1978, p. 157.

12. In the early 1980s, 694,000 of the state's 6.7 million nonagricultural workers were in unions. If agricultural workers are added to the work force, the number of unionized Texans declines to around 10 percent. *Texas Observer,* July 31, 1986.

13. The national figure for union members is an estimate because under the Reagan administration union membership figures are no longer collected.

14. *Texas Observer,* July 31, 1986.

15. Clifton McCleskey, Allan Butcher, Daniel E. Farlow, and J. Pat Stephens, *The Government and Politics of Texas,* 6th ed. (Boston: Little, Brown, 1978), p. 383.

16. Figures are from Geoffrey Rips, "The Battle for Farmworker Compensation," *Texas Observer,* January 13, 1984, pp. 7–15.

17. John Davidson, "A Harvest of Poverty," *Texas Observer,* February 3, 1978, p. 5.

18. Discussed in Dan Kelley, *New State Rules on Agricultural Pesticide Use,* House Study Group, # 114, May 20, 1985.

19. A thorough discussion of the Starr County farmworkers' strike is presented in Julian Samora, Joe Bernal, and Albert Pena, *Gunpowder Justice: A Reassessment of the Texas Rangers* (Notre Dame, Ind.: University of Notre Dame Press, 1979), ch. 8.

20. Statement of Bexar County (San Antonio) Commissioner Albert Pena made during the Starr County struggle. Quoted in ibid., p. 141.

21. The events are covered in ibid., ch. 8.

22. *Allee v. Medrano,* 416 U.S. 815 (1974).

23. Ibid, p. 814.

24. LBJ School of Public Affairs, *The Use of Public Services by Undocumented Aliens in Texas: A Study of State Costs and Revenues* (Austin: LBJ School of Public Affairs, 1984).

25. Wayne A. Cornelius, *Mexican Migration to the United States: Causes, Consequence, and U.S. Resources* (Cambridge: Center of International Studies, Massachusetts Institute of Technology, 1978), pp. 19–20 and 82.

26. LBJ School of Public Affairs, *The Use of Public Services,* p. 9.

27. Figures come from ibid.

28. Wayne A. Cornelius, *Mexican Migration to the United States,* p. 56.

29. Gilbert Cardenas, "Manpower Impact and Problems of Mexican Illegal Aliens in an Urban Labor Market" (Ph.D. diss., University of Illinois at Champaign-Urbana), p. 195.

30. Cornelius, *Mexican Migration,* p. 60.

31. Jorge A. Bustamante, "Commodity Migrants: Structural Analysis of Mexican Migration to the United States," in *Views Across the Border: The United States and Mexico,* ed. Stanley R. Ross (Albuquerque: University of New Mexico Press, 1978), p. 190.

32. LBJ School of Public Affairs, p. 32.

33. Ibid.

34. Ibid, p. 87.

35. Covered in Cornelius, *Mexican Migration,* p. 75.

36. Gilbert Cardenas, "Manpower Impact," p. 193.

37. Cornelius, *Mexican Migration,* p. 75.

PART V

Economic Elites and Local Politics in Texas

As has been demonstrated in the last part of this book, big businesses operating in Texas have received many benefits from the state government. State funds allocated for welfare, highways, and education have directly and indirectly improved the economic climate in Texas for large corporations. State policy regarding the use of natural resources, the activities of financial institutions, and labor unions and working conditions have also been to the advantage of the corporate world. Texas's major economic entities have thus wisely invested in the politics of the state. Campaign contributions, lobbying efforts, and support for the continuation of a fragmented, decentralized, and generally weak state government have reaped handsome dividends for the giant corporations of Texas.

Does the same pattern of influence exist in local communities in the Lone Star State? Part V addresses this question by describing local government in Texas and then analyzing the impact of economic institutions on these governing bodies.

─────16─────

Local Politics in Texas

Citizens have more contact with local government officials than with any other officeholders in America. One reason for this intimacy is the large number of local entities throughout the country. It is virtually impossible to avoid public school teachers, police, tax appraisers, sanitation workers, and thousands of other municipal and county employees, regardless of how hard one might try.

Local governments abound in Texas. There are almost 4,000 distinct local political bodies within the state. They can be divided into three different types of government: municipal government, county government, and special governing districts (such as hospital districts, water districts, school districts, and sanitation districts).

By far the largest category is the special district. Including school districts (see chapter 11), there are nearly 2,500 special districts in Texas. Next in number are the municipal governments. Each of Texas's 1,100 cities has its own municipal government. Finally, a separate government operates in every one of the state's 254 counties.

This chapter first describes the organizational pattern and political authority of local governments in Texas. It then turns to citizen participation at the local level. The final section traces the political power wielded by corporate interests in various communities of the Lone Star State. ★

LOCAL GOVERNMENT: ORGANIZATION AND AUTHORITY

Governments at the municipal, county, and special district level in Texas vary along three dimensions: their legal basis, their type of structure, and their political authority.

Legal Basis of Local Government

The state government of Texas legally establishes municipal, county, and special district governments. Cities with a total population under 5,000 people are regulated by general laws of the state. These general laws limit the structure of government that small cities may institute and the powers that the municipality may exercise. More populous cities (over 5,000 people), since the Texas Constitution was amended in 1912, have the right to choose their own structure of government if a majority of voters in the municipality so desires. Municipalities that opt for their own government structures are called home rule cities. Altogether, Texas has 249 home rule cities and around 851 general law municipalities.[1]

County government exists under the auspices of the state constitution. Its legal function is to administer general state policies to citizens living within its boundary. Everyday implementation of state laws and formulation of more specific countywide policies are primarily in the hands of the county government. After being given a set of general guidelines, there is not much assistance or interference from Austin in county business.

A special district is a governing unit established by state law. It is specifically designed to handle one particular policy area, such as sanitation, water, education, or hospitals. The number of special districts (excluding school districts) has grown tremendously in Texas, with the total nearly doubling from 733 to 1,425 over the last two decades.[2]

Structure of Government at the Local Level

Local government in Texas is organized into a plethora of political structures.

Municipal Government.   Cities in Texas have one of five forms of government: strong mayor, council; weak mayor, council; council-manager; commission; or commission-manager. The cities with the first two forms are governed by an elected mayor and city council. But, as their names imply, the authority of the mayor differs. Strong mayors are empowered to participate in council deliberations, to veto council proposals, to formulate a budget for the city, and to control the heads of administrative departments in the city through appointment and removal powers. Weak mayors are legally circumscribed in their authority. The mayor participates in the council, but the council has the upper hand in most matters. It can, for instance, override the mayor's veto. Further, it, not the mayor, assumes responsibility for oversight of the operations of the city's administrative departments.

Cities with a commission form of government are ruled by an elected board of commissioners. The board collectively legislates policy for the city. Each commissioner is individually in charge of a specific administrative office in the city.

Council-manager and commission-manager governments are noted for the unique relationship between the elected board and the city manager. The elected city council (including the elected city mayor) or commission appoints a manager to be the chief administrative officer of the municipality. Preparing the budget, directing administrative offices, and implementing city policies are all within the manager's jurisdiction. The manager serves at the pleasure of the council or commission.

Texas's 249 home rule cities may choose the form of government they want. Most (about 82 percent) have picked either a council-manager (165 in total) or commission-manager (40 in total) structure. Seven municipalities are governed by a strong mayor. Three communities are commission governments. The rest are mostly structured around a council, weak mayor form of government.[3]

General law cities must become either council-manager or mayor (strong or weak), council municipalities. Most fall into the latter category. Although state law stipulates that cities are restricted to certain established forms of government, in reality, hybrid political entities have been created in some locales. In Houston, for instance, there is a council, a strong mayor, and a chief administrator (manager) appointed by the mayor to direct the implementation of city policy.

Elections in almost all of Texas's cities are nonpartisan; that is, the names of candidates seeking local office are not affiliated with any political party. In addition, until recently, elections for local races were at-large. That is, candidates were chosen by the entire electorate regardless of the office. The federal government, through the efforts of the Justice Department, has of late been forcing Texas cities to select council members from geographically distinct districts.

Larger cities (population size over 100,000) are gradually abandoning at-large elections. Indeed, some of these cities, for instance, San Antonio, Fort Worth, and El Paso, have fully instituted district representation. Others, including Houston and Dallas, retain a mixed at-large and district form of election. Medium-size cities (25,000 to 100,000 people) usually have a mixed or single district representational system. Most smaller cities continue to select local legislators at-large.[4] Texas's mayors remain the choice of the entire citywide electorate.

County Government.   Basically, the government of every county in Texas is organized in a similar pattern. At the core of county government is the commissioners court, composed of four commissioners and a county judge. The four commissioners are elected from separate precincts in the county. The United States Supreme Court, in a Texas case involving the election of commissioners for Midland County, has ordered that the precincts be equal in population size.[5] The county judge is elected countywide.

County voters also choose the county sheriff, the county attorney, the county tax collector-assessor, the county clerk, the county treasurer, justices of the peace, and constables for the county. The state requires the commissioners court to appoint a health officer for the county. In counties with a population in excess of 35,000, the commissioners must also appoint an auditor to attend to the financial books of the county government. Most of Texas's counties also have an agricultural extension agent and a home demonstration agent to assist residents in farming and homemaking. Each is appointed by the commissioners court.

Special District.   There is a great deal of variation in the governing structures of special districts. Around three-fourths of these districts, including school districts, are governed by boards or commissions elected by people residing within the district.[6] The 68th (1983) Texas Legislature mandated that school board members must no longer be elected on an at-large basis. Each member is to be selected from a unique geographical area of the school district. The remaining special districts are headed by personnel appointed by either the governor, other state officials, mayors of cities, city councils, or county commissioners, depending on the district in question. The size of the board or commission differs from district to district, although school boards uniformly are composed of seven elected members. The chaotic nature of special districts in Texas has prompted one observer to despair that generalizations about them "are certain to be misleading, if not totally false." [7]

Functions and Powers of Local Government

Municipal governments in Texas have authority over a wide range of policy matters. First, they provide citizens with a large number of social services, including police and fire protection, parks and recreational facilities, mass transportation, road construction and repair, sewage disposal systems, and public health amenities. Cities are also responsible for planning the growth of their communities. They may annex new land and thus add to their territorial base. Land within the city is subject to zoning laws that restrict its use. Finally, municipal government regulates a good deal of human behavior. City housing codes, for instance, establish minimum requirements that residences must meet before citizens are permitted to live in them.

Municipal government in Texas is financed by a number of revenue sources. Foremost is the property tax, which accounts for 40 percent of city revenues.[8] Virtually every city government levies a tax on tangible property within its boundaries. Texas law also allows a city to invoke a 1 percent tax on the sales of sundry items and four-fifths of the state's municipalities have approved of the sales tax.[9] About 20 percent of all city revenue comes from this tax.[10] The remaining money to finance city policies is derived from myriad sources, including rent from properties, fees, franchise taxes, and fines from law violators. The federal government, through its revenue-sharing program, is another source of funds. Since 1972, Texas's cities collectively have received around $100 million per year from Washington.[11] Finally, cities may issue bonds to borrow money to finance their programs.

County government in Texas must carry out functions mandated to it by the state. For instance, county officials enforce the laws of the state, build and maintain roads and bridges, construct and repair jails and courthouses, oversee the administration of elections, and keep vital statistics (birth, death, marriage, etc.) of residents. State law authorizes, but does not require, counties to operate public libraries, hospitals, welfare programs, and parks. The most populous counties of the Lone Star State provide all of these services.

About half of the revenue needed to finance county government comes from the property tax.[12] Augmenting the property tax as revenue sources are funds derived from the sale of county property, interest earned on county investments, special fees assessed by the commissioners court, and money transferred to the county from other governments. In this last category, the state of Texas contributes about 10 percent to county government operations and the federal government, through the revenue-sharing program, adds another 6 percent to county coffers.[13]

Special districts are empowered to govern in a specific policy area. School districts, now numbering slightly under 1,100, constitute the single largest category of special districts (see chapter 11). Districts involved in some form of water policy, such as delivery, conservation, navigation, and flood control, total almost 1,000 and form the second largest group of special districts. Housing authorities (some 310), soil conservation districts (almost 200), and hospital districts (112), round out most of the remaining special districts in Texas.[14]

The operations of special districts are financed from a variety of sources. Some, primarily school districts, collect taxes—usually property taxes. Indeed, half of the $8 billion raised through the property tax in 1984 was deployed for schools.[15] Other special districts assess fees for their services. Still others issue bonds and borrow money from private lenders.

LOCAL GOVERNMENT AND CITIZEN PARTICIPATION

Local government in Texas, one way or another, touches the daily lives of virtually every person residing in the state. Most Texans, however, have little say in the formulation of local policy. Rather, they are the subjects of ideas initiated and implemented by a relatively few local decision makers. The very structure of local government in the Lone Star State contributes to this inequitable situation.

In Texas, the fragmented nature of local government precludes widespread public knowledge about local decision making. As is the case with the administrative branch of the Texas state government (see chapter 9), citizens find it very difficult to keep abreast of which local governing body exercises what political authority. Proliferation of political institutions breeds public unawareness, which in turn produces extensive apathy. Organized interest groups with a clear stake in local politics, however, ordinarily gravitate to the correct governing unit and monopolize its time.

The method of electing officeholders to local positions in Texas also dampens mass attention and participation. Nonpartisan elections make it unnecessary to develop popularly based political parties in order to win office. Instead, candidates solicit the support of smaller, more narrowly defined interest groups. A system of at-large elections (more and more being replaced by district elections in Texas) allows people and organizations with robust financial resources to support candidates for all places in local government. This form of representation in effect gives "disproportionately larger shares of representation to white, upper-middle-class areas." [16] In cities where district elections are becoming a part of the electoral landscape, minority community leaders on the whole believe "that the change in electoral systems improves the responsiveness of city government to their needs." [17] In addition, a district system increases community participation (but not voting turnout per se), the diversity of types of candidates seeking local office, the length of local government meetings, the level of conflict in local political bodies, and the work load of local officials.[18]

Finally, most local officials in Texas are part-time and not well paid. With the clear exception of chief administrators (city managers and heads of city departments, for example) in large cities, local governments are generally run by amateurs.

Nonpartisan elections, at-large representation, and amateurism in politics are usually features associated with progressive good government. This is the form of government that is preferred by dominant economic interests. Not surprisingly, the "good government" movement was originally advocated by corporate interests during the early part of the twentieth century. Assessing the impact of this movement, sociologist G. William Domhoff concludes that "The actual goal of these reforms was to reduce working-class influence on city government." [19] Although some changes have occurred recently, the political infrastructure advanced by the movement is still well developed in Texas.

ECONOMIC INFLUENCE IN TEXAS LOCAL GOVERNMENT

This section explores the relationship between economic interests and local politics in Texas. Specifically, it looks at the impact that large-scale companies have on local government. As such, the investigation is restricted to locales in Texas that are important to giant companies. Areas that do not provide businesses with marketable resources, an abundance of labor, and/or customers able to purchase products and goods are automatically excluded. This analysis is further limited by the lack of information about corporate involvement in the state's local politics. Few systematic studies have been performed on this topic, and these few are dated.[20]

Nonetheless, a few communities in Texas, especially the large cities, are extremely important components in the national corporate network. Some observers have suggested that Texas's cities (and other Sunbelt metropolitan areas) are on the verge of eclipsing the urban centers of the Northeast and Midwest in overall economic importance.[21] In recent years there has been a substantial transfer of corporate operations from other regions into Texas cities, especially Houston and Dallas. Corporate headquarters, funds, and facilities have been transplanted into the Lone Star State. The early Texas industrial empire, begun with the discovery of oil, has been augmented by this recent upsurge of corporate interest in the state.

Local government has been at the center of the corporate expansion into Texas, for local policies can stimulate or discourage corporate activity within a vicinity. The basic amenities that companies seek from local governing bodies are public services (fire and police protection, water, sewage plants, sanitation, and storm drainage, among others) and local regulation (such as favorable zoning and tax decisions) that furthers the financial interests of the business. In order to better understand the relationship between the corporate community and local government, the remainder of this section will investigate the corporate power structure in some of the state's major cities, the political linkage forged between the corporate world and local officials, and a sampling of local public policies that benefit business interests.

Local Economic Power Structures in Texas

Houston is the largest city in Texas. Its economy is based on agriculture, real estate and land development, some heavy manufacturing, aerospace technology, and, most emphatically, petrochemical industries and financial institutions. Some of the country's biggest energy producers (Exxon, U.S.A., Tenneco, and Shell, for instance) are headquartered in this city. Exxon's impact is doubly felt since it is the city's largest landowner, possessing 2 percent of Harris County's land surface.[22] For many years, two of the state's top five bank corporations and most of its wealthiest savings and loan firms have operated out of Houston. Many of these economic interests are interlinked.

The two largest banks in the city—First City and Texas Commerce—have tied the Houston economic elite together. Representatives from the city's major corporations, agribusinesses, land developers, savings and loan firms, and insurance companies sit on the boards of directors of these banks. The banks themselves are secondarily interlocked. That is, a nonbanking business has directors from the large banks sitting together on its board. For instance, in 1985 Texas Commerce and First City had representatives on the boards of Houston Industries, Texas Eastern, Panhandle Eastern, American General, and Houston Natural Gas (now a part of ENRON).

The three big law firms of Houston—Fulbright and Jaworski; Baker and Botts; and Vinson, Elkins, Searls, Connally, and Smith—also forge a common bond among major corporations. Interestingly, these three law firms have been tightly tethered to the major Houston banks. The late Leon Jaworski, of Fulbright and Jaworski, was the chairman of the board of Southwest Bancshares (now owned by Dallas's M Corp). James Elkins, the son of the founder of Vinson, Elkins, was the First City board chairman. Lawyers from Baker and Botts and Fulbright and Jaworski hold positions on Texas Commerce's board. In addition, the big three law firms represent the legal (and political) interests of Houston's major corporations.

The banking/corporate/law firm nexus constitutes the heart of the economic power structure in Houston. It has been, in the words of one observer, "Houston's quintessential Establishment." [23] Beyond the economic and legal connections, executives of these businesses mingle socially. For decades the leaders of the biggest corporations, law firms, and banks composed the 8F Crowd (see chapter 5), a group of people who met regularly in the late George Brown's suite of rooms in Houston's Lamar Hotel. As the structure of the 8F Crowd faded, its role of coordinating the business community in Houston transferred to the city's chamber of commerce. Spearheading the chamber is its president Louie Welch, former member of the city council and mayor and current board director of Gibralter Savings, Houston's foremost savings and loan outfit, and the Texas Water Development Board. The directors of the chamber are men from leading corporations. It has a seventy-person staff and a sizable budget. The chamber endorses a "philosophy [which] is essentially that of the 8F Crowd. [It] seek[s] to protect a massive investment, stimulate even greater ones, and, in the process, build Houston to [its] own specifications, with as little interference from the public, and as much help from city hall, as possible." [24]

Much of the structure of Houston's political and economic foundation is cracking, however. The recent economic troubles of the state have hit the city's elite very hard. Several of its leading firms have been acquired by out-of-state enterprises. Houston Natural Gas has been merged with Omaha's InterNorth to form the ENRON company. United Energy, a major natural gas firm, has become a property of MidCon. The El Paso Company now belongs to Burlington Northern. The crash that afflicted the petroleum business and the real estate market dramatically affected major banks that had substantial loans in these economic arenas. Indeed, First City has been routinely recording substantial losses in recent years, and Texas Commerce has been taken over by the large New York bank, Chemical. Savings and loan firms have also faltered.

It is too early to assess what effect these economic changes will have on the elite structure of Houston. More than likely, the local elite will become either supplanted by or firmly affiliated with economic interests outside the city. Penetration of a more national economic elite into Houston seems in the cards.

Dallas is the second largest city in the state. It has a diversified economy, the principal sectors of which revolve around manufacturing of aerospace, military defense, electronics, and oil equipment; retailing of goods; generation of electricity; processing and distribution of food; real estate development; and, especially, insurance, and banking. Dallas is considered by many to be the financial center of the Southwest. It is the home of many of the leading corporations in the state (and nation). Among those with headquarters in the city are: Texas Instruments (electronics); Halliburton and Dresser (oil equipment); Southland of which 7–Eleven is a subsidiary (retailer of food); LTV (aerospace, steel, and meat packing); Texas Utilities (electricity); ENSERCH (Lone Star Gas); Lomas and Nettleton (home mortgages); Southland Financial (insurance); and M Corp and First Republic (bank holding companies).

Corporate interests in Dallas are linked together through interlocking directorates and civic organizations. Corporate interlocks are as common in Dallas as they are among the big firms of Houston. Banks again serve as common meeting grounds for executives from the major companies of the city; virtually every major Dallas corporation is interconnected vis à vis the banks. The largest banks themselves are interlocked. InterFirst and Republic have recently announced a proposed merger. M Corp was in 1985 interlocked with InterFirst through the board of directors of Lomas and Nettleton and with Republic through the board of ENSERCH.

Civic associations also bring together the corporate elite. The foremost civic group is the Dallas Citizens Council, which was chartered in 1937. Only board chairmen and company presidents are eligible for membership. The 200 to 250 members are "to study, confer, and act upon any matter, civic or economic in character, which may be deemed to effect the welfare of the city of Dallas, or the state of Texas." [25] The goal of the council "is to promote unified thinking on a problem or issue" facing Dallas.[26] The dominating force of the council is its board of directors, usually composed of senior executives from the city's largest corporations and banks. The bulk of Dallas's leadership "comes primarily from the business and financial sector of the community" [27] through the mediating efforts of the Citizens Council.

In short, as is the case with Houston, there is a power structure in Dallas. Its roots are firmly planted in the highest echelons of the corporate world: "Dallas' influential bankers and corporation heads joined together to control virtually all major political and economic developments in Dallas from 1937 to the present." [28]

There are signs of power structures in each of the other large Texas cities. As a rule, giant companies that have a prevailing influence on the state (and national) economy are not headquartered outside of Dallas and Houston. Some large conglomerates do have operations in the other metropolitan areas of Texas, however. But unless a policy matter bears directly on the company, the absentee board of directors shuns involvement in local affairs. Homegrown businesses in these urban centers usually don't have the economic clout (in terms of sales, assets, and number of employees) of the corporations of Dallas and Houston. Nonetheless, local companies do cluster together in San Antonio, El Paso, and Fort Worth to form a network of economic power.

The Good Government League (GGL) of San Antonio has been described as "a power structure's power structure." [29] The GGL was formed in 1955 and held together for two decades. Some 2,000 San Antonians were in the league at its peak, although the 36–member executive committee guided its activities. It was composed of the leading economic notables in the Alamo City.

El Paso also has a Good Government League. It too is composed of a coterie of business executives. Prior to its inception some thirty years ago, officials from businesses situated in this border city came together in the Committee of Fifty.

Fort Worth's economic elite coalesces through "Seventh Street," a loose confederation of business leaders in the city. Over the years, the major figure behind Seventh Street had been octogenarian H. B. "Babe" Fuqua. Fuqua was a former executive for Gulf Oil and founder of an energy firm in Fort Worth, as well as the prime developer of the city's First National Bank, the principal unit in the First United Bancorporation.

Corporate Linkages to Local Politics

The mere existence of an economic power center in a locale does not automatically mean that it has political power in the area. It is true that the sheer size and economic importance of companies—especially when they are unified in outlook—cannot be ignored by local officials. Corporate decisions to enter or leave an area can have a drastic impact on the community at large. The effect reaches beyond economic ramifications (such as jobs gained or lost) to include political fallout (such as local taxes gained or lost). In this section, however, the direct path linking businesses to local government will be traced. The primary connections are through local elections and through lobbying of interest groups.

Elections.   As mentioned earlier, local elections in Texas are nonpartisan. That is, candidates do not identify with a political party. One of the major consequences of this type of electoral system is that political parties barely exist in local politics. In their absence, economic organizations have assumed electoral functions, such as candidate recruitment and financing campaigns, that are usually performed by parties.

Each of the above-mentioned economic groups in Texas's most populous cities has been deeply involved in local electoral politics. Fort Worth's Seventh Street "orchestrated campaign financing to elect conservative city council candidates who would keep taxes low and downtown healthy." [30] During the 1950s and 1960s, El Paso's Committee of Fifty, according to its most influential member, "would urge people to run and finance their campaigns." [31] That city's Good Government League continues the tradition today. League member Judson Williams (former regent of Texas Tech University and ex–board director at Southern Union Gas) describes the screening process employed by his organization:

Somebody says "Let's get together and encourage people to run." They'd sit down and have a brainstorming session, "Here's an area"—a name would be discussed. If the feeling was they should be encouraged they'd be talked to and asked [to seek office].[32]

The Good Government League of San Antonio, over the course of its twenty-one-year existence, had a clear political goal: "Candidates for the [city] council, including the mayor's position [were] carefully screened, selected, and 'nominated' by the ... GGL."[33] Even in 1975, when the league was on the decline, it "screened over one hundred citizens interested in the GGL's nine endorsements and financial backing."[34] The City Charter Association (CCA) of Dallas, which is the political offshoot of the previously discussed Citizens Council, has "undertaken to persuade 'qualified' men to run for office, and then backed their campaigns financially."[35] Electoral politics in Houston "has long been dominated by a pro-growth establishment consisting of developers, realtors, architects, engineers, the construction industry, and downtown banks and law firms that service these other industries."[36] In the past, the 8F Crowd coordinated these economic interests; today, the chamber of commerce directs the economic meddling into local electoral politics in the Bayou City.

The success rate of these organizations has been quite impressive. Over the years, a large majority of candidates sponsored by each association has won political office. In Dallas, until the early 1970s, only a handful of candidates secured seats on the city council without the support of the City Charter Association. Throughout its existence, the Good Government League of El Paso "has seldom failed to get its favorite into the mayor's post."[37] From 1954 to 1973, seventy-eight of eighty-one local council seats in San Antonio were occupied by candidates recruited and supported by that city's Good Government League. According to political scientist Robert Lineberry, even "the most hard-headed pluralist could not ignore the potent electoral influence of the Good Government League. The electoral success of the organization would rival that of the strongest old-style urban machine."[38] Finally, the clout of Fort Worth's Seventh Street has been so overwhelming that "no politician could endure without its imprimatur."[39]

Over the years the success of economic groups has been at the expense of representation of people from other backgrounds in local political decision-making units in Texas. Very few women, blacks, Mexican Americans, or lower-income people sought, let alone won, political office in the large cities. In the two decades prior to 1979, nineteen blacks or Mexican Americans, for instance, ran for a place on the Houston city council: only one of these candidates was victorious.[40] As we shall soon discuss, installation of district electoral systems in many of these cities has somewhat altered this exclusionary pattern.

Lobbying.   Political associations also exert pressure on local governments in order to affect political decisions. In many instances, lobbying begins with the group advancing new ideas to the government. This phase of lobbying is most clearly seen in Dallas.

The Dallas Citizens Council, now headed by a woman, is the major force behind the adoption of new policies in the city. Individual leaders, usually from the highest ranks of business, bring their policy ideas to the full council, which then discusses the matter and decides whether or not to advocate the idea. All resolutions finally adopted by the council are given unanimous support. This stage of the policy process may take years. Backing for the proposition is then solicited throughout the community. Luncheons, policy discussion groups, and the media are utilized by the council to rally communitywide approval. Only then is the idea presented to the political officials of Dallas. Describing the policy-making role of the city council, it has been concluded that it

> often makes its decision on crucial and controversial community issues only after a relatively long period of debate. The solutions to issues are crystallized and power to implement them mobilized by the real leaders of the community, usually within the Citizens Council. When this has occurred, the City Council acts—if legal action is required.[41]

The Citizens Council also formulates policy for the Dallas school system. One key informant about Dallas bluntly notes that

> the Board of Education would not think of proposing any bond issue, or doing anything without first clearing it with the Citizens Council. This body has the power to make or break any idea or proposal that certain groups come up with. It is such a powerful group that nothing can succeed without its support.[42]

It was the council that initiated Dallas's school desegregation program.[43]

Seventh Street in Fort Worth and the Good Government Leagues in San Antonio and El Paso have also initiated policy proposals to city officials in their locales. Large corporations, bank holding companies, and their law firms have been very active in directing public policy in Houston. A partner in the huge Vinson, Elkins, Searls, Connally, and Smith law firm suggests that "if you thought something needed to be done in Houston, the managing partners of the big [law] firms would be the logical place to start."[44]

In sum, corporate interests are primarily transmitted to local governing officials by influencing the choice of elected officials and by lobbying. At times, other methods of linkage are evident. For instance, some economic notables become political officials, but this is not a frequent occurrence since members of the economic elite usually avoid actually holding local public offices. In Dallas, however, Erik Jonsson, founder of Texas Instruments and a member of the Citizens Council, was mayor for seven years during the 1960s. On other occasions local officials later became corporate executives. After his tenure in office, a former mayor of Fort Worth assumed the president's chair at the city's First National Bank. Similarly, James Aston was city manager of Dallas between 1939 and 1941. He subsequently served as chairman of the executive committee of the Republic of Texas bank until the early 1980s. He has also served on the board of directors of American Airlines, Zale, Lone Star Steel, Allied Finance, Dallas Power and Light, Wyatt Industries, and the Times Mirror Company. Houston's chamber of commerce uses a multidimensional strategy in its attempts to shape local politics. In pursuit of its goals the chamber operates "through frequent interchanges of its personnel with city government, informal meetings and social contacts, the co-option of potential opponents, the dissemination of propaganda, the provision to policymakers of research findings, and intensive lobbying." [45]

Policy Outputs From Local Governments

People associated with big business have generally benefited from the decisions reached by local governments in Texas. The benefits come in many forms. Most are tangible and quite obvious.

In San Antonio the continuous annexation of new land into the city has been a concrete benefit to many land developers, real estate agents, and the institutions (banks, mortgage companies, and savings and loan firms) that financially underwrite the home building industry.[46] There is some evidence that public services provided by local government are better in the affluent Northwest part of San Antonio than in other parts of the city, especially the relatively impoverished West side.[47] Although another study fails to find a social class pattern to the delivery of goods and services in the Alamo City, it is conceded that "the power structure is superordinate with respect to the tax rate, and the revenue rate strongly determines the aggregate level of expenditures." [48]

Houston's generous annexation of outlying areas has enhanced the fortunes of some economic interests. For instance, many unannexed areas around the city are new housing subdivisions that incur large debts in order to construct sewage lines, flood control projects, and water delivery systems. It is quite difficult for residents of these areas to pay off the debts without a substantial increase in their property taxes. Annexation by the city of Houston passes payment of the debts along to all of the city's residents. Among the major beneficiaries of this scheme are the bankers who are guaranteed debt repayment at a very high interest rate. For years, Walter Mischer, who is chairman of Allied Bancshares (third largest bank in Houston), was heavily involved in these annexation scenarios. He, along with other interested parties, would establish debt-ridden water districts, lend money to land developers building in these districts, urge the city of Houston to annex these areas, and collect the almost certain high interest on the notes now covered by Houstonites.[49]

The corporate bias in local policies leaves few benefits available for other interests. Remarkably small amounts of money, for instance, are spent in Houston for public parks. Public transportation in most Texas cities is a low-priority item. Police departments in many of the larger cities are understaffed and the personnel who take these jobs are often underpaid.

POLITICAL CHANGE AT THE LOCAL LEVEL

On the surface, city politics in Texas appears to be in the midst of change. The primary impetus for this phenomenon has been alteration of the selection procedures for electing local officials. Introduction of district elections in the place of at-large elections has meant that more candidates must be drawn from the geographic area that they seek to represent. Gone are the days when virtually all local politicos came from the same middle- to upper-middle-class section of the city and from the same race (white Anglos) and gender (male). More and more women, blacks, and Mexican Americans are found in the governing circles of major Texas cities. Kathy Whitmere is currently the mayor of Houston; Henry Cisneros holds the same title in San Antonio. A majority of the Alamo City's council seats has, in recent years, been occupied by Mexican Americans. In 1979, four members of the Houston's fifteen-person council were from minority groups. That same year recorded the election of three minority members to the Dallas council.

In addition, community groups emerged from neighborhoods traditionally overlooked in the local political process. The foremost example is the rise of COPS (short for Communities Organized for Public Service) in San Antonio. Throughout the 1970s, various organizations from the West side of the city came together—under the financial and spiritual backing of the local Catholic church and because of the mobilization skills of a few people—to form COPS. The greatest initial successes of COPS were improvement of the woefully inadequate city services (drainage, sidewalks, street lights, and so forth) in poor areas of San Antonio, recruitment of some victorious candidates for city office, and, along with the voter registration efforts of the Southwest Voter Registration Education Project, increasing the voter turnout of Mexican Americans. By the end of the decade COPS had become "firmly established in San Antonio as a major political force— some would say *the* major political force." [50] A COPS-style organization, EPISO, spread to El Paso in the early 1980s. Affiliated organizations are to be found now in Fort Worth (Allied Communities of Tarrant County), in Austin (Austin Interfaith Sponsoring Committee), in Houston (The Metropolitan Organization of Houston), and in communities in the Rio Grande valley (Valley Interfaith).

Finally, the face of local politics has been altered by the inability of economic power centers to remain monolithic. The Good Government League in San Antonio, for instance, is now defunct. The economic power structures in other cities, including Dallas's seemingly impregnable Citizens Council, have been rife with internal fissures. Some of these problems are the result of the legal changes in choosing city officials coupled with the challenges raised by community organizations. Stress has also been precipitated, as was the case with the GGL of San Antonio, by the inability of the old economic elite to effectively absorb the nouveau riche in their areas. Local economic structures in some of Texas's cities have also gone through a transformation. Banks once held by local influentials are now owned by the state banking elite with headquarters in Houston or Dallas. El Paso's two leading banks (State National and El Paso National) formed the core of that city's power elite, for instance. Each of these banks has recently been acquired by a major bank holding company (El Paso National went to Texas Commerce and State National is the property of M Corp). Such changes disrupt the personnel who compose elite groups.

Whether disunity in economic elites, new community organizations, and alterations of election methods will combine to uproot the hegemony enjoyed by corporations in local politics is problematic for several reasons, however.

First, economic elites are often able to adjust to challenges. The demands to run blacks, Mexican Americans, or women can be met by screening and recruiting just such people. Gender and racial or ethnic background alone does not make a person an opponent of the corporate status quo. Lila Cockrill, San Antonio's first female mayor, was sponsored by the Good Government League. When Henry

Cisneros first attained a seat on the city council in the Alamo City, his support base was in the GGL.

Control by economic elites is still possible because of the expense of running for city office. A councilmatic position in Houston requires almost $100,000 to cover campaign costs; the mayor's race will cost a serious candidate over $1 million. Mayor Kathy Whitmere spent around $800,000 in her 1981 victory. A cursory examination of campaign contributions reports (filed with the secretary of state) reveals heavy donations from the stalwarts of Houston's economic community to her candidacy. In her recent reelection bid, she received $136,000 (8 percent of total contributions) from political action committees, including those of Brown and Root ($5,000); Vinson, Elkins, Searls, Connally, and Smith ($5,000); and building contractors in the city ($8,000).[51]

A recent study of leaders in cities that have experienced a change in the social background of elected representatives through implementation of district electoral schemes finds that "the overwhelming majority of respondents ... recognize the business community, or some portion of it, as the most powerful force in city politics regardless of electoral systems."[52] Electoral reform does not necessarily mean the future demise of economic elites. Community leaders feel that "business and development interests will probably adapt to the new electoral system and will remain the most powerful groups in city politics."[53] Interestingly, some leaders representing local neighborhood groups also find fault with district elections. COPS of San Antonio, for instance, apparently believes that the new electoral system will undermine its growing political strength since the reform will limit the group's political activity to geographic districts and not the city at large.[54]

Second, defeat for the candidates of local economic power structures does not necessarily signal a liberal or radical change in government. For instance, the demise of San Antonio's Good Government League electorally was a product of internal division within the pillars of the economic elite. As pointed out by one observer of the GGL's 1973 loss of the mayor's office: "By no stretch of the imagination ... could the challengers to the old hegemony be described as more liberal than the GGL."[55]

Finally, the new faces and new organizations that have come forth in Texas cities are not in general mounting a challenge to the corporate dominance found in the state. Even those most identified with a desire to alter the status quo aim their arguments at redressing the lack of government services provided to many economically and politically impoverished citizens in the past and not to a profound restructuring of the political and economic system. When more radical calls for change are made, the fragility of coalitions that sometimes form to fight economic power structures in Texas cities is revealed through internal bickering and disintegration.

CONCLUSION

Local government—like state government—in Texas is greatly influenced by economic elites. The various forms of local government in the state are easily penetrated by these notables. Through effectively screening candidates, financing their campaigns, and lobbying them once in office, economic leaders exercise convincing clout in local political affairs. The payoff is public policy that is beneficial to the high standing of these economic interests. Although the rumbles of change have been felt in many of Texas's cities, it is doubtful that a major restructuring of the corporate bias in local politics is in the offing.

NOTES

1. *Texas Almanac and Industrial Guide: 1986–1987* (Dallas: A. H. Belo, 1985), p. 656.

2. Richard Kraemer and Charldean Newell, *Texas Politics* (St. Paul: West Publishing Company, 1979), p. 346.

3. *Texas Almanac and Industrial Guide,* pp. 663–64.

4. Discussed in LBJ School of Public Affairs, *Local Government Election Systems* (Austin: LBJ School of Public Affairs, 1984), pp. 17–19.

5. *Avery v. Midland County,* 88 S.Ct. 1114 (1968).

6. Clifton McCleskey, Allan Butcher, Daniel E. Farlow, and J. Pat Stephens, *The Government and Politics of Texas,* 6th ed. (Boston: Little, Brown, 1978), p. 289.

7. Woodworth G. Thrombley, *Special Districts and Authorities in Texas,* Public Affairs Series, no. 39 (Austin: University of Texas, 1959), p. 6.

8. Beryl E. Pettus and Randall W. Bland, *Texas Government Today,* rev. ed. (Homewood, Ill.: Dorsey, 1979), p. 284.

9. McCleskey et al., *Government and Politics of Texas,* p. 278.

10. Pettus and Bland, *Texas Government Today,* p. 284.

11. James E. Anderson, Richard W. Murray, and Edward L. Farley, *Texas Politics: An Introduction,* 3d ed. (New York: Harper and Row, 1979), p. 262.

12. Pettus and Bland, *Texas Government Today,* p. 294.

13. Richard Kraemer and Charldean Newell, *Essentials of Texas Politics* (St. Paul: West Publishing Company, 1983), p. 139.

14. Pettus and Bland, *Texas Government Today,* p. 302.

15. Legislative Budget Board, *Fiscal Size Up: 1986–1987* (Austin: Legislative Budget Board, 1986), p. 25.

16. LBJ School of Public Affairs, *Local Government Election Systems,* p. 45.

17. Ibid., p. 44.

18. Ibid., passim.

19. G. William Domhoff, *The Powers That Be* (New York: Random House, 1978), p. 155. Also see his discussion in *Who Really Rules?* (Santa Monica: Goodyear, 1978), pp. 160–68.

20. El Paso is the subject of William V. D'Antonio and William H. Form, *Influentials in Two Border Cities* (Notre Dame: University of Notre Dame Press, 1965). Dallas is investigated in Carol Estes Thometz, *The Decision Makers: The Power Structure in Dallas* (Dallas: Southern Methodist University Press, 1963).

21. See Kirkpatrick Sale, *Power Shift: The Rise of the Southern Rim and Its Challenge to the Eastern Establishment* (New York: Random House, 1975); and David C. Perry and Alfred J. Watkins, eds., *The Rise of the Sunbelt Cities* (Beverly Hills: Sage Publications, 1977).

22. Jim Chiles, "Who Owns Texas?" *Texas Monthly,* June 1980, p. 129.

23. Tony Castro, "Power and Money in Houston," *Texas Observer,* July 4, 1975, p. 3.

24. Wendell M. Bedichek and Neal Tannahill, *Public Policy in Texas* (Glenview, Ill.: Scott, Foresman, 1982), p. 286.

25. From the charter of the Dallas Citizens Council. Cited in Thometz, *The Decision Makers,* p. 123.

26. Ibid., p. 38.

27. Ibid., p. 31.

28. Harry Hurt III, "The Most Powerful Texans," reprinted in *Texas Monthly's Political Reader* (Austin: Texas Monthly Press and Sterling Swift Publishing, 1978), p. 112.

29. Robert Lineberry, *Equality and Urban Policy: The Distribution of Municipal and Public Services* (Beverly Hills: Sage Publications, 1976), p. 56.

30. Tom Curtis, "Who Runs Cowtown?" reprinted in *Texas Monthly's Political Reader,* p. 241.

31. The statement is Sam Young, Sr.'s, who, during his prime, was reputed to be the most important figure in El Paso by two sources: D'Antonio and Form, *Influentials in Two Border Cities,* p. 62; and Carey Galernter, "Young's Power: More than a Banker's," *El Paso Times,* December 18, 1979, pp. 1 and 12. Quoted in Paul Sweeney, "The League Is Weaker: But Still a Force," *El Paso Times,* December 20, 1978, p. 1.

32. Quoted in Sweeney, "The League Is Weaker," p. 15.

33. Bill Crane, "San Antonio: Pluralistic City and Monolithic Government," in *Urban Politics in the Southwest,* ed. Leonard E. Goodall (Tempe, Arizona: Institute of Public Administration, Arizona State University, 1967), p. 134.

34. Arnold Fleischmann, "Sunbelt Boosterism: The Politics of Postwar Growth and Annexation in San Antonio," in *Rise of the Sunbelt Cities,* ed. Perry and Watkins, p. 167.

35. Thometz, *The Decision Makers,* p. 39.

36. Kent Tedin, "The 1981 Election for Mayor of Houston," *Texas Business Review* 56 (November-December 1982): 285.

37. Sweeney, "The League Is Weaker," p. 15.

38. Lineberry, *Equality and Urban Policy,* p. 55.

39. Curtis, "Who Runs Cowtown?" p. 241.

40. Bedichek and Tannahill, *Public Policy in Texas,* p. 282.

41. Thometz, *The Decision Makers,* p. 40. Thometz calls the Citizens Council the "Civic Committee" in her work. I have given the real name of the group in the quote.

42. Quoted in ibid., p. 37. Again I have taken the liberty of substituting Citizens Council for "Civic Committee" in the quote.

43. Discussed in ibid., pp. 66–8.

44. Griffin Smith, Jr., "Empires of Paper," reprinted in *Texas Monthly's Political Reader,* p. 33.

45. Bedichek and Tannahill, *Public Policy in Texas,* p. 286.

46. For a good history of annexation in San Antonio, see Fleischmann, "Sunbelt Boosterism."

47. Discussed in Peter A. Lupsha and William J. Siembieda, "The Poverty of Public Services in the Land of Plenty: An Analysis and Interpretation," *Rise of the Sunbelt Cities,* ed. Perry and Watkins, ch. 7.

48. Lineberry, *Equality and Urban Policy,* p. 159.

49. Discussed in Harvey Katz, *Shadow on the Alamo: New Heroes Fight Old Corruption in Texas* (Garden City, N.Y.: Doubleday, 1972), ch. 9.

50. Paul Burka, "The Second Battle of the Alamo," *Texas Monthly's Political Reader,* p. 245. Emphasis in the original.

51. Mike Snyder, "PACs Flex Their Muscles in City and State Politics," *Houston Chronicle,* January 13, 1986.

52. LBJ School of Public Affairs, *Local Government Election Systems,* p. 46.

53. Ibid., p. 47.

54. Ibid.

55. Lineberry, *Equality and Urban Policy,* p. 83.

—— Epilogue ——

Texas Politics: A Note on Change

If political power is economically structured in Texas, what does this suggest about the possibility of change in the state's political system? What follows is a tentative and clearly incomplete answer to this question; nonetheless, it will pursue the implications of the economic rule model for the future of Texas politics. Because speculation about the future must be based on an analysis of the present, a brief summary of this book's contents will first appear. ★

A RECAPITULATION

Control over the economy of Texas is vested in the hands of a relatively few corporations. This pattern is evident in the production, conversion, and delivery of agricultural items and petroleum by-products, as well as in the financial exchanges occurring in the state's banks, insurance firms, and savings and loan associations. Most of these major corporations have come into the state to avail themselves of its riches; others have developed from within the state. Regardless of their place of origin, these corporations now dominate the economic sectors of Texas.

Moreover, these companies are economically interconnected. They share a commitment to growth in profits and recognize that stability within the business community—a stability that frequently quiets any competition among rival businesses—is necessary for such expansion. More directly, common ownership and interlocks among various boards of directors consolidate the business world of the state.

The commanding position held by a large company alone is usually enough to give it leverage in the Texas political system. In concert, corporations become a formidable opponent in any contest with the government. The hegemony of the business community in society, with its control over valuable resources including jobs and goods and services, virtually guarantees a favorable disposition—a positive mind-set—among officials in government. In other words, even without direct communication—overt promises or threats—political leaders will frequently do the bidding of large corporations in anticipation of promoting social, political, and economic harmony. Consequently, government has tacitly and quietly entered into a symbiotic partnership with big business, an agreement in which "government is clearly the junior partner in the newly combined firm." [1]

This is not to say that big companies remain aloof from the everyday world of political decisionmaking. Quite the contrary. In order to maximize the likelihood of translating ideas sponsored by business into public policy and to minimize the possibility that groups rivaling corporations might catch the attention of government officials, dominant economic interests are continuously involved in the affairs of the state. They influence the selection of government personnel and lobby officials holding political positions.

Candidate recruitment begins with the screening of aspirants for electoral office. Economic notables or their representatives, such as legal firms, play a major role in selecting candidates. Persons sponsored by the corporate sector are recipients of large campaign contributions, most of which are donated legally. The electoral hopes of candidates and parties not in harmony with the corporate outlook are dampened by neglect and, at times, overt opposition. The appointment of government officials is also influenced by economic elites; indeed, corporate executives frequently front up to fill key administrative posts. Consequently, most of the personnel holding elected and appointed offices in Texas are very sympathetic to the interests of the state's dominant businesses.

Organized corporate interest groups actively apply pressure to government officials. These groups hire lobbyists—primarily former members of the state government—to directly contact political leaders. They also feed crucial information to decision makers, the vast majority of whom—at least in the legislature—are without the resources needed to adequately gather data vital to the formulation of public policy. On occasion, corporate interest groups rally the public behind their cause. Overall, they exert a tremendous influence over the course of government in Texas.

The structural design of Texas government facilitates the political clout of well-organized interest groups. The constitution of the state creates a generally weak government, one unable to counter pressures emanating from the private sector. Moreover, the constitution has been occasionally amended to guarantee privileged status to policies that benefit certain corporate interests. Hence, even though the current constitution was originally formulated to prevent the concentration of power in the hands of government and corporations, it has met with only limited success in achieving this aim.

The legislature of Texas has proven to be very receptive to corporate interests. Legislators work only part-time without much money or staff assistance. The organization of the legislature is hierarchical with extensive power vested in the offices of the speaker and lieutenant-governor. It is through their leadership that corporate interests are most able to influence the direction of the legislative body. Once the speaker and lieutenant-governor are on board the corporate ship, most business-oriented proposals sail through the legislature smoothly.

The administrative branch of Texas government, including the governor, other elected administrators, and a multitude of appointed bureaucrats, is easily penetrated by corporate interests. Most of these offices and agencies are autonomous from each other; each is able to work within its sphere of influence without much concern about overall coordination or public accountability. It is an ideal setting in which well-organized groups are able to influence the implementation of public policy. Dominant economic interests exert their influence primarily through the exchange of personnel, campaign contributions, and the development of a close working relationship with the agency in question. Consequently, economic notables are frequently found to be in the forefront in the creation of agencies, are well-represented on administrative boards and commissions, continuously offer expertise and research to administrators, and provide the chief support base for any friendly administrative unit under attack.

Even the courts in Texas are not immune from the influences of economic notables. The structure of the court system with its multiple levels of jurisdiction ensures that those with wealth are best able to comprehend and master the nuances of the system. Furthermore, most of the major participants in the judicial process, ranging from judges to jurors, are similar in background to economic influentials. Again, campaign contributions bridge the electoral aspirations of some of Texas's judges with the interests of economic organizations. An imbalance results in the distribution of justice, leaving Texans without wealth at a disadvantage.

Indeed, the whole of public policy in the Lone Star State slants in the direction of corporate interests. Whether it be in areas budgeted by the state (education, transportation, or welfare) or in activities regulated by government (natural resources, finances, or labor), the corporate sector is the primary beneficiary of political action.

The public school system provides a work force suitable to corporate Texas as well as money (through the Permanent University Fund) and research (through universities) that fuel the expansion of big business. The state's magnificent highway network promotes the economic interests of automobile, petroleum, construction, and insurance corporations while doing little for the impoverished. The poor are only partially assisted through the state's welfare program. The thrust of welfare policies is to provide direct aid to corporations and wealthy individuals who attend to some of the needy. The corporate sector benefits indirectly through the creation of a source of cheap labor and the containment of a potentially hostile mass of impoverished people. For all the benefits they receive, affluent Texans pay little in taxes.

The consumers of the state, thanks to corporate-oriented government regulation, are faced with high prices for petroleum products, electricity, insurance, and the privilege of borrowing money. Moreover, while underwriting some basic costs of industrialization, Texas consumers often pay a high price to live in an environment filled with the noxious wastes of big business.

Even labor laws that improve the lot of most of the state's workers greatly assist corporate employers. The state lacks strong unions, is without full government protection of all employees, and assumes only limited responsibility for the plight of unemployed or injured workers. For these reasons Texas businesses, primarily large ones, operate within a labor environment that allows maximization of profits, occasionally at the financial and physical expense of their employees.

Corporate influence in Texas further extends to local politics, especially in the state's largest cities and in outlying areas within the financial ambit of major companies. Through their sheer presence, their selection and sponsorship of local political officials, and their organized lobbying efforts, economic notables are at the top of community power structures. Local policies often result, especially in areas such as taxation, that are favorable to corporations.

IMPLICATIONS FOR POLITICAL CHANGE

There are two avenues that may be taken to change the nexus between economic dominance and the distribution of political power in Texas. One involves fundamentally altering the economic system. For reasons that appear below, the likelihood of fundamental change occurring in Texas is slight. The other form of change does not aim at total renovation of the economic structure, but attempts to democratize the state through expansion of the political power of those outside the economic elite. Change along this line is possible.

Fundamental Change

Reordering the economic system would require a major transformation of the institutions that control the means of production and distribution of goods and services in Texas. The foothold of large corporations would have to be uprooted. Economic control would have to be transferred to small-scale businesses, cooperatives composed of average citizens, or government bodies. A number of reasons combine to make such radical change very unlikely, at least in the near future.

First, most Texans are probably content with the current corporate control of the state's economy. The large mass of skilled white-collar workers in the state (and many blue-collar workers, as well) believes that their favorable economic status is the direct result of corporate dominance. This feeling, coupled with a strong distrust of government intervention in the economy and little preparation or inclination to collectively or individually assume control over the economy, results in overwhelming support for the corporate status quo. What might happen if all workers were to suffer greatly from inflation, unemployment, and other economic maladies that routinely plague the lower classes is conjectural.

Second, economic notables would, naturally, strongly resist any attempt to undermine their privileged position. Economic reprisals against persons, groups, or communities seeking fundamental change could easily be deployed. Threats of job layoffs, actual unemployment, cutbacks in the production or delivery of services, and movement out of locales are but some of the retaliatory options available to dominant corporations. In addition, companies and their leaders can rely on the government to combat calls for radical change.

Third, state and local governments in Texas would probably respond to attempts to restructure the economy by penalizing those advocating such proposals. Government, with its near monopoly on resources of coercion, could legitimately imprison, harass, intimidate, injure, or kill proponents of fundamental overhaul of the economic (political) system. Civil liberties, political participation, and general freedom might all be curtailed if a systematic attempt were made to uproot the economic/political structure of power now existing in Texas.

In short, fundamental change would be resisted by most of the Texas populace, by economic notables, and by the government. Unless a large number of

Texans could be mobilized to counter the power of corporations and government leaders, calls for radical change are doomed to failure. Any significant attempt to ferment such change might result in fascism, "the joining of big capital—the ruling class or major segments of it—in a formal alliance with the state for the purpose of preventing capitalist collapse, organizing the work force to endure austerity, increasing productivity and profitability, and preserving social order." [2]

Nonfundamental Change

There is a good chance that more people can gain a greater, albeit limited, share of political power through nonfundamental change. This form of change does not require a complete restructuring of the economic control exerted by large corporations. Rather it attempts to broaden the base of political power without undoing the economic and political hegemony of these corporations. As such, nonfundamental change goes only so far in democratizing the state. Sources of nonfundamental change lie within three arenas: the economic system of the state, the intervention of outside political authorities in Texas politics, and the people of Texas themselves.

Change From Within the State's Economy.   Change can occur during times of economic expansion and contraction. Texas has experienced both within the last decade. When the economy was growing, among other things, more people with greater skills and relatively high salaries were being integrated into the work force of Texas. Some of these people came from outside the state to take advantage of the economic opportunities available to the middle classes of Texas. The lot of the indigenous population, which supplies other needed personnel, was also somewhat improved. The new work force had to be accommodated politically. The reemergence of the Republican party in Texas has been, in part, a response to the political orientations of new residents moving into the state. The attempt by the Democratic party to incorporate more minority members has been a recognition of the improvement in the social standing of some blacks and Mexican Americans. Although these political changes increased the power of upwardly mobile groups, they certainly did not set in motion a threat to the lofty status of corporations.

Fissures within the corporate community also increase the possibility of change in the distribution of political power. Although these splits are rare, they effectively weaken corporate strength. When, for instance, Texas trial lawyers and corporations disagreed over consumer protection legislation and tort liability matters, the result was policy beneficial to consumers and workers (see chapter 14). Breaches within the business community require compromise and obligate the disputants to seek new allies. Competition thus usually broadens the basis of power.

Anything that appeals to the self-interest of the business community has a good chance of bringing about nonfundamental change. The appeal might be threatening or accommodating. The important point is that it must be compelling enough to convince the elite that change is within its field of interest.

During the recent period of contraction in the state's economy a somewhat different set of forces have been put into motion. Economic crisis has led to the pursuit of corporate self-interest (for the sake of organizational survival) and division within the business community. In such situations, new organizations can often gain access to the political arena. However, many Texans, now worried about their economic status, are just as likely to act to conserve the political/economic system as to alter it. Moreover, resolution of the corporate crisis afflicting the Texas business community will probably mean fewer companies dominating more of the state's economic and political life. What is more, the companies that survive the turmoil will most likely be more national in scope. Texas firms will be reduced.

Change From Outside Political Authorities.   Decisions imposed on Texas from external political authorities at times have the effect of increasing the political clout of some groups and individuals. Bans on restrictions on voting (see chapter 4) and on racial and sex discrimination have improved the status of many Texans. Recently, for example, the 1975 Voting Rights Act passed by the federal government empowered the Justice Department to review the forms of representation used in cities throughout the country. Any time a city seeks to annex land, change its charter, or alter its laws on voting, it must first receive the approval of the Justice Department. In 1976, the attorney-general of the United States ruled that San Antonio's plan to annex new land was unacceptable because the city effectively denied representation to Mexican Americans living in the city. This decision forced the city to alter its method of electing local officials. Now aspirants for posts on the city council are chosen from distinct geographic districts created for each part of the city. The result has been a major shift in the composition of members of the city council. In 1977, five Mexican Americans and one black were elected: "minority group members composed a majority of city council for the first time in the city's history." [3]

Whereas intervention from external authorities improves the status of some people, it does not necessarily mean a complete renovation of the economic and political structure of Texas. The federal government has never been noted for altering the dominance of major corporations over state economies.

Change by the People of Texas.   A final source of change is the citizenry of Texas. Although Texans are usually apathetic and defer to authority, there have been times when they have banded together to promote political change. On various occasions, groups—for instance, Mexican Americans (through such organizations as LULAC and the G.I. Forum), consumers (in ACORN, for example), and noncorporate farmers (as in the American Agricultural Movement)—have demanded a greater say in decision making. Indeed, a constant theme in the history and culture of Texas has been the inclination toward populism—the belief that the people should rule. The Populist movement appeared in the mid–1870's, influenced the writing of the Texas Constitution (see chapter 7), and has reemerged on several occasions throughout the last one hundred years.

The liberal-populist theme permeated campaigns during the 1982 statewide election. Several victorious candidates, especially Governor Mark White, Attorney-General Jim Mattox, and Commissioner of Agriculture Jim Hightower, overtly made appeals to consumers and others who previously have been without much say in state politics. Blacks and Mexican Americans claim, with some justification, that their votes tipped the electoral balance to the advantage of these candidates. Hence the atmosphere became ripe for new policies and people from different backgrounds (e.g., women, minorities, consumers, environmentalists, academics, or those of lower social status) to enter into the political decision-making process. There are some signs that more women, blacks, Mexican Americans, and consumer-oriented people did receive appointments to state administrative positions.

Also a tremor of shift in public policy can be detected, at least in the field of public education financing. The Texas legislature and Governor White were urged in 1983 by COPS, the grass roots community action organization originating from San Antonio (see chapter 16), to drastically improve the financial basis of school districts that serve the poor of Texas.[4] The legislature enacted bills (approved by the governor) during its 1984 special session that at least partially met this challenge. Money directed at securing financial equality between rich and poor districts has been increased. The maximum that a fiscally disadvantaged school could receive is on the rise. Finally, the method of distributing the basic state grant to each school district was altered to guarantee that impoverished areas garnered a larger allocation than wealthy districts.

Politicized groups, individuals, and leaders are faced with difficult decisions if and when they confront the interests of dominant economic elites. If they try to radically alter the status quo, *or even appear to be radical,* hard times and bitter losses usually follow. If they couch their demands and phrase their suggestions for change in terms not threatening to the lofty position of economic notables, only a partial victory is likely. Although nonfundamental success certainly may improve the power and standing of some people and organizations, it does so well within the corporate framework.

In short, the possibility of thoroughly renovating the economic foundation of political power in Texas appears very remote. Changes made by people working *within* the corporate capitalist system seem more obtainable. Hard work, political awareness and involvement, and a willingness to join with others thus may produce some benefits for the relatively powerless—even in a state as dominated by corporate politics as Texas is.

NOTES

1. Kenneth M. Dolbeare, *Political Change in the United States: A Framework for Analysis* (New York: McGraw-Hill, 1974), p. 26.

2. Ibid., p. 59.

3. Charles L. Cotrell and R. Michael Stevens, "The 1975 Voting Rights Act and San Antonio, Texas: Toward a Federal Guarantee of a Republican Form of Government," *Publius* 8 (Winter 1978): 87.

4. Geoffrey Rips, "COPS Comes to Austin," *Texas Observer,* January 14, 1983, pp. 1 and 10–14.

INDEX

*

ABOUT THE AUTHOR

James W. Lamare received his Ph.D. in American Politics from the University of California, Los Angeles, in 1972. For more than a decade, he taught at the University of Texas at El Paso. Currently, he is head of the Department of Political Science of the University of Canterbury, Christchurch, New Zealand. During the 1988 academic year, he is a visiting Associate Professor of Government at the University of Texas at Austin.

His articles have appeared in several academic journals, including *Public Opinion Quarterly, Journal of Conflict Resolution, International Migration Review, American Politics Quarterly,* and *American Journal of Political Science.* His recent book, *What Rules America?* (West Publishing Company), investigates the impact of economic forces on the political process of the United States.